ECOLOGY OF SEASHORE

RECENT ADVANCES IN ENVIRONMENTAL ECOLOGY SERIES—3

Ecology of Seashore

A. P. DIWAN
D. K. ARORA

ANMOL PUBLICATIONS PVT LTD
NEW DELHI-110 002

ANMOL PUBLICATIONS PVT LTD
4374/4B, Ansari Road
Darya Ganj, New Delhi-110 002

First Edition, 1995

ISBN 81-7488-112-3

Printed in India

Published by J. L. Kumar for Anmol Publications Pvt. Ltd., New Delhi and Printed at Amit Enterprises, 518/14, Anup Mkt., Maujpur, Delhi.

Preface

Although we speak generally of the seashore it is not just one habitat but several, depending on the type of substratum: rocky shore, shingle shore, sandy shore, muddy shore, because each supports its own purticular communities. The various factors which control these communities are tides, desiccation, temperature, substratum, wave action, salinity and light.

It is desired to stress the unity of ecology and the necessity for including the influence of both plants and animals as well as the physical forces as part of the environment. The potential scope of ecology is very great, and no attempt at any exhaustive treatment of the subject is made here.

This book consists of twenty six chapters on various aspects of seashore ecology.

AUTHORS

Contents

1

Introduction

Although it constitutes by far the smallest area of all in the world's oceans, existing as an extremely narrow fringe a few meters in extent between high and low water, the intertidal zone is perhaps the best known and studied of all areas of the sea because it is the most accessible to humans. Here, and only here, can direct observations be made of aquatic organisms during the period of low tide, without special equipment. The intertidal zone has been of interest and use to humans since prehistoric time.

Despite its extremely restricted area, the intertidal has within the greatest variations in environmental factors of any marine area, and these can occur within centimeters of each other. Coupled with this is a tremendous diversity of life, which is greater than that found in the more extensive subtidal areas.

It should be emphasized that this area is truly an extension of the marine environment and his inhabited almost exclusively by marine organisms. Although this area is terrestrial as much as half the time, the terrestrial fauna and flora have not invaded it to any extent, except at the uppermost fringes.

The richness, the diversity of environmental factors, and the case of access act together to attract to this area an inordinate amount of scientific attention. More knowledge is thus available for this small area and its organisms, and their interactions are better known than in any other area. Thanks to such interest and knowledge, this area has produced more unifying concepts with respect tc the organization of marine communities than any other.

ENVIRONMENTAL CONDITIONS

In part, the tremendous array of environmental factors and ranges found in the intertidal is due to the fact that this zone is exposed to the air for a certain amount of time during the year and most physical factors show greater range in air than in water.

Tides

The periodic, predictable rise and fall of the level of the sea over a given time interval is called a *tide*. Certainly, this is the most important environmental factor influencing life in the intertidal zone. Without the presence of the tide or some other means of inducing a periodic rise and fall in the water level, this zone would not exist as it is, and many of the other factors would cease to be of influence. This is because the great range observed in many of the physical factors in the intertidal is a result of alternating exposure to air and to water. If there were no tide, these great fluctuations would not occur.

With very few exceptions, most shore area of the world experience tides. The only major seas that virtually lack tidal action are the Mediterranean and the Baltic. In these areas, the water level on the shore line fluctuates primarily due to the effects of wind action pushing water. This does not mean, however, that all seashores experience the same tidal range, or even the same type of tide. The reasons for the occurrence of different tides and different ranges are complex, having to do with the interaction of the tide-generating forces, the sun and moon, the rotation of the earth, the geomorphology of the ocean basins, and the natural uscillations of the various ocean basins. Most of the explanation is beyond the scope of this text, but a simplified explanation will be given here.

Tides occur due to the interaction between the gravitational attraction of the sun and the moon on the earth and the centrifugal force generated by the rotating earth and moon system. As a result of these forces, the water in the ocean basins is pulled into bulges. Gravitational attraction of one body for another is a function of the mass of each body and their distance apart. In the case of the sun and the moon, the gravitational generating force of the moon on the earth is about twice that of sun, even though the sun is many times more massive than the moon. This is due to the great distance of the sun from the earth relative to the moon.

The earth and moon form an orbiting system that revolves around their common center of mass. Because of the large size of the earth relative to the moon, this point is located inside the earth. The revolution of the earth-moon, system creates a centrifugal force (acting outward) which is balanced overall by the gravitational force acting between the two bodies. However, gravitational force is much stronger than centrifugal force on the side of the earth facing the moon than on the side opposite. As a result, the side facing the moon has the water pulled into a bulge (=high tide). On the opposite side of the earth, the gravitational force of the moon will be the least, and the stronger centrifugal force will pull water into a bulge away from earth (another high tide). Thus, we have the two high tides. These then circle the earth following the position of the moon as the earth revolves on its axis once every 24 hours. Low tides are about halfway between the high tides.

The system as described above would give two high tides and two low tides of equal magnitude each day. As we know, however, tides are not equal, nor are there always four tides per day. How do these discrepancies arise ? In part, this is due to the fact that the earth is not vertical with respect to its plane of orbit around the sun. It actually is inclined 23½° from the vertical. As a result, during the earth's rotation on its axis, a given point on the earth's surface is subjected to different tidal heights. It should also be noted from that, at the highest latitudes (polar seas), only a single high tide would occur. Further changes in the height of the tides result from changes in the moon relative to the earth as the moon moves in its orbit around the earth. Since the orbit of the moon is not circular but elliptical, there are times when the moon is close to the earth (*perigee*) and others when it is further away (*apogee*). Tides are greater at perigee ahd diminished at apogee.

The effect of the sun is seen in spring and neap tides. Spring tides are tides that show the greatest range (both high and low) and result when the moon and sun are directly aligned so these two forces are combined. Neap tides, on the other hand, are tides showing minimum range and result when sun and moon are at right angles to each other and thus counteract each other.

Differences both in number of high and low tides per day and in height in various parts of the world are due to peculiarities of the various ocean basins in which the tides occur. The well-known extremely high tides of the Bay of Fundy or Cook Inlet in Alaska are the result of the basic tide forces acting in the geometry of the basin.

Tides that are expressed as a single low and high per day are called *diurnal tides* (Fig. 1-1). Tides that have two highs and lows per lunar day are termed *semidiurnal tides.* Where there is a mixture of diurnal and semidiurnal we have what are called *mixed tides.* The heights of the highs and low vary from day to day as the positions of the sun and moon relative to each other change, each being alternately fully aligned and 90° out of alignment every 14 days.

Perhaps the most significant effect of the tide with respect to intertidal organism and communities is that it subjects them to periodic exposure to the air, with its considerably wider range of physical parameters. It is this exposure to aerial conditions that necessitates most of the adaptations required by intertidal organisms in order to inhabit this zone. Physical factors, the extremes of which are reduced for organisms inhabiting water, become limiting or lethal when the insulating water is removed.

Tides in combination with time can, however, have two significant direct effects on the presence and organization of intertidal communities. The first effect results from the time that a given area of the intertidal is exposed to the air relative to the time that it is submerged in water. It is the *duration of exposure* to air that is most important, because that is when the marine organisms will be subjected to the greatest temperature

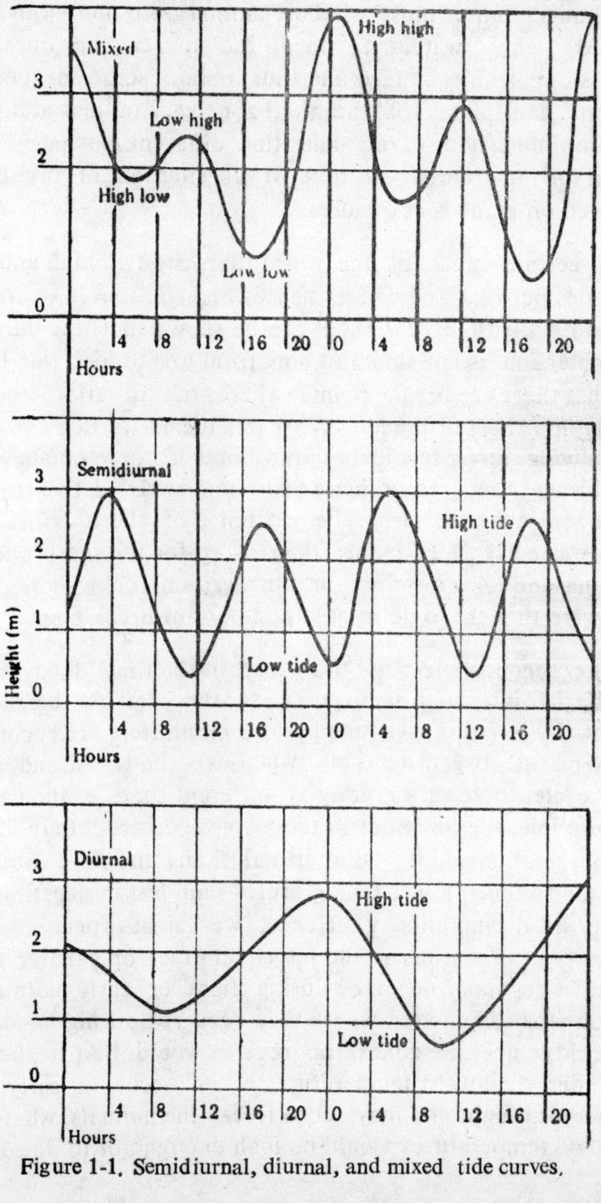

Figure 1-1. Semidiurnal, diurnal, and mixed tide curves.

ranges and the possibility of desiccation (=water loss). The longer the duration of exposure, the greater the chance for encountering a lethal temperature of desiccating beyond tolerable limits. Since most of these animals also must wait until covered with water to feed, the longer the duration, the less opportunity to feed and thus obtain sufficient energy. Animals and plants of the tidal zone vary in their ability to tolerate immersion in air and this differential is part of the reason for the different pattern of distribution of organisms observed on many rocky shores.

In certain areas of the world there are two high and two low tides per day, and where the two highs or two lows are not equal (areas with *mix tides*), it can be shown that the duration of immersion is not smooth going from low to high tide levels and that there are break points where the duration changes greatly in a short distance. What this means is that an organism living just a few inches above one of these points would be subjected to a greatly increased immersion relative to one just a few inches below. The existence of these *critical tide levels* was early suggested as the reason for the sharp changes in fauna and flora distribution observed on rocky shores since they were thought to delineate an important break point.

The second effect is the result of the time of day during which the intertidal is exposed so the air. As before, the potentially lethal ranges for physical parameters are encountered by marine organisms only when exposod to air and in any daily cycle, these vary greatly at different times of the day. If, for example, the low tides in the tropics occurred only during the hours of darkness, the intertidal fauna and flora would be exposed to much lower temperatures and less desiccation than if exposed during midday. Hence, we might expect a greater diversity of organisms in the intertidal of a tropical area where the tides regularly occurred during night or early morning or evening than in an area where they occurred during midday. In the cold temperate zones, the reverse would be true, because in winter, the lowest temperatures would occur in early morning or at night and may act to freeze the animals, whereas at midday, temperatures would be high enough not to do so.

A final effect of the tide is that, because of its predictability, it tends to induce certain rhythms in the activities of shore organisms. These rhythms may be with respect to time of spawning such as that seen in the grunion, a fish of the Pacific coast of the United States that spawns on the beach only on certain nights of the highest spring tides, or with respect to feeding or other activity. Most intertidal organisms are quiescent when the tide is out and resume normal activity, such as feeding, only when the tide is in.

Temperature

Because of its inherent physical characteristics, water, particularly large bodies of water such as the oceans, shows a minimum range of change in temperatue. Furthermore, this range rarely exceeds the lethal limits for the organisms. Intertidal areas are, however, regularly subjected to aerial termperatures for varying periods and these temperatures have a much wider range, on both a daily and a seasonal basis. The range may often exceed the lethal limits of the marine organisms. Should low tide occur when the air temperature is at a minimum (cold temperate, polar) or a maximum (tropics), the lethal limits may be exceeded and the organisms will die. Even if death does not occur immediately, the organisms may be so weakened by the extreme temperatures that they cannot resume normal activities and will suffer mortality from secondary causes.

Temperature also has an indirect effect. Marine organisms are subject to death by desiccation. Desiccation may be hastened by increased temperatures.

Wave Action

It is in the intertidal zone that wave action exerts the most influence on organisms and communities of any area in the sea. This influence is manifested directly and indirectly. Wave action affects shore life directly in two major ways. In the first place, it has a mechanical effect, which acts to smash and tear away objects with which it makes contact.

One can appreciate this action by noting the many pictures and stories of destruction wrought upon man-made structures due to storm waves of varying types. The action is similar in the intertidal zone, and hence, any creature that inhabit this zone must be adapted to this persistent force in some way. On shores that are made up of loose sand or gravel, the wave action is even more profound in that it moves the entire substrate around, influencing the actual shape of the zone. Wave exposure may thus prove to be limiting for certain organisms that are unable to sustain the force, and necessary to others that cannot exist other than in heavy wave areas.

Secondly, wave action acts to extend the limits of the intertidal zone. It does this by throwing water higher on the shore than would normally occur as a result of the tide alone. This continual splashing allows the marine organisms to live higher in wave-swept areas than in calm areas within the same tidal range.

Wave action has some other, perhaps minor, effects also. It acts to mix atmospheric gases into the water, thus increasing the oxygen content so wave-washed areas never lack for oxygen. Because of the constant interaction with the atmosphere and the formation of bubbles plue the stirring up of the substrate, wave-swept areas may have decreased penetration of light. This is, however, of little ecological significance.

Salinity

Salinity changes may occur in the intertidal in two situations that may affect the organisms. In the first place, the intertidal may be exposed at low tide and subsequently fiooded by heavy rains or runoff from heavy rains. This means they will be subjected to greatly reduced salinities. In certain cases, this reduction in salinity may exceed the limits and the organisms may die, as most intertidal organisms show a limited tolerance to decreased salinity. The second situation has to do with tidepools, those areas that retain sea water at low tide. These may either be flooded with fresh water runoff from heavy rains, thus reducing salinity, or they may show increased salinity when exposed to heavy evaporation during the day.

Other Factors

Different substrates—rock, sand, mud—have very different faunas and community structure in the intertidal, but these are taken up separately in this chapter. Oxygen seems not to be a factor exerting a limiting effect except in certain special cases and pH and nutrients are also unimportant to organisms and community structure.

ADAPTATIONS OF INTERTIDAL ORGANISMS

Since the intertidal organisms are primarily marine in origin, the adaptations that we observe have to do primarily with avoiding or minimizing the stresses imposed by the daily exposure to the terrestrial environment. The major stress from the marine environment is wave action.

Resistance to Water Loss

As soon as marine organisms are removed from the water into air, they begin to lose water. If they are to survive in the intertidal, this loss must somehow be minimized and/or the organisms must have body systems that will tolerate considerable losses during the hours of exposure to the air.

The simplest mechanism for avoiding water loss is seen in mobile animals such as crabs. These animals simply move from the exposed surface areas of the intertidal into very moist cracks, crevices, or burrows, where water loss is reduced or absent. Alternatively, they may seek refuge under the moist covering of algae. In other words, these animals avoid the adverse environmental condition of the shore by actively selecting suitable microhabitats. A similar situation occurs in some species of anemones such as *Anthopleura xanthogrammica* of the Pacific coast of North America. It is soft bodied, with no way of perventing water loss. However, it normally, is found only among barnacles or in crevices where water loss is reduced. Physiological adaptation is not needed.

Another simple mechanism is that seen in several of the high intertidal algae genera such as *Porphyra*, *Fucus*, and *Enteromorpha*. These plants connot move and have no mechanism to avoid water loss. They simply are adapted to withstand a severe loss of water from their tissues. Specimens of these genera can be found that are dry and brittle after a long exposure at low tide, yet will quickly take up water and resume normal body processes when the tide returns. Kanwisher (1957) found that they can tolerate as much as a 60-90 per cent loss of water and still recover. A similar tolerance to great water loss is see in some intertidal sedentary animals. Boyle (1969), for example, reports chitons can tolerate a 75 per cent water loss and limpets, according to Davis (1969), from 30–70 per cent, depending on the species.

Many species of intertidal animals, in contrast to the above, have mechanisms for prevention of water loss. These mechanisms may be structural, behavioral, or both. Barnacles of many species are predominant members of the intertidal zone all over the world. These animals are sessile and avoid water loss by closing up within their shells at low tide. Here, the presence of an impermeable shell cuts down the evaporative water loss. Limpets of the genera *Patella*, *Acmaea*, and *Collisella* are also dominant animals of the rocky intertidal. Certain species of these limpets have a "home scar" into which their shells exactly fit. At low tide, they return to these "homes" and by fitting into these grooves, greatly reduce water loss. Other limpets that have no scar simply clamp down tightly against the rock so no tissue is exposed, only shell. Other gastropods such as the periwinkles (*Littorina*) have opercula which completely seal off the aperture to their shells. At low tide, they may pull into the shell, closing the aperture with the operculum and thus reduce water loss. Certain bivalves, such as *Mytilus edulis*, are able to survive in the intertidal because of their ability to close their valves tightly to prevent water loss. Still other organisms, such as the anemone *Actinia* and the hydroid *Clava squamata*, produce mucus that prevents water loss. Many inhabitants of sand or mud simply burrow into the substrate to prevent desiccation.

Maintenance of Heat Balance

Intertidal organisms are also exposed to extremes of heat and cold and show behavioral and structural adaptations to maintain their internal heat balance. Though deaths by freezing have been recorded for intertidal organisms, extreme low temperatures seem to be less of a problem to shore organisms than high temperatures. This may be due to the fact that organisms are often living much closer to their upper lethal temperature than to their lower lethal one. Hence, most mechanisms for heat balance concern the avoidance of too high temperatures. This may be accomplished by (1) reducing heat gain from the environment and (2) increasing the heat loss from the body of the animal. Heat gain from the environment is reduced in several ways. One way is to have a relatively large body size when compared to similar species, either lower in the intertidal or in the subtidal. Large body size means less surface area relative to volume and hence, less area to gain heat. At the same time, a larger body takes longer to heat up than a smaller one. It has been recorded for gastropod mollusks such as *Littorina littorea* and *Olivella biplicata* that the large individuals occur higher in the tidal zone and the smaller ones lower. Yet another mechanism to reduce heat gain is to reduce the area of body tissue in contact with the substrate. This is, however, difficult to achieve for most intertidal animals, since they need the extra purchase provided by a large area of tissue in contact with the substrate to avoid being swept off by waves. Yet, there are some shore animals that do have such a small area of attachment or none at all. These occur where wave action is not severe, and, in those animals that lose attachment, the ability to reattach as the tide comes in is well developed.

Heat loss can be attributed to a number of causes. One mechanism, found in hard-shelled organisms such as mollusks, is greater elaboration of ridges and other sculpturing on the hell. These act as radiator fins and facilitate heat loss. Examples of such sculptured mollusks are best found in the tropics and include *Tectarius muricata* and *Nodolittorina tuberculata*. Enhancement of heat loss occurs when the organism is light in color. (Dark organisms gain heat by absorption.) Many tropical and subtropical snails of the high intertidal such as *Nerita peleronta* (Caribbean) and *Littorina unifasciata* (New Zealand) are much lighter in color than their lower level relatives, presumably then, facilitating heat loss.

Finally and most importantly, heat loss can occur through evaporation of water. Unfortunately, again, intertidal organisms must face the problem of desiccation and can ill afford to cool themselves through evaporation or else chance a lethal desiccation. Many intertidal organisms show a strategy of adaptation that allows them some cooling by evaporating water and, at the same time, avoiding excessive desiccation (see Segal and Dehnel, 1962). To facilitate this balance, many intertidal animals have an extra water supply from which cooling may take place. This extra water is held in the mantle cavity of barnacles and limpets, ond it is above the amount the animal needs to survive desiccation. Secondly, most high intertidal animals can withstand a remarkable amount of desiccation and finally, many animals have the ability to reduce the rate of water loss from the tissues when necessary.

Mechanical Stress

As noted previously, wave action reaches a zenith in the intertidal zone. As a result, it is necessary for any organism that lives intertidally to adapt in order to resist the smashing and tearing effects of waves. Waves action has different effects on rocky shores as opposed to sandy shores and requires different adaptations. which are discussed subsequently. However, some generalities may be noted here.

In order to maintain position in the face of wave action, several adaptations have been developed by intertidal organisms One such adaptation, observed in barnacles, oysters, and serpulid polychaete worms, is simply to become fixed to the substrate. Similarly, the majority of algae in the intertidal are fused via a holdfast to the bottom.

Still other organisms develop attachments that are strong but not permanent, thus giving limited movement. Such attachments are the byssal threads of *Mytilus,* which anchor the animals securely but still can be broken and remade to allow limited slow movement.

The dominant intertidal mollusks sueh as the various limpets and chitons, resists wave action through a strong, enlarged foot which clamps them to the substrate.

Motile organisms such as crabs have no structural mechanism to resist being swept away and survive only because they seek shelter from the waves in crevices or under rocks.

Most intertidal mollusks are adapted to wave skock by possessing thicker shells than their subtidal relatives and lack delicate sculpturing which is easily broken in the waves.

Respiration

Since the animals inhabiting the intertidal are marine, they have respiratory surfaces adapted to extract O_2 from water. Usually, these are thin-walled extensions from the body surface. These respiratory organs are thus very susceptible to desiccation in air and do not function unless immersed in water. Such organs would be a distinct disadvantage in the intertidal. Among intertidal animals, there is a tendency to enclose the respiratory surfaces in a protective cavity to prevent them from drying. This is seen particularly in various mollusks where the gills are in mantle cavity, which itself is protected by the shell. A similar situation prevails in barnacles where the mantle tissue acts as a respiratory organ.

Because animals with protected respiratory organs must also conserve water at low tide, they often close up (operculum) or clamp down (chitons, limpetes)such that gaseous exchange is reduced. Thus, to conserve O_2 and wnter, most animals are quiescent during low tide.

Feeding

All intertidal animals must expose the fleshy parts of their bodies to feed. This means exposing those parts most susceptible to desiccation. As a result virtually all intertidal animals are active only during the time the tide is in and they are covered with water. This is true whether the animals are grazers, filter feeders, detritus feeders, or predators.

Salinity Stress

As noted above, the intertidal zone may be subjected to flooding by fresh water, which would create an osmotic stress on the intertidal organisms adapted to be submerged only in sea water. This is particularly true since most intertidal organisms do not show adaptations to tolerate salinity changes, certainly not like estuarine organisms do. Most have no mechanism to control the salt content of their body fluids and hence, are *osmoconformers.* The only adaptations observed are the same as those for preventing desiccation, such as closing up valves or shells in barcles and mollusks. Perhaps this is why there are records of catastrophic mortality of intertidal organisms following heavy rain or runoff. Apparently, however, such events are so rare or unpredictable that special mechanisms have not evolved.

Reproduction

Because so many of the intertidal organisms are sedentary or sessile, they must rely upon eggs and/or larvae that are free floating in the plankton for dispersal. Hence, we see a high incidence of planktonic larvae among intertidal organisms. These larvae are of many types.

A second reproductive adaptation attributable to the intertidal position is that most organisms have a breeding cycle that is closely synchronised with the occurrence of certain tides, such as spring tides. An example is *Mytilus edulis,* in which gonads mature during periods of spring tides and spawning occurs on subsequent neap tides. In *Littorina neritoides,* the egg are spawned at time of spring tides.

Rocky Shores

Of all the intertidal shores, those composed of hard material, the rocky shores, are the most densely inhabited by macroorganisms and have the greatest diversity of animal and plant species. They stand in strinking contrast to the almost barren appearance of sand and mud shores. It is these densely populated, topographically diverse, and species rich rocky areas that have fascinated marine biologists and ecologists for many years. In recent years, these areas have been subject of several classic studies that have enhanced our understanding of how these associations of species interact with each other to maintain or change the community.

Zonation

On of the most striking featurer of any rocky shore anywhere in the world, when seen at low tide is the prominent horizontal banding or *zonation* of the organisms. Each zone or band is set off from those adjacent by differences in color, morphology of the major organism, or some combination of color and morphology. These horizontal bands or zones succeed each other vertically as one progresses up from the level of the lowest low tides to true terrestrial conditions (Fig. 1.2). This zonation observed on intertidal rocky shores is similar to the zonation pattern that one observes with increasing elevation on a mountain, where the different horizontal zones of trees and shrubs succeed each other vertically until, if one progresses far enough, permanent snow cover is reached. The major difference between these two areas is the scale, mountain zones being perhaps kilometers in width as opposed to intertidal zones extending a few meters vertically.

Rocky intertidal zones vary in vertical extent, depending upon the slope of the rocky surface, the tidal range, and the exposure to wave action. Where there is a gradual slope to the rock, individual zones may be broad, whereas under similar tidal and exposure conditions on a vertical face, the same zone would be narrow. In the same manner, exposed areas tend to have broader zones than protected shores, and shores with greater tidal range have broader vertical zones.

Of course, these striking bands may be interrupted or altered in various places along a rocky shore wherever the rock substrate itself shows changes in slope, composition, or irregularities that change its exposure or position relative to the prevailing water movement.

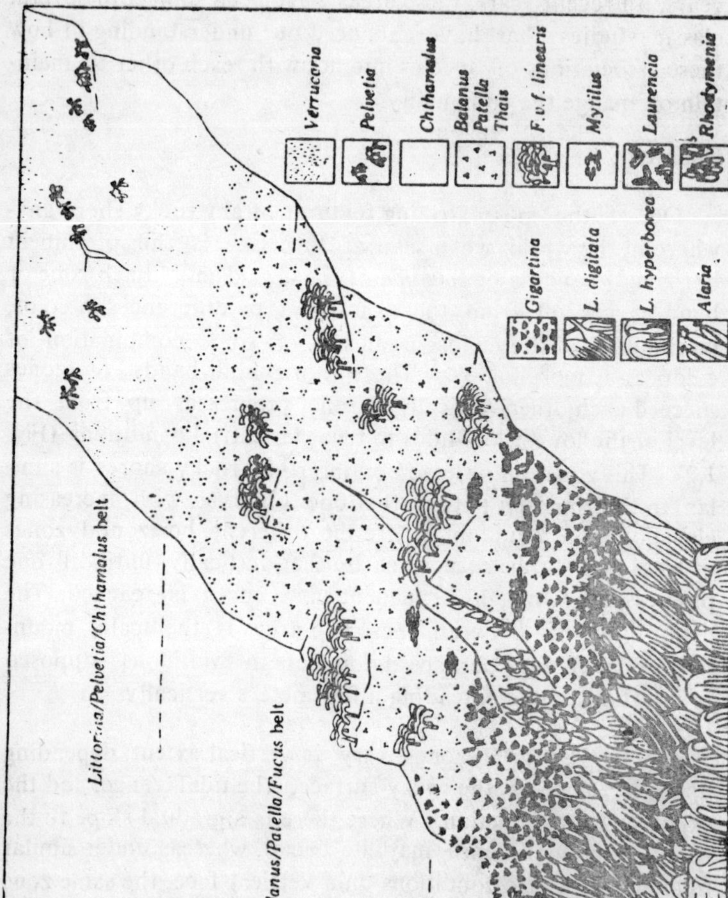

(A)

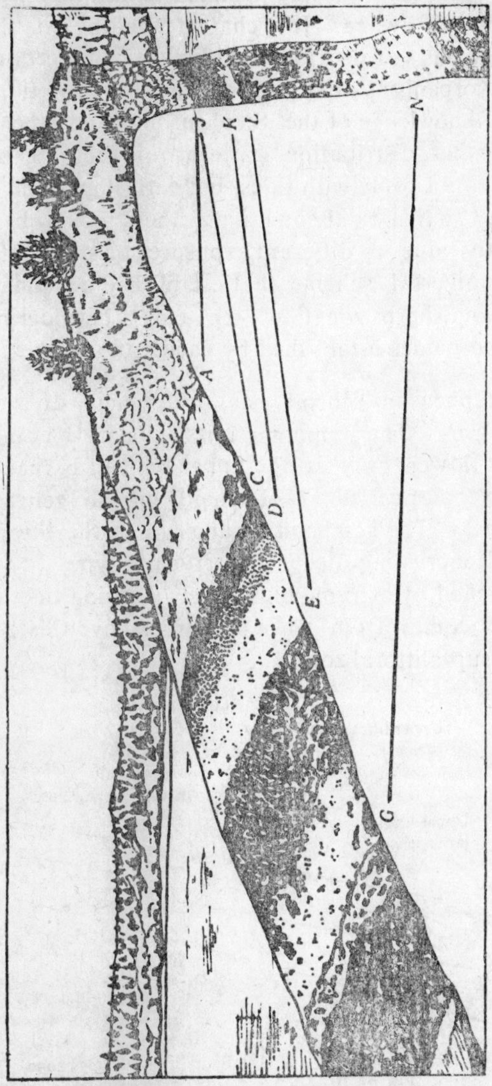

Figure 1 2. Zonation in the rocky intertidal.

The fact that these prominent zones can be observed on nearly all rocky shores throughout the world under many different tidal regimes led the team of Stephenson and Stephenson (1949) to propose, after some 30 years of study, a "universal" scheme of zonation for rocky shores. This "universal" scheme was really a framework using common terms that would allow comparison of diverse. It is characterized by establishing the zones on the basis of distributional limits of the certain common groups of organisms and not on the basis of tides. It thus reflects the knowledge of the Stephensons, and other intertidal ecologists, that distribution patterns of the organisms and zones vary not only with tides, but with slopes and exposure. Thus, under similar tidal conditions, there could be different band widths due to different exposures or slopes of rocks. It was this universal scheme that established a standard format for describing shore zonation, replacing a bewildering host of schemes and names established by earlier biologists.

The Stephenson scheme has three main divisions of the intertidal area. The uppermost is termed the *supralittoral fringe*. Its lower limit is the upper limit of barnacles, and it extends to the upper limit of snails of the genus *Littorina* (periwinkles). The dominant organisms are the littorine snails and black encrusting lichens (verrucaria type). Part of this zone is reached by extreme high water of spring tides, but must of its water comes from wave splash. Above this zone is the terrestrial supralittoral zone.

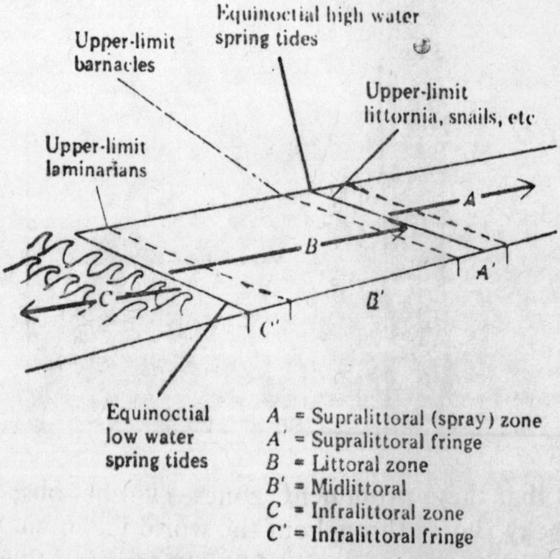

Figure 1.3. The Stephenson "Universal" scheme of zonation for rocky shores.

The middle part of the intertidal is termed the ***midlittoral*** zone and is the broadest in extent. Its upper limit is coincident with the upper limit of barnacles, while its lower limit is that point where large kelps reach their uppermost distribution. This zone is often subdivided and contains a host of different organisms. Perhaps the only universally present dominant group are the barnacles.

The lowermost zone of the scheme is the ***infralittoral fringe,*** which extends from the lowest low tide up to the upper limit of the large kelps. This is an extremely rich zone composed of organisms that can tolerate only limited exposure to air. It is really an intertidal extension of the *infralittoral zone* or what we know as the sublittoral area.

Although the above scheme does set forth a means for describing zonation on rocky shores, it does not offer an explanation as to why the zonation occurs. It is this explanation of zonal patterns that intrigues current marine biologists.

Causes of Zonation

Whereas it is fairly easy to recognize and measure the extent of the zones on a rocky shore, it is more difficult to came up with suitable explanations as to why organisms are distributed into these zones. Two sets of factors can be considered to explain the phenomenon : physical and biological. We shall take each up in turn.

Physical Factors : The most obvious explanation for the occurrence of the zones is that they are a result of the tidal action on the shore and therefore reflect the different tolerances of the organisms to increasing exposure to the air and the resultant desiccation and temperature extremes. One difficulty with this explanation is that the rise and fall of a tide tends to follow a smooth curve with no obvious sharp breaks, which would correspond to the often sharp boundaries observed in the intertidal zones. If, however, one observes a whole series of such tidal curves, such a series of breaks does become apparent. gives a typical tidal curve for a mixed tide area on the California coast gives the maximum time of continuous submergence for various tide levels. As can be seen from the graph, there are certain points on this curve that reflect sharp increases in exposure to air. This can also be deduced which represents a single typical lunar tide cycle. Consider an organism at point X on the graph. At this point, the tide will cover the organism at least once every six hours. If, however, the organism moves up only a few inches, the tide will not cover it for 12 hours. Thus, there is a great change in exposure time with a very short vertical movement. Points exhibiting sharp increases in exposure time over short distances have been termed *critical tide levels* by Doty (1946) and were offered as one of the early explanations for the zonation patterns described above. In this explanation, it is important to remember that it is not the tide per se that causes the limit, but rather the fact that, at these critical points, the organisms are subjected to greatly increased time in the air and hence to greater temperature fluctuations and desiccation.

The critical tide hypothesis has been tested in various places by several scientists since its original promulgation by Doty in 1946. In general, it is difficult to find good correlations, particularly at the lower tide levels. This lack of good correlations, can be partly attributed to the varying topography of the various shores and to the variation in exposure. Thus, a species may well be able to exist above the critical tide level if t e rocky shore is exposed to persistent violent wave action, which would throw water up higher and thus decrease desiccation. Similarly, caves, overhangs, and crevices remain moist when exposed areas are dried out, thus allowing persistence of organisms above the level predicted by the citical tides. The effects of these topography and exposure differences suggest, however, that the real upper limits are set by certain physical factors, namely desiccation and temperature.

Since the intertidal organisms are marine, desiccation is a serious problem. Several natural observations as well as field experiments have suggested that desiccation can set the upper limits to organisms and zones. In the North Temperate Zone, for example, rocks which have a north-facing slope often have the same organism occurring higher than do adjacent south-facing slopes. Since such rocks experience no difference in wave exposure or tides, the only reason for the height difference is that north faces dry out more slowly than south faces. Similarly, field experiments by Frank (1965) and others in which water was slowly dripped down slopes have resulted in the organisms extending higher up (Fig. 1.4). In other experiments organisms were transplanted above their normal positions. Notable in this respect are barnacles which, of course, cannot move. When transplanted by Foster (1971) above their normal tidal height, they died, with younger ones dying more quickly than older ones. Again, desiccation can be suspected.

Along with desiccation and often acting in concert with it, temperature is the other major physical limiting factor. As noted previously, aerial temperatures have ranges that may exceed the lethal limits and hence, intertidal organisms may

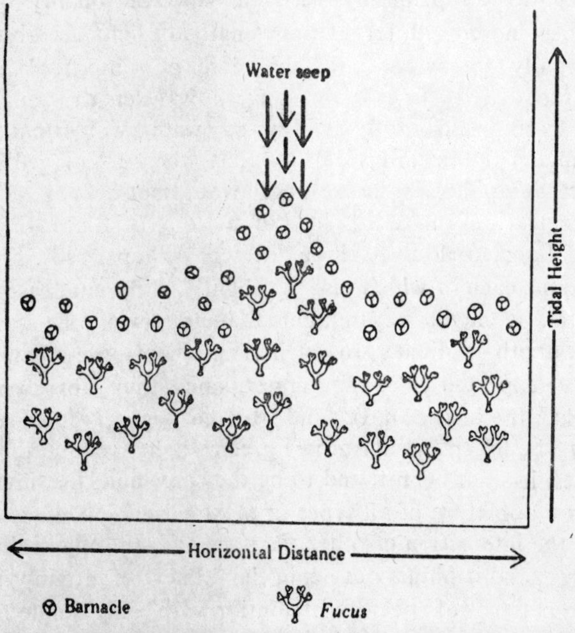

Figure 1.4. Zonation change in the presence of a water seep.

die from either freezing or "cooking". Upper limits to zones may therefore be partly attributable to the tolerable temperature limits of the intertidal organism. In addition, high temperature promotes desiccation, and the synergistic effect of these factors may be even more devastating than each acting alone.

Finally, sunlight itself may act adversely to limit organisms on the shore. Sunlight includes wavelengths in the ultraviolet region that are deleterious to living tissue. Water quickly absorbs these wavelengths and so serves to protect most marine animals. However, intertidals animals have direct exposure to such rays at low tide. The higher an organism is in the intertidal, the greater the exposure to these rays. At the present time, there is little information concerning whether such UV radiation is active in controlling distribution of organisms, but the possibility remains. Light also has been suggested as a regulator of the distribution of intertidal algae. This has to do primarily with the spectral quality of the light. As noted different wavelengths of light are absorbed differentially by water. In the case of intertidal algae, those that need light of longer wavelength (reds) and that are absorbed most quickly by water would tend to be found higher in the intertidal so that when submerged (when they actually photosynthesize), they would not be too deep for the penetration of red light (about 2 m). Since the main intertidal algae belong to three different groups, reds, browns, and greens, each of which has a slightly different absorption spectrum, it might be thought that they would be arranged along a depth gradient. In such a gradient, the green algae would be expected to be the highest, since they absorb mainly red light ; the brown next; and the red algae, which absorb mainly the deep, penetrating green light, deepest. This, however, has not been found to be the case, aud the intertidal algae are a mixture of all types at most levels. This is likely due to the interaction of other factors and the physiology of the algae, and it points out again the fallacy of attempting to explain patterns of species distribution with only single factors when a multitude are acting at all times.

We can summarize the above by stating that it appears that physical factors are strong determinants of the upper limits of the distribution of intertidal organisms.

Biological Factors : Although the early work in the intertidal focused on the importance of physical factors in setting the zonal patterns, more recent work has begun to clearly establish the great importance of various biological factors in setting various observed distribution patterns. In general, these biological factors are more complex, often subtle, and closely linked to other factors, which is probably why we have only recently begun to understand how they act. The major biological factors are *competition*, *predation*, and *grazing* (=herbivory). We shall take them up in order.

Competition for a certain resource does not occur if the resource is so plentiful that adequate supplies of it are available for all species or individuals. In the rocky intertidal zone, only one resource is commonly in limited supply and that is space. This is perhaps the most restricted area in the marine environment in terms of physical dimensions ; at the same time, it is densely populated, at least in the temperate zone. As a result, there is an intense competition for space. This has resulted in observed zonal patterns. On the intertidal shores of Scotland, there is a distinct zonation of barnacles with the small *Chthamalus stellatus* living in the highest zone and the larger Balanus *balanoides* occupying the major portion of the mid-intertidal. Studies done by Connell (1961) showed that *Chthamalus* larvae settled out throughout the zones occupied by both barnacles, but survived to adulthood only in upper zones. The reason for the disappearance in the midlittoral region was due to competition from *Balanus balanoides*, which either overgrew, uplifted, or crushed the young *Cathamalus*. *Balanus* was prevented from completely eliminating *Chthamalus* because it did not have the tolerance to drying and high temperatures that prevailed at the higher tidal levels and hence did not survive there, whereas *Chthamalus* could survive there. Here, then, is a case where the zonation is at least partially a function of biological competition.

A more complex example concerning competition is that among the mussel *Mytilus californianus* and several species of barnacles on the Pacific coast of North America. In this case, studies by Dayton (1971) have shown that *M. californianus* is the dominant space competitor on open coast shores Given enongh time and freedom from predators, the *M. californianus* eventually overgrow and outcompete all other macroorganisms and take over the substrates throughout most of the mid-intertidal. *Mytilus californianus* takeover is, however, slow. Wherever open space occurs, it may be rapidly colonized by other organisms, including three species of barnacles, *Balanus glandula, B. cariosus,* and *Pollicipes polymerus* These, in turn, displace any rapidly growing algal species. The barnacles persist only until the mussels enter. The mussels outcompete and destroy the barnacles by setttling on top of them and smothering them. Since nothing appears to be large enough to settle and smother the *M. californianus,* they remain in control of the intertidal space. Given this competitive edge, it would appear that eventually, the rocky Pacific coast of North America would be a monotonus band of *M. californianus.* It is also curious that *M. californianus* forms dense clumps or bands only in the intertidal, though it is perfectly capable of living subtidally. Since it is a premier space competitor, why this abrupt lower limits ? The reasons for this have to do with other biological factors which act to prevent such resource monopolization and may be grouped under the term ***predation.***

Intertidal algae, particularly those on temperate shores, also often show abrupt limits to their upper and lower distribution. Earlier, these limits were ascribed to critical tide levels, but it has also been suggested that this could be due to competition for space and/or access to light. Unfortunately, very little information is available concerning actual or potential competition among algal species to test these hypotheses. In two experimental studies none on the Pacific coast of North America, evidence was found for competition. The first study by Dayton (1975) was directed at the larger kelps, and he found that the dominant kelps, *Hedophyllum sessile,*

Laminaria setchelli, and *Lessionopsis ltitoralis* all outgrew and outcompeted certain smaller species in the lower intertidal. These smaller species were generally fast-growing species, which quickly colonized open areas. As noted they are *opportunistic* or *fugitive* species. In turn, among the three dominants, *Hedophyllum* was outcompeted by the other two such that they came to dominate the areas. The second study was actually done in the subtidal, where Vadas (1968) found that the giant kelp *Nerencystis* outcompteted and overgrew the brown alga *Agarum*. On the New England coast, similar studies by Lubchenko (1978) directed at tidepool algae indicated that *Enteramorpha intestinalis* was a dominant space competitor as opposed to *Chondrus crispus*; in the absence of grazers, *E. intestimalis* would quickly outcompete *Chondrus* and take over the space. These few studies suggest that competition among algal species may be more widespread than originally assumed and may be a fertile ground for future ecological work.

The role of predators in determining the distribution of organisms in the intertidal, and hence, the zonal patterns, is best documented for the Pacific coast of North America and is discussed here as an example of how complex biological interactions serve to give the prevailing observed distributions.

The dominant abundant intertidal animals on the Pacific coast other than the space-dominating *Mytilus californianus* are the barnacles *Balanus cariosus* and *Balanus glandula*. These latter two species occur abundantly in the intertidal region, despite the fact that they are competitively inferior to *M. californianus*, because a predatory starfish, *Pisaster ochraceus*, preys upon *M. californianus*, thus preventing it from completely ovegrowing the barnacles *Pisaster ochraceus* is a voracious predator of muscles, consuming them at a rate that effectively prevents them from occuping all the space.

At the same time, *Balanus glandula* is found primarly as a band of adults in the high intertidal, while *Balanus cariosus* occurs as cattered, large individuals or clumps in the mid-intertidal. This pattern, as Connell (1970) has shown, is also due to predation. *Balanus glandula*, like *Chthamalus* in England, is capable of living throughout the intertidal zone and indeed settles throughout. The same is true for *B. cariosus*. That both show a restricted distribution is due to predation by three species of predatory gastropods of the genus *Thais* : *T. lamellosa*, *T. emarginata*, and *T. canaliculata*. The abundance and motility of these predators is such that they are capable of completely consuming all the young *B. glandula* settling out in the mid-intertidal in 12-15 months. *Balanus glandula* survives only in a narrow band at the top of the intertidal, where the *Thais* species are prevented from entering because of excessive desiccation. In the case of *B. cariosus*, however, the situation is somewhat different. There is no high level refuge for this barnacle, but, as with *B glandula*, the youg are consumed by the *Thais*. The refuse for *B. cariosus* is that once it reaches 2 years of age, it is too large for *Thais* to attack. The only problem, as yet unresolved, though it may have to do with periodic events like big freezes at low tide, is how it manages to survive the *Thais* for two years. As a result, the pattern of distribution for *B. cariosus* is random clumps of large, older barnacles.

It is not known for certain what regulates *Thais* populations, but they are preyed upon by large *Pisaster* and are also vulnerable to periodic events such as freezing during winter low tides. Such periodic events may reduce the population by such a significant amount that the *Balanus cariosus* could successfully establish themselves in an area. This may explain the differences among various shores with respect to the abundance of this barnacle.

Pisaster ochraceus can consume *Thais* and barnacles of any size and is the primary predator of small and medium-sized *Mytlius*. It is the top predator in the system. Because of its ability to influence the structure of the entire community in the intertidal—through its ability to consume *Mytilus* and therefore prevent monopolization of the space—it has been called by Paine (1966) a *keystone species*.

The reasons that refuges from predator occur in the upper

intertidal is that both *Pisaster* and *Thais* can feed only when the tide is in, and they require a long period to successfully attack their prey. The short period of immersion of the upper intertidal does not allow sufficient time for them to make successful forays into that area. In subtidal areas, unlimited time is available ; hence the starfish have sfficient time to atack and consume any prey item. It is probably for that reason that *Mytilus*, for example, do not extend into the subtidal areas, even though they can certainly live there ; hence, the reason for the sharp lower boundaries to the zonation of this species.

Lubchenco and Menge (1978) have also demonstrated that predation is important in setting zonal patterns in the intertidal of the North Atlantic Ocean. In the low intertidal of New England, the competitive dominant species is *Mytilus edulis. Mytilus edulis* is able to outcompete and eliminate the barnacle *Balanus balanoides* and the alga *Chondrus crispus*. It is prevented from doing this by the starfish *Asterias forbesi* and *Asterias vulgaris* and the snail *Thais lapilius*, all of which prey upon *M. edulis*. In the areas where these predators are absent namely the most exposed, wave-beaten areas, *M. edulis* eliminates *Balanus* and *Chondrus*. Thus, the exposed wave-beaten areas exhibit a zonal pattern where the low intertidal is a *M. edulis* band, while in protected areas, a diverse lower zone exists with *Mytilus, Balanus*, and *Chondrus* present (Fig. 1.5)

The role of *grazers* or herbivores in regulating upper and lower limits of algal species is less well studied documented, but evidence suggests this process may also be considerable importance. The dominant groups of intertidal grazers are the various limpets, sea urchins, and littorine snails. In the tidepools and on the shores of New England studied by Lubchenco (1978), one of the dominant is *Chondrus crispus*. In the tidepools, but not on the exposed intertidal, it is out competed by the green alga *Enteromorpha intestinalis*, but it is able to persist in those pools that have a high population of the grazer *Littorina littorea*, because the latter preferentially consume *E. intestinalis*. Similarly, in England, when Jones (1948) removed all the limpets (*Patellavulgata*) from an intertidal strip,

strip was densely settled by the algae and appeared in marked contrast to the surrounding barer areas. Since the only alteration was the removal of the main grazers, this suggests their great importance in determining at least the abundance of

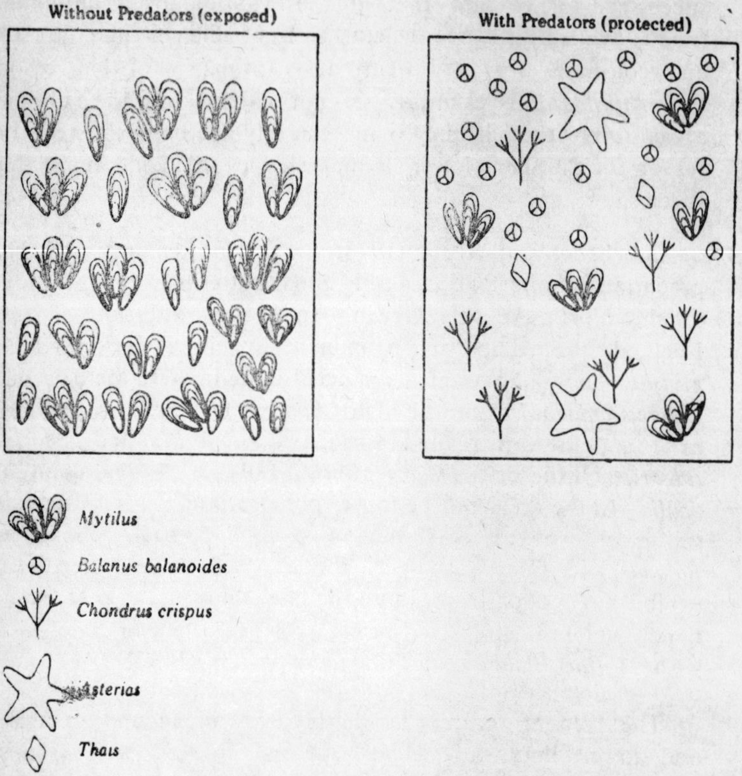

Figure 1-5. Composition of the low intertidal in the North Atlantic Ocean with and without mussel predators.

algal species. In this same study, after a few years, the limpets again returned (*via* settlement) and the algae were consumed until the area appeared like the rest of the shore. In somewhat similar studies on the Pacific coast of North America, dimination of limpets (*Acmaea, Collisella*) from intertidal areas has resulted in heavy algal growth where none, or little, had been before.

Sea urchins are large grazers and often occur on shores in dense aggregations. Removal experiments with sea urchins in both the Atlantic Ocean (England) by Jones and Kain (1967) and the Pacific Ocean (Washington coast) by Dayton (1975) have had similar results. In both cases, removal resulted in dense growth of algae where there had been sparse or no growth before. In all of these cases, the small, rapidly growing opportunistic algal species were the first to settle, and later, they were replaced by the dominant, larger algae. What is important here is that the algae that settle in these areas often differ from those in the immediately surrounding areas. This suggests that the urchins prefer to eat certain species, leaving others, and thus effectively alter the appearance of those areas of the intertidal that they occupy. In spite of this evidence as to their ability to remove certain algae and determine the composition of the zones, there is as yet, no direct evidence that they set the limits to the distribution of any species.

Small Scale Distribution Patterns

Although the major large-scale patterns of organism distribution in the rocky intertidal, the zonation, can be explained through some combination of exposure, desiccation, temperature, competition, predation, or grazing acting separately or together, these vertical bands are never perfect. Often small-scale local variations occur that act to alter the bands and affects the immediate local distribution of certain organisms. Such small-scale or *local distribution* patterns can result from either biological or physical factors.

Perhaps the easiest of these local distribution patterns to explain are those that result from physical factors, primarily the variation in the nature, slope, and exposure of the rock surface. Existence of a different rock type in a local area as compared to the surrounding shore almost always means the presence of different organisms, or at least different abundances. An outcrop of sandstone among an otherwise granite rock shore usually means a different complement of organisms.

Similarly, slopes facing south and those facing north often have different organisms, or the densities and/or levels to which the organisms are found differ. This reflects the different amount of desiccation and harmful effects of direct exposure to the sun's rays (=insolation). On the Pacific coast of North America, for example, two limpet species. *Collisella* (*Acmaea*) *digitalis* and *Collisella* (*Acmaea*) *scabra* inhabit the high intertidal zone, but, as Haven (1971) has shown, their local distribution within the zone reflects their reaction to the small-scale changes in the substrate. *Collisella scabra* is found primarily on horizontal surfaces where it has a home "scar" or depression in which it remains during periods of low tide. *Collisella digitalis* has no scar and is found on the cooler, moist shaded vertical slopes. *Collisella scabra* is able to survive on the drier horizontal rocks because of its depression or scar, in which the fit is tight enough to prevent desiccation at low tide. *Collisella digitalis*, on the other hand, without the increased desiccation protection of the scar, must live where desiccation is not a intense (*i.e.*, north-facing slopes and crevices). Similarly, certain species do not prefer to settle on vertical faces or overhangs. These area are then settled by other species unable to compete on the flat surfaces.

Much small-scale patchiness probably results from the destructive effects of wave action and wave-borne objects, such as logs, that may be hurled against the shore, smashing into small areas and clearing them of organisms. Such battering was studied by Dayton (1971) in the state of Washington, and it was found that any point on an open shore had a 5-30 per cent chance of being hit by a log within a three-year period. An additional effect of wave action is that it produces aggregations of mobile species, such as snails and crabs, in crevices or other protected areas. Heavy wave action from storms, even if unaccompanied by battering of objects, also is responsible for removal of organisms from the intertidal. Thus, Menge (1976) found in the exposed intertidal in New England that winter storms could clear as much as 90 per cent of the intertidal, whereas during summer and fall, less than 10 per cent of the same space was free of organisms.

The premier space competitors, *Mytilus edulis* in New England, or *M. californianus* on the Pacific coast of North America, both tend to form large clumps that grow out from the substrate. As a result, as the clumps get larger, fewer mussels are attached directly to the substrate through their byssal threads and more are attached to each other. This creates an unstable situation in which the battering waves are more likely to tear off a clump, and hence, older, larger clumps become more vulnerable.

Creation of such open spaces in any zone usually resu ts in quick colonization by a series of *opportunistic* or *fugitive* species. These species quickly settle an open area, mature, and reproduce before the slower growing dominant species retake the open space and force them out through competition. The most common of these opportunists are the smaller filamentous green and red algae and smaller animals such as hydroids. These initial species are then replaced successively by competitively better species until the competitives dominant in the area takes over. In any one zone, then, there may be many of these patches, which, depending on the time since their initial clearance, will be in differing stages of *succession* towards the dominant community characterizing the zone. This accounts for the differences one observes in different patches in the same zone in the same area.

Small scale distribution anomalies may also be the result of biological interactions of various types. Some of these are *passive*, such as the fact that many species of animals must inhabit moist arears in order to survive the exposure of air and hence shelter under the fronds of various intertidal algae. The patchiness of these forms follows the distribution of the algae, but it is not due to any direct action of the algae. Removal of the algal canopy also results in the disappearance of the sheltering organisms.

Other biological effects are more direct and lead to definite distribution patterns, which can be observed. Thus, for example, the intertidal anemone *Anthopleura elegantissima* of the Pacific coast of North America tends to occur in large clumps, uniformly separated from each other. Each clump has resulted from the continued asexual division of the original anemone, such that each clump consists of genetically identical individuals, a *clone*. Francis (1973) discovered that the sharp boundaries that exist between adjacent clones are the result of active fighting between the outer individuals of each clones. In these fights, special tentacles called acrorhagi are employed and are able to inflict massive tissue damage to other anemones. The result of such clonal "border wars" is the separation of clones by anemone-free strips, which are just the width that prevent two anemones from reaching each other. Thus, clumps of anemones are always separated from other such clumps.

Yet another example of biological interaction that produces spacing is the phenomenon of *territoriality*. Territoriality is defined as an individual or group of individuals actively keeping other members of the same or different species out of an area. This phenomenon is well known among various birds and mammals, but it also occurs among certain invertebrate organisms. On the north Pacific coast of America, the largest limpet in the intertidal is *Lottic gigantea*. Stimson (1970) has shown that individuals of this species create a territory in the intertidal, which they actively defend against other *Lottia* and other limpets. Should other limpets invade this territory, the resident *Lottia* pushes the interloper out. In this way, each *Lottia* keeps a small patch of rock free of potential competition and ensure that all algae growing on the site will be consumed by itself.

Another type of interaction producing small patches is that observed by Dayton (1973) in the alga *Postelsia palmaeformis*, which occurs in isolated clumps in the most wave-swept portions of the Pacific coast. This alga creates its own patch by sacrificing a portion of its offspring. Young *Postelsia* plants always settle close to the parent plants. Usually, this means settling on various barnacles, algae, or *Mytilus*. As they grow in the wave-swept area, they eventually produce so much surface of resistance to the wave battering that the young are pulled free at the same time, removing the barnacle, alga, or

Mytilus to which they were attached. This creates a new open area, which is then invaded by a second wave of *Postelsia* sporelings, which this time attach directly to the rock surface and grow up into adults. Thus, the space around a *Postelsia* maintained, and competitive dominants do not force *Postelsio* patch is out.

Predation and grazing can also create small patches or patchy distribution. Predation is the reason for the occurrence of *Balanus cariosus* in small clumps in the intertidal ; grazing by sea urchins may result in tidepools free of algae, while others without urchins have an abundant growth. On the New

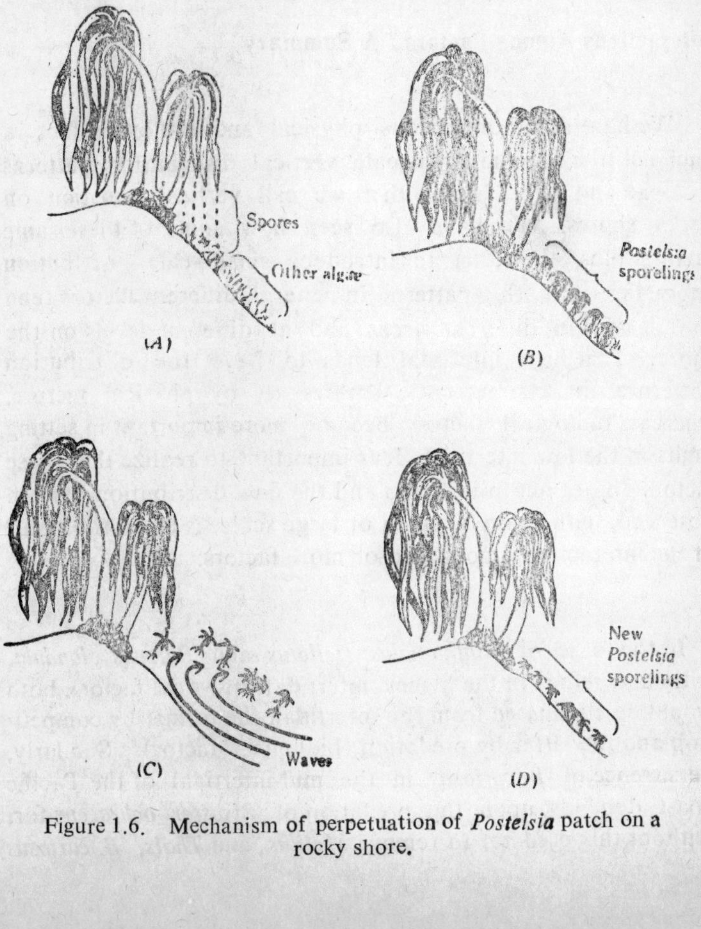

Figure 1.6. Mechanism of perpetuation of *Postelsia* patch on a rocky shore.

England coast, as noted above, tidepools without *Littorina littorea* are dominated by *E. intestinalis* whereas those with the snail have *Chondrus crispus*.

A final biological factor contributing to the patchiness, both large- and small-scale, is the preference for settlement shown by various intertidal invertebrate larvae. Most intertidal invertebrates have a larval stage that is free swimming or floating, which serves to allow dispersal of the otherwise sessile or sedentary adult. Over the years, a great number of studies have been done on various invertebrate larvae.

Interactions Among Factors : A Summary

We have seen how various physical and biological factors each act to cause the large-scale vertical distribution patterns of algae and invertebrates that we call vertical zonation on rocky shores. We have also seen how some of these same factors, plus others, act to introduce small-scale distribution anomalies into this pattern. In general, different factors tend to operate in different areas and at different levels on the shore. The high intertidal tends to have the distribution pattern of its characteristic species set by physical factors, whereas biological factors become more important in setting limits in the low intertidal It is important to realize that these factors do not act in isolation and the final distribution pattern observed, either on a small or large scale, is often the result of the interaction among two or more factors.

In the case of *Chthamalus stellatus* and *Balanus glandula*, without a refuge in the highest intertidal (physical factor), both would be eliminated from the intertidal, the former by competition and the latter by predation (biological factor). Similarly, persistence of *B. cariosus* in the mid-intertidal of the Pacific coast depends upon the predation of *Pisaster ochraceus* for, without this predator to remove *Mytilus* and *Thais*, *B. cariosus* would be outcompeted by *Mytillus* or completely consumed by *Thais.*

On the coast of Scotland, where *Balanus balanoides* and *Chthamalus stellatus* occur, the competition between the two barnacle species is ameliorated by the activity of the predator *Thais lapilus*, which consumes *Balanus.*

When several factors begin to act simultaneously, the picture becomes even more complicated and we can begin to appreciate the real complexities that act to give the observed patterns. One the best examples is the aforementioned patterns worked out for the New England intertidal by Lubchenco and Menge (1978) and summarized here. In the low intertidal of New England, the dominant space competitor is *Mytilus edulis*, which can outcompete other space occupiers such as *Balanus balanoides* and the alga *Chondrus crispus.* On open, exposed rocky headlands, no predators exist for *M. edulis* and hence, it outcompetes the barnacles and alga to dominate the low intertidal. *In* protected areas, three predators occur : *Thais lapillus, Asterias forbesi* and *A. vulgaris*, all of which prey upon *M. edulis*, with the result that *Chondrus* is able to persist because *M edulis* never becomes abundant enough to monopolize the space. The only major herbivore in this system, *Littorina littorea*, prefers to graze on ephemeral algae that compete with *Chondrus.* Thus, the presence of the herbivore reduces competition by other algae on *Chondrus*, allowing it to persist and dominate protected areas. In this same system, the high intertidal is dominated by *B. balanoides.* Its lower limits are apparently set in exposed areas by competition with the lower-living *M. edulis* and in protected areas by predation by *T. lapillus.* The mid-intertidal in this system has a distribution pattern in exposed areas that is determined primarily by competition between *B. balanoides* and *M. edulis*, but modified by wave action. Thus, winter storms clear much open space, which is first settled by *B. balanoides* in the spring. The barnacles are, in turn, outcompeted by the *M. edulis*, which settle in the s ummer so that by the onset of winter again, the area is dominated by *M. edulis.* In protected areas, predators become abundant and heavy predation by *Thais* prevents either the barnacle or the mussel from monopolizing the space. Thus, in this relatively simple system, the final structure of the intertidal and its changes depends upon the interaction of wave action, predation, grazing, and several levels of competition. As we learn more about the intertidal in other parts of the world, it can be anticipated that more such examples will come to light.

Horizontal Distribution Patterns

As we noted in the preceding section, the appearance of the various vertical bands or zones changes as one moves from areas of high wave exposure to protected and quiet water. This is true not only for the New England example, but for other areas as well. Partly, this is due to the action of water restricting certain species in or out of wave-swept areas. In other words, some species of algae or invertebrates simply cannot tolerate the wave action and are absent from wave-swept areas. Usually, these are species with delicate structure or with poor means of holding on to the substrate. In a similar fashion, certain species cannot tolerate quiet water areas. This may be due to their inability to complete, to lack of enough or proper food, or to the presence of predators that are not present in wave-swept areas. Thus, we have seen that *Mytilus edulis* outcompetes *Balanus balanoides* and *Chondrus crispus* in exposed areas of New England because no predators can tolerate the wave action ; in protected areas, predators reduce competition allowing the barnacle and algae to exist and thus altering the appearance of the zones.

Succession

Succession, as defined is an ecological concept referring to the orderly progression of communities or *seres*, in which one community or association of species occupies a site and somehow modifies its conditions before the next one can take over. This replacement of one association by another continues until reaching the last or *climax* community, which persists indefinitely under a given climatic regime. Thus, in any one area, when open space appears, there is an orderly, predictable sequence of communities that develops on that site, which will be culminated by a known climax community. A fundamental requirement of this concept is that certain species must be present before others in order to modify the environment for subsequent ones. Does such a prodictable sequence occur in the rocky intertidal ?

Current thinking has it that succession, as defined above, does not occur in the rocky intertidal. When areas are cleared in the rocky intertidal, there is often a sequence of species that occurs, but in other instances, there is not. The discrepancy appears to be with the size and location of the cleared area. If the area is small and near the dominant association for that part of the intertidal, it is quickly overgrown by the dominant. If, however, the area is large, there may well be a sequence of species occupying it before the dominant species again reoccupy the area. Usually, these initial species are those that we have termed opportunistic or fugitive, and they are gradually replaced by the better competitors. In this sequence, usually the first settlers on cleared area are colonial diatams or fast-growing small algal species. These are followed by barnacles and tube worms, which are followed by the dominant large algae and/or mussels. The reason for the sequence is not, however, that the earlier species must be present or modify the substrate, but simply that their larvae are more quickly produced and dispersed and hence, arrive first. *Mutilus*, for example, is perfectly capable of settling on newly cleared areas.

Age Structure

As we noted terrestrial communities or associaations consist of a matrix of long-lived plant species, which allow us to characterize terrestrial communities on the basis of the dominant plant species. In the marine environment, especially the intertidal, the long-lived species tend to be various invertebrate animals, whereas the plants and the various algal species tend to be more short lived. We, in turn, tend to name zones in the intertidal on the basis of animals—*Mylitus* zone, barnacle zone, and so forth. Even though the potential longevity is great for various marine invertebrates, it is well to consider under what conditions such longevity is achieved and what the age structure of the animals actually is.

A noted previously on the Pacific coast of North America, the high intertidal has a band of *Balanus glandula* ; below that, any of these species found are usually less than 2 years old. If the age structure of the large barnacles in the band is analyzed, it is generally found to consist primarily of a single age class. Why ? Because the physical conditions are so harsh in this area that most years, the juvenile barnacles simply do not survive. As a consequence, the barnacles there result from a single good year in which conditions allowed survival through the vulnerable juvenile stage. Once adult, the barnacles can survive succeeding harsh years. The reason that all of the lower level *B. glandula* are less than 2 years old is that in two years, *Thais* completely consumes all mid-tide barnacles. Similarly, *B. cariosus* populations in the mid-intertidal consist primarily of animals less than 2 years old. However, there are a few that may be large and many years old. Again, the majority are less than 2 years old, because that is the time period during which *Thais* consume them. The few large, old individulas are those that somehow avoided predation until they were 2 years old and thus invulnerable to *Thais*. Unless consumed by *Pisaster*, these individuals may live for many years. Thus, under very stringent environmental conditions or under optimal conditions low in the intertidal, the age structure of the dominant organisms is mainly of single-year classes.

Predators also seem to consist mainly of older individuals. Examples are *Pisaster ochraceus* and *Thais lamellosa.*

Herbivores such as *Lottia gigantea* and the turban snail *Tegula funebralis* also have populations dominated by older individuals. Why this should be the case is not known at the present time.

Tidepools

A characteristic feature of many rocky shores is the presence of tidepools of various sizes, depths, and locations. Certain conditions affecting life of tidepools differ markedly from the surrounding intertidal and hence, necessitate a separate discussion here. Tidepools can, of course, occur at any level in the intertidal ; however, low-level pools often are little different from the surrounding sea and are essentially extensions of the sublittoral. They will not be considered here. Only in midlittoral and infralittoral pools do we observe the conditions that characterize these areas. Our remarks here will be restricted to those pools that undergo a complete interchange with the ocean water during the tidal cycle.

At first glance, tidepools would appear to be more or less ideal places for aquatic organisms seeking to escape the harshness of the intertidal during its exposure to air. In reality, however, escape from certain physical factors such as desiccation may mean exposure to others that operate more severely in tidepools.

Tidepools, of course, vary a great deal in size and, hence, volume of water which they contain. Since water is a great moderator of harsh physical conditions, the larger the pool and the greater the water volume, the less the fluctuations in physical factors.

Three major physical factors are subject to variation in tidepools. The first is temperature. Whereas the ocean itself is a vast reservoir that heats and cools very slowly and usually within very narrow limits, the same is not true of tidepools. These relatively small bodies of water are subject to considerably more rapid changes. Shallow tidepools exposed to the sun on warm days may quickly reach lethal or near lethal temperatures. Similarly tidepools in cold temperate or subpolar regions may have temperatures in the freezing range in winter. An additional problem is this : The pool may either heat up or cool down over a several-hour period while exposed to the air, but when the tide returns, it will be flooded at some point with ocean water at quite a different temperature ; this will suddenly change the temperature of the whole pool. Thus, any organism inhabiting such pools must be adapted to considerable sudden fluctuation.

The second factor to vary in pools is salinity. During exposure at low tide, tidepools may heat up. When that happens, evaporation occurs and the salinity increases. Under hot tropical conditions, the salinity increase can be dramatic enough in some instances to reach the point of precipitating out salt. The opposite situation is the case when heavy rains occur at low tide and flood pools with fresh water, dramatically lowering the salinity. Again, tidepool animals and plants may have to be adapted to wider ranges in salinity than typical marine or intertidal organisms. As before, when the tide returns, the pool will be flooded with sea water at some point and again, there will be a sudden, abrupt return to normal conditions.

The final physical factor undergoing change in pools is oxygen concentration. Since the amount of oxygen that can be held in sea water is a function of temperature, it follows that those pools that heat up during exposure to the air will lose oxygen. Under normal conditions, this may not be serious enough to produce oxygen stress, but if the pool is crowded with organisms, it may well produce a stress situation. For example, a pool filled with algae that was exposed at night would produce a situation in which the lack of photosynthesis coupled with high respiration could reduce the oxygen level significantly. Oxygen has been recorded as falling to 18 per cent of saturation in topical tidepools.

Tidepools are thus areas of refuge from desiccation for intertidal organisms, but, in turn, these organisms suffer from rapid changes in temperature, salinity, and occasionally oxygen, thus restricting the fauna and flora to those organisms that are able to tolerate such ranges.

SANDY SHORES

Intertidal sand beaches are common throughout the world and are certainly better known than rocky shores to most humans, because they are the substrate of choice for various recreational activities. At the same time, they present a very marked change from the previously described rocky shores because, in contrast to the crowded life on the latter, sand beaches appear devoid of macroscopic life. They are not, of course, but the environmental factors acting on these shores create conditions where virtually all organisms bury themselves in the substrate.

In this section, we shall explore the action of physical factors on sand beaches and see how these factors act to impose certain adaptations upon the larger organisms found in this area. The very specialized conditions and organisms existing in the tiny spaces between the sand grains are the subject of the next chapter.

Environmental Conditions

As with rocky intertidal shores, sand beaches are subject to a similar array of physical factors, but the relative importance of these factors in structuring the community and their effect on the substrate differ.

Perhaps the most important physical factor governing life on sand beaches is *wave action* and its attendant effect on *particle size.* Anyone who has visited marine beaches is aware of the fact that the particle size of the sand can differ among beaches and also among seasons on the same beach. Particularly in the temperate zone, the profile of the beach also changes between winter and summer. The particle size of sand on a beach is a function of wave action on that beach. Where wave action is light, the particles are fine, but where wave action is heavy and strong, the particles are coarse, forming deposits called gravel or shingle rather than sand. The importance of the particle size to organism distribution and abundance rests with its effect on *water retention* and its suitability for burrowing. Fine sand, through its capillary action, tends to hold much water above the tide level in its interstices after the tide has retreated. Coarse sand and graval, on the other hand, allow water to drain away quickly as the tide retreats. Since the organisms inhabiting the intertidal are aquatic, they are well protected against desiccation in a fine sand beach but subject to desiccation in a coarse gravel beach. This make the latter less hospitable. Fine sand is also more amenable to burrowing than coarse gravel.

A second important physical factor in sand beaches, which was not of concern in rocky shores, is also the product of wave

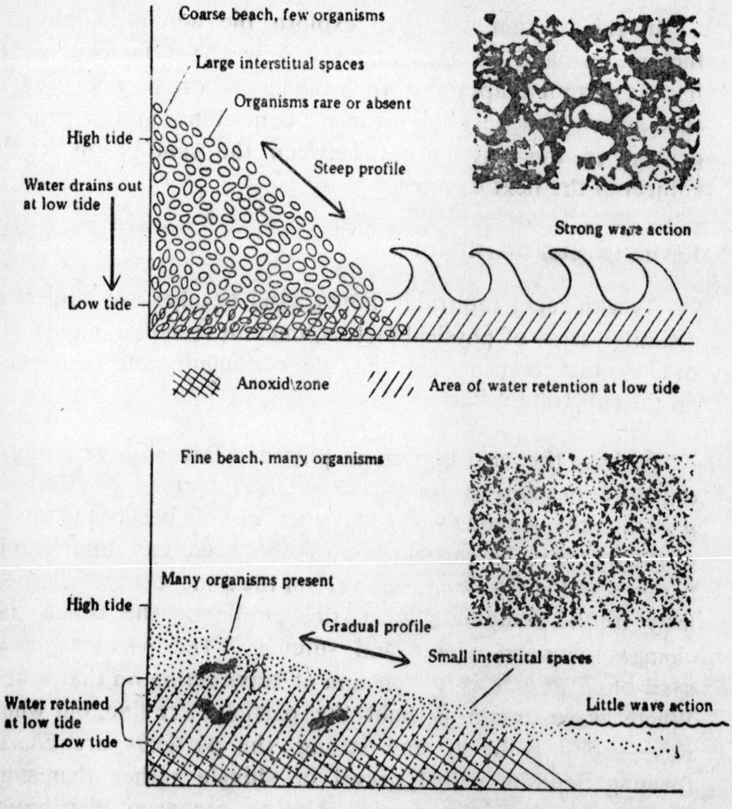

Figure 1.7. Comparison of the physical conditions between fine-grained and coarse-grained beaches.

action. That is wave-induced ***substrate movement.*** The particles on sand or gravel beaches are not large enough to be stable when waves strike the shore. As a result, with each passing wave, the substrate particles are picked up, churned in the water, and redeposited. Particles are thus being continually moved and sorted. The reason that fine sand beaches occur only where wave action is light and coarse ones where it is heavy is that, in heavy wave action, the smaller particles remain in suspension so long that they are carried away from the beach, leaving only those heavy enough (=coarse) to settle immediately. Light wave action also means that a smaller depth of particles is affected by the passage of a wave, whereas

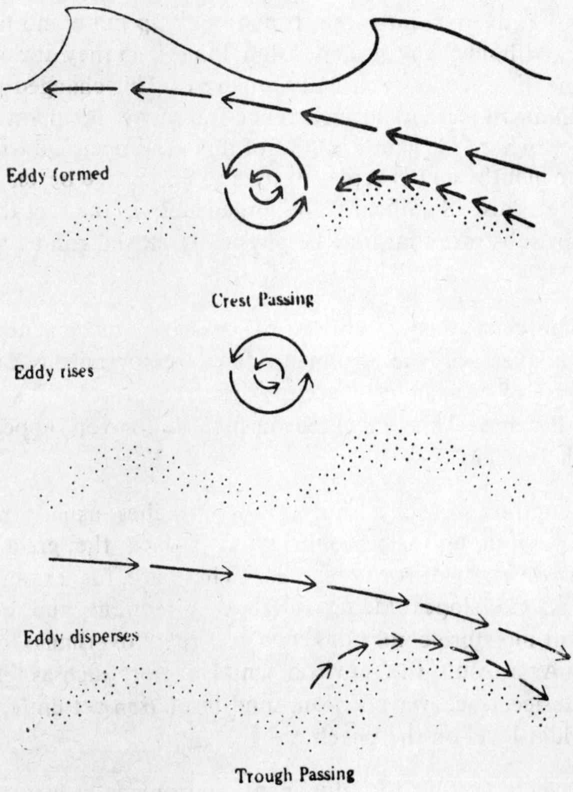

Figure 1.8. Transport of sand particles by wave action.

heavy wave action disturbs the substrate to a greater depth. Many beaches show a gradation of particle sizes from fine near low water to coarser at the high tide mark. This reflects the distribution of wave energy on the beach, being greater near the high tide mark, where waves break more often, and lesser with increasing depth in the tidal zone.

Since the substrate itself, at least the surface layers, is in constant motion and be picked up and held for greater or lesser amounts of time in suspension, depending upon the strength of the waves ; it follows that any change in wave intensity on a given beach will mean a change not only in grain size, but also in the profile or shape of the beach. This comes about when gentle wave action is replaced by heavier waves, which dig deeper into the beach, pick up more and heavier grains, and hold them in suspension longer, so they are deposited some distance away, usually, offshore. This changed profile is a common seasonal occurrence on many temperate zone beaches, where a gentle slope of fine sand occurs during the summer months and is replaced by a steep, coarse beach during winter storms. Significant for organisms is the fact that the depth of substrate that may be physically moved can be several feet !

Because of this condition of ceaseless movement of the surface layers of the sediment, few large organisms have the capability of permanently occupying the surface of sand or gravel beaches. This is the reason for the barren appearance of such beaches.

In contrast so rocky shore, sand beaahes usually have a rather smooth, uniform profile and thus lack the great topographic diversity of rocky shores. There are, for example, no crevices, no slopes facing different directions and offering different moisture conditions, nor are there overhangs or tidepools. As a result, the environmental factors such as temperature, desiccation, wave action, and insolation act uniformly at each tidal level on the beach.

Wave action is the dominant environmental factor acting on the sand beaches, creating the special conditions that make it difficult, or impossible, for many organism to inhabit this area. At the same time, sand beaches offer some positive advantages to marine organisms with respect to other physical factors. Sand is an excellent buffer against large temperature and salinity changes. Measurements of temperature with depth on sand beaches at low tide have demonstrated that, below the first few centimeters, the temperature is very nearly that of the surrounding sea water. The amelioration of temperature is partly due to the insulating properties of sand itself and partly due to the water held in the interstices of the deeper layers. In a similar manner, salinity changes are also minimal below 10 or 15 cm on beaches, even if the upper layers have fresh water flowing over or falling on them. Again, this is due to the fact that the water held in the interstices is salt water, which has a higher density than fresh water. As a result, the fresh water remains perched on the surface. Sand is further a barrier to any harmful effects of exposure to direct sunlight (insolation) for any organism living in the sand, simply because the sand is opeque to light and reflects or absorbs it in the surface layers. Desiccation is not a problem as long as the beach sand is fine enough to hold water by capillary action during periods of low tide. Thus, any organism burrowing into the sand will be constantly moist.

A final physical factor acting on beaches is *oxygen content.* Oxygen is never limiting in the water bathing the beach because the turbulence of wave action ensures constant saturation. Where it might become limiting is in the substrate itself. The water held in the beach and responsible for ameliorating the changes in temperature and salinity also contains oxygen, which is available for use by the organisms. This supply, however, is used up by respiration of the organisms and must be replenished. This replenishment comes through interchange of the water with the sea above, and is dependent on the fineness of the sediments. Fine sediments have a slow rate of exchange and coarse sediments a rapid exchange. Thus, in fine-grained beaches, water interchange is slow and may result in reduced oxygen supplies.

Adaptations of Organisms

The dominant environmental factor acting on sand beaches is wave action, which creates the unstable, constantly moving substrate. In order to inhabit this area, organisms must first be adapted to tolerate these features. There are two routes that may be taken by organisms in adapting. The first is to burrow deeply enough into the substrate such that the organism is deeper than the depth of sediment affected by the passing wave. This strategy is employed by many large clams such as *Tivela stultorum*, the Pismo clam. Such animals are usually also aided by developing a very heavy shell, which helps in keeping the animal down in the substrate. The only difficulty with this type of adaptation is that a very severe storm may generate waves large enough to pull these animals out and throw them on the beach. This is the reason for the catastrophic destruction that occasionally occurs in these forms.

The second route of adaptations is the ability to burrow in very quicky as soon as the passing wave has removed the animal from the substrate. This appears to be more common mechanism and is employed by many annelid worms, small clams, and crustaceans. A good example of this type of adaptation can be found in the various sand crabs of the family Hippidae found in many beaches around the world. These animals have a short body with limbs highly modified to dig quickly into wet sand. As soon as they are pulled out of the substrate by a passing wave, they reburrow before the water motion can carry them off. Small clams of the genus *Donax* also do the same thing, and razor clams of the genus *Siliqua* are extraordinarily fast at reburrowing.

Other adaptations are correlated with the above. For example, most burrowing mollusks tend to have very smooth shells that reduce the resistance to burrowing into the sand. SImilarly, shore echinoderms such as sand dollars have much reduced spines to allow them to burrow into the sand.

A special adaptation observed by Chia (1973) in small sand dollars (*Dendraster excentricus*) is that they tend to accumulate iron compounds in a special area of their digestive tracts, which serve as a "weight belt" to keep them down in the presence of wave action.

A final set of adaptations has to do with the problem of preventing clogging of respiratory surfaces by the resuspended sand. In order to prevent this from occurring, the intake siphons of sandy beach clams are often fitted with various screens, which prevent entrance of sand but allow passage of water. Similarly, in the sand crabs, the antennae held together form a tube to the surface through which water enters the branchial chamber. These are densely clothed clothed with closely spaced hairs designed to prevent entrance of sand.

Types of Organisms

The most noticeable group that is absent from sand beaches is the large plants. No macroscopic plants occur on open sand beaches, presumably because there is no way for them to attach and maintain themselves in the wave action. Small benthic diatoms, however, may be present on the sand grains. The second major group of organisms conspicuous by its absence is the sessile animals such as barnacles and mussels, so dominant on rocky shores. Again, there is no place for them to attach. The sand beach is dominated by represenatatives from three invertebrate classes : polychaete worms bivalve mollusks, and crustaceans. Various combinations of species from these three groups dominate sand beaches throughout the world.

Feeding Biology

The absence of large multicellular plants means that there is very little primary productivity. Although diatoms are present, the opaqueness of the sand ensures that even the diatom population is restricted to the very surface layers. As a result, there are no macroscopic herbivores on a sand beach. Since there is virtually no primary productivity, the animals living on the beach must depend for food upon either the phytoplankton carried in sea water above the beach, the organic debris brought in by the waves, or consuming the other beach animals. There are relatively few true carnivores among beach animals, because to be such would require active movement across the substrate in search of prey. This is probably not feasible in the face of the heavy wave action. As a result, most of the organisms in a beach are either suspension or detritus feeders.

Suspension feeding animals are those that filter particles out of the water column. These particles may be plankton organisms or, particularly on the sand beach, they may be various organic particles resuspended from the bottom by the passing waves. The dominant group of suspension feeders on sand beaches are the bivalve mollusks such as razor clams (*Siliqua, Ensis*), surf clams (*Tivela, Spisula*) and coquinas (*Donax*).

Sand beaches tend to have lesser amounts of organic detritus than muddy shores, but enough debris from various sources finds its way to the beach to be a reliable source of food for certain organisms. Since this detrital material is often carried up and down the beach suspended in the wave wash rather than being deposited on the bottom, the mechanisms employed by detritus feeders on the beach are aften different from those employed by detritus feeders on muddy shores.

The sand crabs of the family Hippidae, such as *Emerita analoga* and *Blepharipoda occidentalis* of the Pacific coast of America, employ a unique mechanism to trap debris in the wave wash. MacGinitie and MacGinitie (1949) observed that *Emerita* orient so that their heads point shoreward. They remain completely buried as the incoming wave passes over them shoreward. After passage, as the water begins to run down the beach, they stick out their very large second antennae. These are highly clothed in hairs forming a net that, when spread into the backwash, intercepts all particles within a certain size range. The particles are then wiped off by the mouth and ingested. As the tide rises and falls, the position of the wave wash front also moves. These crabs take advantage of this to maximize their feeding time by being moved up and down the beach with the tide. Movement is effected by surfacing as a wave rolls in and being carried up some distance by the wave and then quickly reburrowing. In a similar manner, as the tide recedes, they emerge and roll down the beach before reburrowing and commencing feeding.

A similar method of feeding is employed by the gastropod mollusk *Olivella columellaris* on the coast of Central America. In this case, a mucus net is produced by the animal and held across the wave backwash. This net acts like a filter and captures small particles. Since the animal feeds by consuming the entire net with particles, it must produce a new net at frequent intervals.

Most sand beaches also include one or more polychaetes, which burrow through the sand ingesting the sand digesting out the organic particles. Much like earthworms on land, however, they are rarely abundant on open sand beaches because the amount of organic material is less than in mud shores.

Sand dollars, one of the echinoderms common on sandy beaches, are generally deposit or detritus feeding animals. These animals generally burrow through the sand. As they do so, the finer organic particles, but not the sand grains, fall down between the short spines, are trapped in mucus, and carried to the mouth. Some species, such as the Pacific coast *Dendraster excentricus*, according to Timko (1976), have even modified this basic feeding process to remove suspended particles by projecting part of the body up into the water column.

Carnivores are rare but the few found usually are polychaete worms or gastropod mollusks. The polychaetes, such as species of the genera *Nephtys* and *Glycera*, actively burrow through the sand and small prey items with their eversible proboscis. The carnivorous gastropods are represented most commonly by burrowing snails of the family Naticidae (moon snails). These animals burrow slowly just below the surface layers of the sand in search of bivalve mollusks, which they consume by boring holes through the shell and eating out the contents. A number of transient predators also occur. At low tide, various shorebirds actively feed on beach organisms, and at high tide, fishes invade the area.

Zonation and Community Organization

Since there are no organisms visible on the surface of the intertidal sand beaches, these areas do not display the surface zonation patterns so obvious on rocky shores. Furthermore, since the various physical factors such as desiccation and temperature that act to limit organisms on rocky shores are of far less importance to organisms living in the sand, it might be suspected that zonation of organisms would be reduced or absent. In fact, there is a zonation of sandy shore organisms, but it is neither as clearly defined nor as well understood as that for rocky shores. The lack of clear zonation patterns is due partly to the habit of some dominant organisms moving up and down the beach for feeding and partly to the dearth of studies on the determinants of distribution patterns in this area. Certainly one of the major contributors to the lack of understanding is the inability of researchers to set up field experiments is this area to determine the results of excluding certain organisms. Wave action precludes such work.

From the few data that are available, it is possible to establish a three-zone division of most sandy beaches that follows quite closely the universal scheme of Stephenson's mentioned earlier. The highest parts of the sandy beach, corresponding to the supralittoral fringe, are usually inhabited by talitrid amphipod crustaceans (beach hoppers) in the temperate zone and by the fast-moving ghost crabs (*Oxypode*) in the tropics. Both groups excavate burrows and are scavengers. The broad mid-littoral area, which corresponds to the area inhabited by barnacles and mussels on rocky shores, is much more variable. One group found here is isopods of the family Cirolanidae.

Also coming into this zone when it is the area of wave swash are the various sand crabs and those other animals that feed in a similar way (see previous section). The lowest zone, or infralittoral fringe, is inhabited by the greatest number of species, including the large surf clams (*Tivela, Spisula*), sand dollars (*Dendraster*), various polychaete worms, a host of crustaceans, and the larger carnivorous snails (*Natica, Polinices*).

In direct contrast to rocky shores, where experimental work has demonstrated the importance of physical factors, competition, and predation in determining the observed zonation patterns, the explanations for the establishment of the pattern in sandy beaches have not been subjected to rigorous experimental analysis. As a result, we know little of the factors or

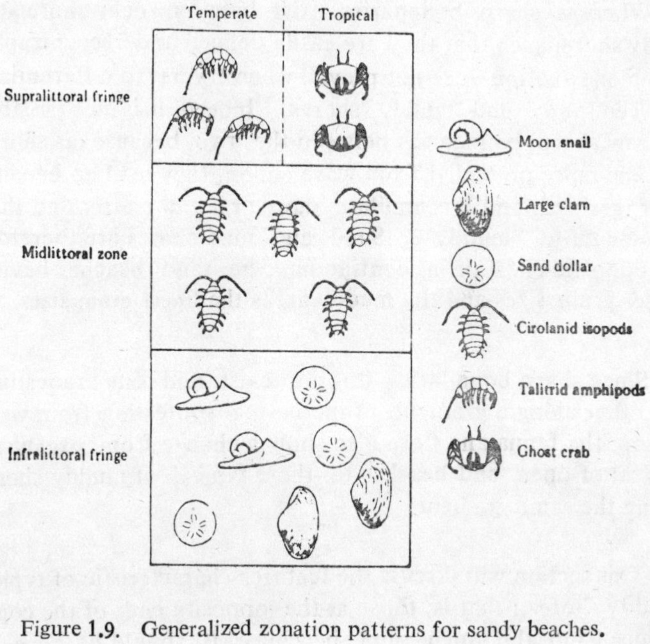

Figure 1.9. Generalized zonation patterns for sandy beaches.

their interactions that establish the sandy beach distribution patterns.

The extremely crowded conditions for organisms observed on rocky shores are not found on sand beaches. Indeed, the fauna is very sparse and certainly not occupying all available space. This immediately suggests that competition for space is not a major contributor to the observed distribution pattern. Competition for food also appears negligible, since the sparse populations and abundant plankton make competition unlikely. Similarly, there are relatively few indigenous invertebrate predators, and it seems unlikely that they are responsible for any major distributional pattern. The effect, however, of large vertebrate predators such as birds and fishes remains to be investigated. This leaves the physical factors as probable major contributors to the patterns observed.

MUDDY SHORES

Whereas sharp boundaries exist between rocky shore and sandy shore, such that they are easily defined and recognizable, a similar situation does not prevail when trying to differentiate between sandy and muddy shores. Indeed, it is not possible to draw sharp boundaries between the two, because as shores become more protected from wave action, they tend to become finer grained and accumulate more organic matter and thus become more "muddy". Sand and mud shores are therefore the opposite ends of a continuum, the sand beaches having larger grain sizes and the muddy areas the finest grain sizes.

Since sharp boundaries do not exist and one grades into the other along a gradient of increasing protection from wave action, the fauna and flora also show a change from organisms typical of open sand beaches to those typical of muddy shores along the same gradient.

This section will discuss the features characteristic of typical muddy shores ; that is, those at the opposite end of the continuum from the open sand beaches. It should be borne in mind, however, that various transitional communities exist that will show mixtures of organisms from both extremes. Since muddy shores are also composed of sediments, similar factors will apply here as did with sandy shores and will not be repeated.

Muddy substrates are also characteristic of estuaries and salt marshes. Indeed, most of the muddy shores of the world are associated with estuaries and similar embayments. Hence, many of the types of organisms and adaptations are similar between the two areas. To avoid the problem of overlap in discussing these two areas, this section will treat the infaunal organisms of mud flats, their adaptations, feeding biology, and trophic structure. These considerations will, of course, apply to the estuarine infauna. The role of other organisms, productivity and ecological relationships are taken up.

Physical Factors

The major contrast with open sand beaches is that muddy shores cannot develop in the presence of significant *wave action.* Therefore, muddy shores are restricted to intertidal areas completely protected from open ocean wave activity. Muddy shores are best developed where there is a sources of fine-grained sediment particles Muddy shores are located in various partially enclosed bays, lagoons, harbors, and especially estuaries.

Since these areas are developed where water movement is minimal, the slope of mud shores tends to be much flatter than that observed for sand beaches. This is why these areas are often referred to as "mud flats."

The very fine particle size coupled with the very flat angle of response of these sediments means that water in the sediments does not drain away and is held within the substrate. This long retention time for water, coupled with a very poor interchange of the interstitial water with the sea water above and a high internal bacterial population, usually results in complete depletion of the oxygen in the sediments below the first few centimeters of the surface. *Anaerobic* conditions thus prevail within the sediment and this is one of the most important characteristics of the muddy shore.

Muddy shores tend to accumulate organic material, which means that there is an abundant potential food supply for the resident organisms ; but the abundant small organic particles "raining" down on the mud flat also have the potential to clog respiratory surfaces.

Adaptations of Organisms

As we noted for sandy shores, the surface of muddy shores is also often rather barren, as few animals inhabit the surface of the mud flat. Most organisms inhabiting these areas show an adaptation to burrowing into and through the soft substrate or else inhabit permanent tubes in the substrate. In contrast to sand beaches, however, the presence of the organisms in the mud flat is advertised on the surface by the presence of various holes of differing sizes and shapes. Thus, one of the primary adaptations of organisms in mud flats is the ability to burrow into the substrate or to form permanent tubes.

A second major adaptation concerns the anaerobic conditions that prevail in the substrate. If organisms are to survive while burrowed into the substrate, they must either be adapted to live under anaerobic conditions or else must have some way of bringing the overlying surface water with its oxygen supply down to them. Since most multicellular organisms cannot survive in the absence of oxygen, the latter is the more common adaptation. It is to obtain this oxygen-rich surface water and food that the various burrows, holes, and tubes appear on the surface of the mud flat.

Although most mud flat organisms are intolerant of completely anaerobic conditions, many have adaptations that permit them to exist at lower oxygen tensions than similar forms that live on open sand beaches. The most common adaptation to low oxyen supply is the development of carriers (e.g., hemoglobin) that will continue to pick up oxygen at concentrations well below that of similar pigments in other organisms.

Since wave action is essentially absent on these mud flats, there is no necessity for development of either rapid burrowing or heavy bodies to maintain positions, as is the case for sandy shores.

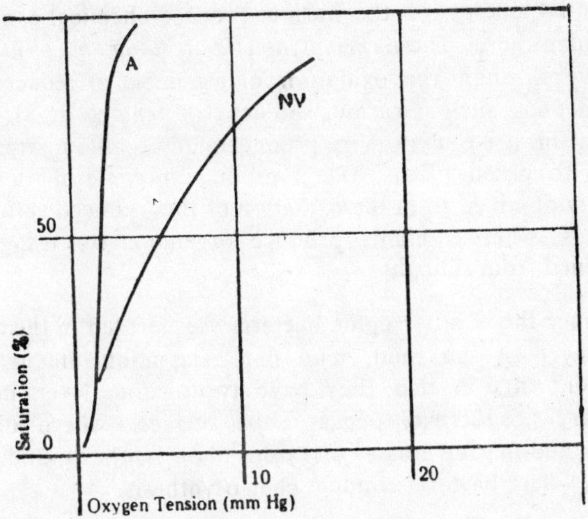

Figure 1.10. Oxygen dissociation curves for the blood of *Arenicola* (*A*) and *Nephtys* (*NV*).

Types of Organisms

In contrast to sand beaches, muddy shores often develop a substantial growth of various plants. On the bare mud flats, the most abundant plants are diatoms, which live in the surface layers of mud and often give a brownish color to the surface of the mud at low tide. Other plants include large macroalgae such as species of *Gracilaria* (red algae), *Ulva* and *Enteromorpha* (green algae). These large algae often undergo seasonal cycles of abundance, becoming common in the warmer months and virtually disappearing in colder months. Other areas, particularly the lowest tidal levels, may be covered with a growth of various sea grasses such as the genus *Zostera*. As a result of the occurrence of these various primary producers, there is substantial primary productivity in the mud flats.

Mud flats contain large numbers of bacteria, which feed on the abundant organic matter. Bacteria are the only abundant organisms found in the anaerobic layers of the mud shore and constitute a significant biomass. Among the dominant bacteria inhabiting this area are a number capable of utilizing the potential energy of the various reduced chemical compounds abundant here. These *chemosynthetic* or *sulfur bacteria* obtain energy through the oxidation of a number of reduced sulfur compounds, such as various sulfides (for example H_2S). These organisms are thus primary producers of organic matter analogous to green plants. They produce organic matter using energy obtained from the oxidation of the reduced sulfur compounds, whereas plants produce organic matter using energy obtained from sunlight.

Since these autotrophic bacteria are located in the anaerobic layer of the mud, mud flats are unique among marine environments in that they have two separate layers in which primary productivity occurs : the surface, where diatoms, algae, and marine grasses carry on photosynthesis, and a deep layer, where bacteria conduct chemosynthesis.

The dominant macrofaunal groups on muddy shores are the same as those encountered on sand beaches ; namely, various polychaete worms, bivalve mollusks, and small and large crustaceans, but of quite different sorts.

Feeding Biology and Trophic Structure

Because of the greater amount of organic matter present in and on muddy shores and because of increased productivity due to both bacteria and plants, there is vastly more food available on muddy shores than on sand beaches. This permits more large organisms to live on mud shore and, indeed, mud flats may be very densely populated.

The dominant feeding types on mud flats are deposit feeders and suspension feeders, a situation similar to that on sand beaches. Deposit feeders are particularly abundant due to the large amount of organic material and the large populations of bacteria in the sediments. Deposit feeding polychaetes are represented by genera such as *Arenicola* and *Capitella.* Both feed by burrowing through the substrate, ingesting it and digesting out the organic matter (or bacteria), and passing out the undigested material through the anus. *Arnenicola* spp., however, from a U-shaped burrow in which one arm of the U is a permanently open shaft to the surface, while the other arm is filled with sediment that the worm ingests. The worm consumes sediment from the filled shaft, passes it through its gut, and then moves up in the open burrow to defecate at the surface, leaving characteristic mounds. Capitellids, on the other hand, form no permanent tubes, but move like aquatic earthworms through the surface layers of the substrate, ingesting it.

Deposit feeding bivalves are also common in these areas. Temperate zone mud flats often have large numbers of small tellinid clams of the genus *Macoma* or *Scrobicularia.* These bivalves have siphons that are separated. Each clam lies buried in the substrate with its siphons extended to the surface. There, the intake siphon is moved over the surface like a vacuum cleaner, ingesting organic particles and bringing them down to the clam for digestion.

Suspension feeders include various other species of clams, some crustaceans, and numbers of polychaetes. Suspension feeding mechanisms are not different from those observed in other areas. There is, however, some question as to how exclusively these forms are feeding on suspended plankton. The fine sediment particles are easily stirred up on mud flats and remain resuspended in the water. Hence, suspension feeders may possibly take in amounts of these particles in addition to various plankton organisms. Perhaps most of the suspension feeders on mud flats also partially take in re-suspended sediments and hence, are actually feeding on both deposited and suspended material.

In general, deposit feeders are more common in fine-grained shores and suspension feeders become more abundant in coarser sediments, where there is little organic matter.

The major carnivores on mud shores are often the fishes, which feed when the tide is in, and the birds, feeding when the tide is out. Indigenous mud flat predators include a few polychaete worms such as *Glycera* spp., moon snails (*Polinices, Natica*), and crabs.

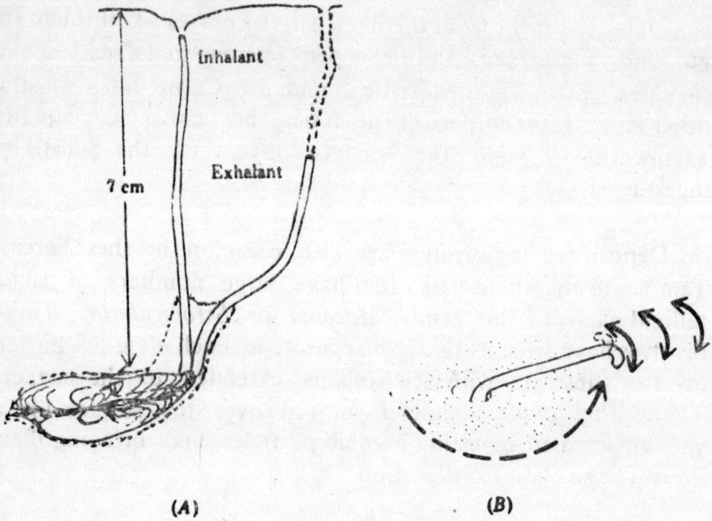

Figure 1.11. (*A*) *Macoma nasuta* in the substrate. (*B*) *Macoma nasuta* feeding with its incurrent siphon

Despite the relative abundance of plant material on muddy shores, there are very few herbivores, and most plant material finds its way into the food chains only after it has been broken down into small pieces to enter the deposit feeding food web.

Thus, the tropic structure of a mud flat is often built up from two bases : a detritus-bacteria base and one based on plants. The detritus base web is derived from plants and other organic sources and includes the bacteria that live upon the detrital particles. Detrital particles can thus either be taken in directly by the large macrofaunal invertebrates or else be consumed by bacteria. An additional bacterial component at the base of this tropic pyramid is the sulfur bacteria.

Bacteria are consumed commonly by various nematode worms, which thus occupy a position similar to that of herbivores in other areas. Bacteria are also consumed by deposit feeders as they ingest the organic particles upon which the bacteria are found. Nematodes and deposit feeders are, in turn, consumed by various carnivores, including predatory invertebrates (moon snails, (*Glycera*) as well as birds and fishes.

A second food web is based primarily on the microscopic diatoms as the autotrophic base. The diatoms are consumed by several different polychaetes, mollusks, and crustaceans. These, in turn, are consumed by the large predatory birds and fishes.

Zonation

Little information exists regarding the zonation of mud flats. The very gentle slope of these areas means that the intertidal is often very extensive, more so than rocky or sandy shores. The upqer area, the supralittoral fringe, is often inhabited by various species of crabs, many of which burrow into the substrate. The very extensive midlittoral area is the home of most of the common species of clams and polychaetes. There is no sharp boudary with the infralittoral fringe, and similar organisms are ecountered.

The role of physical factors and biological factors in structuring these communities has been little studied. Some studies have demonstrated a separation among the species by depth in the substrate, implying a "niche" separation. Experimental removal of a species or increased densities usually has resulted in corresponding changes in density of other species, which suggests some sort of biological interaction. However, this is not well worked out at this time, and hence, we are not able to discuss how this interaction may produce the pattern we have observed. Since this area is often similar to the substrate found in shallow water subtidal soft bottoms, and estuarine areas, it is likely that a similar set of factors is acting.

INTERTIDAL FISHES

Whereas a great deal of research has been concentrated on the ecology of invertebrates and plants of the intertidal zone on all three types of shores, there are very few accounts of the fishes of these areas or of the role they may play in community organization as grazers or predators. Since fishes are often present in considerable numbers in the intertidal and since it is known that they have a significant effect on other communities such as coral reefs, it is reasonable to assume that future research may elucidate their role here as well.

2

The Sea Shore Environment

The seashore of Britain is some seven thousand miles in length, but in area it is a very limited habitat as it extends only from the topmost sea-washed point of the beach down to the lowest point uncovered by the tide, a region amounting to approximately 0.75% of the land area of the British Isles. Nevertheless, life is very abundant on the seashore and this intertidal region is one of the most exciting habitats to explore for it supports such a great variety of organisms. Here are to be found representatives from nearly all the invertebrate groups of animals (a selection that cannot be found in any *one* land habitat), though fish are the only truly intertidal vertebrates and the plants are limited to seaweeds.

All these varying forms of life have to tolerate ever-changing conditions and of these the tide is the prime factor. Its rise and fall twice a day means that at one time the surrounding medium is water and at another air ; as all the shore inhabitants have migrated from the sea, this poses the problem of resistance to desiccation during the period of exposure. This, in turn, is affected by climatic conditions, as is the force with which the waves break on the shore. Geographical position and geological structure of the shore also govern the populations.

Although we speak generally of *the seashore* it is not just *one* habitat but several, depending on the type of substratum ;

rocky shore, *shingle* shore, *sandy* shore, *muddy* shore, because each supports its own particular communities The various factors which control these communities will now be dealt with in detail.

Tides : If we could imagine the world without gravity, the oceans would be spread evenly around the earth's surface as shown in (*a*) of the following diagram. However, our

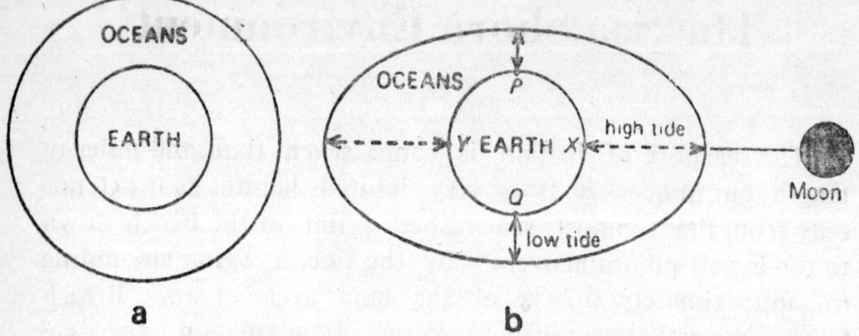

Figure 2.1. (*a*) No gravitational effect, (*b*) moon overhead at *X* gravitationally attracts oceans and earth to give high tides at *X* and *Y*, and low tides at *P* and *Q*.

planet comes under the influence of the gravitational effect of the moon, and when the moon is overhead at *X* its gravitational attraction on the oceans causes a pile up of the waters ; high tide occurs at *X* as shown in (*b*). The moon also attracts the earth but, as the earth is a solid mass, it is not so strongly affected as the freely moving oceans and is pulled only slightly away from the water on the opposite side at *Y*, thus causing high tide here at the same time as at *X*. Simultaneously, low tide occurs at the regions from which the water has been withdrawn, that is halfway between *X* and *Y*, at *P* and *Q*, as shown in (*b*).

This gravitational attraction of the oceans occurs at every point on the earth when the moon is overhead. Therefore, as the earth rotates on its axis once in twenty-four hours, high tide occurs *twice* in every twenty-four hours—once when the moon is overhead and once when overhead on the opposite side of the earth. However, the interval between high water is not exactly twelve hours because the moon circles the earth. The interval is approximately 12 hours 25 minutes; if high water is at 11·00 a.m., the next high water occurs at 11.25 p.m. and the following at 11.50 a.m. the next day.

The extent to which the tide rises and falls varies giving *spring* tides and *neap* tides. The use of the word *spring* has nothing to do with the season, but is derived from a Norse word meaning to *swell*, and *neap* from a Norse word meaning *scarcity*.

At *spring* tides the sea reaches the farthest point up the beach at high water and the lowest point down the beach at low water. For the spring tides of greatest range these points are known as *Extreme High Water Springs*, EHWS, and *Extreme Low Water Springs* ELWS. At *neap* tides the sea flows to the lowest point up the beach for any high tide and ebbs to the highest point down the beach for any low tide. For the neap tides of least range these points are known as *Extreme High Water Neaps*, EHWN, and *Extreme Law Water Neaps*, ELWN. The whole intertidal area exposed between EHWS and ELWS is called the *littoral* region. However, as extreme spri g tides and neap tides occur only occasionally, that is at the time of an equinox, it is more convenient to refer to the *Mean High Water Springs*, MHWS, *Mean Low Water Springs*, MLWS, *Mean High Water Neaps*, MHWN and *Mean Low Water Neaps*, MLWN. These are the average of all HWS, LWS, HWN, and LWN, respectively.

Two spring tides occur each lunar month, once a day or two after new moon and the other after full moon. Similarly neap tides occur twice each month, a day or two after the first and last quarter of the moon. Between spring and neap tides there is a gradual day-to-day variation in the ebb and flow between these limits. The greatest area of the shore exposed and submerged occurs at spring tides and the least at neap tides, as shown below.

This variation in the height of the tide is the result of the gravitational attraction of the moon *and* the sun. At full and new moon, the moon and sun exert gravitational pulls along the same diameter, but at the first and last quarter of the moon the gravitational pulls oppose each other.

As the movements of the sun, earth and moon are known, it is possible to predict the time and height of the high tide at any given place on the surface of the earth. This information is compiled for each year and published in the form of tide tables.

If tide tables are studied, it is found that MHWS accurs in any particular region at about the same time of day. On the south-west coast of Devon MHWS occurs at approximately 6 00 a.m. and 6.00 p.m. G.M.T., and MLWS falls at midday and midnight. This means that the shore is uncovered during the hottest and coldest periods in the twenty-four hours, so the shore populations have to tolerate extreme conditions of expo sure. In contrast, on the south-east coast of Britain, between

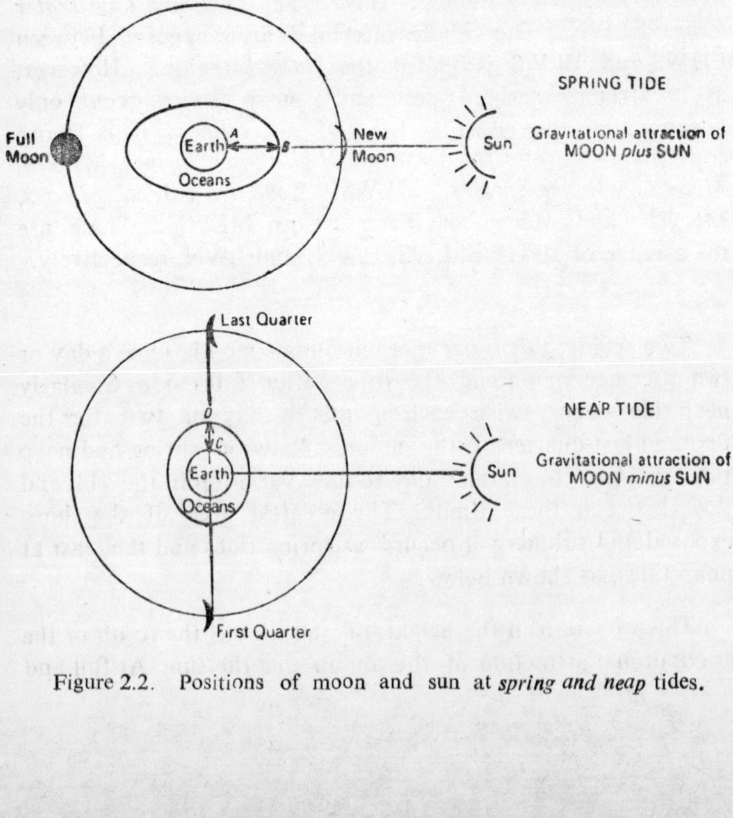

Figure 2.2. Positions of moon and sun at *spring and neap* tides.

Dover and Harwich, MHWS occurs about 12.00 a.m. and 12.00 p.m. G.M.T., and MLWS at 6.00 a.m. and 6.00 p.m., so that here the exposure temperatures are comparatively moderate. Obviously the time of day at which the shore is uncovered plays a considerable part in determining the inhabitants.

The height to which the tide rises is not the same at every point along the coast but varies according to the geological structure of the coastline. In the Bristol Channel, the rise and fall varies from 6 metres near the entrance at Milford Haven to 12 metres in the upper regions at Avonmouth and Bristol, whereas on the east coast, at Lowestoft, the rise and fall in only 2.1 metres.

The rate of ebb and flow of the tide is not constant throughout the whole six-hour period, a fact apparent to anyone waiting for the tide to go out. It seems a long time before it starts to fall then suddenly races away down the beach ! This is because the rate of ebb is very slow in the first hour, speeds up a little during the second hour and reaches a maximum in the third and fourth hours, when half the overall fall occurs in just two hours. The rate then slows down again in the fifth and sixth hours.

Another fact which also affects the height of the tide is the wind. If there is an onshore wind the sea flows much farther up the beach than anticipated at high water—a fact familiar to people who live near the coast when, during winter gales, promenades are flooded and damaged. On the other hand, if the wind is offshore, then the tide does not rise as high as indicated in the tide tables.

Within the region of the littoral zone the period of exposure varies, so that the inhabitants near MHWS mark are normally exposed to the atmosphere except at high water spring tide, while those near MLWS mark are normally submerged except at low water spring tide ; this accounts for the very different living conditions in these two areas. Between these two extremes variations occur down the shore, and it is possible to divide the littoral area into zones or regions of similar conditions. Beginning at the top, the area above EHWS mark, although not normally covered by the tide, receives spray from the sea so is called the SPLASH ZONE. From EHWS to MEAN High Water (average of the high water levels ranging from springs to neaps) the shore is exposed for long periods and is covered only when the tide is higher than the Mean, and is referred to as the UPPER SHORE. The MIDDLE SHORE ranges from MHW to MLW (average of the low water levels from spring to neap tides) where 90% of the area is exposed and submerged daily. The LOWER SHORE extends from MLW down to ELWS, a region which is exposed only when the tide falls below the Mean. This is shown in the following diagram.

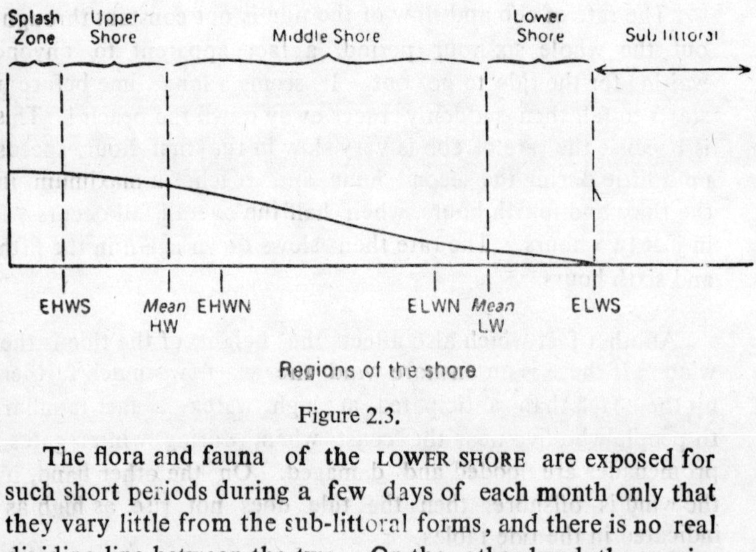

Figure 2.3.

The flora and fauna of the LOWER SHORE are exposed for such short periods during a few days of each month only that they vary little from the sub-littoral forms, and there is no real dividing line between the two. On the other hand, the species of the UPPER SHORE have undergone considerable modifications to adapt themselves to the long periods of exposure. The small periwinkle, *Littorina nerioides*, which lives in rock crevices in the SPLASH ZONE, has the gill chamber modified for air-breathing, whereas the edible periwinkle, *L. littorea*, which lives on the MIDDLE SHORE, has the normal gill structure enabling it to absorb oxygen from the water in which it is submerged for some 50% of its life.

Desiccation : All plants and animals of the sea shore have to face the hazard of desiccation when exposed to the atmosphere by the ebbing tide. Water is all important to living organisms, ourselves included. We feel the effect of desiccation, or dehydration, on extremely hot summer days when so much water is lost from our bodies in the form of sweat that we seem to be continually thirsty. All living tissue, or *protoplasm*, consists of at least 70% water, so even the slightest loss upsets the delicate balance.

Wind and sun are responsible for this 'drying out' effect, so most of the shore animals hide in crevices,under rocks and seaweeds or bury themselves when the tide reccdes. As seaweeds cannot take this evasive action they wilt, becoming almost brittle if exposed for long, dry periods, though usually they regain their normal turgor once the tide returns. The brown wracks of the upper shore survive these conditions quite happily, but the more delicate red seaweeds would succumb and these are found inhabiting the lower regions of the shore.

Besides taking evasive action, many shore animals have, through the ages, become modified in some way to combat water loss. The periwinkle, the snail of the shore, is a good example. When the tide ebbs it retreats within its shell, closing the entrance behind it with a special horny disc attached to the rear portion of its body, thereby reducing water loss by evaporation to a minimum.

Temperature : As all the animals of the shore are *cold-blooded*, even small changes in temperature affect their activities and, if sudden, may prove fatal. The sea temperature varies very little in comparison with the air, so this factor is another hazard facing the littoral fauna during the period of low water. However, the animals cope with the situation quite effectively by reducing their activities to a minimum and, if mobile, retreating into sheltered positions under rocks and stones or below the sand. Gradual changes of temperature do not seem to affect the animals, but when a *sudden* rise or fall occurs many may die The young, or larvae, are even more sensitive to changes, so a high fatality rate at this stage affects the size of future populations.

The extreme temperatures of a hard winter or very hot summer take their toll. For instance, before the hard winter of 1963 one could drag a net over the rocks along the bottom of Torquay breakwater and be certain of bringing up many velvet swimming crabs (Plate 27), but for several seasons after that time no crabs were to be found. These crabs did not begin to recolonize the area for three years, and it was not until 1968 that their numbers were comparable to those of the years before 1963.

Temperature also has a definite controlling effect on the geographical distribution of shore populations and this explains why some Mediterranean species are found in the extreme south-west of Britain but nowhere else around our shores. Each species can endure a certain minimum and maximum temperature so an animal, such as the edible periwinkle, found on all coasts, is living within the centre of its range; it is a creature of temperate seas. As the largest of the acorn barnacles, *Balanus perforatus,* (Plate 23) is confined to the south-western peninsula, this is evidently the northerly limit of its temperature range or, in other words, its minimum survival temperature. On the other hand, another acorn barnacle, *Balanus balanoides,* inhabits most coastal regions, but *not* the southernmost tip of Cornwall, so here, presumably, the southerly limit for the species has been reached, that is its maximum survival temperature.

It is worth noting that the temperature of the sea around the British Isles is higher than would be anticipated in such latitudes. The reason for this is that warm waters from the Gulf of Mexico are carried to our coasts by the North Atlantic Drift (the Stream).

Substratum : There are two principal types of substratum : *stable* rocks or *unstable,* movable particles of shingle, sand or mud. Of the two, the stable environment supports the greater variety of flora and fauna as it is only here that seaweeds and sedentary animals find suitable surfaces for attachment.

The nature of the rocks varies greatly from the chalk cliffs of Dover to the rugged granite of Land's End, but the mineral content has little effect on the colonizers as they are interested in the rocks only as a medium for attachment. However, the texture of the surface is most important. If it is very smooth, or readily crumbles, few organisms settle but, in contrast, a rugh surface with numerous cracks and crevices supports large populations.

To some animals, such as the piddocks, hardness is the controlling factor because these bivalves bore into the rock and then remain within for the rest of their lives. Hardness also determines the degree of erosion caused by the continual battering action of the waves ; the softer the rocks the more readily they become eroded and deposited on the shore as s ingle or sand.

The unstable habitat of a single beach supports very little life owing to the continual friction between the pebbles, but a sandy beach contains hidden populations buried below its surface. Burrowing animals also inhabit muddy beaches, although the variety of species is limited by the fineness of the particles which would block the gills of many sand-dwellers.

Wave Action : Most of us, through first-hand experience or the medium of the press, are fully aware of the devastating effect the force of waves, whipped up by onshore gales, has on our coasts : breaches in sea walls with consequent flooding, damaged promenades, cliff falls due to undercutting of the lower layers, etc.

This pounding action obviously affects shore populations, and on the most exposed rocky coasts only truly tenacious animals survive. Examples are sedentary acorn barnacles and limpets which, though mobile, cling closely to the rocks with their powerful, muscular foot. The growth of seaweeds, if any, in such positions is stunted and the modifications developed by some organisms to withstand these unfavourable conditions often complicate identification.

On sand and mud, the survival of fauna from wave action depends entirely on deep and rapid burrowing as the surface layers of the substratum become displaced, Even on sheltered shores the littoral fauna is subject to some wave action, but the way in which the animals overcome this problem will be considered in the sections on habitats.

The relative exposure of a coast depends on the *fetch* of the waves, that is the distance over which they travel before breaking on the shore. In the British Isles the west-facing coasts suffer the greatest exposure, for here the waves are swept across miles and miles of the Atlantic Ocean before reaching the obstruction of the land.

The continual abrasive action of waves wears away rock faces and changes the shore form, though the extent of erosion depends on rock hardness. On unstable shores rough seas churn up the sand and mud, and deposit it in different positions, thus altering the sites of sand-banks, sand-bars and channels.

Salinity : When rock pools are uncovered by the tide, heavy rainfall may dilute the water slightly ; not sun causes evaporation and increases the salt concentration, but normally these minor variations in salinity cause no hardship to the littoral plants and animals, although sub-littoral species could not tolerate such changes. The same applies to the buried inhabitants of sand or mud, when rain percolates through to the lower layers. However, in estuaries, where fresh water mixes with sea water, the variation in salinity is sufficient to have a controlling effect on the populations.

Light : Many of the littoral animals are negatively phototropic, that is they move away from light and hide under stones or seaweeds, in cracks and crevices, or bury themselves below the surface. These reactions are the same as those displayed in response to other stimuli, but they are all inter-related and concerned with survival when the shore is uncovered by the tide. Other animals are just the opposite and prefer well-illuminated areas. To some, light is necessary for feeding because they seek their food by sight, while others track their food by touch or smell, and feed as efficiently in light or darkness. The latter animals frequently confine their feeding to the hours of darkness in order to escape the notice of predators, and themselves remain hidden from their prey.

Seaweeds, as all green plants, require light for *photosynthesis,* the process by which plants manufacture organic compounds from simple substances.

The intensity of light is the important factor to most organisms. Each species prefers a certain amount of illumination and therefore attempts to remain within its optimum light intensity. We shall see an interesting effect of this on plankton in Section 2.

All the factors mentioned in this section influence the lives of shore populations, and the balance between them determines the most beneficial niche for each species. A zonation of the fauna and flora of the littoral region therefore becomes apparent

3

The Shore and the Sea

Life on the shore cannot be considered in complete isolation from the sea for all the inhabitants have, through the ages, migrated from the sea. Some, such as channelled wrack and periwinkles, have become completely littoral in habit, but others such as Laminarians and rocklings, live both on shore and in shallow seas.

As in any other habitat, the animals of the shore are basically dependent on the plant life as a source of food and energy. Green plants are the only organisms with the ability to capture the energy of sunlight and use it to be bind together simple inorganic substances into complex organic compounds. The green pigment *chlorophyll* absorbs the energy which is then used to combine chemically water and carbon dioxide into sugar, i.e. the energy is stored in the sugar molecules. This process is called *photosynthesis* and the waste product of the reaction is oxygen. With other nutrients absorbed from the surrondings some of the sugar mulecules are converted into complex proteins. Green plants are thus referred to as the PRODUCERS. Animals can only feed on organic matter so they are dependent directly or indirectly on plants. They are thus referred to as the CONSUMERS. The consumer which feeds directly on plants, a herbivore, is the *primary* consumer ; the carnivore which feeds on the herbivore is the *secondary* consumer. Thus plants are the source of energy as well as material for the build up and maintenance of animal protoplasm. The energy stored in food is made available to the organisms by respiration, an oxidation process in which carbon dioxide and water are the waste products. The sea contains the nutrients so important for plant growth ; thus it is true to say that all shore populations depend on the sea for nutrition.

Seaweeds are the plants of the shore but, although some animals feed on them, the basic source of food for the majority is the floating life of the sea—the *plankton.*

The term *plankton* refers to all drifting and floating organisms whatever their size, but in most instances it is taken to mean the minute and microscopic plants and animals of surface waters.

Phytoplankton : The plants of the plankton, the *phytoplankton,* are mostly microscopic algae of two types, diatoms and dinoflagellates, both of which reproduce simply by dividing into two—an asexual method of reproduction called *binary fission.* When conditions are favourable the populations increase rapidly, particularly the diatoms, as they can divide three or four times a day. All phytoplankton are found in the surface waters where they can absorb the sunlight necessary for photosynthesis.

Although individual plants of the plankton cannot be seen with the naked eye, when massed in their millions they form a brown, red or green scum on the sea ; occasionally some of this is left as a thin film on shore by the receding tide.

Phytoplankton are the principal producers in marine life, whether offshore, inshore or seashore.

Zooplankton : The animals of the plankton, the *zooplankton,* vary in size. Many are microscopic, but others, such as sea-gooseberries, are readily visible. Some of these creatures are permanent members of the plankton, such as the copepod crustacean *Calanus* which is the main food of the herring, while others are only temporary members. These latter are the larval stages of marine animals, including many littoral species such as zoea larvae of shore crabs or veliger larvae of gastropods.

These small animals of the plankton are capable of swimming, but their movements are not sufficiently powerful to transport them against water currents, so they just drift along. However, they can swim up and down in a vertical migration. Research shows that zooplankton move upwards during the afternoon until dusk, scatter randomly throughout the hours of total darkness, rise again at dawn, then move downwards until midday. Why zooplankton move up and down in this way is not fully understood, but it is believed that each species prefers a certain light intensity and swims to keep within this optimum as its position varies with the rising and setting of the sun.

Many of these tiny creatures are phosphorescent, and on a quiet night their myriad glowing lights flicker over the surface when the water is disturbed.

Food Chains and Webs : Only a few animals feed on seaweeds and most of these are gastropods, such as periwinkles, topshells and limpets, so the phytoplankton are the principal producers. Many zooplankton feed on them directly and are thus primary consumers. However, some eat other zooplankton so are secondary or even tertiary consumers, or they may be omnivorous in their habits, feeding on phyto-or zooplankton, whichever is nearer.

Secondary consumers are any of the suspension feeders, either of the sea, such as the herring already mentioned, or of the littoral zone. Many seashore animals are sedentary and cannot forage for food, therefore they feed when the tide is in by filtering plankton from the sea. Various devices have been evolved for this purpose, as we shall see in the next section.

Tertiary consumers are the carnivores who eat the suspension feeders, and quaternary and later consumers are any other carnivores. This linkage is referred to as a *food chain* and below are a few examples.

Producer	Primary Consumer	Secondary Consumer	Tertiary Consumer
Seaweeds	Edible periwinkle	Man	
Seaweeds	Flat periwinkle	Fish	Man
Phytoplankton	Zooplankton	Barnacle	Blenny
,,	,,	Mussel	Starfish
,,	,,	Cockle	Man
,,	,,	Star sea-squirt	Cowrie
,,	,,	Breadcrumb sponge	Sea-lemon
,,	,,	Mysid	Pipefish

Many links in these food chains are interconnected and form a food web as shown in the following diagram.

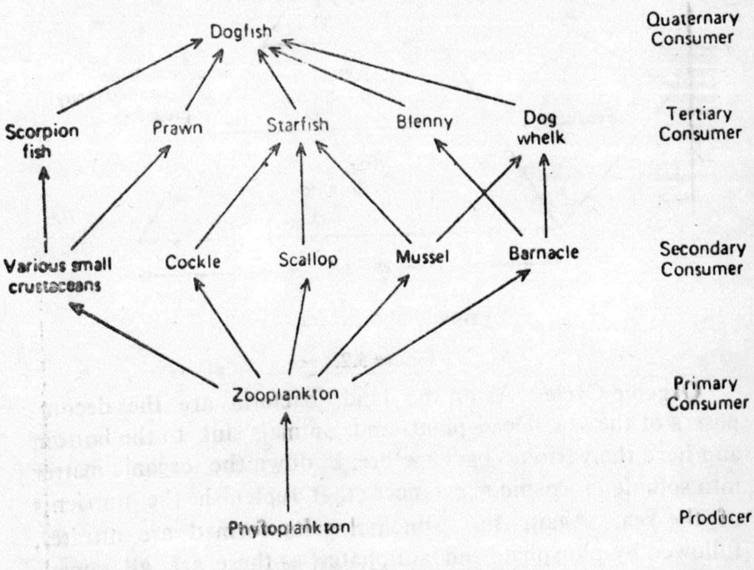

Food web of the seashore

Figure 3.1.

The transfer of organic material in a food chain is far from efficient. At each link the loss in bulk is approximately 90%, so enormous numbers of primary consumers are necessary to support one tertiary consumer. For instance, presuming each consumer in the chain feeds on one type only, a blenny must eat 10 grammes of barnacles to increase its weight by 1 gramme. These barnacles must consume 100 grammes of zooplankton and the latter 1000 grammes of phytoplankton. In other words, 1000 grammes of phytoplankton are necessary to support 1 gramme of blenny !

The primary consumers are small and abundant compared with the final predator, those in between being larger and fewer in number at each step. Such a relationship is referred to as the *pyramid of numbers*, and is shown opposite.

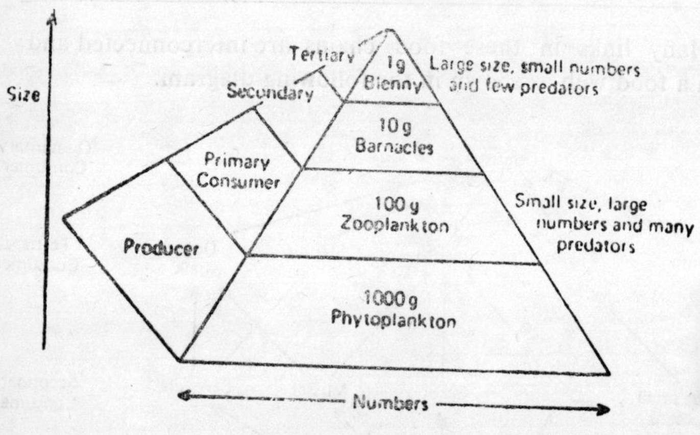

Pyramid of numbers

Figure 3.2.

Organic Cycle : As on the land, bacteria are the decomposers of the sea. Dead plants and animals sink to the bottom and here the various bacteria break down the organic matter into soluble inorganic substances that replenish the nutrients of the sea. Again the principal salts formed are nitrates, followed by phosphates and sulphates, as these are all constituents of proteins. Thus the organic cycle of the sea is comparable with that on land.

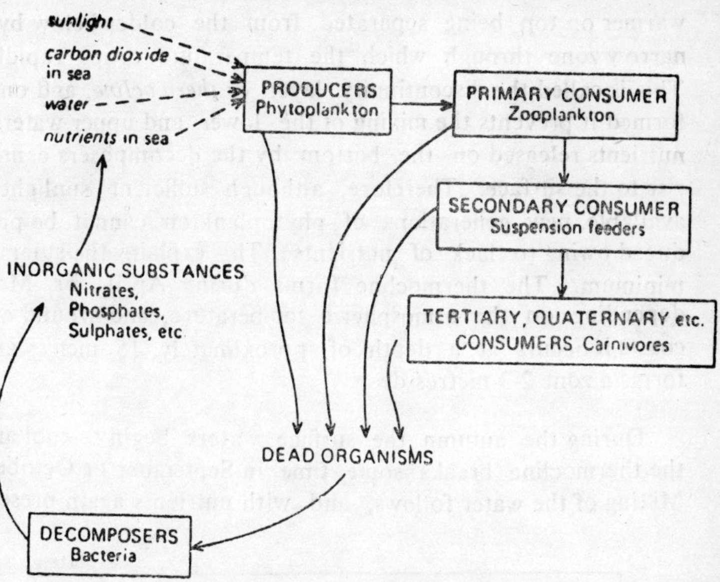

Figure 3.3. Organic cycle of the sea.

Plankton Cycle : The abundance of plankton throughout the seasons is not constant. During the winter months it is at a minimum, but in early spring a sudden outburst of phytoplankton occurs, the conditions being at an optimum for growth and reproduction. After only a few weeks the numbers fall away drastically until another slight increase in the autumn, before falling to the winter minimum. Fluctuations in zooplankton follow this pattern, though their numbers do not decrease so rapidly.

In spring the rise in temperature and increase in light intensity give the favourable conditions for phytoplankton to utilize the nutrients of the sea for rapid growth and reproduction. About this time many of the creatures of the sea and shore are ready to spawn This produces a large influx of zooplakton which voraciously feed on the phytoplankton and greatly deplete the plant numbers.

As summer approaches and the sun's intensity increases, the surface waters warm up and the distinct layers form, the warmer on top being separated from the colder below by a narrow zone through which the temperature drops rapidly. This is called the discontinuity layer or *thermocline*, and once formed it prevents the mixing of the lower and upper waters ; nutrients released on the bottom by the decomposers cannot rise to the surface. Therefore, although sufficient sunlight is available, new generations of phytoplankton cannot be produced owing to lack of nutrients This explains the summer minimum. The thermocline forms during April or May, depending on the atmospheric temperature, and around our coasts it occurs at a depth of approximately 15 metres and forms a zone 2-3 metres deep.

During the autumn the surface waters begin to cool and the thermocline breaks some time in September or October. Mixing of the water follows, and with nutrients again present

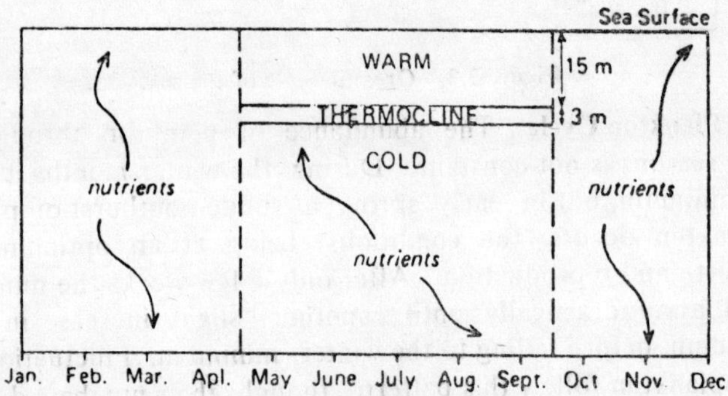

Figure 3·4. Distribution of nutrients throughout the seasons. Note the thermocline separating the warm and cold layers during the summer months.

in the surface layers, phytoplankton increase in number. However, this is short lived because the temperature and light intensity soon fall too low and the plankton decrease to their winter minimum.

Throughout the cold months decomposition continues on the bottom and the released nutrients spread evenly throughout the sea, ready for the spring phytoplankton explosion.

Fertility of the Sea : As shown by the plankton cycle, the fertility of the sea varies with the seasons, but it also varies from area to area as on land. Fertility depends on the carbon dioxide, oxygen and nutrient content, light intensity, salinity and temperature. There is no shortage of nutrients in the oceans, but they are of use to plants only when present in the illuminated surface waters. For a region to be fertile, water movements must occur for distribution of these nutrients from below to above. The high fertility of British seas is mainly due to the mixing of the waters caused by the flow of the Gulf Stream around our coasts, coupled with the additional nutrients brought by it from the Atlantic Ocean.

Dispersal of Shore Animals : Many shore animals are also dependent on the sea for development of their young and dispersal of the species. The larvae are minute free-swimming creatures which form the temporary plankton of our seas. Here they feed, grow and drift with the currents until they are ready to take up adult life on the shore.

4

Feeding Mechanisms

The ways in which our sea shore creatures feed can be divided broadly into five categories :

1. Plankton Feeders
2. Detritus Feeders
3. Seaweed Feeders
4. Predators
5. Debris Feeders

1. Plankton Feeders

These animals, also referred to as suspension feeders, sieve plankton from sea water, and the shore inhabitants exhibit many different modifications of structure for this function.

(*a*) *Gills* : Water flows over the gills for breathing purposes as in all fish, but additionally the gills may be adapted for trapping the plankton drawn in with the water current. By special mechanisms, the entangled food is then transferred to the mouth. Some bivalves, such as cockles and mussels, feed in this manner.

(*b*) *Appendages* : Some crustaceans filter-feed by sieving the water through stiff hairs on their appendages. Usually the maxillipeds are concerned in this method, but in the barnacle the tr e (thoracic) legs carry out this function.

(*c*) *Pores* : Minute holes in the surface of sponges allow tiny particles to be drawn in with the water current.

(*d*) *Tentacles.* Some animals bear a crown of tentacles covered with fine hairs for trapping the plankton. Many sedentary polychaetes and polyzoans feed in this way.

(*e*) *Perforated Pharynx.* In sea-squirts the first region of the gut behind the mouth, the pharynx, is perforated by tiny slits, bearing cilia at their edges, and when water is drawn through for breathing purposes any plankton present becomes entangled in this meshwork.

(*f*) *Cilia.* The arms of some echinoderms baer cilia whose beating directs water containing plankton, towards the mouth.

2. Detritus Feeders

These animals, also referred to as deposit feeders, feed on the microscopic particles of decaying organic matter that form a thin film over the surface of sandy and muddy bottoms. When detritus is disturbed from the bottom, as occurs in storms or by movements of animals, suspension feeders may also filter out these fine decaying particles, but they may not feed on them.

(*a*) *Gills.* Certain bivalves filter out the detritus by means of ciliated gills, and their siphons (extensions of the inhalent and exhalent apertures) are especially long and flexible for covering as wide a circle of the surface as possible to obtain detritus. The tellins of sandy shores and peppery furrow shells of muddy shores use this method.

(*b*) *Tentacles.* Some animals have mucus-secreting tentacles and as these are moved over the bottom, minute particles stick to them. The detritus is then transferred to the mouth. Some sedentary polychaetes and sea-cucumbers bear such tentacles.

(*c*) *Ingestion by swallowing.* Some burrowing ploychaetes simply eat mouthfuls of surface sand or mud from which they digest the contained detritus. Other animals just swallow up detritus as they move over the bottom.

3. Seaweed Feeders

Comparatively few animals feed exclusively on seaweeds.

Gastropods such as limpets, periwinkles, topshells and sea-hares are the principal herbivores which browse on seaweeds, and each has a radula bearing many minute teeth for rasping the weed from rocks. A few other animals may eat a little seaweed, but not as their main diet.

4. Predators

Apart from simply staking and grabbing the prey with open mouth, shore animals display several ingenious ways of catching and eating a victim.

(*a*) *Shell borers*. The predator bores a hole, either mechanically or chemically, into a shell and then sucks out the flesh of the prey from within. Many carnivorous gastropods use this method.

(*b*) *Shall openers*. This is a tussle between the strength of the predator and the adductor muscles of a bivalve (muscles which keep the two halves of the shell closed). Starfish are adept at this, and when they have succeeded in opening up the valves they extrude their stomach over the flesh of the prey and digest it *in situ*. Other animals just crush the shells to obtain the juicy contents.

(*c*) *Paralysis of prey*. These predators inject poison into their victims. This reduces the struggling ability of the prey but does not kill it Sea-anemones and their relatives have special stinging threads which are minute, but when a whole battery are released at once they quickly paralyse the prey. Some fish, such as weevers, have poison glands at the base of their spines, and cephalopods secrete a venom their salivary glands.

(*d*) *Capturing devices*. Cuttlefish and squids each have two long, thin tentacles which are normally retracted, but when stalking prey they suddenly shoot them out and grab the victim. Some polychaetes extrude their pharynx which bears chitinous jaws for gripping the victim, and other animals have an eversible proboscis which is prehensile and grips the prey by coiling around it.

5. Debris Feeders

These are the scavengers which feed on decaying organic matter of macroscopic size (large fragments as opposed to the minute particles which form detritus). Some animals just swallow the debris, but others grip and tear up the food material before it is passed to the mouth. Many decapod crustaceans (crabs and their relatives) use this latter method.

5

Rocky Shores

It is easily observed that plants and animals on tidal rocky shores characteristically occupy bands or zones parallel to the water's edge. It is widely held that the cause of this zonation is the regular emersion of the shore by the tidal ebb. Those organisms intolerant of exposure to air remain low on the shore and those able to withstand desiccation often live higher on the shore. Surprisingly, perhaps, tides are *not* the principal cause of zonation.

Distribution on the shore is primarily the result of a gradient of physical conditions on either side of an air/water interface. In non-tidal conditions there are still recognizable, if compressed, patterns of shore zonation. Above the air/water boundary there will be evaporation at the surface giving graded vertical changes in air moisture content and on splashed marine shores a fine layer of salt may coat exposed rock surfaces. Below this boundary, penetration of light decreases with depth and the amount of dissolved and suspended matter derived from the land decreases remote from the shore and at depth. The net result of these physical gradients is to create supra —and sublittoral zones. Superimpose on this tideless shore the effect of wind-driven waves and this results in an in-between or midlittoral zone. This is the situation which exists in the virtually tideless Mediterranean with a compressed midlittoral zone where changes in sea-level are controlled by changes in barometric pressure and wind force. An additional tidal rise and fall simply extends, and allows sub-division of, the midlittoral zone. Tides do not therefore initiate zoning but they do influence the pattern that the zones take.

Physical factors influencing rocky shore zonation

Tidal Heights : The landward boundary of the intertidal area is extreme high water of spring tides (EHWS) and the lower limit is extreme low water of spring tides (ELWS). At spring tides more of the bottom of the shore is exposed at low water and more of the top covered at high water. Some organisms living at the top of the shore may be wetted only twice a month while others at the bottom of the shore may be exposed only briefly twice in a month. The neap tide levels—mean high water neap tides (MHWN) and mean low water neap tides (MLWN)—are also important in controlling distribution because intertidal organisms between these levels on the shore will always be submerged again within 10 hours to 12 hours at most. Adaptations to combat this degree of desiccation are of a different order from those necessary to withstand desiccation for a fornight or longer. However, predicted tidal level are often exceeded simply because onshore winds in combination with low barometric pressure may have the effect of raising sea-level, but calm, anticyclonic conditions with high barometric pressure tend to depness sea-level.

Temperature : The main feature that tides impose on the shore is the regular alternation of periods of immersion and then drying our during emersion. When the tide is in, organisms experience more or less uniform temperature governed by the prevailing temperature of the inshore water mass. When the tide is out, however, air temperature, which is at once more variable and usually different from sea temperature may cause stress to certain stenothermic (tolerating only a narrow range of temperature) organisms and restrict their distribution to low on the shore. In summer, air temperature is often higher than the temperature of sea water with the reverse applying in winter. Intertidal organisms of rocky shores need to be able to tolerate widely fluctuating temperatures at every ebb and flow of

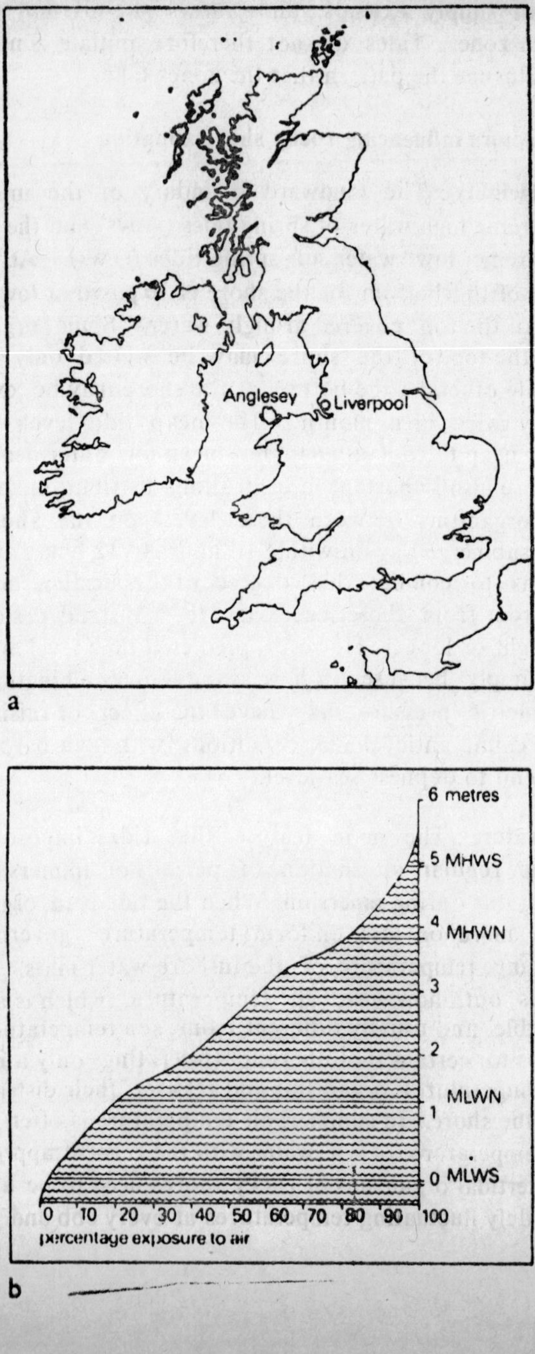

Figure 5.1. (*a*) Locality map for Figures 5.1 (*b*) and 5.2 (*b*) The percentage of time that various levels on the shore at Holyhead on Anglesey in North Wales are exposed to the air.

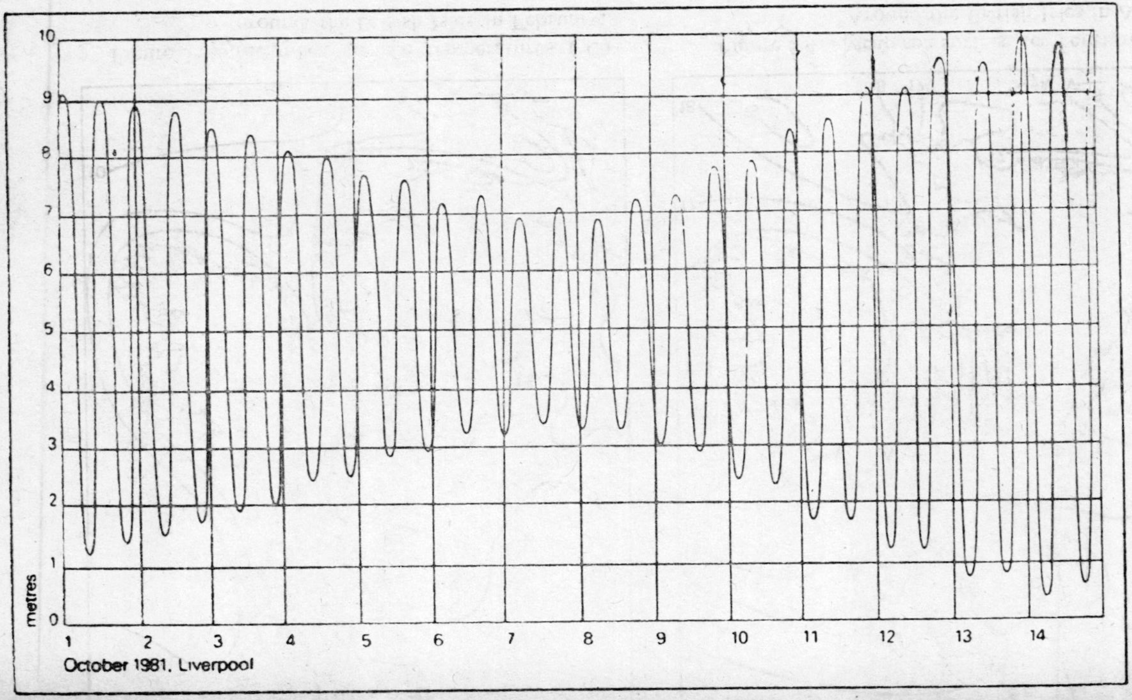

Fgiure 5.2. The spring/neep tidal cycle drawn from predictions (for locality map see Figure 5.1 (*a*).

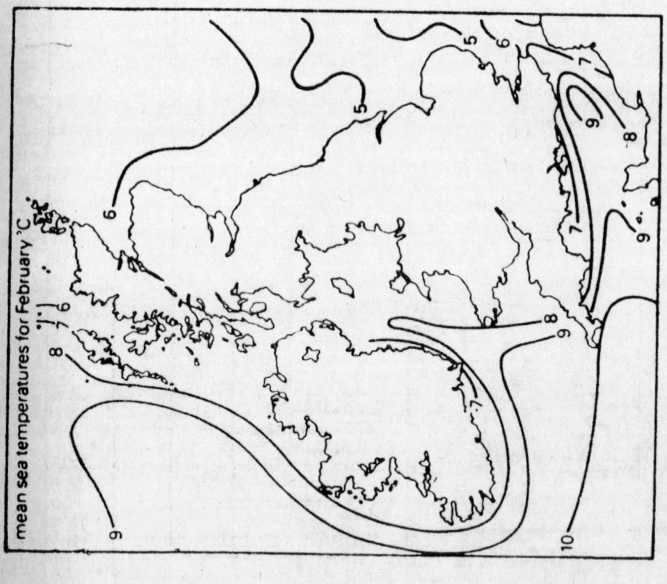

Figure 5.3. Mean sea surface temperatures (°C) around the British Isles in February.

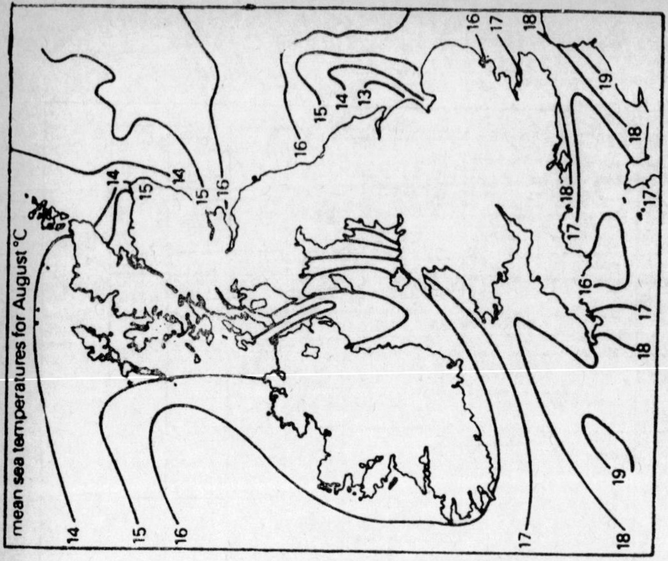

Figure 5.4. Mean sea surface temperatures (°C) Around the British Isles in August.

the tide. A low tide during the day in summer, exposidg intertidal rocks directly to the sun's rays, may cause rapid rises in body temperature in organisms attached to the surface. The heating process is enchanced if the rock is a heat absorbing dark colour. Conversely, at night at low water in the winter, organisms may be exposed to the risk of frost.

The level at which intertidal species live is not an infallible guide to their temperature tolerance. If the rocky shore is irregular, south and south west facing slopes (in the northern hemisphere) receive the full heating and drying effect of the sun, whereas nearby north facing slopes and areas of overhang are shaded and remain cooler. The common European periwinkle *Littorina littorea* is able to withstand the potentially lethal heat of the summer sun, and body tissue temperatures may be only a degree or so lower than the 40°C recorded from the rock face. Heat death does not occur in this species until 46°C – at 30°C most other shore molluscs begin to show signs of distress—the sudden fall in temperature as the tide rises stimulates the animals to activity.

Desiccation : Dehydration causes stress in organisms and water loss is increased in bright sunlight and in windy conditions. Organisms at the top of the shore have adaptations to overcome this problem. These adaptations include a coating of mucus in the beadlet anemone *Actinia equina* and also the operculum in prosobranch molluscs. The operculum in periwinkles consists of a horny plate impregnated with calcium and effectively closes off from the outside world those soft parts within the spiral shell.

The limpet *Patella vulgata* homes in at low tide and remains stationary in a definite position on the rock. The foot muscle anchors the animal firmly with a pull of up to 3.5 cm^{-2}. The edges of the conical shell fit perfectly with small indentations in the rock. Water is retained in the mantle cavity just inside the shell and while firmly clamped to the rock the animal suffers little desiccation. Adult limpets living high on the shore have taller shells than those near low water mark or in rock

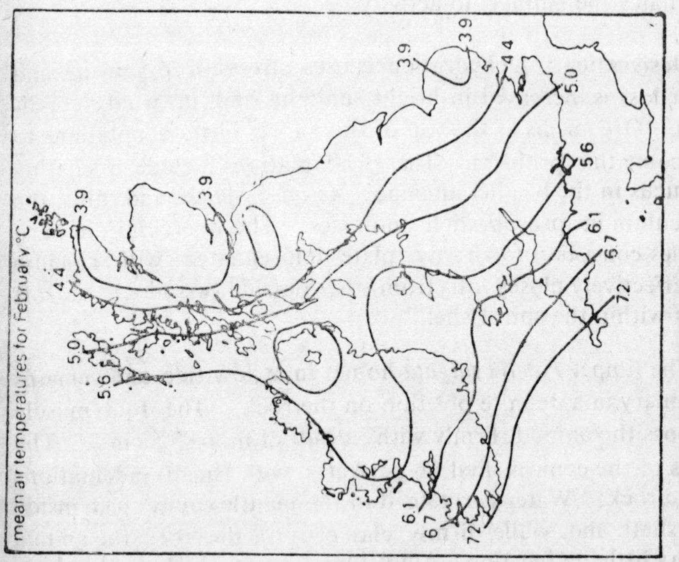

Figure 5.5. Mean air temperatures (°C) over the British Isles in February.

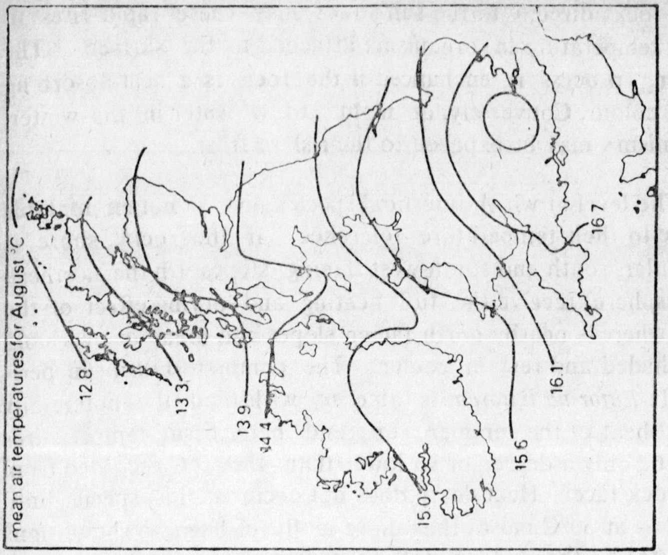

Figure 5.6. Mean air temperatures (°C) over the British Isles in August.

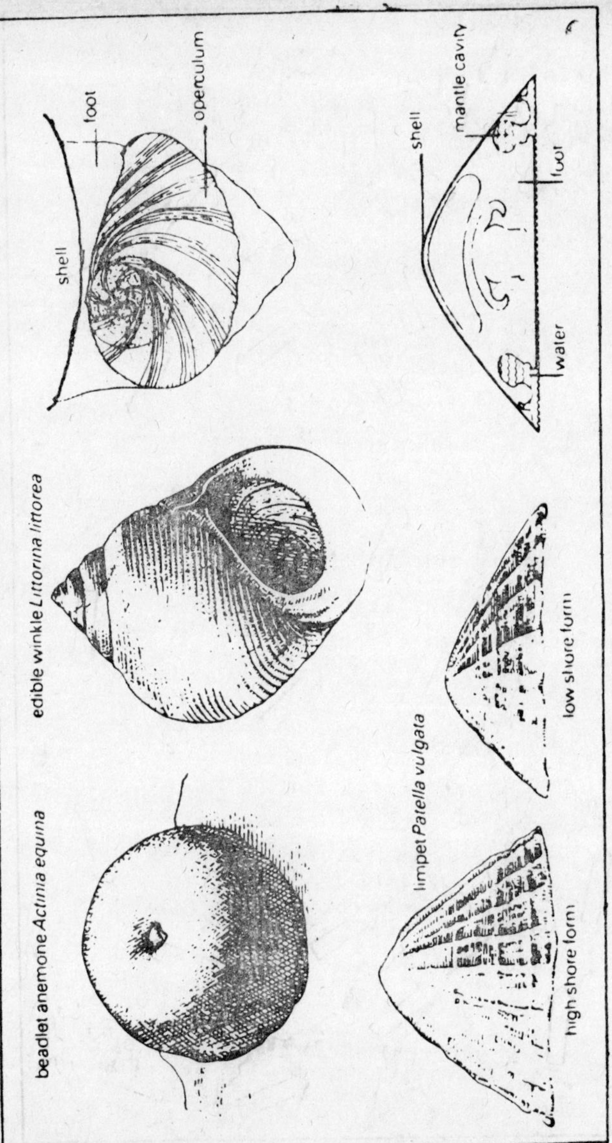

Figure 5.7. Some adaptations to withstand desiccation.

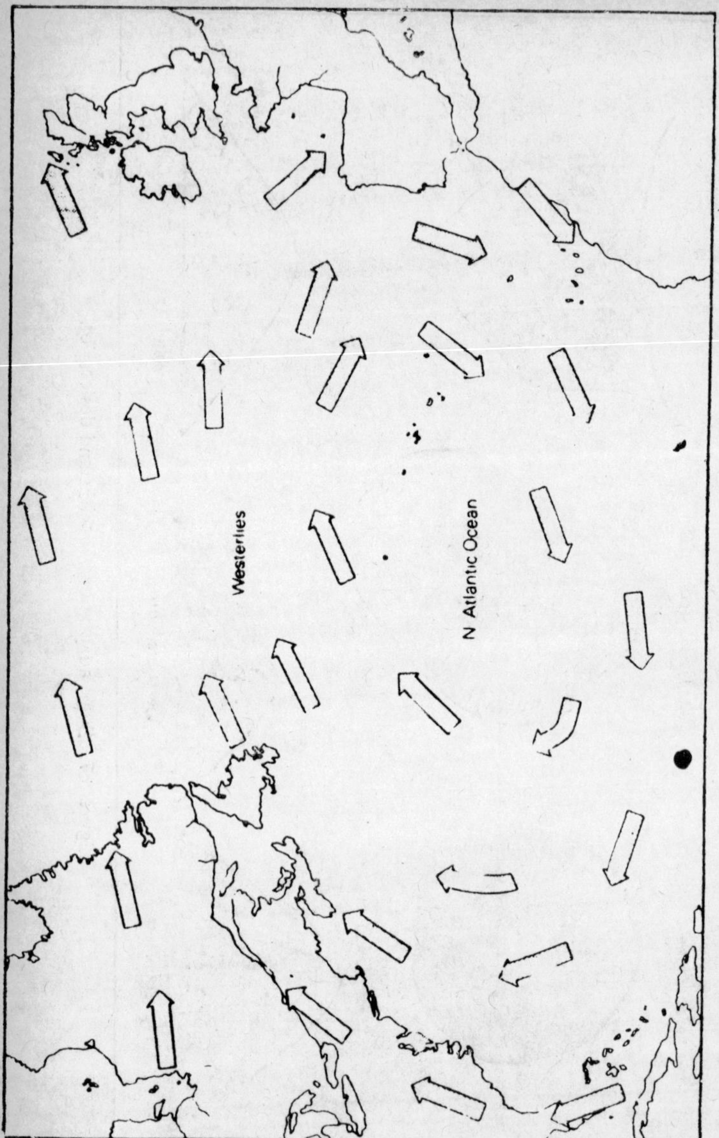

Figure 5.8. Prevailing westerlies blowing over the North Atlantic.

pools. It seems likely that the tall shell with a narrow base is produced by long periods of clamping down tightly on the rock to prevent desiccation. The mantle is responsible for new growth of the shell at its margin and the continual downpull of the foot muscle also has the effect of pulling in the mantle. Lower on the shore or in rock pools the shell muscles are relaxed for longer periods and the mantle spreads more widely, producing a flatter shell

Exposure : The distance of open sea over which the wind may blow — the fetch — governs the degree of wave action to which a coast is 'exposed'. The longer the fetch, the greater the wave action. Headlands, receiving the full brunt of the prevailing south westerlies across the North Atlantic such as those jutting out to sea in western Ireland, will suffer from greater exposure than the leeward side of an island. Associated with large oceans are oscillations in water level that give rise to

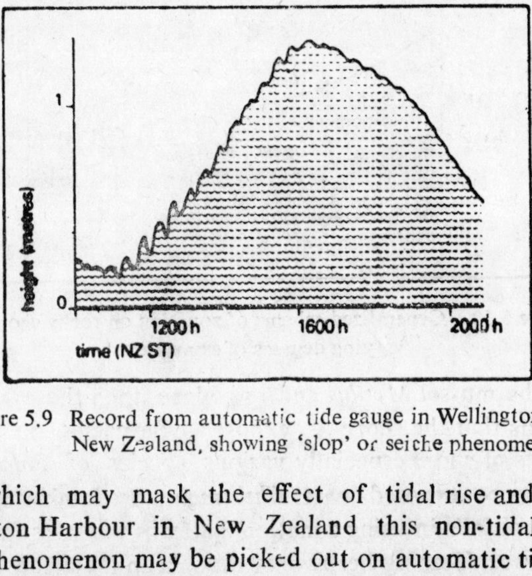

Figure 5.9 Record from automatic tide gauge in Wellington Harbour, New Zealand, showing 'slop' or seiche phenomenon.

'swell' which may mask the effect of tidal rise and fall. In Wellington Harbour in New Zealand this non-tidal 'slop' or seiche phenomenon may be picked out on automatic tide gauge recordings and is the result of a pendulous motion of water generated by storms or by earth tremors which have often taken place at great distance from the site where the effects are observed.

In general, slightly sloping, sheltered areas have a low exposure rating but open coasts with deep water close inshore and vertical cliff faces provide the most violent conditions with a high exposure rating. It is possible to use the width of a particular zone, such as the black lichen *Verrucaria* at the top of the shore, to assess the degree of exposure. If it is a narrow band confined within tidal limits and lower on the shore there is a mass of the brown alga knotted wrack *Ascophyllum nodosum* (on European coasts), then in combination, these suggest sheltered conditions. If there is a wide band of *Verrucaria* lying above the normal tidal range and in the midshore region

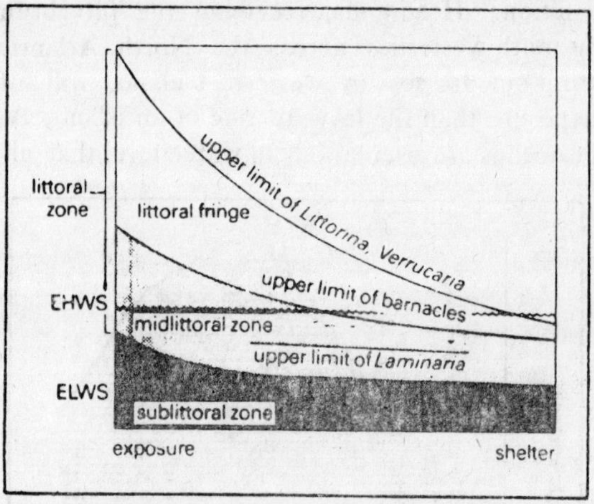

Figure 5.10. Generalized scheme of zonation on rocky shores of varying degrees of exposure.

there is the mussel *Mytilus* and red algae, then these are good indications that the shore is exposed. Barnacles do well on both kinds of shore especially various species of *Balanus*, but on the more exposed coasts *Chthamalus* predominates. There are some pitfalls in using zonation patterns to assess the degree of exposure. Grazing herbivores may keep the algae in check to such an extent that a shore may give the impression of more exposure than is really the case. Moderate oil pollution through reduction or loss of certain species loads to an apparent shift towards greater exposure on exposed coasts and towards more shelter on sheltered shores.

The position in the food web and factors affecting the distribution of some on the common inhabitants of rocky shores are examined below.

Algae : Primary producers

Green : Sea lettuce *Ulva lactuca* is found commonly on rocky shores, often in brackish (a mixture of sea and fresh water) conditions. This alga has a life cycle which includes two free-living stages—gametophyte and sporophyte. In cosmopolitan *Ulva* the two stages in this alternation of generations look alike, the green coloration of the plants resulting from the pigment chlorophyll contained in chloroplasts.

Brown : Brown algae contain photosynthetic pigment which include fucoxanthin giving the characteristic brown colour to to the plants. Giant kelps such as *Macrocystis pyrifera* may reach 60 m or more in length and are harvested off the coasts of California, South Africa and the Falkand Islands for use in the alginate industry. In Europe, the kelps, species of *Laminaria* attain lengths of only a few metres. These are the sporophyte generation but there is also a tiny filamentous gametophyte generation. Other brown algae such as Neptune's necklace *Hormosira banksii* which occurs in southern seas and, more common in the northern hemisphere, the fucoids such as bladder wrack *Fucus vesiculosus* have only one main stage (sporophyte) in their life cycle.

Relatively sheltered shores on either side of the Atlantic are dominated by the brown seaweed family Fucaceae. On European coasts a distinct pattern of zonation of the fucoids is apparent with channelled wrack *Pelvetia canaliculata* occurring just below the *Verrucaria* belt. Spiral wrack *Fucus spiralis, Fucus vesiculosus* and/or *Ascophyllum nodosum* occupy the upper and midlittoral zones respectively, with a band of serrated wrack *Fucus serratus* just above low water mark. Below this and extending into the sublittoral are the kelps such as *Laminaria saccharina*, the oarweed *Laminaria digitata* and *Laminaria hyperborea*,

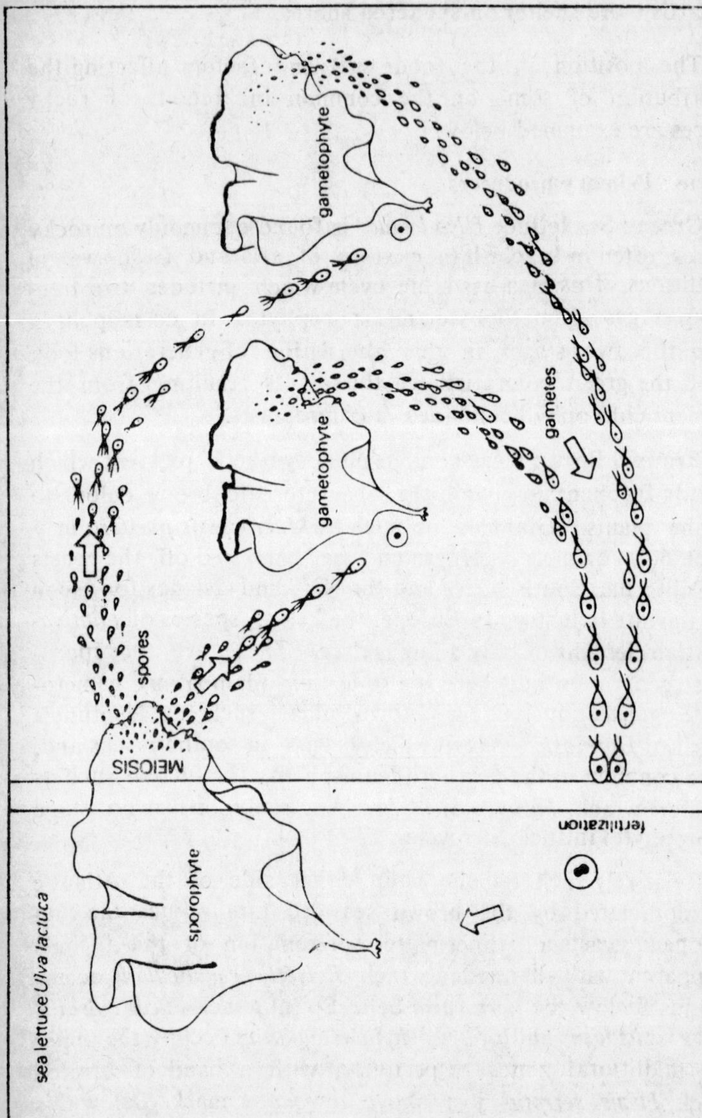

Fig. 5.11. Life cycle of the green alga sea lettuce *Ulva lactuca* with an isomorphic alteration of generation which look alike.

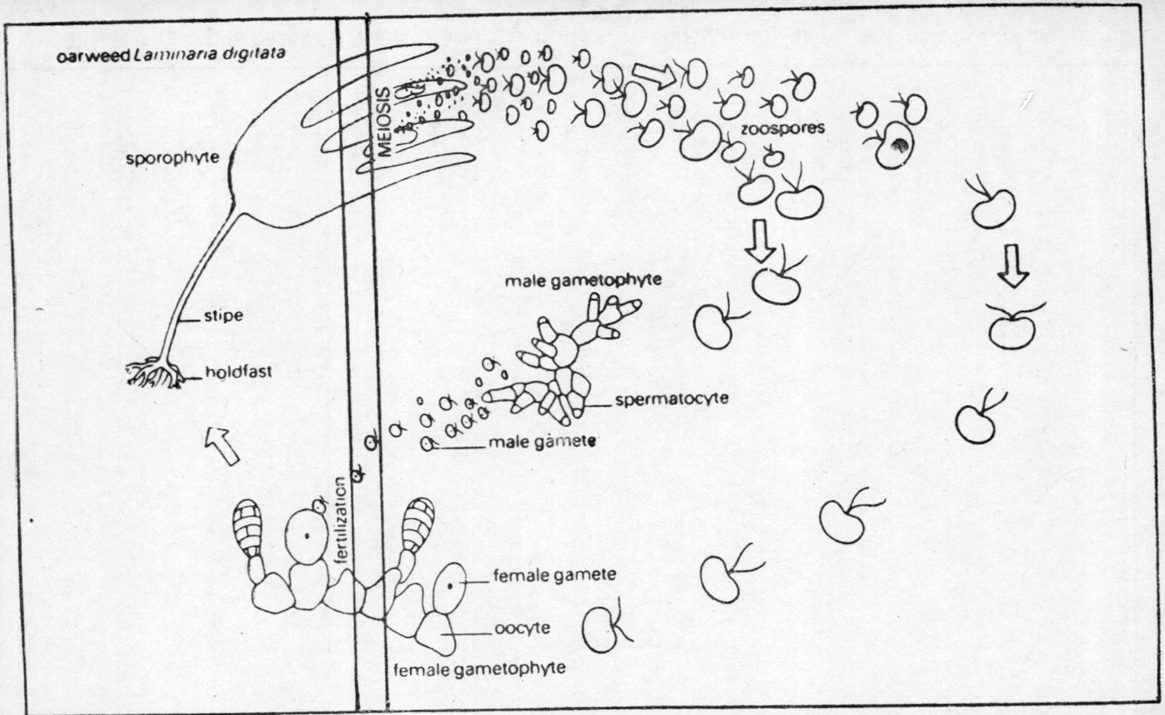

Figure 5.12. Life cycle of the brown alga o..rweed *Laminaria digitata* in which there is a heteromorphic alternation of generations, a small gametophyte and a large sporophyte.

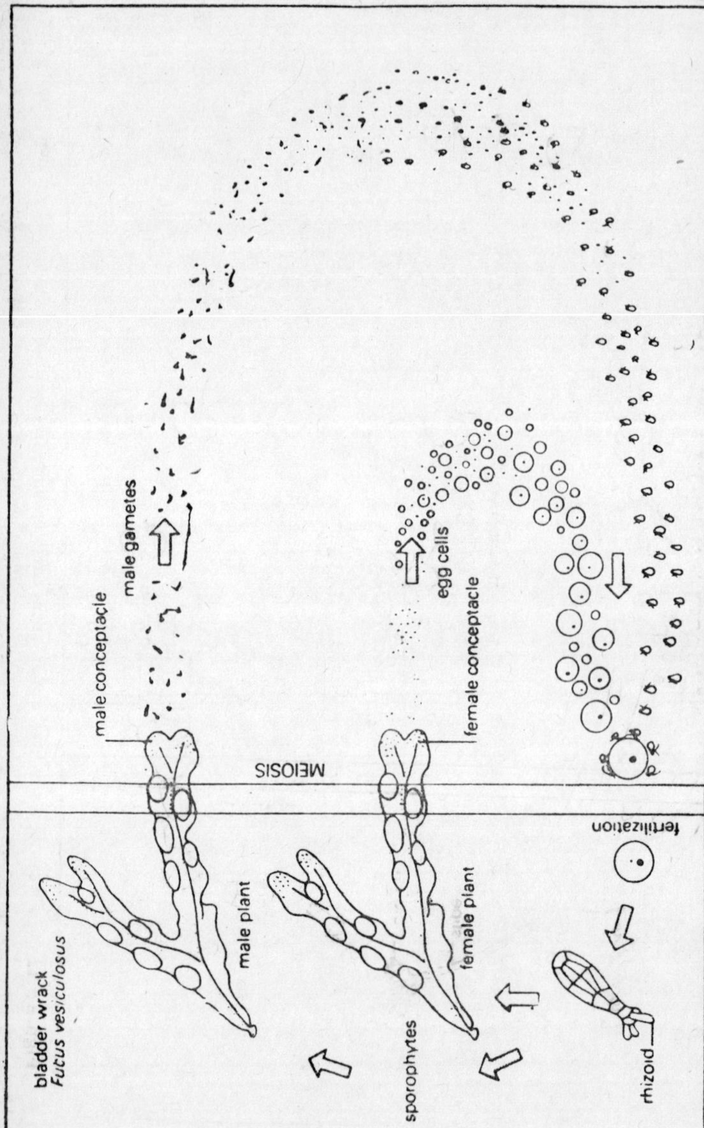

Figure 5.13. Life cycle of a fucoid brown alga bladder wrack *Fucus vesiculosus* with one free-living stage, the sporophyte.

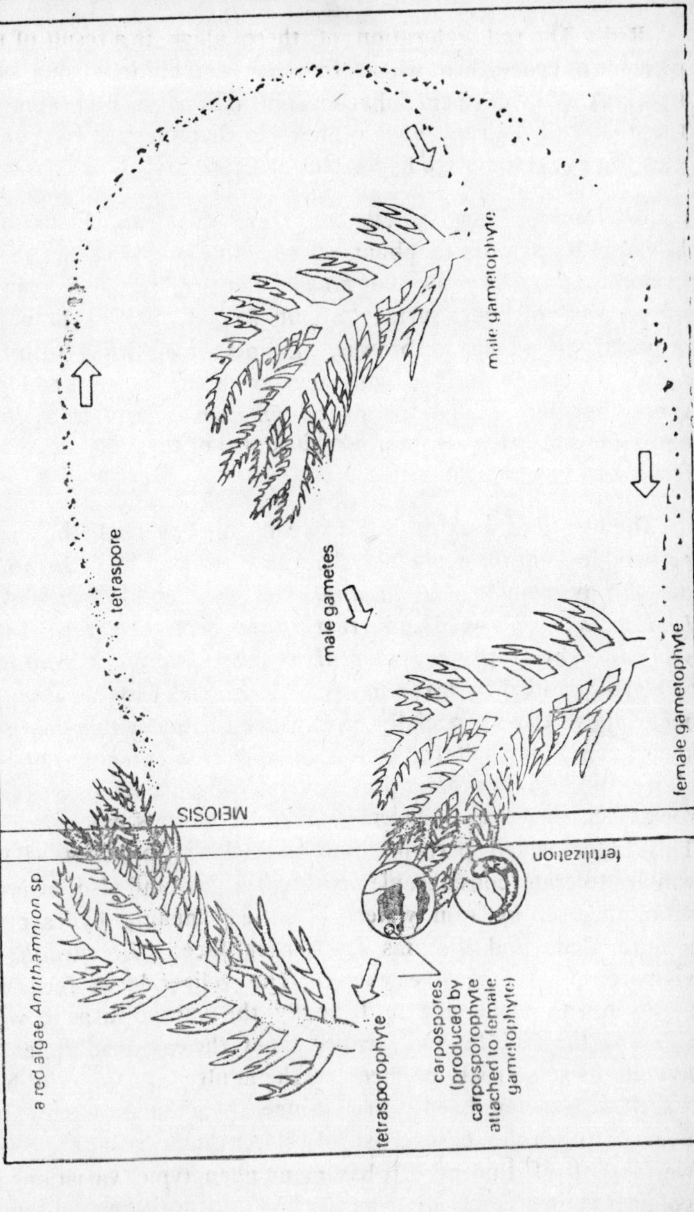

Figure 5.14. Life cycle of a red alga *Antithamnion* with a third generation—the carpo-sporophyte.

Red : The red coloration of these algae is a result of the pigment phycoerythrin which bleaches quickly in strong sunlight. A blue pigment phycocyanin may also be present in these so-called 'red' algae. They are characterized by a complex life cycle some are harvested for agar.

Molluscs : Many gastropods graze on algae Planktonic larvae of limpets settle about MLWN but higher on the shore in pools and damp shaded areas. During the first year of life an area of rock surface about 75 cm^2 cm^{-3} of limpet is required on which to browse. Limpets rasp away with the radula (a horny tongue with rows of teeth) at settling algal spores but larger algal plants of *Enteromorpha*, *Ascophyllum* and *Fucus* are eaten also during the course of their 60-cm zigzag feeding traverses at high tide.

The littorinid winkles of European shores such as the small periwinkle *Littorina neritoides*, the rough periwinkle *L. saxatilis*, the flat periwinkle *L. littoralis* and the edible periwinkle *L. littorea* are zoned in that order from the top of the shore. The species *saxatilis* and *littoralis* continue to be re-classified by taxonomists. *L. neritoides* and *L. saxatilis* occur above EHWS especially in exposed regions with a marked splash zone. In sheltered conditions they may extend no higher than MHWS. *L. neritoides* prefers very exposed, steep, creviced rock faces whereas *L. saxatilis* generally prefers more shelter. This latter rough periwinkle extends down to ELWN. Both winkles tolerate considerable exposure to air and also lowered salinity caused by rain water ; both feed mainly by rasping minute algae and diatoms from rock faces. *L. saxatilis* is viviparous, hatching live young. The veliger larva feeds on albumen within the egg until finally the embryo rasps its way free with the radula and escapes from the egg membranes to live in the same rock crevices as the adults. *L. littoralis* has a shell with a depressed spire (hence the common name) and lives both on the east coast of North America and on the west coast of Europe. It has many phenotypic variations in colour ranging from a citrina (yellow) form through aurantia (red—orange) to olivacea (derk green). In combination with

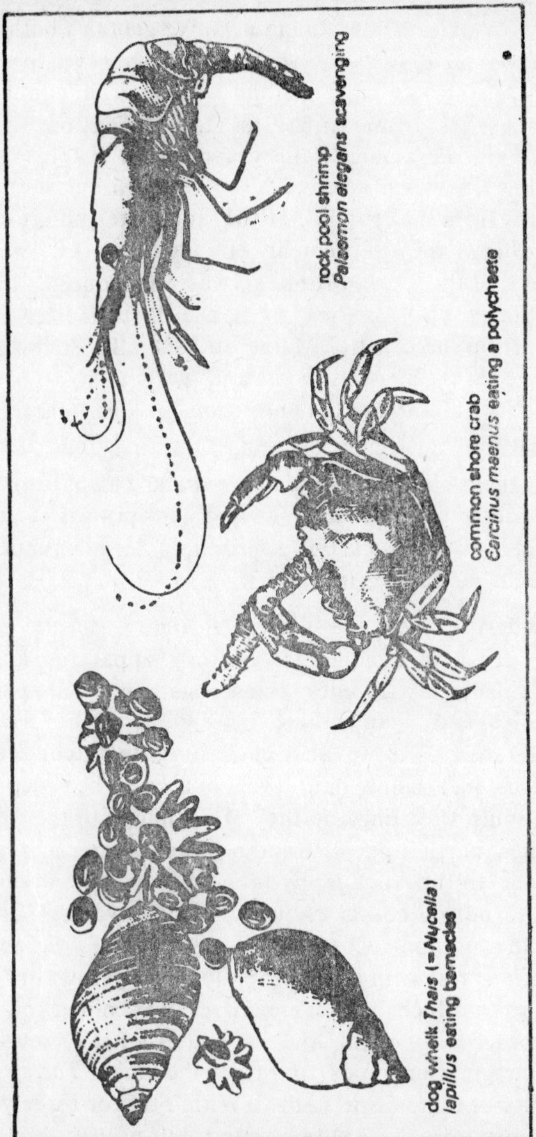

Figure 5.15. Secondary consumers (not all drawn to the same scale).

zigzag banding and stripes in contrasting colours 12 varieties have been recognized. This species lives in association with the algae *Ascophyllum* and *Fucus* which provide both shelter and food. Winkles show strong negative geotaxis both in and out of the water ; desiccation reverses this, however, preventing them from rising too high on the shore. The edible winkle *L. littorea* ranges from MHWN to ELWS living on rocks and among gravel. Permanent clusters of up to 950 m^{-2} may be found at low tide when inactive. They feed on micro-organisms and detritus from the surface of the substrate and are effective in controlling the settlement of algal spores by rasping with the radula. *L. littorea* was introduced into the United States of America from the British Isles and was recorded from the coast of Maine in 1868. By 1880 it had dominated the Massachusetts coast and is thought to have been esponsible for eliminating the indigenous *L. palliata* from New England shores.

Top shells such as *Mondonta lineata* are also browsers but rtend to prefer more shelter, having poor powers of adhesion If disturbed, *Gibbula cineraria* produces large quantities of sticky mucus perhaps to increase its grip.

Echinoderms : The sea urchin *Echinus esculentus* is also a browser. It has a complex masticatory apparatus known as Aristotle's lantern. Twenty calcareous pieces are connected with muscles and ligaments to five mobile teeth. These rasp organisms such as algae and encrusting invertebrates. This species lives just below tidal levels but may be uncovered at ELWS. In south west England they are confined to the sublittoral but further north appear on the lower shore and in pools. Attachment to the rock is by tube feet and the urchin's presence on turbulent coasts shows how effective these are in anchoring the urchin. Continuous removal of *Ecbinus* from experimental test sites leads rapidly to the growth of a dense algal sward. Much the same effect was noted on certain Cornish beaches following the reduction of the browsing limpet population after the oil spill from the tanker *Torrey Canyon* and the use of toxic dispersants. Within two or three years the rocks were covered by a rich intertidal growth of algae ; the limpets took tonger to recover.

Secondary consumers

Molluscs : The preferred diet of the dog whelk *Thais*

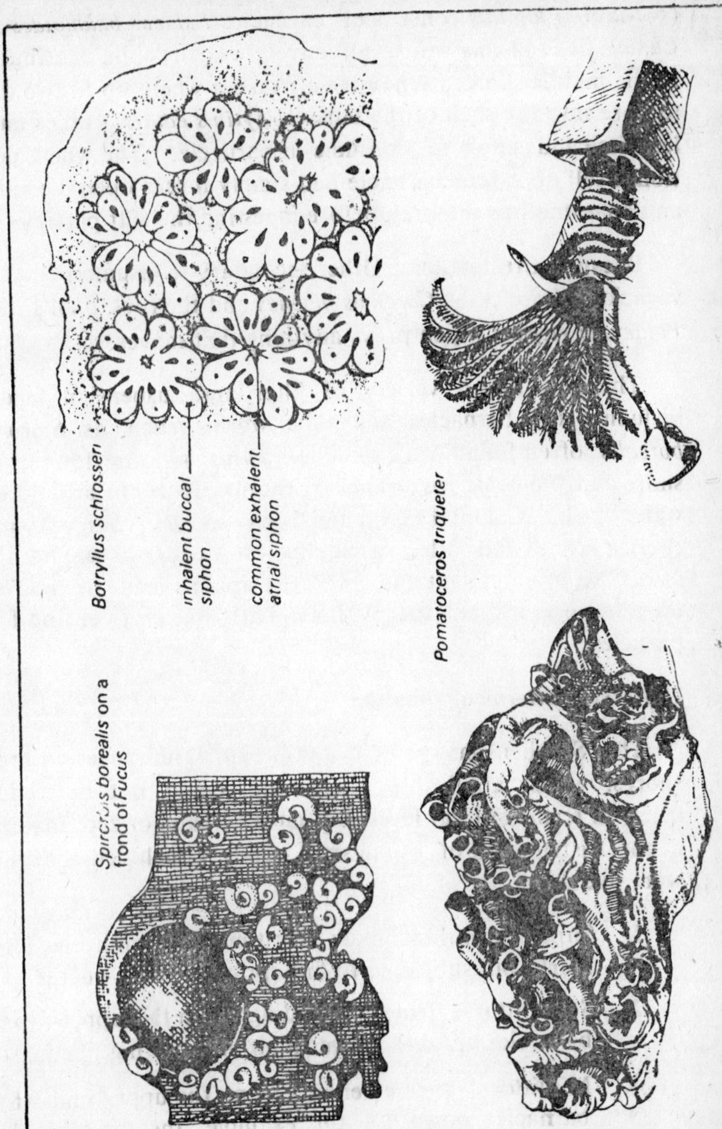

Figure 5·16. Filter and suspension feeders

(=*Nucella*) *lapillus* consists of barnacles *Balanus balanoides* and *Chthamalus stellatus* which effectively restricts its distribution to the middle shore. While it may take a whelk up to two days to bore into the shell of the mussel *Mytilus edulis* it takes much less time and effort to consume a barnacle. The whelk positions itself above the barnacle and simply forces open the valves and anaesthetizes the prey before ingesting the soft parts.

Decapod Crustaceans : Other secondary consumers include voracious shore crabs *Carcinus maenas* and the rock pool shrimp *Palaemon elegans* which preys anything that moves.

There is also a variety of filter and suspension feeders including the barnacles and tube worms such as *Spirorbis borealis* often found on fronds of *Fucus serratus* low on the shore and *Pomatoceros triqueter* encrusting rocks around low water mark. Colonial ascidians such as *Botryllus schlosseri* encrust stones and other ascidians low on the shore, and filter feed. Minute inhalent and exhalent siphons lead to and from the pharyngeal filter that is lined with mucus to entrap food particles.

Universal patterns of zonation

The Stephensons pointed out in 1949 that zones on rocky shores, whilst applicable world-wide, could not be defined solely in terms of tidal levels but must be categorized in terms of the distribution of organisms. They concluded that there were five zones :

1. Superalittoral zone or maritime belt lying above tide marks but subjected to fine spray in rough weather.
2. Superlittoral fringe extending from the upper limit of barnacles up to the lower limit of flowering plants.
3. Midlittoral zone extending from the upper limit of the barnacles down to, for example, the top of the kelp belt.
4. Infralittoral fringe extending from the top of the kelp belt to ELWS.

5. Intralittoral zone extending from ELWS to the lower limit or seaweed or even to the edge of the continental shelf.

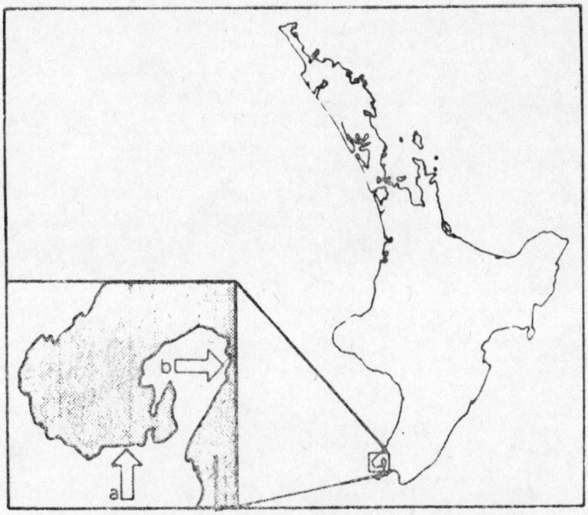

Figure 5.17. Wellington Harbour New Zealand.

That these zones are universally applicable (at least in cool temperature waters) may be shown by comparing typical patterns of zonation on exposed and sheltered British rocky shores with similar shores in New Zealand. Most of the individual species are different with the barnacle *Chamaesipbo* replacing the northern *Balanns.* Brown fucoids are less in evidence in the New Zealand midlittoral, Neptune's necklace *Hormosira banksi* forming the replacement together with a more diverse green algal cover than is usually found on shores in the northern hemisphere. But the delimiting upper level of barnacles and the upper limit of the low shore kelps are present with only minor variations on all cool temperate marine rocky shores (in polar regions these are no barnacles, in the tropics, no kelps).

Rock pools

Those organisms particularly sensitive to desiccation are often able to extend their range upshore in shaded damp

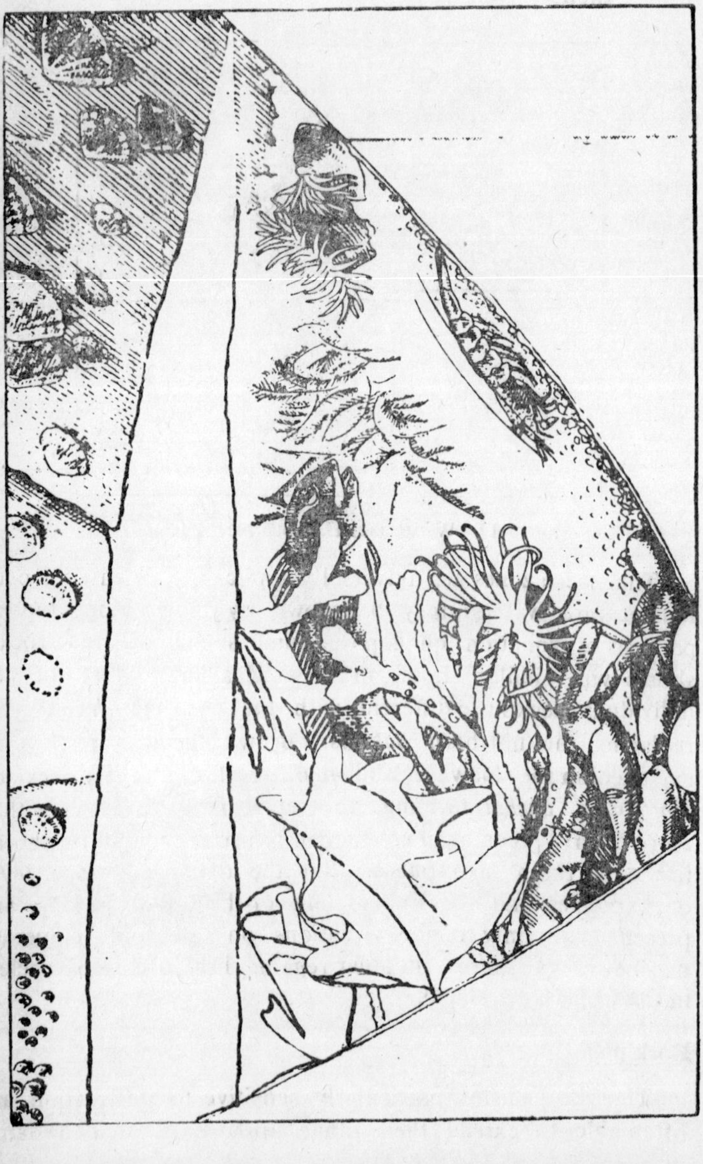

Figure 5.18. Midshore rock pool.

crevices. A permanent presence of water in rock pools might be expected to extend the range of those species to even higher levels on the shore. However, apart from a few red coralline algae such as *Corallina* and the limpet *Patella aspera* for which desiccation appears to be the limiting factor, this range extension rarely materializes. Rock pools have their own physical characteristics - unshaded shallow pools will show marked changes in temperature, salinity, oxygen and pH levels. Special physiological adaptations may be necessary to cope with such widely fluctuating changes as those that occur in a high-level pool that is exposed to sunlight and/or rain for a fortnight and is then suddenly inundated by a high spring tide.

Nevertheless rock pools on the low and middle shore which experience a regular tidal change of water often contain a rich and varied selection of shore organisms, a feature explored for generations by the fossicking net and bucket brigade.

6

Plants of Rocky Shores

Of the several seashore habitats, rocky shores exhibit the greatest variety of animal life and are the only type to support large plant populations. The latter, of course, consist of the seaweeds.

The words *rocky shore* conjure up in the mind's eye a different picture for each of us depending on the particular region of the coast we have visited. If our journeys have taken us to the west coast of Cornwall where the shore and cliffs suffer the continual onslaught of Atlantic rollers, the picture presented is bleak, with barren areas of rock only sparsely clothed with vegetation. On the other hand, if we are familiar with some of the sheltered bays of South Devon the picture envisaged is of rocky expanses covered with luxuriant growths of sea-weeds varying in colour from bright green, through green-browns to red.

First of all, why do seaweeds grow in such profusion on rocky shores ? The answer is quite simple ; rocks are stable and form a suitable base for attachment. Unlike terrestrial plants, seaweeds do not need a root system because they absorb nutrients directly from the sea, but they do possess a 'rootlike' structure, called the *holdfast*, for anchorage. This holdfast grows into rock cracks and crevices, thus gaining a firm enough grip to prevent dislodgement by the pounding action of waves.

Seaweeds belong to the non-flowering class of plants called *ALGAE* and all contain chlorophyll, though its presence is sometimes masked by other pigments, as is the case in the brown and red seaweeds. Ail photosyhthesize and therefore require plenty of sunlight. For this reason seaweeds are confined to shores and shallow seas.

Seaweeds are the producers in certain marine food chains but, although they are the staple diet of some shore dwellers, many animals depend on them, principally for protection from desiccation when exposed by the ebbing tide and for shelter from wave action when the sea returns. Numerous creatures take advantage of this amenable habitat, but before studying them we must first give our attention to the seaweeds themselves.

Classification As already mentioned, there are seaweeds of varying colours, and for classification purposes they are divided into

CHLOROPHYCEAE—greens

PHAEOPHYCEAE —browns

RHODOPHYCEAE —reds

The Chloruphyceae are usually bright green and very easy to recognize, but in the Phaeophyceae and Rhodophyceae there is often colour variation brought about by the bleaching action of the sun so that a red weed, such as carragheen or Irish moss, *Chondrus crispus*, may appear dull green, or even a yellowish white if exposed for a sufficient length of time. This bleaching is particularly prevalent with detached seaweeds thrown up on the shore and can cause considerable confusion in identification. Brown seaweeds are not typically brown but vary from olive brown to dark green.

Structure : In comparison with the familiar plants of the garden the physical structure of seaweeds is very simple, and the whole plant is called the *thallus*. The thallus is anchored by the *holdfast*, from which arises the stem or *stipe*, and at the tip this develops into a flattened or cylindrical *frond,* whose size, shape and texture varies from species to species. When the tide is in the complete plant is submerged, and at this time the exchange of gases and other substance occurs by diffusion over the whole surface of the thallus.

Reproduction : There are no flowers, but most seaweeds reproduce sexually. The minute male and female gametes are usually released into the sea, where fertilization occurs, and the zygote so formed may be dispersed some distance by the water currents before it deposits on the bottom and develops into a new plant. Even though zygotes may be carried to other regions of the shore, only those that deposit on the correct zone develop to maturity.

Vegetative reproduction occurs in many seaweeds, but the actual method varies with the different types. In some simple forms, such as the sea-lettuce, the frond just divides into two or more and each part continues to grow, while in the large oarweeds new growth occurs at the tip of the stripe, and when the new frond is well developed the old one is broken off by the force of the waves.

Some seaweeds also reproduce asexually by means of spores, which appear as slight swellings on some part of the found, and when released germinate into new plants.

As there are several hundred different species of seaweeds, it is possible for us to consider only the most common forms found around the costs of Britain.

Brown Seaweeds and Zonation : The greatest amount of cover is given by the tougher types of brown seaweeds, called the *wracks,* and, as each can withstand certain periods of exposure only, their positions down the beach are zoned.

Starting at the top of the shore, the first brown seaweed encountered is channelled wrack, *Pelvetia canaliculata,* with fronds terminating in divided tips 5—15 cm long, hanging from the rocks in dense clusters. The edges of the fronds are inrolled, a feature which, besides making identification easy, serves the useful purpose during exposure of trapping moisture in the channel formed between the frond and rock surface. The fronds branch in a very definite manner, termed *dichotomous* branching. One frond divides into two ; each of these in turn divides twice, and so on to the tips. This form of branching is typical of most wracks.

During neap tides some areas of the upper shore remain exposed for several days and at these periods, particularly in the hot dry months, the normally olive-brown fronds become shrivelled and almost black, though they quickly regain their usual turgor when next submerged. *Pelvetia* may survive in the splash zone, but here growth is very stunted.

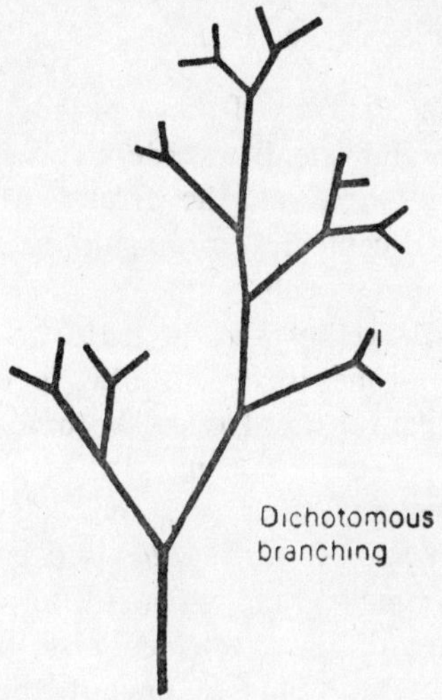

Figure. 6.1.

The reproductive structures, the *receptacles,*, develop at the tips of the fronds and when ripe appear yellowish orange. They contain both male and female gametes ; that is *Pelvetia* is a hermaphrodite.

Flat or spiral wrack, *Fucus spiralis,* occupies the next belt down the beach, overlapping the lower edges of the upper shore and the upper region of the middle shore. The flat fronds, up to 12 mm in width, have a smooth edge, a midrib, divide at the tips and are generally between 12 and 20 cm long, although they may reach 35 cm in length. The ripe receptacles are very distinctive oval, orange-brown swellings at the tips of the fronds and, like *Pelvetia*, contain both male and female gametes.

The middle region of the shore supports two wracks bearing air bladders for buoying their fronds up near the surface when the tide is in. These are bladder wrack, *Fucus vesiculosus*, and knotted wrack, *Ascophyllum nodosum* and both are confined to this region because their bladders could not withstand the increased pressure at greater depths of water. Sometimes they live side by side, but more frequently one species is present on a particular shore.

F. vesiculosus has a frond from similar to *F. spiralis*, but with a wavy margin and small bladders on either side of the midrib, arranged in pairs, and the fronds may be from 30—120 cm long. The receptacles are again at the tips of the fronds, but they contain only gametes of one sex, the female receptacles appearing yellow and the male bright orange when ripe. In winter months it is not always easy to identify bladder wrack because the fronds become badly damaged during storms. Ofter only the midrib survives above the holdfast, bearing just a few torn shreds of fronds with no signs of air bladders. *F. vesiculosus* is capable of colonizing many varied environments and in adapting itself becomes so modified that it is difficult to recognize, particularly as air bladders may be absent. This is one of the tricks of nature which leads the methodical man a marry dance !

Ascophyllum nodosum is very different. The frond is narrow, like a thick flattened cord, with no midrib, but containing large egg-shaped air bladders arranged singly down the centre at intervals of around 7—10 cm, depending on the size of the plant. *A. nodosum*, unlike the other wracks, branches irregularly and grows to a great length, maybe to 3 metres in its most favourable situation—a well-sheltered shore. On exposed shores it gives way to *F. vesiculosus*, which is a much hardier plant.

The reproductive bodies of *A. nodosum* are borne at the tips of special short side branches arising along the length of the fronds, and when ripe these receptacles are bright yellow in the male plants and yellow olive in the females.

Quite frequently, knotted wrack is camouflaged by a tufted covering of the red seaweed, *Polysiphonia*. When looked at through a hand-lens, *Polysiphonia* is seen to consist of a lattice-work of fine branches arising in a tuft from the holdfast, which is firmly attached to the *Ascophyllum* frond. A plant which

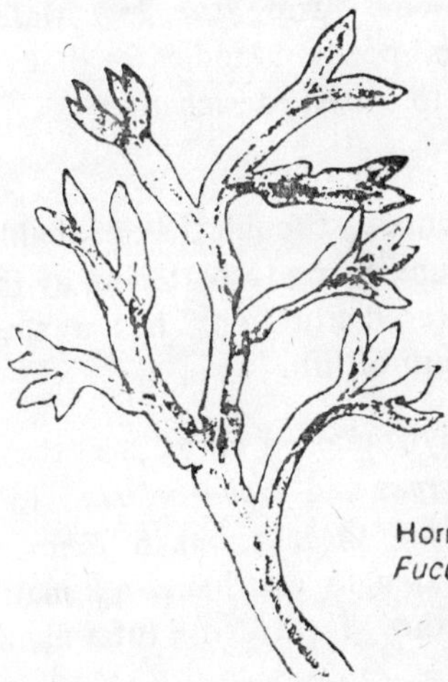

Horned wrack.
Fucus ceranoides

Figure. 6.2.

attaches itself to another plant, but absorbs *no* nourishment from it, is called an *epiphyte* ; many seaweeds exhibit this epiphytic habit.

Horned wrack, *Fucus ceranoides*, is another inhabitant of the middle shore, but *only* where *fresh water* is present. Obviously we shall find this seaweed is a common member of estuarine flora. The fronds have a definite midrib, divide dichotomously and bear narrow, pointed receptacles at their tips.

Intermingled with *F. vesiculosus* on the lower regions of the middle shore the last of the fucoids, serrated wrack, *F. serratus*, appears as a flat matlike covering to the rocks. The fronds are distinctly flat with a midrib, but the margins are serrated or toothed, hence the common names of serrated or saw wrack. The receptacles do not form swollen bulbous structures as in the other wracks, but extend as a flattened, blistered area over the terminal 2—4 cm of the frond, those of the male plant appearing bright orange when ripe. Sometimes sterile structures in the form of small, fine, white hairs are dispersed over the fronds. *F. serratus* is one of the commonest British seaweeds and clothes a wide belt of rocks, extending down on to the lower shore where it is exposed only for brief periods during the low water spring tides. Its preference for this position indicates that *F. serratus* is not so well modified to resist desiccation as the other wracks.

The fucoids are perennials, though they probably survive no more than three seasons owing to battering by the waves, but *Ascophyllum*, in its sheltered situations, has a slower rate of growth and a longer length of life.

Two epiphytes commonly found on *Fucus* are the filamentous brown seaweeds *Ectocarpus* and *Sphaecelaria*. In each the hairlike fronds branch into fine threads, but in *Ectocarpus* they may be up to 25 cm in length and hang in a matted mass, wheareas in *Sphaecelaria* they form dense tufts about 2.5 cm long.

Now we have reached the zone which is little different from the sub-littoral region and here are found the largest and toughest of the brown seaweeds. There are the oarweeds whose extensive holdfasts harbour a multitude of small organisms. These holdfasts are very tenacious, but on occasions they are attached to insecure rocks so that in rough seas the rock, holdfast and oarweed are carried up the shore, thus giving the interested beachcomber an opportunity to study the wealth of life sheltering within the confines of the holdfast. These oarweeds are rarely completely exposed; more frequently the stipes stand out of the water, but bend over so that the frond droops into the water. If there are deep pools in the lower regions of the middle shore these oarweeds may grow in profusion around the edges, trailing their fronds below the surface.

Tangle, *Laminaria digitata*, has a very thick, smooth, cylindrical stipe that is flexible enough to allow the large leathery fronds to sway with the moving currents as the tide ebbs and flows. In a young plant the frond is entire, but as it grows it divides into many straplike sections and somewhat resembles a hand. The number of straps varies according to the environmental conditions, the more sheltered the area the less the number of divisions. Sometimes this species is replaced by cuvie, *L. hyperborea*, which has the same type of frond, but the stipe is hard with a rough surface and stands upright for 60-90 cm when exposed.

Sea belt, *L. saccharina*, has a much narrower, shorter stipe *L. digitata* and the frond, rather more yellowish in colour, extends into a long, narrow, wavy belt, about 10-15 cm in width, but extending in length to 1½ metres or more. When exposed the fronds drape horizontally along the rocks, but when partially submerged float outstretched, moving gracefully to the motion of the tide. This oarweed is also found in deep pools on the lower middle shore and its specific name is derived from the sweet-tasting substance which exudes from the dry fronds. It is this seaweed which children love to take home for a weather guide, the belief being that rain is about when the frond is moist and limp, and sunny weather when it is firm and dry.

Another oarweed somewhat similar to *L. saccharina*, but found only on very exposed coasts, is dabberlocks, *Alaria esculenta*, which is recognized by its prominent midrib.

Very low on the shore a few isolated furbelows, *Saccorhiza polyschides*, may be exposed and this species is identified by its large bulbous holdfast from which arises a tough, flattened stipe, very twisted and frilled at first, but widening into a massive frond divided like *L. digitata*, though much larger.

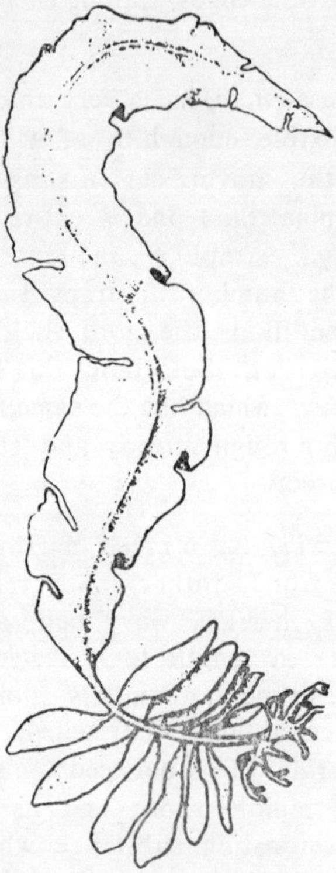

Figure 6.3. Dabberlocks. *Alaria esculenta.*

This shows a gradation in size down the shore with the smallest seaweeds inhabiting the upper regions and the largest the lower and sub-littoral regions. In other words, those with the smallest surface area survive the longest periods of exposure ; they are the adapted to withstand desiccation. The large weeds on the lower shore are uncovered for so short a time that desiccation is no problem, but when the tide is in their fronds are well below the surface so the light received is of reduced intensity ; thus they are specially adapted to contend with this problem.

Rock Pool Vegetation. Rock pools vary in size, depth and situation, and each type supports its own special community.

Deep Pools : As already mentioned, deep pools of the middle shore may be bordered by the oarweeds, *Laminaria saccharina* and *L. digitata*. Another tough, leathery brown seaweed, in the form of long, narrow, flat straps, floats outwards from the edge of pools where it arises from green-brown button-like structures. This is thongweed, *Himanthalia elongata*, and the unique feature of this species is that these long, dichotomously branched straps are the reproductive structures, epuivalent to the small receptacles at the tips of fucoid fronds. The thongs range from 1 to 2½ metres in length and when ripe appear blotched. Thongweed may also be found low on the shore where it must not be mistaken for the round, unbranched bootlace weed, *Chorda filum*, whose fronds are slimy, reaching

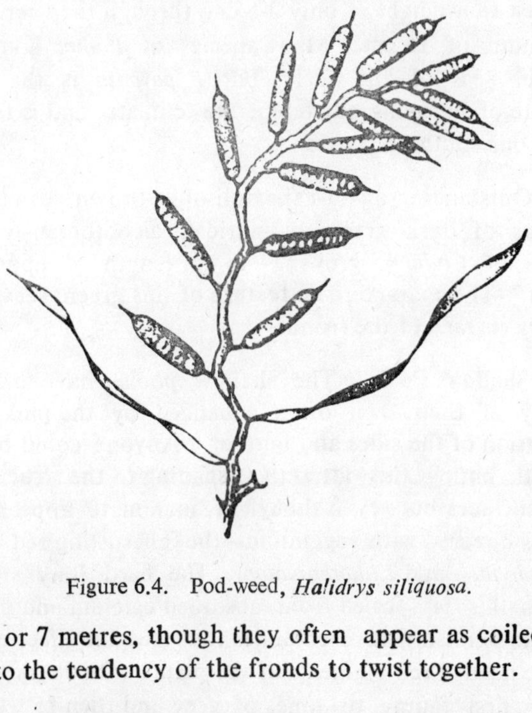

Figure 6.4. Pod-weed, *Halidrys siliquosa.*

up to 6 or 7 metres, though they often appear as coiled masses owing to the tendency of the fronds to twist together.

On the south and west coasts of Britain, from the walls of pools from the middle shore downwards, the yellowish olive dichotomously branched fronds of *Bifucaria rotunda* float outwards in masses, always remaining covered with water. Near by the submerged fronds of the bushy *Cystoseira tamariscifolia* may appear bright blue, but as soon as this seaweed is removed from the water its beauty is lost. The pod-weed, *Halidrys siliquosa,* may abound in the same pool. This is another brown seaweed, much branched and quickly recognized by the pod-shaped air bladders. It also inhabits the lower shore and it is often found among the debris of the driftline.

The most attractive of our brown seaweeds, popularly called peacock's tail, *Padina pavonia,* lives on the verges of these middle shore pools. The fronds are flat, firm, fan-shaped, concentrically marked and rise stiffly from the holdfast to a height of only 2-5 cm, through they can grow to a maximum of 15 cm. Many species of *Padina* flourish in the warmer seas of the world, but *P. pavonia* is the only one capable of surviving our temperate climate and is found only along our southern coasts.

Outstanding against the dull olive-brown seaweed are the clusters of dark green, cylindrical, dichotomously branched fronds of *Codium,* growing to a length of approximately 30 cm. The characteristic feature of this green seaweed is the velvety surface of the fronds.

Shallow Pools. The shallow pools have a particular beauty of their own often enhanced by the pinkish mauve coloration of the sides and bottom. Anyone could be forgiven for attributing this attractive shading to the structure of the rock surfaces but, even though of inanimate appearance, the area is covered with vegetation—the encrusting red seaweeds, *Lithophyllum* and *Lithothamnion.* The hard limy structure of the thallus is formed from absorbed calcium and magnesium and the pinkish mauve colour is the resultant effect of the lime on the normal red pigments of the plants. On death this colour is lost, first fading to tones of grey and then to white. The two forms are very similar, but the thallus of *Lithothamnion* has more fluted edges.

Corallina officinalis is another calcareous red seaweed commonly bordering pools, but this has a normal thallus and grows in tufts ranging in colour from deep mauve, pinkish mauve, yellowish pink to white, depending on exposure. The branched fronds, usually 2-7 cm long, though they may reach a maximum of 12 cm, grow in stiff tufts from a small calcified encrusting holdfast up to 1 cm in diameter, and the limy skeleton is segmented, a feature which makes identificaion simple. The tufts often appear edged in a lighter colour because fading first occurs at the tips of the fronds. *Corallina* is to be found on most rocky shores of Britain, from the middle shore downwards.

Purple tinted fornds of *Chondrus crispus* may glisten just below the surface, but this iridescent beauty is lost once the plant

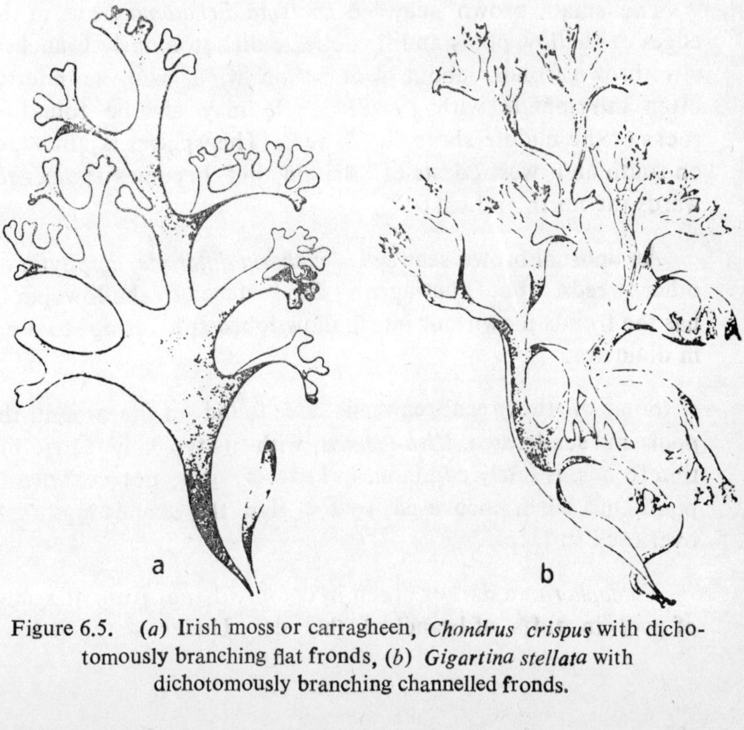

Figure 6.5. (*a*) Irish moss or carragheen, *Chondrus crispus* with dichotomously branching flat fronds, (*b*) *Gigartina stellata* with dichotomously branching channelled fronds.

is lifted clear of the water. This red seaweed in not entirely confined to pools and may be found over a wide area from the middle shore down to the edge of the sub-littoral zone. The flat fronds, about 1 cm wide, branch and termiante in short dichotomous divisions with rounded tips giving a characteristic form 7-15 cm in length. However, difficulties in identification do arise because this species has several variable forms ; for instance, in exposed positions the fronds are narrow and appear nearly cylindrical. Normally *Chondrus crispus* is dark red, but it can be pinkish red and turns green at the tips when exposed for long periods in hot sun, finally bleaching to yellowish white. The important feature to remember is that the fronds are flat and their edges *never* inroll ; this distinguishes *Chondrus* from *Gigartina stellata C. crispus* was, and still is, collected for use in the manufacture of jellies and blancmanges, and as the main source was the rocky coast of Ireland it acquired the popular name of Irish moss or carragheen.

The small brown seaweed *Dictyota dichotoma* grows at the edges of shallow pools and its delicate dichotomously branched, olive-brown fronds, about 4 or 5 mm wide, with no midrib, often intermingle with *Corallina.* It may also be found on rocks of the middle shore and lower. This species is abundant on south and west coasts of Britain, but becomes sparser towards the north and east.

An unusual brown seaweed, *Leathesia difformis*, epiphytic on other weeds, but floating on the surface of shallow pools, has the fronds blown out into hollow lobed spheres up to 4 cm in diameter.

Some of the green seaweeds are found in the around the pools and sea-lettuce, *Ulva lactuca*, with its typically broad but thin fronds, is fairly common. However, it is not confined to pools and when uncovered by the tide the fronds lay limply over rock surfaces.

Cladophora, a darker green in colour, hangs from the sides of pools in tufts of branched threads. Under water it has a delicate traccry, but when exposed or handled the threads form an indistinct mass about 7 cm long.

Enteromorpha is the bright green seaweed which forms a slippery covering over the rock suıfaces in all regions and also extends into some pools, where it is attached to stones or other seaweeds such as *Corallina,* or even to slow-moving animal inhabitants such as the limpet. *Enteromorpha* is most conspicuous in late winter and early spring when it may carpet large expanses of rock, particularly where fresh water mingles with sea water. These grass green seaweeds are annuals and by the end of the summer the dying fronds become bleached.

Red Seaweeds. It is obvious that the brown wracks and

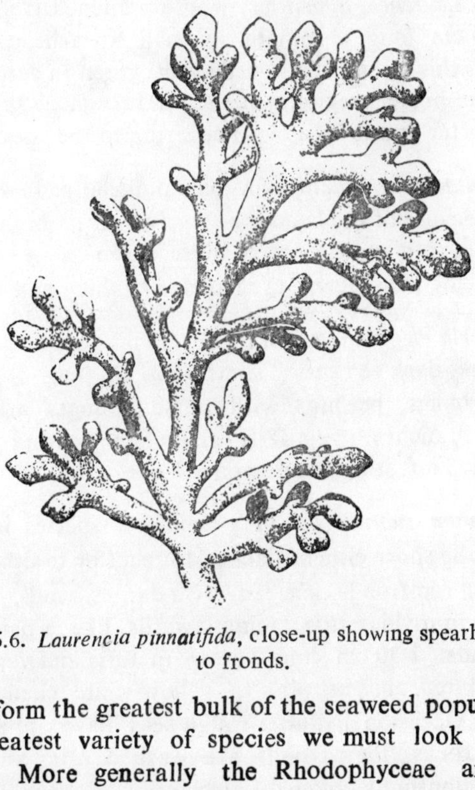

Fegure 6.6. *Laurencia pinnatifida*, close-up showing spearhead tips to fronds.

oarweeds form the greatest bulk of the seaweed population, but for the greatest variety of species we must look to the red seaweeds. More generally the Rhodophyceae are located lower down the shore, many in rock pools, indicating they are not very tolerant of exposure. This is understandable because they do not have the tough, leathery structure exhibited by the wracks and many obtain shelter beneath the fronds of *Fucus serratus.*

On the middle and lower zones *Gigartina stellata* may be abundant. It is very similar in size and structure to *Chondrus crispus,* but *Gigartina* has channelled fronds formed by the inrolling of the edges and it also may bear short, knoblike outgrowths over the surface and edges ; these are the reproductive structures.

In the same area, quite large epxanses of rock may be covered with *Laurencia pinnatifida* whose branched fronds, although oniy 7-10 cm long, terminate in small spearheads. Normally dark red, this weed turns yellowish green in sunny situations and in the higher regions of the middle shore the plants are much shorter and form a close covering to the rocks.

Lomentaria articulata is a pale pinkish red weed, unmistakable because of the beadlike struclure of its branched fronds. It grows in tufts on the lower shore, often as an epiphyte, and, besides being constricted, the fronds are shiny and delicate.

Plumaria elegans is often found alongside *Lomentaria.* hanging in lank, dark red tufts, some 5-10 cm long from sheltered rock overhangs, perhaps with purse sponges attached to it. *Plumaria* branches irregularly and when floating in water the fronds have a feathery appearance.

Ceramium rubrum is a very common species inhabiting all levels of the shore either attached to rocks or to other seaweeds. Its pinkish red fronds, marked with darger bands, are fine and terminate in divided tips facing inwards like a pair of forceps. The fronds, 7-30 cm long, grow in tufts and very in colour from dark red, bright pink to yellow-white when bleached by the sun. Occasionally, after rough seas have ripped the plants from the rocks, their fronds are washed ashore in masses to form an unusually colourful display.

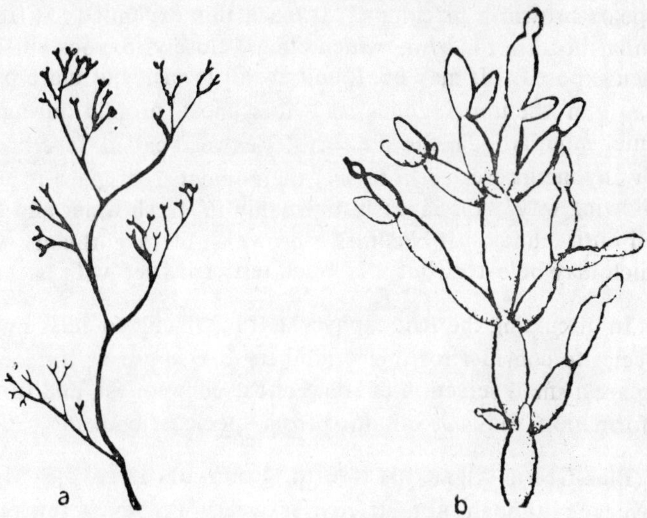

Figure 6·7. *Ceramium rubrum,* with forcipate tips to fronds, (*b*) *Lomentaria, ar ticulata* close-up showing constrictions of fronds.

Dulse, *Rhodymenia palmata,* another common red weed, grows in clusters on the lower shore either attached to rocks or to oarweeds and wracks. The flat fronds, arising from a very short stipe, gradually increase in width in the shape of a V, then divide either dichotomously or into several branches of equal size (palmate). Often very small fronds grow outwards from the edges of the main fronds ; the overall length of the plant may be as much as 30 cm.

Two attractive inhabitants of the lowest regions are *Delessaria sanguinea* and *Phycodrys rubens* growing on rocks or epiphytically on *Laminaria.* Both may reach a length of 25-28 cm and have a distinct midrib in the leaflike fronds. *Delessaria* fronds have a continuous edge whereas those of *Phycodrys* are indented and resemble oak leaves ; on this account the latter is often called the sea oak. The detached fronds of thsese two species become deposited higher on the shore and this is where they are most likely to be encountered.

Laver, *Porphyra umbilicalis,* although a red seaweed, usually appears brownish in colour. It has a thin expanded flat frond, similar in form to *Ulva,* which clings closely to rock surfaces when exposed. It may be found at all levels, but more particularly in the upper zones and it is most prolific during the winter months. This is the edible seaweed called 'laverbread'. For anyone interested in testing their palate, prepare it in the following way. First wash thorughly in fresh water and then boil until tender. It becomes a brownish-black glutinous mass which may be eaten, but it is much testier if fried with bacon.

In discussing the Rhodophyceae it is difficult to decide which species to consider for their numbers are so great ; the foregoing are a small selection of some of the commonest, and further information may be obtained from specialist books.

Blue-Green Algae. A fourth group of algae, the Myxophyceae, although not strictly seaweeds, do have a few representatives on the shore. These blue-green algae are single-celled though they form colonies, some being filamentous, such as *Calothrix confervicola* which grows in minute tufts on other small algae. Others form small gelatinous masses, such as *Rivularia atra* which grows in hemispherical jellylike black-green blobs up to 4 mm in diameter on rocks and stones. This is the most primitive group of algae ; they have no sexual method of reporduction and contain a blue pigment which combines with chlorophyll to give the blue-green colour.

Litchens. Seaweeds are the main plant colonizers of rocky shores, but another form of vegetation also grows on some rocks—the *lichens.* Out of each of the tide, but within range of sea-spray, *Xanthoria porietina* adorns the rocks in bright yellow-orange foliaceous patches and on the upper shore the encrusting film of *Verrucaria maura* may be mistaken for black pathces of tar. *Lichina pygmaea,* a larger commoner lichen, grows in black tufts of up to 2.5 cm high, over a wide area extending from the upper shore down to the mean tide level. It is fairly tolerant of wave action and therefore often grows in sufficient abundance to give a dense covering to the more exposed rocks.

The lichens, which are found in many varying habitats, are unique forms of plant life, consisting of two unrelated species growing together in close association. This partnership of mutual benefit is called *symbiosis*, and in the lichens the two partners are a fungus and an alga.

The grey-green stiff tufts of *Ramalina* grow best when regularly sprayed with sea water and bridge the gap between the seaweeds of the intertidal zone and the flowering plants of the fringing cliffs.

Flowering Plants of Rocky Coasts. As a habitat, the cliffs of our rocky coast do not present a very hospitable environment because in such exposed positions the colonizers have to counted with both wind and weather. Even when out of direct reach of sea-spray the atmosphere is so heavily laden with salt, and the salinity of the soil so high, that special modifications in the structure of the plants are necessary for their survival. Plants capable of absorbing water from such salty soil solutions are called *halophytes*. The slope of the cliffs and their aspect, and the nature of the rock strata are also controlling factors in this habitat.

On some rocky coasts the sea does lap the base of the cliffs and here we may find a few flowering plants growing on the rocks themselves though, of course, only in crevices and depressions where a little soil has collected. Along the south and west coasts of Britain rock samphire *Crithmum maritumum*, adapts itself to this situation with its long, tough roots capable of penetrating deeply into the cracks and its succulent leaves which store water. It is a perennial with a stem of about 30 cm tall, but this tends to bend, spreading the branches outwards close to the rock surface. The fleshy leaves are divided into narrow leaflets and the yellow flowers, in umbels, appear from July to September.

Cliff spurrey, *Spergularia rupicola*, rock sea lavender, *Limonium, binervosum* and thrift, *Armeria maritima*, also survive on rocks where soil is at a minimum. All are perennials with long woody root systems capable of penetrating cracks and crevices.

Cliff spurrey, a very low-growing plant, with trailing, slightly downy stems, bears small five-petalled pink flowers from June to September and is more commonly found in the south and west of Britain.

Rock sea lavender is similar to the common sea lavender of salt-marshes but the stems are shorter, the leaves smaller and narrower, and the deeper mauve flowers arranged more closely on the flower spikes. It is in bloom from July to September.

Thrift, or sea pink belongs to the same family as sea lavender, but the tubular, five-petalled, pink flowers are crowded together in clusters at the tips of leafless flower stalks. The leaves are rather fleshy and form a cushion-like mat on rock surfaces which feel springy underfoot. The flowering period extends from April to October.

Some cliffs are so sheer and the crevices so few that little vegetation can find a foothold. but others tumble away in gentler slopes with many ledges and sheltered dips that are colonized by plants. Here again the beautiful thrift may flourish as it is one of the commonest and most adaptable of our coastal flowers. Sea campion, *Silene martima*, happily takes root on ledges where only small amounts of soil become deposited and its low form enables it to survive the force of the winds in such exposed positions. Sea campion is not confined to this habitat and a mass of its white flowers is a common sight on shingle beaches throughout the summer.

On many cliff-tops the cultivated farmland extends within a short distance of the edge so the coastal plants are confined to a narrow belt. Mixed in with rough grass the flowers of sea pink, sea plantain and kidney-vetch make a colourful show.

Sea plantain, *Plantago maritima*, is a perennial belonging to the same family as the troublesome weed of our lawns. The flowers are in a spike and the yellow anthers appear first at the base; as these winter, those above ripen. All stages of the flower may be seen during June, July and August.

Inland plants which are found growing within reach of sea-spray often exhibit minor modifications and in the kidney-vetch, *Anthyllis vulneraria,* the clustered, small pea-flowers range from the normal yellow to orange or bright red, while the leaves become more fleshy.

Two other members of pea family, sea clover, *Trifolium squamosum*, and hare's-foot clover, *T. arvense*, tolerate a salty atmosphere and the later may be found only a metre or two above high water level. Both are annuals and flower during midsummer.

Throughout the summer the cliff-tops may be adorned with masses of the white daisy-like flowers of scentless may-weed, *Tripleurospermum* (=*Matricaria*) *maritimum*. This species, very tolerant of exposure, is found along the whole of the Atlantic seaboard, but only rarely along the east coast.

Wild carrot, *Daucus carota*, both subspecies *carota* and subspecies *gummifer*, frequent cliff-tops, sometimes side by side. They have the common cow-parsley form of inflorescence, but often the central florets are a deep pink red when first opened, though they gradually fade and blend with the outer yellowish white florets.

The inland relative, fennel, *Foeniculum vulgare*, is sometimes found among the grasses of cliff-tops. but only in situations well away form sea-spray. The compound leaves consist of fine, narrow leaflets which form a delicate tracery; the yellow flowers appear in July and August. This species may grow to a height of 1 or 1½ metres, if in a reasonably sheltered position, and when cultivated its seeds are used for flavouring and its leaves for garnishing food.

A delightful flower which may enhance the beauty of the

Atlantic seaboard is the spring squilla, *Scilla verna.* Its dainty blue flowers raise their heads only 5-10 cm above the surrounding turf but, nevertheless, are a conspicuous and lovely sight when carpeting large patches of cliff-top. Squilla grows from a bulb and has the long, narrow leaves with parallel veins typical of the lily family. It blooms in April and May.

It is not possible to list even a small number of the flowers one *may* find on cliff-tops simply because so many of the inland species survive here, provided they are not within direct reach of the sea-spray.

7

Animals of Rocky Shores

Exploring a rocky shore is one of the delights of many a town-bred boy or girl for here may be seen many fascinating and, to them, weird creatures, but to the zoologist it is an unusual and happy hunting ground because rocky shore populations include representives from nearly all the phyla or groups of invertebrate animals (animal without backbones). This great diversity of fauna is due to the many micro-habitats within the one environment, for here animals live under rock overhangs, beneath boulders and stones, buried in sand or gravel below stones, among seaweed fronds, in rock pools, within rock crevices, in their own rock borings and on bare rock ; but wbatever their habitat, all are adapted to survive the rigours of periodic exposure and submergence.

From topics discussed in the first section it is obvious that the variety of fauna differs from one rocky shore to another, but if we follow the ebbing tide down a sheltered shore a fair selection of the commonest populations may be encountered.

As we clamber down from the cliff-topes the first animals to catch our eye are acorn barnacles, not single ones, but large populations, together showing up as a white band along vertical rock faces. The width of this band varies with the slope of the shore and species of barnacle. With the two commonest, *Chthamalus stellatus* and *Balanus balanoides*, the upper limit of this belt is approximately high water springs in the former, but mean high water in the latter and should both be present on one shore, *B. balanoides* is found below *C. stellatus.*

Closer study reveals that each barnacle is a small, boxlike structure, formed of several limy plates, with its base fixed to the rock, but exhibiting no signs of life. The animal, a crustacean, is tucked away inside and will not protrude its body until covered by the tide and then it simply flicks its legs in and out to trap plankton. Their cementing technique is so efficient that some species survive the constant onslaught of ocean breakers on the most exposed shores of out coastline.

Despite their protection, barnacles fall prey to other animals and one predator, the dog whelk, *Nucella lapillus*, can always be found crawling over and around them. It feeds by forcing its special toughened tongue, or radula, between the movable surface plates of the barnacle and then sucks up the juicy flesh from inside. The shell of dog- whelks feeding entirely on barnacles is a dirty-white colour and as this biends with their prey, they may be somewhat difficult spot. During the spring, clusters of their yellow, vase-shaped egg capsules abundant in rock crevices.

Empty barnacle shells offer shelter to minute creatures and the small bivalve *Lasaea rubra* may be found hidden here as well as among the lichen, *Lichina pygmea*. Its white, oval shell, only about 1·5 mm long, is tinged with red.

Above this barnacle belt, hidden away in rock cracks in the lichen area, tiny, grey black, smoothshelled small periwinkles, *Littorina neritiiodes*, may live. These small periwinkles are terrestrial in most of their habits, but remain dependent on the sea for dispersal, protection and development of their eggs, which are shed during the winter months when rough seas reach these splash zone rocks.

In some of the same crevices young rough periwinkles, *L. saxatilis*, may also be found; these are easily recognized by their grooved shells. Rough periwinkles may be white, cream, brown or grey and larger specimens abound on rocks and in shallow pools of the upper shore.

In some of the small rock hollows we may see a mass of blue-black valvet floating on the surface of the trapped sea water. This is a cluster of one of the few insects found on the beach, the springtail, *Anurida* (=*Lipura*) *maritima*.

The high water level is always marked by the depris left behind by the receding tide and if we disturb a clump of decaying seaweeds our feet are enveloped in a host of small jumping creatures—the shore hoppers *Orchestia*. These crustaceans 'hop' by flexing their tails.

Limpets dot the bare rocks and on soft sandstone deep circular grooves form where limpets constantly clamp down their shells on the same site each time the tide ebb. This habit prevents desiccation, and if we try to dislodge a limpet the tightness of its grip soon becomes apparent Limpets, like periwinkles, are univalves, but their shell is just simple cone, sometimes tall and at other times flat. It is believed that this variation in shape is related to an individual limpets home ground. For instance, if it lives on exposed rock, constantly buffeted by the waves, the shell is laid down in a high cone, but if in a sheltered pool. the shell is deposited in a more flattened form, the difference being controlled by the extent of contraction of the lownward pulling adductor muscles which alter the position of the shell-secreting mantle. Rocks on which limpets have established themselves are usually bare as these molluscs browse on sea-weeds when submerged.

Dark red or greenish-brown fleshy blobs under the edges of rocks, and in crevices, are closed beadlet anemones, *Actinia equina*, but in nearly shallow *Lithophyllum* encrusted pools, these coelenterates display their flowerlike beauty with spread tentacles, ready to catch any passing prey. Some of the beadlets, usually those a little farther down the shore, have their crimson columns spotted green and these are known as 'strawberry' anemones.

The columns of beadlet anemones often harbour the sea-spider *Pycnogonum*, a small, eight-legged, pale brown animal which may also be found among the debris at the top of the shore.

Wherever sea-anemones abound, the grey sea-slug, *Aeolidia papillosa*, is sure to be near by as it feeds solely on anemones. Its skin is extended into tubular papillae giving the appearance of a shaggy coat.

On south and west coasts the toothed topshell, *Gibbula lineata*, crawls over rocks browsing on seaweeds around mean high water level, but does not venture much farther down the beach.

In the middle shore zone, in open, shallow, sunny pools. may be seen the gracefully waving tentacles of snakelocks anemones, *Anemonia sulcata*. Unlike beadlet anemones, the tentacles of snakelocks cannot be withdrawn and when uncovered by the ebbing tide hang limply from the column, their brown colour blending with the rocks. Small snakelocks may be found in clusters in shallow crevices on the surface of rocks, and sometimes when the animals are in full sunlight the tentacles are apple green with mauve tips.

Daisy anemones, *Cereus pedunculatus*, also live in shallow pools, but their namerous short tentacles soon withdraw and disappear below the surface when touched or when the pool dries out. They are attached to rocks beneath the floor of the pool, so contraction of the column pulls them downwards.

Another good place to search is under loose stones and rocks, especially those resting on other stones, for these give plenty of room for animals to crawl in and out, and provide excellent protection. After looking beneath a rock *always* return it to its original position before dislodgement to ensure that all plants and animals are restored to their normal surroundings. If this is not done, many may die.

One of the commonest of all rocky shore inhabitants, the common shore crab, *Carcinus maenas,* crawls away sideways to new cover when disturbed in its hideout below a stone. Beware of the nippers, and if you want to pick up a crab, grasp its carapace between your thumb and first finger just behind the attachment of its chelae legs. In this way the nippers cannot reach your hand. If a female, she may be carrying eggs on her abdominal appendages, but look carefully to see they are eggs and *not* the sac-like structure of the parasitic barnacle, *Sacculina.*

Broad-clawed porcelain crabs, *Porcellana platycheles,* have a flattened body and chelae for adhering flush agains, the undersurface of rocks ; when disturbed they are relatively sluggish in their movements compared with shore crabs. They are hairy, and mud particles stick to them so that they appear a dirty brown in colour. Long-clawed porcelain crabs, *P. longicornis,* have a typically smooth, round carapace. They have no hairs and long antennae, so they cannot be mistaken for the broad-clawed from.

Pirimela denticulata is a pretty little crab-found under and around stones on clean gravel. It is about 12 mm broad and the carapace may be green, brown purple or red, and may even be motled.

Gommaric locusta, a close relative of the shore hopper, is abundant under stones, but does not 'hop'. When disturbed it just wriggles away on its side with its tail tucked underneath.

When we dislodge certain stones an unpleasant occur may reach our nostrils, and the gravel or sand beneath is found to be blackened. This is caused by bacteria which rapidly develop wherever the oxygen content is low. A similar condition occurs a few centimetres below sand and mud, appearing as a black lyer when the sand is dug.

Turning over a stone on muddy gravel may display many actively coiling and twisting fine, yellowish-red threads. These are the tentacles of the burrowing polychaete worms commonly called redthreads, *Audouinia* searching for food particles, but once exposed ihese are quickly withdrawn. Tentacles of another burrowing polychaete, *Amphitrite,* may be uncovered, and if we scaleworm, *Harmothoe lunulata,* sharing the same burrow. This type of togetherness where one animal benefits from the association but in no way harms or helps the other is called *commensalism*. *H. lunulata* is happy to live in a similar way in the tubes of other burrowing animals, but it is also discovered on its own under rocks.

As another stone is turned an unattractive, slimy, coiled black mass may be laid bare end attempts to uncoil it will show it to be the very long body of the bootlace worm, *Lineus.* Although somewhat wormlike in appearance, this is no an annelid (true worm) because it is unsegmented ; it is one of the nemertines (ribbon worms).

Chitons, or coat-of-mail shells as they are sometimes called, cling closely to the undersurface of stones with their large foot, but if irritated they bend bend their flexible bodies into balls, rather like woodlice. Chitons are molluscs, but their shells are formed of eight overlapping plates.

Flatworms, flat-bodied creatures, some 2—3 cm long, may be seen gliding over upturnad rocks, but they are not easy to detect as they blend well with the background. Some species also live amongst seaweeds, and if the placed in a bucketful of sea water the flatworms emerge in their full glory, swimming gracefully by undulating body movements.

Squat lobster are small crustaceans similar to lobsters, but with the abdomen tucked firmly under the body, more like crabs, though it can be flexed to jerk the animal backwards through the water. Two species may found under rocks, but the smaller one, *Gelathea squamifera,* with its inconspicuous brownish green is the commonest. *G. strigosa* with its colourful blue and red carapace, is larger, but found only occasionally very low on the shore.

Several echinoderms lodge themselves beneath rocks and the common starfish, *Asterias rubens,* probably needs no introduction. Globular, spiny creatures are sea-urchins, *Psammechinus miliaris* being the commonest. Its green spines may be mauve tipped and are frequently covered with small pebbles or pieccs of shell, probably for camouflage, though few predators can relish a mouthful of their spines ! Sea-urchins move slowly on these spines ; they go in search of small encrusting animals which they dislodge by means of five strong teeth surrounding the mouth. Brittlestars have five long, thin arms radiating from a small central disc so are easy to distinguish from starfish. *Ophiothrix fragilis* is the commonest species, but it is a very fragile creature and must be handled carefully as bits of its arms readily break off. Sea-cucumbers, *Cucumaria,* shelter under stones, but they are not easily recognized as relatives of starfish because the body is elongated and the mouth surrounded by a circlet of tentacles. One species, *C saxicola,* is commonly called the sea-gherkin, so this gives some idea of the shape.

By now we have almost reached the water's edge and on turning loose stones a splashing and slithering means a shore fish is retreating in search of new cover. Common blennies, *Blennius pholis* are frequently found as they enjoy a period of exposure to the atmosphere. If you watch them in an aquarium some are sure to be resting on their paired fins with the head well clear of the water. The butterfish or gunnel, *Pholis (=Centronotus) gunnellus,* is recognized by its elongated, sideways flattened body with about a dozen large, white-ridged dark sports on each side below the dorsal fin.

The bullhead or sea-scorpion, *Myxocephalus (=Cottus) scorpius,* is a ferocious-looking fish with its broad, flattened, spiny head and spine-bearing operculum. Needless to say, unpleasant pricks can be received from these spines. Rock gobies, *Gobius paganellus,* are typically goggle-eyed with the caudal fin rounded, so are easily identified. On turning a stone a small flattened, reddish fish, with two large black spots surrounded by yellow circle on its back just behind the eyes, remains steadfastly in the same position This is the pretty Cornish sucker, *Lepadogaster lepadogaster* (=*L. gouani*), which has its pelvic fins modified into a large sucker so that it can firmly grip the rocks. Or we may find the two-spotted sucker, *Diplecogaster* (=*Lepadogaster*) *bimaculata*, with its orange body marked with reddish V-shaped bands and a black spot behind each pectoral fin. Occasionally the deep-water lumpsucker, *Cyclopterus lumpus*, is stranded at low spring tides in the spring when it comes ashore to spawn. It is a bulky fish without scales, but its body is covered with tubercles.

Our attention has been fixed on life beneath stones, so now we must return to the middle shore and work down again, this time looning for creatures on the rocks and sheltering among seaweed fronds.

Univalve molluscs are prolific on rocky shores. Some, such as the edible periwinkle, *Littorina littorea*, are immediately

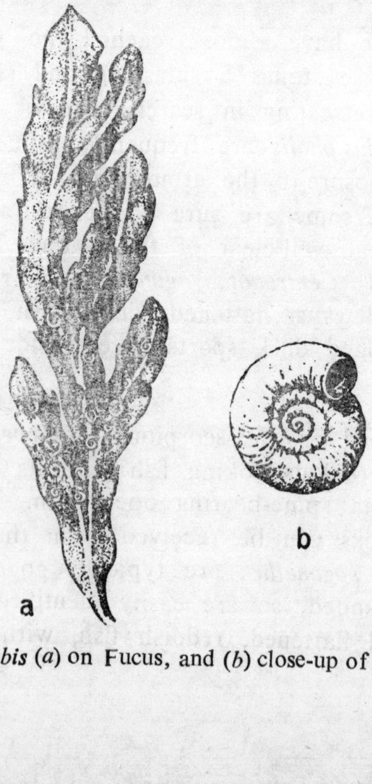

a b

Figure 7·1. *Spirobis* (*a*) on Fucus, and (*b*) close-up of coiled limy tube

obvious as they remain on the bare rocks after the tide has fallen, their bodies being completely withdrawn to avoid desiccation. However, some will be observed crawling along the bottom of shallow pools, over and amongst seaweed and wherever there is sufficient moisture to prevent dehydration. *L. littorea* overlaps the lower limit of *L. saxatilis*, but is abundant on the lower half of the middle shore where large populations congregate in rock crevices. The fourth periwinkle the species, *L. littoralis*, inhabits approximately the same area though it extends a little farther into the lower shore zone where serrated wrack gives it sufficient cover. This periwinkle exhibits a great colour range from white, yellow, orange, brown to back, has a flattened spire giving the shell a more oval shape and resides amongst the fronds of bladder and serrated wrack. On the former its shape gives some form of camouflage as its shell could be mistaken for an airbladder of the weed. In spring its egg capsules form small, oval, closely adhering jelly masses on fucoid fronds, especially *Fucus serratus.*

Some of the fronds of these wracks may be dotted with white limy circles about 2 mm in diameter ; these are the homes of the tube-building polychaete worms *Spirorbis* and a close relative, *Pomatoceros,* builds its elongated, ridged tubes on rocks and stones in the same area.

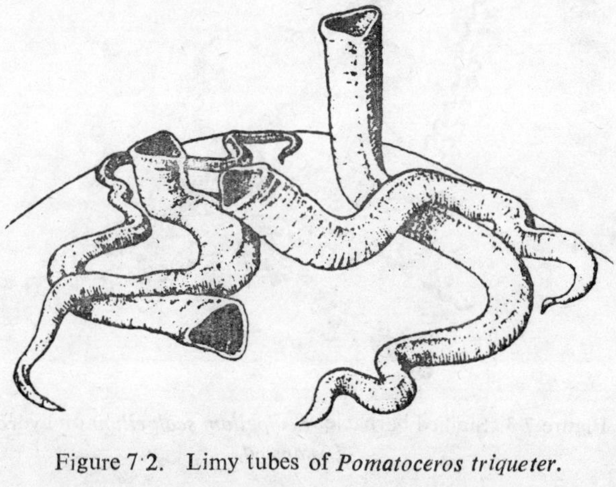

Figure 7·2. Limy tubes of *Pomatoceros triqueter.*

Hydrodis fix themselves to fuciod weeds, seeming to form a plantlike tracery even through they are animal colonies related to sea-anemones. However, to admire their flowerlike beauty they must be viewed under water with a magnifying glass. *Obelia genticulata* and *Dynomean* (= *Sertularia*) *pumila* are two common species and these in turn may act as supports for other animals. The small stalked barnacle, *Scalpellum scalpellum*, is one such *epizooic* animal (an organism which attaches itself to an animal, in the same way that an epiphyte attaches itself to a plant, instead of to rocks or stones).

Other univalve molluscs to be found on this middle region are the flat or purple topshell, *Gibbula umbiltcalis*, whose purple-striped, flattened cone can be seen over the whole area, and the grey topshell, *G. cineraria*, whose silver-grey conical shell is confined to the lower middle and lower shore.

Mussels, *Mytilus edulis*, attach themselves by strong threads to exposed rocks where they leisurely filter their food from indrawn sea water when covered by the tide. These are one of the few non-burrowing bivalves, and where mussels abound, dog-whelks and starfish are near at hand as both are partial to a mussel diet. Dog-whelks feeding on mussels secrete a brown

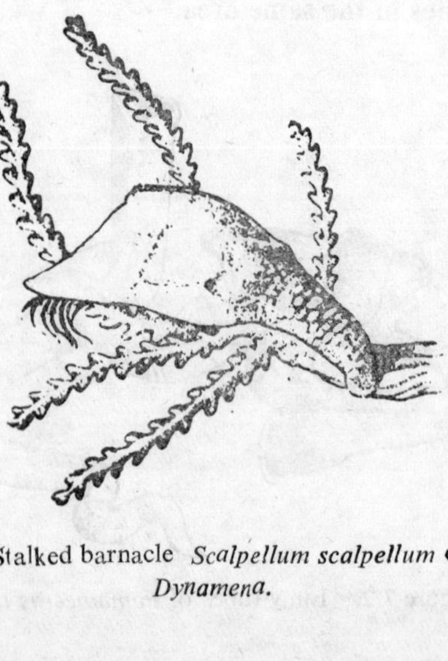

Figure 7 3. Stalked barnacle *Scalpellum scalpellum* on hydroid *Dynamena*.

shell as opposed to the white shell as opposed to the white shell of barnacle feeders, but some have a brown and white banded shell, the results of periodic diet changes. Slipper limpets, *Crepidula fornicata*, will probably be on some mussel shells and on loose stones and empty shells in this zone. They are filter feeders like the mussel and therefore compete for the same food. *Crepidula* is a pest on oyster-beds.

During late spring the sub littoral sea-hare, *Aplysia punctata*, ventures on shore for the sole purpose of laying its eggs. On exposed rocks the sea-hare curls up and looks like a dark brown or purple fleshy blob, but in a shallow pool it expands and raises its lateral fleshy lobes above its back in swimming.

Crawling over rocks, but sheltered by seaweeds, we may find the bright green paddleworm, *Eulalia viridis*, but more conspicuous are its egg capsules, which hang from *Fucus* as bright green globes.

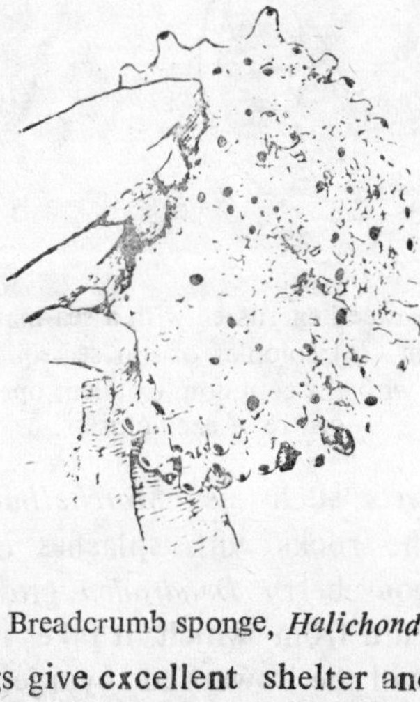

Figure 7·4. Breadcrumb sponge, *Halichondria panicea*.

Rock overhangs give excellent shelter and as the tide ebbs from the lower regions of the middle shore a colourful array of encrusting animals gradually comes into sight, intermingled with some of the more delicate red seaweeds. The green or buff breadcrumb sponge, *Halichondria panicea* with its exhalent openings situated at the top of minute volcanoes, is easy to identify and alongside may be the beautiful orange *Hymeniacidon.* These are both colonial sponges as is the urn sponge, *Sycon,* whose cylindrical from protrudes from the surface. Solitary forms such as the flattened purse sponge *Grantia compress,* hang downwards among the red seaweeds, sometimes attached to weeds instead of rocks.

Patches of deep red superimposed with cream stars are colonies of the compound star sea-squirt, *Botryllus schlosseri,* which also encrust fucoids alongside boxlike covering of the sea-mat, *Membranipora membranacea.*

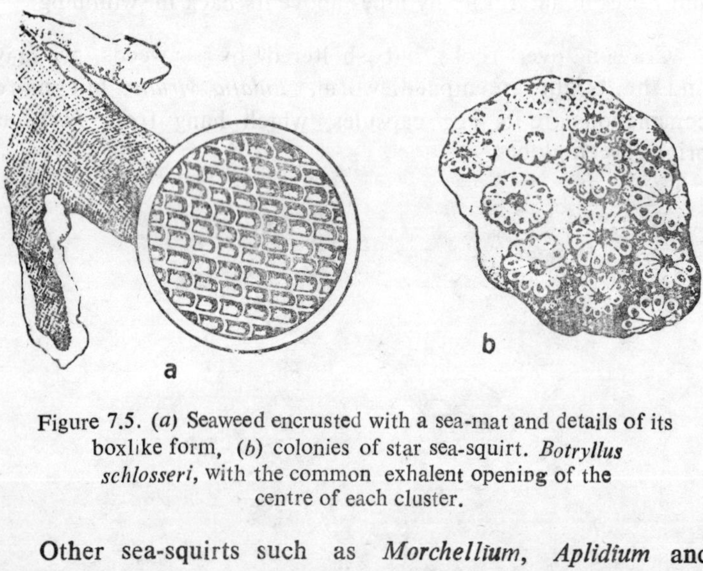

Figure 7.5. (*a*) Seaweed encrusted with a sea-mat and details of its boxlike form, (*b*) colonies of star sea-squirt. *Botryllus schlosseri*, with the common exhalent opening of the centre of each cluster.

Other sea-squirts such as *Morchellium, Aplidium* and *Sidnyum* adorn the rocks with splashes of red, yellow and orange. The red gooseberry, *Dendrodoa grossularia,* looks very much like the fruit from which it takes its name, but if you touch one you will be rewarded by a jet of water splashing your face ! This explains the common name 'sea-squirt' given to this group of animals. Less colourful are the solitary forms such as *Ciona,* but these larger species show off their internal organs through their transparent outer covering or test, as it is called. *Clavelina lepadiformis* is a most attractive animal but must be searched for diligently as it is not so abundant as the other sea-squirts.

Many small creatures, such as the queer-looking skeleton shrimp, *Caprella*, the two small British cowries, *Trivia arctica* and *T. monacha*, the common or painted topshell, *Calliostoma zizyphinium* and the long-legged spider crab, *Macropodia*, crawl over and hide in the crevices of these encrusted rocks. Here also, plodding along on its large foot in search of the bread-crumb sponge, we may detect the sea-lemon, *Archidoris pseudoargus*, in its coat of yellow, specked with red. This gives splendid camouflage on *Halichondria*, its staple diet. White, coiled bands alongside are its egg ribbons. Another much smaller sea-slug, *Goniodoris*, may be near by, feeding on sea-mats and sea-squirts.

Fronds of some seaweeds may be so covered with coloneis of the sea-mat *Flustrellidra* (=*Flustrella*) *hispida* that it is difficult to identify the plant beneath, and another colonial polyzoan, *Bugula*, hangs freely emulating many of the hydroids.

On south and west coasts the small, short-armed starfish, the cushion star, *Asterina gibbosa*, may be located on these lower rocks, but its dull greenish-red colour makes it inconspicuous on its rocky background. Near by we may be lucky enough to find one of the most dainty and attractive echinoderms, the feather-star, *Antedon bifida*.

Below rock overhangs in gullies and crevices, particularly where there is some sand, the dahlia anemone, *Telia felina* spreads its tentacles in a wide circle close to the surface as its column is short though very broad. Plumose anemones, *Metridium senile*, are occasionally encountered on the lowest rocks, but these are only small specimens as this is a sub-littoral species. Only rarely the parasitic anemone, *Calliacus parasitica*, is found on rocks far it normally lives in deeper water on the back of edible whelk shells occupied by hermit crabs.

Small clumps of the yellowish-white soft coral, dead men's fingers, *Alcyoninum digitatum*, may be exposed at lowest spring tides only, as this is a sub-littoral species. It looks most un-unattractive, but when placed in sea water it becomes transformed into something of beauty as the tiny polyps emerge.

When hunting around the rocks of the lower middle shore look out for the ferocious velvet swimming-crab, *Macropipus* (=*Portunus*) *puber*, in its handsome armour. If it is irritated, it poises itself with chelae outstretched in a most menacing manner.

Low on the shore the small hairy crab, *Pilumnus hirtellus*, may be discovered and easily recognized by its covering of hairs. Here, too, a stranded spiny spider crab, *Maja* (=*Maia*) *squinado*, may be found sheltering in a rocky crevice. Another decapod crustacean, *Athanas nitescens*, only about 2 cm long, lobster like in shape, but red in colour with a longitudinal white stripe, may be found sheltering amongst seaweeds of the lower shore.

Small saddle oysters, *Anomia ephippium*, live on rocks and stones low on the shore. Like mussels these attach themselves by threads, but their valves are flattened and circular growing close to the rock surface.

On south-west coasts a lucky find on stones of the lower shore is the dainty Chinaman's hat, *Calyptraea chinensis*. It belongs to the same family as the slipper limpet and, like it, is a filter feeder—an unusual method for gastropods. The shell is a circular, rising to a point at the centre, hence its common name.

Stipes of some laminarians exposed on the lower shore may be pock-marked with deep gouges in the tissue. These indicate that the pretty blue-rayed limpet. *Patina pellucida*, has been having a meal, and search will soon disclose the culprit. In young specimens the rays are bright electric blue, but with age they lose their brilliance. Laminarian holdfast offer ample shelter to many small animals, and if a laminarian complete with holdfast has been ripped free from the rocks, place it in a bucket of sea water and watch for the creatures to emerge.

The banded chink shell, *Lacuna,* is another gastropod found on laminarian stipes, though it also browses on fucoids of the lower shore.

Now let us turn our attention to rock pools and discover what variety of creatures lurk among the seaweeds lining the walls. Of course, many animals we have already encountered take refuge in pools and in this way are able to survive higher up the shore than usual. Some species are found only on shore in pools, thus indicating that they are incapable of withstanding the hazards of exposure to the atmosphere. However, even in pools, conditions are not as constant as in shallow seas. In hot sun evaporation of water alters the salinity, the rate of photosynthesis increases making the water more alkaline as carbon dioxide is absorbed and oxygen evolved, and the temperature rises. Heavy rainfall also affects salinity and if there is no sunshine the water will be less alkaline. If low water springs is at night, then the carbon dioxide released during respiration of both seaweed and animal inhabitants increases the acidity of pools (carbon dioxide dissolved in water forms carbonic acid). All these changes occur gradually as the tide ebbs, but when it rises the inflowing water soon floods the pools and conditions quickly revert to that of the sea.

In deep pools these fluctuations are not so great, and those very low on shore are not exposed for a sufficient length of time for the inhabitants to suffer hardship, but in the shallower pools, uncovered for several hours, the inhabitants must be able to withstand these wide variations or succumb.

The shallow pools encrusted with *Lithophyllum* and *Lithothamion* (Plate 1) are usually scattered with beadlet anemones, and from crevices daisy anemones may be seen showing their heads. Winklets, topshells and dog-whelks abound in pools of their particular zone and, of course, limpets often with a little green seaweed such as *Enteromorpha* growing from their shell. Univalves are typical of rocky shores, but bivalves are not, (except mussels) although in pools with a sandy or gravel botttom carpet shells, *Venerupis* spp. may sometimes be found.

In shallow pools some of the winklets, topshells and dog-whelks may seem to make jerky movements instead of their usual slow steady crawl and on a closer look we soon see why ; the shells are occupied by small hermit crabs. These animals are shy and quickly withdraw into their borrowed homes when touched. They are the young of the large hermits which live in edible whelk shells in waters offshore, and as they grow they move house to a larger shell. It is entertaining to watch a hermit crab in an aquarium select and move into a new abode. First of all he rolls a shell over to expose the aperture, then gingerly explores it with his large claw to see if it is empty and test it for size. This is an elaborate process, but when he is satisfied it is suitable, he moves it so that the aperture is next to that of his own shell. He then draws out his abdomen and rapidly inserts it into the fresh shell and takes a grip of the columella with his modified abdominal appendages. Finally he jerkily turns the shell over and continues on his way. The hermit crab takes all this care because without a shell he is vulnerable to predators and would not survive for long. Occasionally two hermits choose the same shell for their new home and then a clashing of claws ensues until the vanquished moves off leaving the conqueror to move in. Just to be contrary, the victor may change over to the new shell and then decide that the original was more suitable and move back again, leaving the object of the fight empty !

Ordinary shore crabs occasionally scuttle across the bottom of the pool when disturbed, and among the seaweed fronds long-legged spider crabs hide, often camouflaged with growths of seaweed which the crab itself places in position. These live in the deeper pools. To find them, gently pull a fairly fine-meshed net through the edging weeds and scrutinize the catch carefully, because out of water these crabs tend to fold up their extensive legs.

Crustaceans specifically found in pools are the swimming forms seen shooting through the water as we move some of the seaweed. These are the prawns, *Palaemon* (=*Leander*) *squilla* being the commonest ; it is similar to the common or edible prawn, but considerably smaller. These fast-moving creatures need to be caught with a net and along with them may be trapped the small, prettily coloured chameleon prawn, *Hippolyte varians*, with its back bent typically at a right angle, and also *Athanas nitescens* already mentioned. Cast skeletons of all these crustaceans will also be picked up in the net. Common prawns, *Palaemon* (=*Leander*) *seratus*, are encountered only in the deeper pools very low on the shore, for their normal habitat is around the rocks just below low water mark. These are the edible prawns on sale at the fishmongers, but they are not bright pink when in their natural habitat. Their greyish, nearle transparent bodies blend with the rocky background to help keep them out of sight hungy fish swimming by.

As prawns are a favourite diet of many sea fish they are used by fishermen as bait. To catch prawns the fishermen often use a special circular drop net. This has a mesh of approximately 1 cm and is held open to a diameter of about 60 cm by a metal frame ; frequently an old bicycle rim minus the spokes is used. Three ropes, equally spaced around the

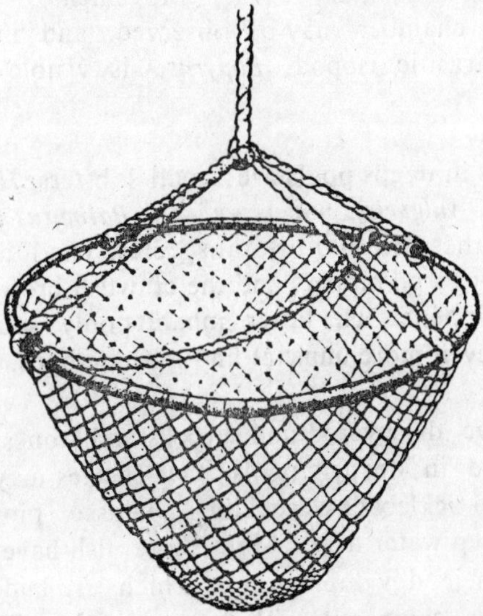

Figure 7·7. Drop net for catching prawns, the bait is attached to the cross string.

edge of the frame, attach the net to the main rope. A piece of heavy string is fastened to the frame so that it stretches across the diameter and to this are fixed fleshy fish bones or other suitable bait. The net is then submerged at the edge of a rock pool, or over the edge of a breakwater, so that it hangs beside the rocks with the frame horizontal. It is left in this position for about ten minutes then drawn out carefully, keeping the frame horizontal ; as it leaves the water any prawns feeding on the bait fall into the bottom of the net.

Prawns are fascinating to watch in an aquarium because they are so meticulous about cleanliness The first two pairs of legs, which terminate in fine nippers, are forever moving over the body to remove any particles or growth on their carapace and they can bend the long second pair around to scratch their backs ! Berried females can be seen moving their abdominal appendages back and forth to aerate thoroughly the developing eggs. Internal organs show up through the transparent exoskeleton and if a prawn has just fed, the food can be seen in its alimentary canal. Movement of the gills in the branchial chamber may be observed, and in an infected prawn the parasitic isopod, *Bopyrus*, is visible within this cavity.

Rare finds in deep pools are small lobsters, *Homarus gammarus* (=*H. vulgaris*), and crawfish, *Palinurus elephas* (=*P. vulgaris*), for these are sub-littoral species The lobster is bright blue with very large nippers and the crawfish brown, spiny and with small nippers. The latter inhabits only south and west coasts. An even more unusual find is an octopus.

The fish we discovered under rocks and stones also inhabit the pools, and in deeper pools other species may be encountered such as sticklebacks, rocklings, wrasse, pipefish and the yound of deep-water fish. Most shore fish have the habit of protecting their developing eggs, which are laid in relatively small numbers compared with deep sea fish. The latter discharge large quantities of eggs but only one or two may survive the rigours of life in the open waters and reach maturity.

Pipefish have long narrow bodies, as their name implies, with an elongated snout adapted for sucking in their food—a most unusual habit. The male fosters the eggs in a special cavity below the abdomen formed by folds of skin ; even after release, the young remain around the male and occasionally re-enter the cavity for protection. The commonest species to be found on shore is the worm pipefish, *Nerophis lumbriciformis,* as all others live around sub-littoral rocks.

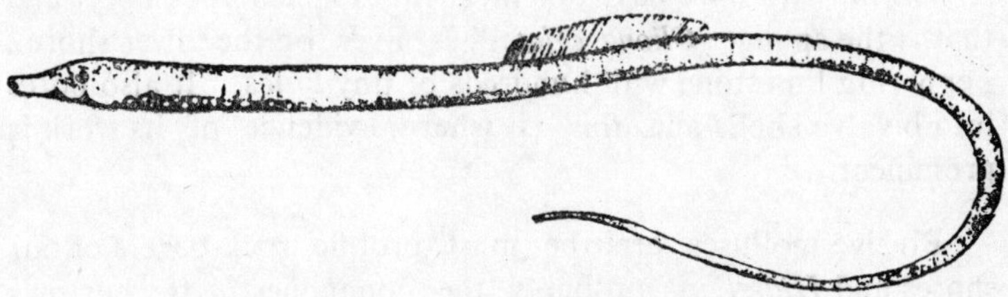

Figure 7.8. Worm pipefish *Nerophis lumbriciformis.*

Wrasse found in pools are the young of the several species inhabiting shallow seas and some are exceedingly pretty in gay colours of green, blue, red, orange and yellow. The adults venture shorewards in the breeding season to make simple nests of seaweed in intertidal rock crevices.

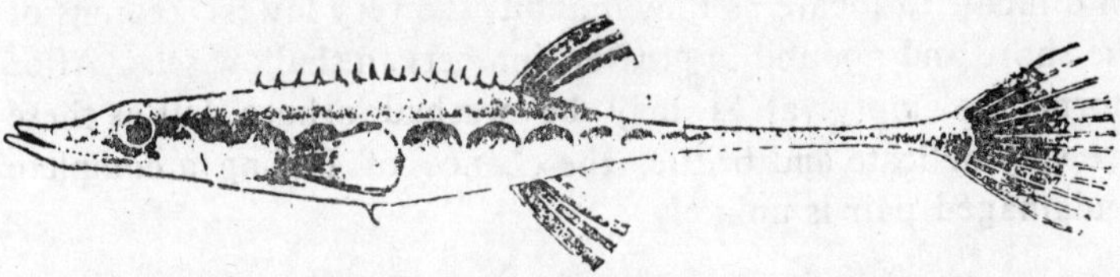

Figure 7.9. Fifteen-spined stickteback, *Spinachia spinachia.*

The fifteen-spined stickleback also makes a nest, but it is the male who carries out the hard work and when it is completed he entices a female within to lay her eggs ; then it is he who stands guard over them until they hatch. In the case of blennies, again it is the male who protects the eggs which are laid under rocks without the shelter of a nest.

Now to the animals which gain the greatest protection—those living deep within rock crevices. Rockworms, relatives of ragworms, extend only their heads from their hideouts when covered by water, and rocks must be split open to find them. The two commonest are *Eunice harassi* and *Marphysa sanguinea*. *Polydora* are small annelids which bore U-shaped tubes into rocks and shells. The only signs of the live worms we are likely to see are their small, fine tentacles extending from the mouth of their tubes in the bottom of a *Lithophyllum* encrusted pool.

On our shore we have one most unexpected rock borer and that is the sponge *Cliona celata*. It lives on the lower shore,. peppering limestone with hundreds of tiny holes. It also bores into bivalve shells and this is where evidence of its work is prominent.

Bivalve molluscs are the most prolific rock-borers of our shores and *Hiatella* is probably the commonest. It burrows into soft rock, mainly limestone but sometimes sandstone, low on the shore and in shallow seas.

The largest rock borer is the common piddock, *Pholas dactylus*, but it is found only in the south-west, which is the northernmost limit of this Mediterranean species. There are several smaller piddocks living in the same area, but they are all difficult to locate as they inhabit the very lowest regions of the shore and abound in greater numbers in shallow seas. After storms the empty valves may be washed ashore, but as these are very delicate and brittle, the chance of finding a complete undamaged pair is unlikely.

8

Sandy Shores

The main difference between sandy shore and rocky shore organisms is that the latter *withstand* desiccation whereas those of sandy shores *avoid* desiccation. In order to do this, they usually burrow. Rocky shores provide surfaces for secure attachment, not present in mobile soft sediments. Relatively few species have adapted to life in sand. Although protected from wave action when the tide is in and from the effects of desiccation at low water, there remain problems of ensuring supplies of oxygen and food and locating a mate. Compared with the richness of many rocky shores, sandy beaches appear barren. Very few plants manage to survive on intertidal sand. The instability of the surface layers make it difficult for plants to become established—diatoms and phytoflagellates are found near the surface but little else survives apart from the distinctive flora of the strand line at the top of the beach (Fig. 8.1). This includes the familiar sea rocket, saltwort and sea sandwort which have thick waterproof cuticles to avoid desiccation and often fleshy leaves in which to store water. The osmotic problems engendered by sea water give these plants the appearance of a desert flora ; water conservation is imperative in both.

The first part of this chapter examines the physical conditions that exist in and on sandy shores and then looks at the special adaptations shown by the animals that live there and the general applicability of their zonation patterns. A small sandy inlet in the south west corner of the Isle of Man in the Irish Sea—Port Erin Bay—is used to illustrate these interactions between physical conditions and the organisms living in the sand.

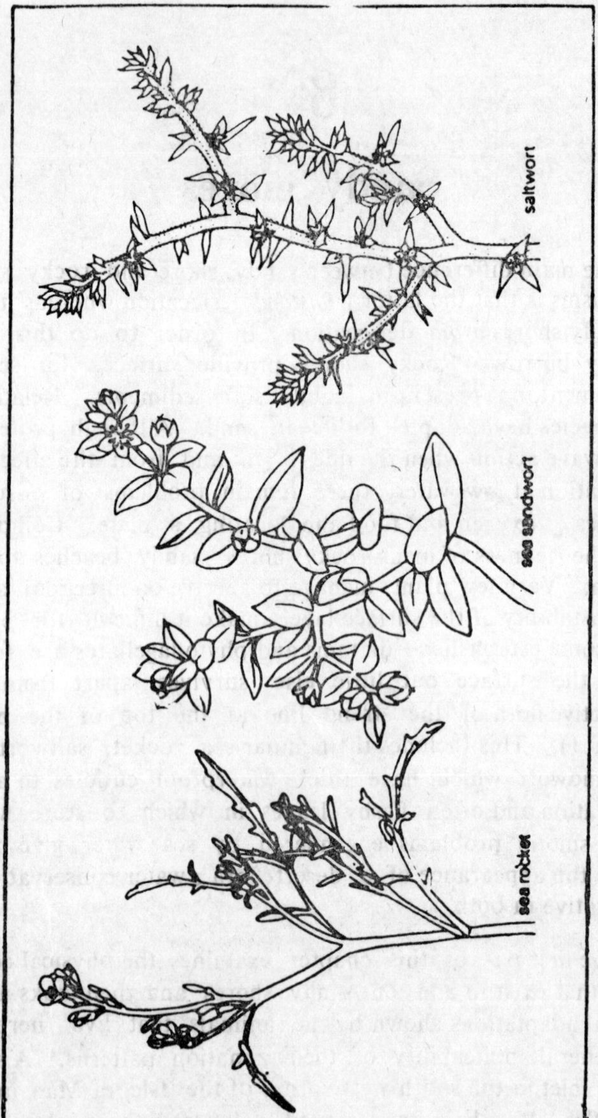

Figure 8.1. Strandline flora.

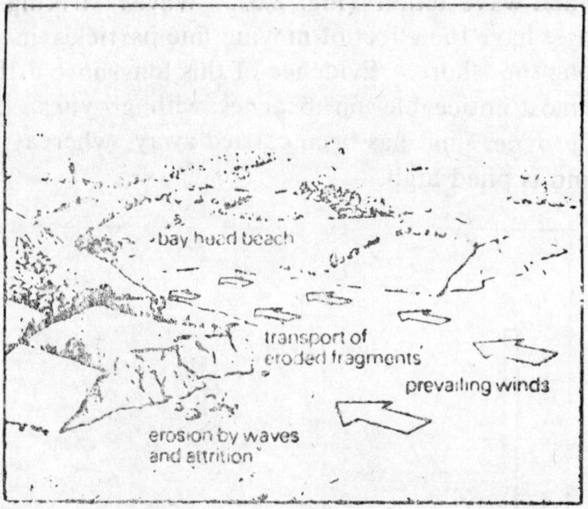

Figure 8.2. Erosion of headlands and deposition of bay head beaches.

Formation and Transport of Sediment

Pockets of air contained in crevices rocky clift faces are forced to contract under the onslaught of the waves. This continual contraction and expansion of air has a weakening effect and pieces of rock at the bases of prominent headlands are broken off (Fig. 8.2). These are then picked up and thrown against the clift by the waves and cause further mechanical erosion. Pebbles are worn down to form shingle until eventually fine sand is formed, mainly of silica fragments. These, of course, will vary according to the source. Banks of shell from dead molluscs may weather into sand consisting almost entirely of calcium carbonate fragments. Atolls and other coral reefs have sandy beaches composed of weathered coral fragments. Some New Zealand sands have very diverse origins including volcanic ash near Mount Maunganui on the east coast of North Island which gives rise to pale pumicecoloured sand. On the north coast of Mount Egmont on the west coast of North Island at Onaero there is a short ironsand beach consisting largely of titanomagnetite and ilmenite and is almost black.

When the substrate has been broken into fragments the fine sediments produced may then be transported by a combination of wind and wave action (Fig. 8.3). Waves striking a shore at an angle have the effect of moving fine particles in a zigzag path along the shore. Evidence of this longshore drift of sediment is most noticeable on beaches with groynes. In the lee of each groyne, sand has been carried away, whereas to windward sand is piled high.

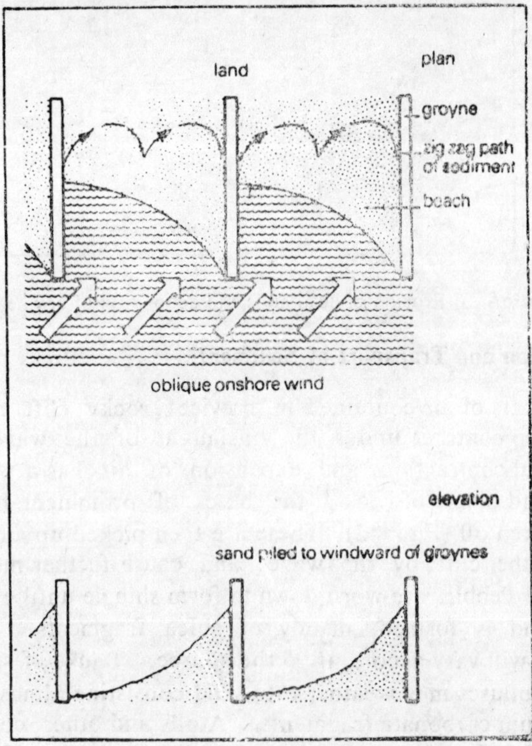

Figure 8.3. Longshore drift of sediments caused by prevailing winds striking shore at an angle.

The degree of water movement is important in determining the kind of sediment deposited ; in very sheltered conditions finer deposits accumulate. This is the overall effect, but there are seasonal differences. Sometimes waves are constructive and the 'swash' up the beach is greater than the 'backwash'. A gently sloping beach reduces wave action, a condition much favoured for holiday resorts. Destructive waves with a weak 'swash' and a powerful 'backwash' are capable of stripping areas of steeply sloping beach ; particularly vulnerable times are the periods of equinoctial gales in spring and autumn. However, constructive conditions, longshore drift and suitable coastal topography may combine to produce spectacular results such as Chesil Beach in Dorest on the south coast of England, linking the island of Portland Bill with the mainland.

Particle size

Many of the other physical factors pertaining to sandy shores are governed directly or indirectly by grain size. This may be measured by passing a dried sample of sand through a stack of sieves graded from the top—coarse to fine. The amount retained on each sieve is then expressed as a percentage of the total weight of the sample and these percentages plotted as a cumulative curve (Fig. 8.4). If the mesh sizes of the sieves

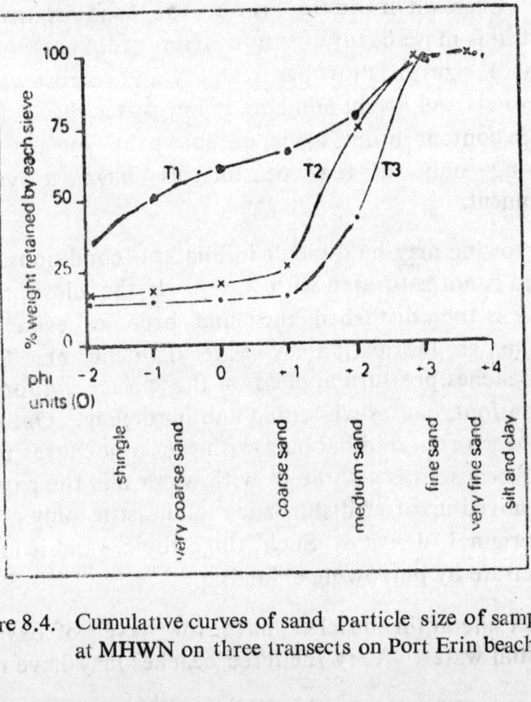

Figure 8.4. Cumulative curves of sand particle size of samples taken at MHWN on three transects on Port Erin beach.

are converted to their phi (ϕ) equivalents (logarithms to the base 2) it is easier to handle the calculations necessary to define the sediment. Median phi diameter ($MD\phi$) at the 50 per cent level on the cumulative curve may be extracted from the graph together with phi quartile deviation ($QD\phi$) for which the 25 per cent (Q_1) and 75 per cent (Q_3) levels on the curve need to be inserted in the formula $QD\phi=(Q_3\phi-Q_1\phi)/(2)$. This indicates if the fractions retained on the sieves are well sorted. If most of the grains are of the same size, the slope of the curve will be almost vertical and the $QD\phi$ will be low (0=perfect sorting with only one grain size). If there is great variation in the size of particles the cumulative curve slopes gently, and this is indicated by a high $QD\phi$.

Water and air content

Sand grains that fit together closely produce small interstitial spaces. This pore space or porosity determines how much water may be held around and between the grains by capillary action. Even when the tide is our the sand retains water but water drains more easily from coarser sediments. Sand with small pore sizes has low permeability and retains water. Even strong winds and bright sunlight at low water have little effect on water content in fine sands, except at the surface. Animals burrowing only a few centimetres have a very stable environment.

Burrowing may be difficult in dilatant conditions, *i.e.* when the sand is not saturated with water. If the close packing of particles is then disturbed the sand becomes even harder to penetrate, as lubrication by water is deficient. On certain sandy beaches pressure applied on the surface by, for example, a human foot, causes whitening and hardening. On other parts of the beach repeated dabbing with the foot causes the sand to soften, because it is saturated with water and the particles tend to be buoyed up after disturbance and settle only gradually to their original density. Such thixotropic sand is much easier to penetrate by burrowing animals.

Most fine-grain beaches have low levels of oxygen in the interstitial water. Very sheltered beaches may have no oxygen present at all, a condition described as anoxic. Coarse-grained beaches have larger air spaces and fewer micro-organisms (which may have a high oxygen demand) and therefore are well oxygenated.

Organic content

Fine sand provides a large surface area for the attachment of bacteria and other micro-organisms. In these sands organic matter often blocks the air spaces between grains, the oxygen is used up and conditions become anaerobic. Certain bacteria such as *Desulphovibrio* thrive in these low oxygen conditions and reduce iron sulphate to iron sulphides. In sheltered conditions, just below the surface there is often a black layer of sand. This is a result of the sand grains being coated with iron sulphides such as mackinavite, greigite and pyrite. At the surface the grains are coated with oxidized iron compounds, such as ferric oxide, which are characteristic of the narrow top layer of yellow sand.

Sampling Equipment

Very little equipment is required to study sandy beaches.

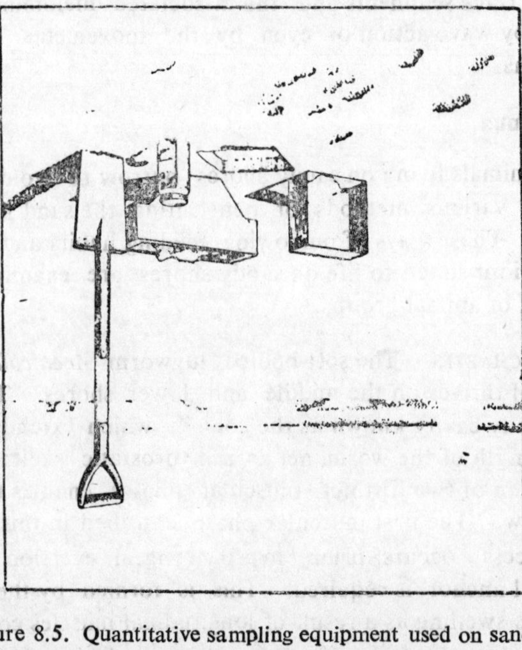

Figure 8.5. Quantitative sampling equipment used on sandy beaches.

For quantitative samples a box quadrat—essentially a biscuit tin with no lid or bottom—is forced into the sand and the contents removed with a spade into a sieve (Fig. 8.5). Animals are retained on the mesh after the sand has been removed from the sample by dunking the sieve up and down at the water's edge. Meiofauna will be lost from sieves that allow the sand to escape; special flushing techniques using upward water currents are needed in order to retain small organisms.

Meiofauna

Certain groups of meiofauna, known collectively as the thiobios, thrive in the black anaerobic layers of sand and include nematodes, gastrotrichs and many rotifers. The whole of the meiobenthos, including the aerobic forms such as crustaceans, coelenterates and higher coelomate invertebrate groups, makes a major contribution to benthic food webs. Meiobenthos is included in the diets of deposit feeders such as many polychaetes, molluscs, crustaceans and young fish. Suspension feeders such as the peacock worm (Fig. 8.6) may utilize surface sediments and the associated meiofauna resuspended by wave action or even by the movements of larger organisms.

Macrofauna

All animals living on sandy shores burrow to avoid desiccation and various methods of penetrating the sand have been evolved. These ways of burrowing, feeding habits and patterns of behaviour suited to life on sandy shores are examined for a selection of animal groups.

POLYCHAETES. The soft-bodied lugworm *Arenicola marina* (Fig. 8.6) thrives on the middle and lower shores. The fluids in the body cavity known as the coelom, which extends for the whole length of the worm, act as a hydrostatic skeleton. The alternation of two distinct muscular phases enables the worm to burrow. The first muscular phase identified in this burrowing process occurs prior to pharyngeal eversion when a 'terminal anchor' is required. This is formed by the anterior segments swelling as a result of longitudinal muscles contracting

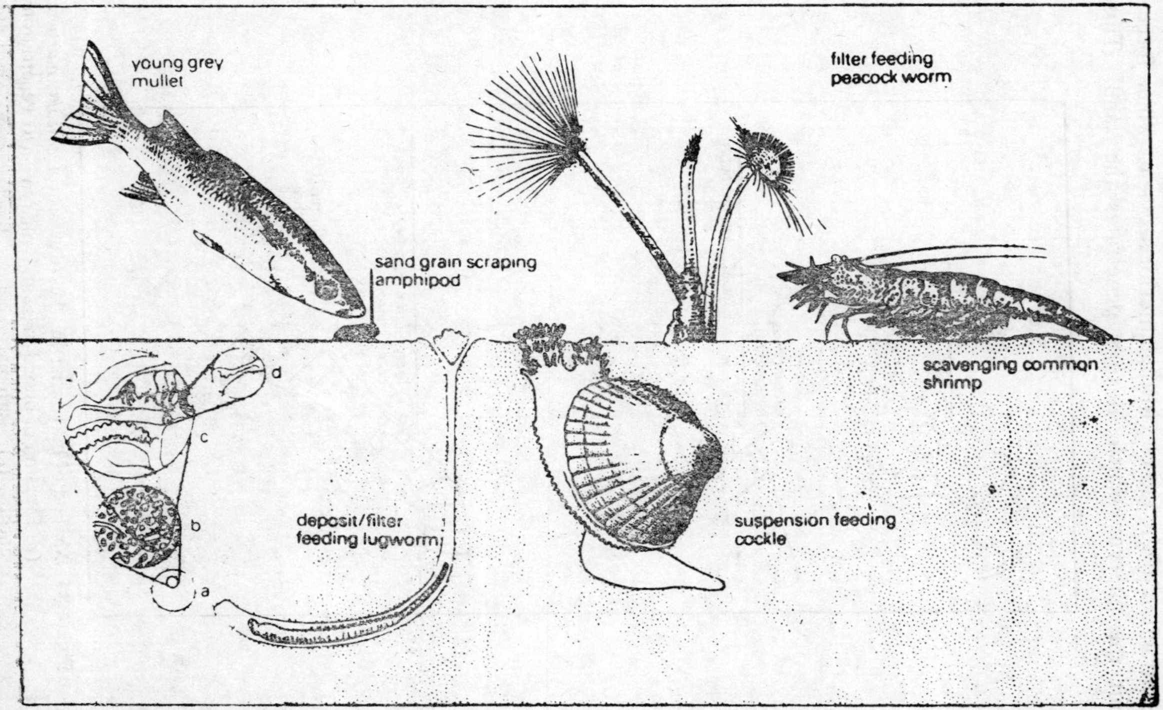

Figure 8.6. Food web inter-relationships between interstitial me ofauna.

just behind this anterior anchor. The second phase involves contraction of the muscles in the anterior segments which forces out the pharynx which in turn penetrates the sand. This

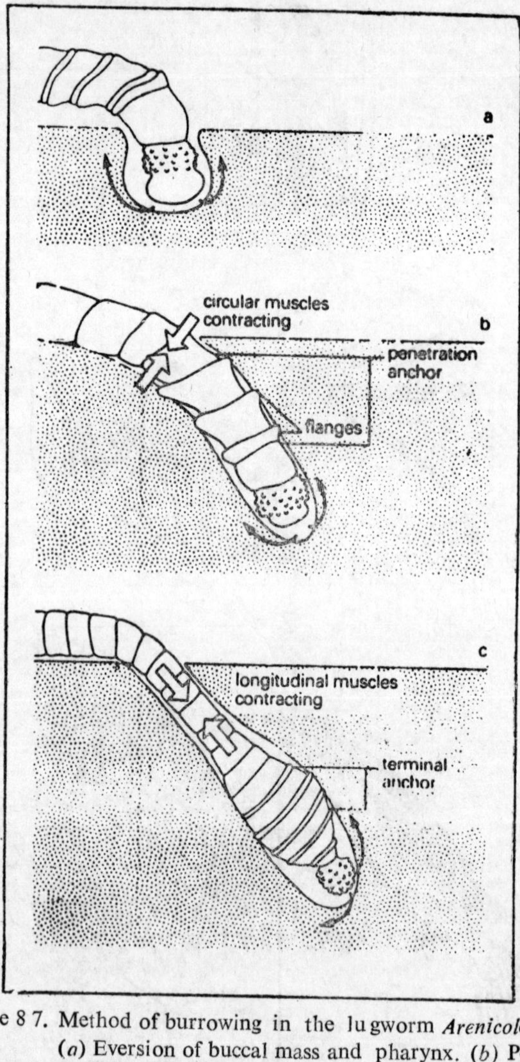

Figure 8 7. Method of burrowing in the lugworm *Arenicola marina*. (*a*) Eversion of buccal mass and pharynx. (*b*) Penetration anchor. (*c*) Terminal anchor. Black arrows indicate movement of sand.

'penetration anchor' is needed to hold the worm firmly and purchase is provided by flanges formed at the posterior edges of the anterior segments. The worm everts (throws forward) its proboscis, the first part to emerge being the buccal mass armed with conical teeth (Fig. 8.7). These teeth thrust sand sideways and then towards the rear of the animal, thus clearing a hole. The rest of the pharynx (anterior part of the digestive tract) is thrown out and resembles a small balloon. This drives out more sand rasped by the buccal mass and has the effect of shaping the walls of the burrow at the same time. Sand is also ingested rhythmically and micro-organisms and organic matter digested.

Errant polychaetes such as *Nephtys caeca* (Fig. 8.8) also use their eversible pharynx for burrowing in coarse clean sand but the body is thrown into waves as if swimming, in order to make an entry into the sand. Their proboscis is armed with jaws used for attacking prey. The ragworm *Nereis diversicolor* lives in fine muddy sand (and in muddy estuaries) and has well-developed sensory tentacles and eyes, and even more powerful jaws.

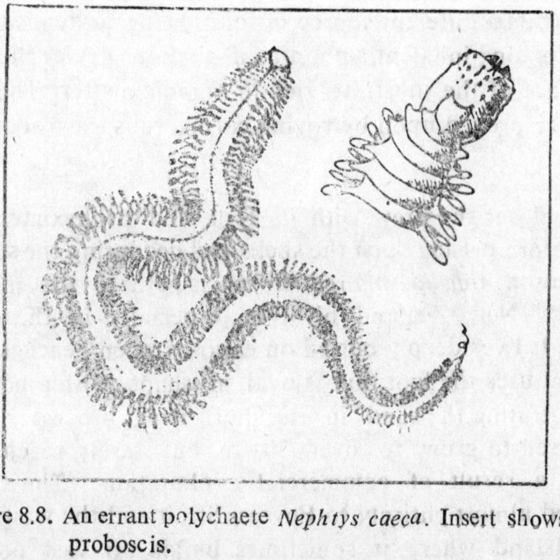

Figure 8.8. An errant polychaete *Nephtys caeca*. Insert shows everted proboscis.

Low on the shore the sand mason *Lanice conchilega* living in clean coarse sand constructs a tube of large sand grains with a ragged projecting fringe at the entrance. The peacock worm *Sabella pavonina* found in finer deposits, lives in a muddy tube that stands up above the surface. *Sabella* feeds by expanding a crown of tentacles at the anterior end of the worm. Cilia on the tentacles carry food particles to the mouth ; fine particles are ingested, large particles rejected, while medium-sized particles are stored in sacs near the mouth ready for tube construction. Two other tube dwelling polychaetes occur low on sandy shores. *Sabellaria alveolata* uses large sand grains to build densely packed tubes. The reefs thus formed provide suitable substrates for fucoid seaweeds to become established. *Pectinaria koreni* builds a cone-shaped tube with the smaller posterior end opening at the surface. The head bears large setae (bristles) used for burrowing.

Molluscs. The cockle *Cerastoderma* (=*Cardium*) *edule*, widely distributed around the North Sea, Mediterranean and Atlantic, filters out suspended matter from the water using inhalent and exhalent siphons. The thin tellin *Tellina tenuis* has a similar geographical distribution but prefers clean sand and exploits a different source of food, being a deposit feeder. It uses its long inhalent siphon as a suction device 'hoovering' the surface of the substrate, rich in organic matter. These small tellins are preyed upon by roving carnivorous gastropods.

It encloses the prey with its foot and asphyxiates the bivalve before prising open the shells and devouring the soft parts. The toheroa *Amphidesma ventricosum* is perhaps the most well known of New Zealand bivalves, especially in the form of soup ! It lives deeply buried on exposed open beaches of fine sand and uses the foot that is oval in shape with a pointed tip for penetrating the sand in the burrowing process. Toheroa shells used to grow to over 30 cm but rarely reach this size now as a result of commercial exploitation. The species is restricted almost entirely to Foveau Strait and the west coast of North Island where it sometimes builds up vast population

Currents carry larvae northwards and digging at the southern ends of beds such as those on Ninety Mile beach is severely restricted to conserve the breeding stock. The smaller tuatua *Amphidesma subtriangulatum* is more widespread occurring between MLWN and MLWS. It is a less powerful burrower and may be washed up and down the shore in conditions of strong swash and backwash.

Crustaceans Peracarids amphipods and isopods often dominate sandy beaches with densities of cumaceans over 25000 m^{-2} recorded from Butterfield's Beach on Stewart Island in New Zealand.

Amphipods are also much in evidence at all levels. The true 'sandhopper' *Talitrus saltator* of European beaches lives during the day among the strandline debris or buried beneath it. Once disturbed these amphipods straighten the normally flexed abdomen and spring away from the source of danger. In the Mediterranean on sandy shores with little tidal influence, these amphipods move inland to forage and navigate back to the strandline by using a sun compass based on polarized light and an inbuilt (endogenous) sense of time Experiments carried out in Britain indicate that the locomotor activity, which may involve movement down the beach on tidal shores, is under the control of a persistent endogenous clock with a 24-h periodicity synchronized by changes day to night, the amphipod being active only during the dark period.

At middle and lower tidal levels, haustoriid amphipods predominate on northern sand shores. *Bathyporeia pelagica* occupies a zone between MHWS and MLWS.

Haustorius arenarius is even more robustly built and swims upside down, a current of water being drawn through a channel formed by the expanded side plates of the legs, by the beating action of the posterior limbs (pleopods)).

Just before entering the sand the amphipod rights itself and 'swims' into the sand expelling sand grains through the ventral channel in the powerful current produced by pleoped action. Burrowing is thus a modification of the swimming activity and the amphipod is incapable of burrowing on dry sand and is confined to the thixotropic lower part of the resurgence zone and the zone of saturation.

The masked crab *Corystes cassivelaunus* also lives buried in the lower shore. Although the body may be lying in black, deoxygenated sand it maintains a respiratory tube to the surface formed by its elongated second antennae.

Echinoderms. The European heart urchin *Echinocardium cordatum* lives low on the shore, extends into the sublittoral in clean sand and often shares its burrow with a small bivalve *Montacuta ferruginosa.* The urchin burrows by means of spatulate (poon like) spines on its underside. It maintains a passage to the surface for respiration by means of specially elongate tube feet. These it extends onto the surface to collect food particles which are then transferred back to the mouth. Perhaps one of the most unusual echinoderms living at low water on New Zealand beaches south of Napier is the biscuit star *Pentagonaster pulchellus* in which the central disc is rigid with short blunt arms covered with a mosaic of smaller plates.

Universal patterns of zonation

In much the same way that rocky shores may be divided up into three basic zones applicable world-wide, so Dahl has suggested that sandy shores may be similarly sub-divided The supralittoral or subterrestial fringe dominated by littorinid molluscs on rocky shores has as its sandy shore counterpart the ghost crab *Ocypode* zone in the tropics and the sandhopper zone in temperate regions. Sondhoppers are probably excluded from this high-level zone in the tropics because their thin exoskeleton makes them susceptible to desiccation and the brooding of their young in a marsupial pouch necessitates a moist environment. The midlittoral, rocky shore barnacle belt si dominated on sandy shores by cirolanid isopod such as

Eurydice pulchra in Europe, *Pseudaega punctata* and *P. subtruncata* in New Zealand. The infralittoral fringe or kelp zone of temperate rocky shores is characterized on sandy shores by haustoriid, oedicerotid and phoxocephalid amphipods and in the tropics by larger hippid crab-like crustaceans.

One taxonomic problem highlighed by Dalh's general classification of sandy shore zonation is that of the difference between the dominant and morphologically distinctive low shore nothern European amphipod family Haustoriidae and the family Phoxocephalidae. The original taxonomic work on which the families were diagnosed was done in Europe. Investigation of antipodean species in the southern hemisphere shows a predominance of phoxocephalids and an almost complete gradation of morphology between the two families. Had the original taxon mic studies been made on New Zealand or Australian shores, a single family would most likely have been erected to include all of these low shore southern species.

When the tide is out almost any sandy beach may be divided into four zones. At the top of the beach is a zone of dry sand where few animals live except under cover of the strandline. Below this is a zone of moderate water retention where the sand remains damp during the period of low water. This is the zone sought by the makers of sand castles. Towards the sea is a zone of resurgence where water flows in and out of the sediment with each tidal cycle. This sand is often too wet for sand castles. The upper limit of the zone may be located by looking for the highest level on the beach where water flow marks are visible on the surface of the sand. The top layers of sediment in this zone are usually well aerated. A zone of saturation extends down to the sea below this critical resurgence zone. This saturation zone has standing pools of water on the surface, supplied by run-off from higher on the beach. The zone may be detected by the presence close to the surface of anaerobic black sand smelling of hydrogen sulphide.

Dunes

Windblown sand may accumulate above the strandline and form unstable heaps. Sea couch grass and marram grass (Fig. 8·9) stabilize these embryo dunes by binding the sand with

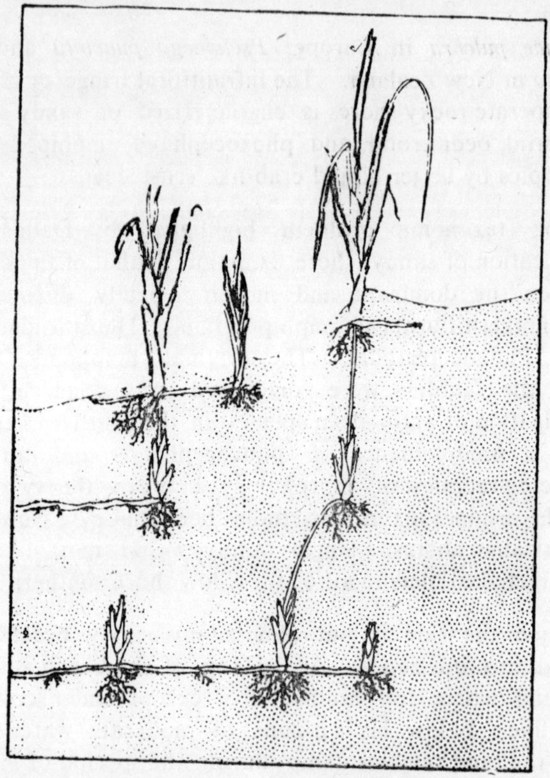

Figure 8.9. Marram grass showing branching rhizome system underground which binds the dune sand.

Figure 8.10. Port Erin Bay, Isle of Man.

their branching underground rhizome systems. As the grasses are covered by fresh windblown sand, so they grow upwards and the new shoots trap further sand and the dune height increases. These are known as yellow dunes as much yellow sand is still visible between the tussocks of grass. Yellow dunes are susceptible to blowouts, stroug winds scouring out hollows where the rhizomes have not yet become fully established. In time a succession of other plants will invade the dunes, further increasing stability. These well-established dunes have an extensive cover of grey linches and at this stage are known as grey dunes which a variety of truly terrestrial animals, especially insects and spiders, colonize.

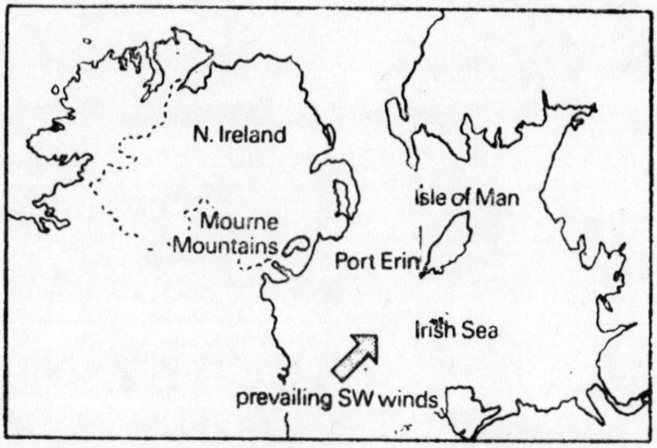

Figure 8·11. Sixty-kilometre fetch across Irish Sea to Port Erin Bay.

Port Erin Bay, Isle of Man

There is a 60-km fetch across the Irish Sea from the Mountains of Mourne on the east coast of Northern Ireland to Port Erin Bay (Fig. 8.10) and waves pound in on this exposed part of the Isle of Man when the prevailing south westerlies blow (Fig. 8·11). A beach composed mainly of silica fragments derived from material eroded from headlands at the entrance to the bay, lies at its head. In Port Irin Bay when the tide flows in it follows a clockwise course. As a result all fine material is picked up and deposited at the south end of the bay.

The anaerobic black layer is much more in evidence at this sheltered southern end. This distribution of grain size is also reflected in the distribution of fauna, for examgle the amphipod *Bathyporeia nana*. This smallest member of the genus is present in dense concentrations at the southern end of Port Erin Bay where it lives in the surface yellow sand at and below low water where it is able to scrape food from the small sand grains. It is effectively excluded from the north end of the beach where the sand grains are too large for the amphipod to manipulate. The predatory errant polychaete *Nephtys caeca* is also more abundant at the southern end of the beach.

9

Life on Sandy Shores

At first glance a sandy shore appears very barren—just an extensive mass of sand, perhaps slightly rippled by wave action, but with no signs of plant or animal life—a very different sight from the rocky shore clothed in seaweeds. However, on walking down the beach a shell or two embedded in the surface sand catches the eye, indicating that perhaps, after all, a living creature is somewhere near at hand. A closer look at the sand shows that the surface is not absolutely smooth but is perforated by small holes. This is the answer—the animals live buried beneath the sand.

A sandy shore is devoid of seaweeds for the simple reason that there is no solid surface available for attachment of their holdfasts. As *no* seaweeds grow here, protection against wave action, desiccation and predators is lacking, so to survive, the animal life resorts to living within the sand. Some animals always remain below in their burrows, but others become active when the tide rises and venture away from their hideouts. Hundreds of microscopic animals, called the *interstitial* fauna, live between the sand particles, but as these cannot be readily observed they do not come within the scope of this book.

At low water springs and old fisherman may be seen walking backwards along the water's edge, every now and then extending what appears to be a stick or thin rod into the sand. Investigation shows that the stick is a metal rod, perhaps 5 or 6 mm in diameter, with the tip ground into a spearhead, which the fisherman inserts into an appropriate hole, twists around and eventually pulls out with a razorshell impaled on the end. It looks very easy when observing an expert, but a novice is lucky to spear even one creature in a couple of hours! The razorshell is a bivalve mollusc with long, narrow valves so that in shape it is somewhat like a large pea pod.

The common large razorshell which the fisherman seeks for bait, or even a tasty meal, is the pod razor, *Ensis siliqua*, in which the two valves are straight. It lives just below the surface and has two short siphons, one for the intake and one for the removal of water via the hole in the surface sand. As soon as the razorshell feels a vibration on the surface it discharges a jet of water and rapidly burrows deeper by means of its foot. The rate at which it can move down through the sand is quite surprising and the explanation for our empty apear. The fisherman's footfalls disturb the razorshell, so by walking backwards he is able to observe the water ejected and note the correct hole down which to probe for his victim.

If a live razorshell is laid on the sand the movement of its foot can be observed. First the foot extends fully, pushing downwards, and then the tip swells as body fluids are pumped into it. This bulbous tip acts as an anchor, so that on contraction of the muscles connecting the foot and shell the animal is drawn into the sand. This process of foot extension, followed by anchorage and muscle contraction, is repeated until the animal is completely below the surface and the siphon hole is the only indication of its presence.

A visitor after dark may find a razorshell protruding a few centimetres above the surface and, if stealthy and quick, succeed in withdrawing it just by grasping and pulling. Another method of obtaining specimens is by placing salt over the hole; this usually brings the razorshell to the surface and the projecting shell can be grasped and extracted as above. The salt acts as an irritant, causing this response in the animal. However, the more useful way of collecting razorshells is by digging, but it is no easy matter to obtain an animal intact because they are so sensitive to the slightest of vibrations.

The siphons of the razorshell are short, and it is a suspension feeder, filtering food particles from the indrawn sea water.

Normally it remains buried, but in rough weather the scouring action of the sea may bulldoze it out of the sand and carry it shorewards to rest finally amongst the pile of debris at the top of the beach.

The sword razor, *Ensis ensis*, has thinner, curved valves and is smaller than *E. siliqua*, so it does not fall victim to the fisherman's spear even though it inhabits the same area.

Many other bivalves inhabit the sandy shore, especially the various members of the trough shell family, Mactridae, whose empty valves are an easy find for the shell collector. Very occasionally what appears to be a small bump on the sand turns out to be a trough-shell with siphons and valve edges exposed. These animals are also suspension feeders, as are the venus shells which live in the same habitat. The striped venus, *Venus striatula*, is the commonest.

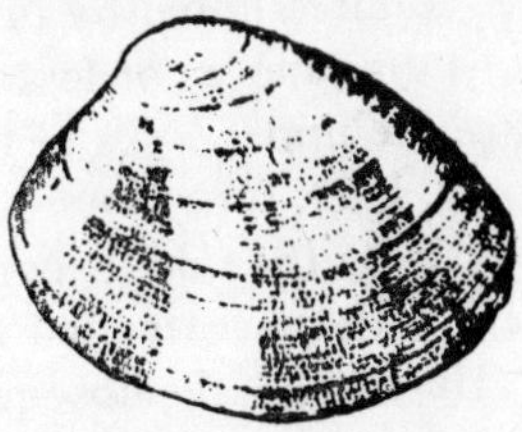

Striped venus, *Venus striatula*

Fi ure 9.1.

The edible cockle, *Cardium edule*, lives just below the surface on the middle and lower shores, but as it also inhabits muddy sand, we shall leave consideration of this species until life on muddy shores is discussed.

Two other bivalves frequently found are the wedge shell, *Donax vittatus* and the tellin shell. *Tellina tenuis*, both with long siphons for deposit feeding. The latter has a very thin, glossy shell which may be white, pale pink, rose or salmon.

No one can resist picking up and admiring attractive empty bivalves scattered on the sand, but sometimes we are disappointed to find that an apparently perfect shell is pierced by a small round hole. The culprit is another member of the molluscs, but this time a univalve, the necklace shell, *Natica alderi*. This animal has a special gland which secretes a chemical substance capable of dissolving the limy shell of its prey. As soon as the shell is perforated, *Natica* inserts its proboscis to feed on the juicy contents. This carnivore burrows in the sand out of sight, but sometimes a sluggish movement in shallow water indicates a specimen pushing its way along on its enormous foot.

The netted dog-whelk, *Nassarius reticulatus* is a univalve which bulldozes its way through the sand with only its siphon above to indicate its presence. As in all whelks, this siphon allows clear water to be inhaled even while *Nassarius* is scavenging in the sand for fleshy food particles.

As we wander down shore towards the receding tide we may find the level surface is interrupted by tube like structures, with fringed edges, protruding more or less upright to a height of 2 and 3 cm. These are the upper ends of the homes of sand-masons, *Lanice conchilega*. Each tube is uniquely formed by the worm itself; when covered by the tide it collects small particles of sand and shell with its extended tentacles and wafts them into its mouth. Here they are subsequently coated with a mucous secretion which sticks them together to form a protective tube.

Keen fishermen are down on the shore at low tide digging for another favourite bait, this time the lugworm, *Arenicola marina* whose presence is obvious from the coiled casts of sand and nearby depressions. The lugworm lives in a U-shaped tube with two openings, one above its head and the other above its tail, but it does not form this tube from particles as the sand-mason does. Instead, the lugworm burrows into the sand and secretes a mucus which holds the walls in position.

The food of the lugworm consists of small particles of detritus and to obtain this it swallows large amounts of sand. The organic material is digested as the sand passes along the worm's alimentary canal, and the unwanted particles are egested through the anus and deposited on the surface above in the form of the familiar coiled worm-cast.

Survival of the lugworm is dependent on an ample supply of oxygen for respiration and this is ensured when the tide returns. A continuous current of water flows into the burrow from the rear end, forward over the gills and out through the head opening, the worm itself maintaining this current by alternate contraction and relaxation of its body muscles. Because of the upward force of water at the head entrance, the particles of sand remain loosely packed and readily subside to form a depression as the worm ingests the lower layers—hence the coiled cast *and* the accompanying depression. The lugworm does not often venture from the safety of its burrow as it is such inviting prey for any carnivorous neighbours. However, as the casts high on the beach are much smaller than those nearer the low water mark, the lugworm must periodically, as it increases in size, leave the safety of its tube and swim seawards before burrowing out a new home.

Several other worms live within the sand, one of the commonest being the white-or cat-worm, *Nephthys hombergi*. This species is a very active swimmer and, unlike the lugworm, does not have a permanent burrow. It is carnivorous and continuously hunts prey such as very small or young crustaceans, burrowing into the sand only when the tide recedes. The flattened, segmented, whitish body has a dark line running along the centre of the back, which makes identification easy. *Nephthys* is found 8 to 10 cm below the surface. *Glycera convoluta*, often dug up with *Nephthys*, is recognized by the round body segments, many in number, narrowing to a point at both ends ; when exposed this worm tends to coil. The ragworm, *Nereis diversicolor*, may be found in sand, but it is much more common in mud its inclusion in the chapter on muddy shores is more appropriate.

On digging down into the sand we find the colour does not remain uniform, but that a black layer shows up a little way below the surface. This indicates poor aeration and the consequent presence of bacterial colonies since these are the only organisms capable of living in situations with such a reduced oxygen content. The position of this black layer varies according to the substratum ; the more permeable the sand, the lower the layer.

Of the sand-burrowing echinoderms the sea-potato, *Echinocardium cordatum*, is the most abundant. Unlike other sea-urchins it is not round, but heart-shaped, and has specially modified spines on the undersurface for digging down into the sand. The only visible sign of this animal is a star-shaped depression in the sand on middle and lower shores, which is the opening of the shaft leading up from its burrow some 20 cm below. This urchin moves sluggishly and it is therefore quite easy to dig up a specimen. After rough seas, empty tests (skeletons) of *Echinocardium* may scatter the beach, but care must be taken in handling them as they are extremely brittle.

The burrowing starfish, *Astropecten irregularis*, normally lives offshore, but occasionally a specimen may be found low on the beach. It digs itself straight down by means of its modified tube-feet and spines, and leaves *no* telltale hole on the surface. However, movement of the marginal spines ensures that a water current passes over the animal for respiratory purposes and this disturbance may leave a faint trace on the sand indicating its presence when the tide recedes.

Two burrowing sea-cucumbers, *Leptosynapta inhaerens* and *Lapidoplax digitata*, may possibly be found in the same area as *Echinocardium*. They differ from rocky shore specimens in having an elongated, wormlike body and no tube-feet. Both species also inhabit muddy shores, but *Lapidoplax* is confined to south-west and west coasts. Frequently the commensal scaleworm, *Harmothoe*, shares their burrows.

Searching for the hidden sand-dwellers is far more rewarding at night, as some of them venture above the surface when darkness hides them from predators, and desiccation from the hot sun is no longer a hazard. In the beam of a powerful torch, or preferably a paraffin vapour lamp, an empty depression about 4 cm in diameter may be seen, with a parallel but winding track leading away, perhaps as far as a metre, to what appears to be a blob of sand. Closer inspection shows this to be the only true sand-burrowing crab in Britain, *Corystes cassivelaunus.* Its common name is 'masked' carb and the reason for this is obvious once the sand has been cleaned off its carapace.

The antennae of masked crabs are especially long and bear two rows of stiff hairs which interlock to form a tube when the two are held together. This special adaptation allows the crab to remain completely buried, with only the tips of the antennae level with the surface of the sand. In this position clear water is drawn down the tube, passed back over the gills for oxygen absorption and finally expelled from the under-edge of the carapace. This flow is in the opposite direction to normal when the crab is above ground. The masked crab inhabits only areas of *clean* sand because the meshwork of antennal hairs would not prevent the entry of very fine mud particles which, if present, would rapidly clog the gills.

The sexes are distinct, the chelae of the male being much longer than in the female. Occasionally a pair of these crabs may be seen with the male fiercely gripping the female in one of his chelae and he may even move around still holding her. The significance of this action is a mystery at present, although it may well be concerned in the mating habits of the species. *Corystes* is found very low on the shore at spring tides, during a few months of the year only, as it is really a sub littoral species. In the south-west it can be found inshore from April to July, but is most abundant during May.

Further hunting after dark may reveal the tentacles of the daisy anemone, *Cereus pedunculatus*, spread flush with the surface, but with the slightest disturbance the tentacles close and disappear below the sand. Small hermit crabs scuttle around in the shallows and here too a dab can be detected hurriedly covering itself with sand as the torch beam picks it out.

An interesting and successful way of collecting some of the inhabitants very low on the shore is by pushing through the shallows a special type of long-handled net, designed by shrimpers of old. This shrimpers' trawl is a long bag of fine net held open by a straight edge of wood or metal at the base, and a half hoop above to which the handle is attached. The straight edge is pushed through the upper 4 or 5 cm of sand to disturb any buried creatures and, by the forward movement, force them into the bag.

On emptying out the net the most prolific animal of the catch is sure to be the common shrimp, *Crangon crangon* (=*C. vulgaris*), the most familiar crustacean to be found on any sandy shore. During daylight hours it usually remains buried, but even when on the surface detection is difficult, the body colour blending with the sand. The shrimp needs this camouflage for it is a favourite food of many a fish and it also helps when stalking prey, for the shrimp is an omnivorous feeder.

The contents of the net will include many other interesting animals, perhaps the little cuttlefish, *Sepiola atlantica*, which so attractively flashes on and off its bright lights, like a neon sign. This luminescence is a feature of cephalopods.

The lesser weever, *Trachinus vipera*, may be in the trawl as this fish buries itself with only the top of its head protruding so that, unobserved, it can keep a watchful eye for its main diet, the shrimp. Care must be taken in handling this fish because it can inflict a painful sting owing to the presence of poison glands at the base of its dorsal fin and opercular spines. On this account it has acquired the local name 'sting-fish'.

The lesser sand eel, *Ammodytes tobianus*, may be in the catch. This fish has an elongated body with no pelvic fins, thus giving it an eel-like appearance. It is not a true sand-dweller like the lesser weever, as it swims in shoals and feeds on young sprats and crustaceans, resorting to the sand only when predators are near at hand. It then burrows by means of its spoon-shaped lower jaw which projects beyond the upper jaws. The greater sand eel, *Hyperoplus* (=*Ammodytes*) *lanceolatus*, is not such a common species, though it may be caught in the same manner.

The sand goby, *Pomatoschistus* (=*Gobius*) *minutus*, also falls victim to the trawl as it lives in the same area as shrimps. Young of the various flatfish are likely to be in the net, ranging in size from a couple of centimetres upwards and, should it be a very low spring tide, even a specimen large enough for the fishmongers's slab may be taken in this way.

The shrimpers' trawl may force out of the sand some stems and leaves of the *one* flowering plant found on the shore, eel-grass, *Zostera.* This plant was prolific on British coasts until the 1930s when it was attacked by an unknown disease which depleted the *Zostera* beds. The leaves are bright green, long and narrow, forming an underwater forest when supported by the water. At last eel-grass is becoming re-established, and at low water springs a few small clumps may be exposed.

On returning up the beach the *driftline* or *strandline* is well worth studying though, of course, most of the creatures found here are dead or dying. However, one crustacean inhabits this region, the sandhopper, *Talitrus saltator.* This amphipod burrows into the sand below the debris during daylight hours and surfaces at night to feed on any available plant or animal material. The sandhopper always remains above high tide mark on account of its inability to survive submergence. Like all amphipods its body is laterally compressed and it appears to 'hop'.

The strandline reflects the inhabitants below the sand in both littoral and sub-littoral regions. In winter, shells of the 'red-nosed' cockles are prolific and after an onshore gale whole live specimens may appear, each extending its long red foot in an attempt to roll into a position where it can burrow. This is the same type of movement as in the edible cockle.

The debris may be dotted with bodies of the sea-mouse, *Aphrodite aculeata*, a deep water annelid (segmented worm), though this is not immediately apparent from its dorsal surface, because the back of its oval-shaped body is covered with a thick mat of long grey bristles When seen in a shaft of sunlight these bristles become iridescent, transforming the dull animal into a creature of beauty.

Several of the offshore crabs become victims of winter storms Examples are the masked crab, *Corysтes,* already mentioned, *Portumnus latipes* another sand-burrower but also active swimmer, shown by the paddle-like fifth pair of legs, the common swimming-crab, *Macropipus* (=*Portunus*) *depurator*, and the angular crab, *Goneplax rhomboides* (=*G. angulata*), readily recognized by the rectangular carapace, twice as broad as it is long. *Goneplax* has its eyes on long stalks which can be setracted into grooves along the anterior edge of the carapace and, like *Corystes*, the male is distinguished by its first pair of legs which are three times as long as the width of its carapace.

Sometimes the edible whelk, *Buccimum undatum*, is washed ashore, but more frequently clusters of its egg-cases litter the strandline and from a distance look rather like bath

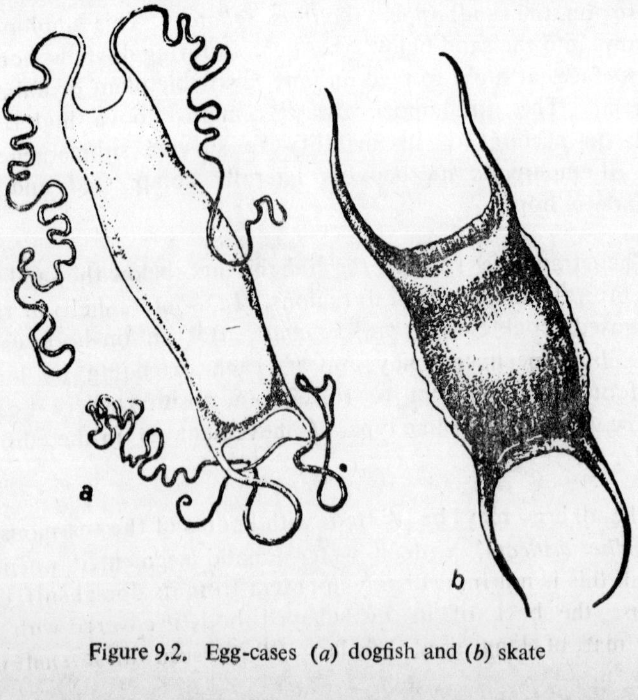

Figure 9.2. Egg-cases (*a*) dogfish and (*b*) skate

sponges. When bright yellow the cases contain developing eggs, and well-formed embryos can be seen moving within when studied with a hand-lens When we turn over some whelk shells in the debris, we find they contain the hermit crab, *Pagurus* (=*Eupagurus*) *bernhardus*. Live specimens of the razorshell and other sand-burrowing bivalves may occur along the strandline as well as their empty shells, together with a few live necklace shells. Fish, too, may be amongst the stranded and also the empty egg-cases of skate and dogfish.

Wood washed ashore comes in all shapes and sizes : branches and tree trunks fallen from cliff faces many miles away ; planks of wood washed overboard from timber-carrying vessels ; broken timber from boats and ships lost at sea. Some may be pieces of wood worn away from nearby piers or groynes which are riddled with small holes and tunnels. This is the work of the gribble, *Limmoria lignorum*, a small crustacean which attacks wooden piers near low water level. This isopod burrows just below and parallel to the surface of the wood, making a tunnel about 5 mm in diameter, with minute borings through the roof. These holes, which allow a water current to flow along the tunnel, indicate the presence of the animal below. Continuous burrowing in the wood by many generations eventually causes weakening and the outer layers break away ; the gribble then penetrates the newly exposed layers and, over the years, gradually reduces the diameter of the pier until it collapses.

Occasionally a piece of timber drifts ashore burrowed with tunnels two or three times the diameter of those of the gribble. These have been formed by the shipworm, *Teredo*. This animal is not a worm but a bivalve that grinds its way through the wood, making a perfectly circular burrow which is its home for life. It is interesting to note that none of the burrows crosses another. There are many species of *Teredo*, but only three are found in British seas.

Goose barnacles, *Lepas anatifera*, are stalked barnacles which attach themselves to floating timber so they are not found unless flotsam bearing them has drifted ashore. They are easily recognized by the stalked attachment and white plates from between which, when below water, the appendages rapidly protrued and withdraw to trap plankton ; thus the feeding mechanism is the same as that of the acorn barnacles found on rocky shores.

These creatures are just a few of the possible 'finds', so in summer or winter a study of the standline can be most rewarding for the enthusiastic beachcomber.

The fauna of a sandy shore is governed by the several factors discussed in Section I, but exposure is of particular importance.

When the wind is blowing on to a wide, open sandy shore the tops of the waves start to break long before they reach the beach, and when they do arrive at the shallows they break with such violence that the turbulence caused results in the transport of the coarser particles up the beach. In this way separation of the different grades of sand occurs with the coarser material high on the shore and the finer near low water mark. Breakwaters are erected on such beaches to counteract this action.

This deposition, however, is in no way permanent as is obvious if one beach is visited regularly over the years. The positions of pools vary and the height of the sand up certain indicators such as breakwaters, groynes or hondrails, shows how the sea plays havoc with the sand particles, piling them perhaps a metre or so high at a certain spot and in a few weeks or may be days, with the change of wind and current, clears them to another section of the beach. This instability of the habitat is quite a hazzed for its inhabitants.

Particle size determines the retentivity and porosity of the sand, the coarser grades drying out more rapidly as the tide recedes. During neap tides the surface sand high on the beach dries out completely and is readily blown by the wind. As has been seen, this is *not* the region the animals inhabit ; they choose to borrow in the area from high water neap tides seawards. Burrowing in this region, they protect themselves from desiccation in hot dry weather as the evaporation of water cools the surface layers and a few centimetres down the sand remains damp and at a fairly constant temperature, so once buried an animal has few worries.

Zonation. Zonation on sandy shores is not so evident as on rocky shores. However, it can easily be shown by simple investigations similar to those suggested in Section 6. For instance, stations may be set up down the shore, and at each a quadrat dug to a predetermined depth. The numbers of each different organism found can be recorded, this information later being transferred to a suitable chart.

Sand Dunes and Their Vegetation. On wide, exposed sandy beaches where onshore winds prevail, large quantities of sand are carried shorewards by the pounding waves, and when dried out the particles are blown landwards, where they pile up into dunes. In this country no dunes are as high and extensive as on the Continent.

The sand carried by the wind is fine and dry, so the plants that colonize this soil need a root system capable of binding and holding together the sand grains. The marram grass, *Ammophila arenaria*, is the dominant species and on some of the smaller dunes the only plant that is immediately obvious. It is a perennial with branching rhizomes which spread rapidly throughout the soil particles and anchor the plant. As the wind whips sand across the surface, the marram grass acts as a windbreak so that this newly blown sand tends to collect around it, thus building up the dune. In gale conditions so much sand may be deposited that the plant becomes burried, but its rhizomes soon develop new shoots which push their way to the surface. With a strong offshore wind *blowouts* in the dunes may appear. These are deep hollows which expose the rhizomes of the marram grass.

The first formed area of the dune adjacent to the shore is known as the *fore-dune*, and in some localities the sea couch-grass, *Agropyron junceiforme*, is encountered within reach of the spring tides. Its creaping rhizome binds the sand particles as efficiently as marram grass, but its upward growth is not so extensive and the dunes formed are not as high as when marram grass is the colonizer.

Lyme-grass, *Elymus arenarius*, is another colonizer found in some areas This plant is also tolerant of sea water, whereas marram grass is not and colonizes only sand that is out of reach of spring tides.

Most plants growing on sand dunes are xerophytes (that is adapted to grow in dry conditions) due to the poor retentivity of the soil, the exposure to gale force winds and the high temperature of the surface layers in hot sun.

The grasses have rolled leaves to contend with these conditions and their specialized structure adjusts the rate of transpiration to the rate of water intake.

The plant population of the fore-dunes is scarce because the habitat is so unstable, but a few of the possible binders are the sea holly, *Eryngium maritimum*, sea sandwort, *Honckenya peploides*, sea spurge, *Euphorbia paralias*, sand sedge, *Corex arenaries*, and sea convolvulus, *Calystegia soldanella*,

To withstand the dune conditions sea holly has a thick cuticle coated with wax, and the leaves are spiny to reduce the surface area. It is a perennial which grows about 30 cm high, but tends to creep over the surface. It is a member of the parsley family with blue and mauve florets borne in dense umbels, surrounded with broad, spiny bracts. It blooms during July and August.

Sea spurge is modified in a different manner. The leaves are succulent, having large, colourless cells capable of storing water towards the centre, with the normal green photosynthetic cells nearer the edges. As transpiration occurs the large cells become flaccid, but soon regain their turgor when water is in ample supply. This perennial is 20 to 30 cm high and the flower is a yellow-green insignificant inflorescence, blossoming from June onwards.

Sea sandwort, another succulent, is often associated with

sea couch-grass along the high water springs mark as it is also tolerant of salt water. Here it may participate in the formation of low dunes for it is a prostrate creeping perennial only a few centimetres in height. Its small, inconspicuous, white flowers appear from May to September.

The sea convolvulus, or sea bindweed, is a creeping perennial with stems, up to only 30 cm, in length, which do *not* twine like the common hedgerow convolvulus. The flowers, however, may be up to 4 cm in diameter, the five pink petals being marked with a central white stripe. These are seen from June to September. The small leaves are succulent, with a waxy surface.

Sand sedge is another perennial with an extensive creeping underground stem, which makes it a good stabilizer. These rhizomes often grow in straight lines, shown by the position of the aerial shoots. The aerial stems, which are three-angled, are up to 30 cm high with stiff leaves rolled for the same purpose as in marram grass. This species is unisexual, bearing male flowers at the tip of the stem and female flowers below. It blooms during June and July.

10

Shingle Beaches

In the latter part of the nineteenth century and the early part of the twentieth, when the 'seaside' became popular as a holiday resort, many a small child taken to a south coast town such as Bexhill or Hastings must have been sorely disappointed when he caught his first glimpse of the beach and found it consisted of pebbles instead of the bright, fine, yellow sand he expected. A little patience on his part though and he would soon be building his sand castles when the receding tide gradually exposed the lower sandy shore. Some parts of the British coast are not so accommodating to the would-be builder of sand castles for even at low water the beach still consists of shingle, the sand being deposited only in the sub-littoral regions. This occurs along the south coast of Devon where places with the attractive names of Blackpool Sands, Slapton Sands or Bee Sands, conjure up in the mind's eye large expanses of golden sand when, in fact, the beaches are formed completely of shingle.

Although the particle size of shingle is many times that of sand, a shingle beach is not stable enough to support the seaweed populations found on rocky shores and therefore it appears very barren. Its looks do not belie it because it supports very little life. Shingle shores usually slope steeply and the bounding action of the waves causes friction between the pebbles which obviously prevents colonization, because any plants or animals would be damaged and die within a short space of time.

However, after rough seas and onshore winds many victims of the storm are washed ashore, thus indicating the plentiful life offshore where the bottom is sandy. The driftline debris is the only humus found on many shingles beaches, but it is sometimes sufficient to support a minimum of plant life on the higher flattened reaches of the shore which are no longer disturbed by wave action. Gradually over the years more vegetation develops, for each season the dying plants themselves increase the humus content.

One of the commonest plants found clinging closely to the surface is the sea campion *Silene maritima,* already mentioned in Section 4. Its low-lying foliage forms a mat over the shingle, thus acting as a stabilizer.

The sea pea, *Lathyrus japonicus,* is another low-lying perennial with small mauve-purple flowers which are in bloom during July and August, but this plant is mainly confined to the south and east coasts. As with all members of the pea family, the roots bear nodules containing nitrogen-fixing bacteria which absorb atmospheric nitrogen and make it available to the plant for protein formation, so the decaying sea pea plants greatly enrich the nitrogen content of the humus.

The yellow horned-poppy, *Glaucium flavum,* is a very distinctive plant found on shingle. Its yellow flowers, which may reach 7 cm in diameter when fully open, are very fragile and with the slightest touch the beautiful petals fall to the ground. It is in bloom from June to September. Its peculiar name is derived from the shape of its podlike fruits which are curved and narrow, and vary from 15 to 30 cm long.

Sea pink, *Armeria martitima,* discussed in Section 4, is probably one of the most familiar flowers of the coast as it grows almost anywhere near the sea, shingle shores included.

The sea radish, *Raphanus maritimus* belongs to the cabbage family and has the typical four-petalled flowers of the group. These are pale yellow and appear from June to August. It is a bushy plant growing to a height of 60 to 100 cm and the fruit pod is most distinctive because it is constricted behind each seed to form a bead chain, the number of seeds varying from one to four. This plant is mainly confined to the south-west coasts of Britain.

Sea-kale, *Crambe maritima,* also belongs to the cabbage family, but the flowers are white and borne in clusters. They are in bloom from June to August. It is a low growing, fleshy perennial, capable of developing underground stems if it becomes buried by shingle. The leaves are cabbage-like and may be eaten as a vegetable.

Sea beet, *Beta maritima,* is a straggly plant which grows to a height of 30 to 60 cm. Its angular stems bear shiny, fleshy leaves. The small green flowers, each arising in the axil of a slender bract, occur in dense spikes and are in bloom from July to September. The young leaves may be eaten and should be cooked in the same way as spinach. Although most commonly found on shingle beaches, sea beet also grows low on cliffs where it is washed by sea-spray.

Several of the sandy shore flowering plants may be found on shingle beaches with some sand content—in particular sea sandwort, sea bindweed and sea spurge.

Where the stable shingle borders the land some of the soil intermingles with the shingle and here, still within reach of the sea-spray, the carline thistle, *Carlina vulgaris,* with its yellow flowerhead and prickly leaves: may occur, the flowers appearing from July onwards. This plant is a biennial which reaches a height of from 10 to 30 cm. and even in winter the dead plants may be found looking much the same as during the summer months. The curled dock, *Rumex crispus,* is abundant in this region growing from 33 to 90 cm. high, with wavy, lanceolate leaves more fleshy than in the inland form. Another inland plant which may grow here is bittersweet, *Solanum dulcamara,* but although the flowers are the same, the form of the plant is modified. Its stems are angular, more branched and prostrate and the leaves are heart-shaped and fleshy instead of oval. Herb robert, *Geranium robertianum,* also adapts itself to this habitat by growing closer to the ground and bearing smaller flowers.

11

Life on Muddy Shores

The muddy inlets and creeks of our coast hold little attraction for the ordinary holiday maker, but there are some interesting creatures which quite happily make their homes in such areas. Mud becomes deposited in sheltered regions where there is little wave action, so the slope of such a shore is very gradual.

If our time of arrival coincides with that of low water we may be sorely disapppointed when we find that we cannot see the sea. However, by the third hour of flow the tide will be racing back up the shore, flooding the boots of any unwary fisherman too engrossed in digging bait to notice the incoming water. This may readily happen around Southend and the rate of flow has to be seen to be believed.

On such a shore the *mud*, as we call it, is really a mixture of sand and mud, but as we progress farther up the estuary we find the sand content decreases as protection from wave action increases. As would be expected, a variation in fauna accompanies this change, though no hard and fast dividing line can be drawn between inhabitants of muddy sand and mud, but when lugworms are no longer present the sand content is at a minimum.

Muddy shores located around river mouths are built up when the outward flow of fresh water is halted by the inward flow of sea water. During its journey from source to mouth the river erodes some of the loose soil of its banks and the finest particles, *silt*, are carried in suspension down to the mouth where they become deposited once the outward flow is checked. In very wide estuaries the shores exposed at low water are so extensive and have such a slight gradient that they are referred to as *mudflats*.

In narrower estuaries a special problem arises for the would-be colonizers because here the mixing of fresh and salt water greatly affects the overall salinity. Each animal is adapted to a particular environment and any change affect its ability to survive. The balance between the body fluids of a marine creature and the surrounding sea water is so fine that when the salinity becomes lowered too much water enters the tissues of the animal ; on the other hand, when a freshwater animal is subjected to increased salinity, water is drawn out from its body tissues. Either is harmful and fauna living here have to control this intake or loss of water —a process called *osmoregulation*, since the water movement is by osmosis.

Thus we have two types of muddy shore, one with constant and the other with variable salinity.

Constant Salinity. A muddy beach appears very barren just as a sandy shore does since the majority of inhabitants live below the surface, but it does not look so inviting as a stretch of golden sand. Unless there is a reasonable proportion of sand, walking over mud is most difficult and not to be recommended unless one is well equipped with thigh boots. Only a few specially adapted species live here because fine mud particles clog the breathing and feeding mechanisms of the majority of animals.

Let us consider the inhabitants of a tidal harbour where the substratum is sandy mud. Here are the telltale casts of lugworms and the protruding tubes of sand-masons which were encountered on sandy shores, and below the surface catworms may be found as they can tolerate the presence of a little mud. Edible winkles abound near stones and leave distinctive tracks as they crawl over soft muddy surfaces.

Attached to odd stones, mooring chains and harbour walls at about mid-tide level we may find a few mussels. These are suspension feeders and if too much sediment is deposited around them they produce longer byssus threads, attaching them at a higher level in order to pull themselves upwards and thus bring their inhalent and exhalent openings above the silt ; during this operation the old threads are torn free. This is one time when the foot of an adult mussel comes into use, for normally the foot is only really active in young mussels when they are moving around searching for a settlement site at the correct level. In estuaries where loose stones are prolific, mussel populations become extensive and form mussel-beds. In a few areas these are cultivated, but in Britain fresh mussels are not a popular delicacy. Great care must be taken to cleanse them thoroughly as they readily harbour bacteria and noxious substances from the indrawn water. This is done by keeping the mussels in clean sea water, or fresh water containing the requisite amount of salt, for several hours ; commercially this is usually for a period of forty-eight hours.

Other rocky shore inhabitants are abundant where there is suitable attachment and cover, and at low water vertical zonation often shows up clearly on harbour walls.

By raking through the surface layers of the middle and lower zones we are sure to dislodge some edible cockles, *Cardium edule*, as they are shallow burrowers. Cockles are suspension feeders with short siphons. However, they have a large foot typical of deep burrowers but, instead of drawing the cockle far below, it is used to roll the shell along the surface. This is accomplished by a sudden straightening movement of the curved foot, provided its tip is in contact with the sand. In favourable environments the populations are dense, forming cockle-beds. Commercial beds are usually situated in sandy-mud estuaries such as the Thames ; here the largest beds are at Leigh-on-Sea.

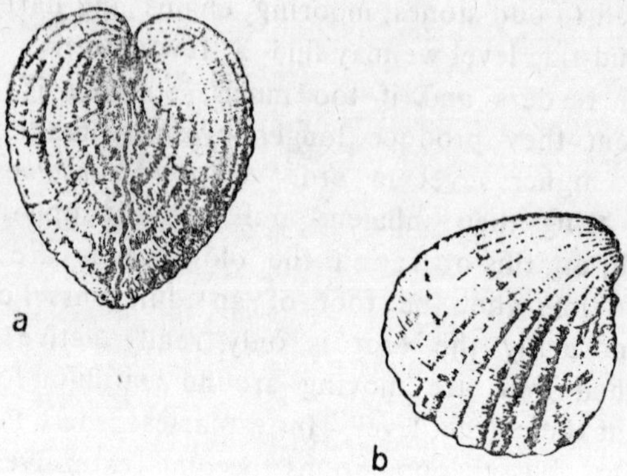

Figure 11·1. Edible cockle, *Cardium edule*.
(*a*) side view showing the two valves and heart-shaped outline and (*b*) single valve.

Other suspension feeders to be found on the lower shore are the various kinds of carpet shell, *Venerupis,* with oval shells, somewhat angular along the posterior edges. The empty valves are frequently found alongside those of cockles.

The sand gaper, *Mya arenaria,* one of the largest shore bivalves. is to be found here in sandy mud. The siphons, which may extend to a length of 30 cm, are joined by a tough sheath These animals are suspension feeders and the fringed

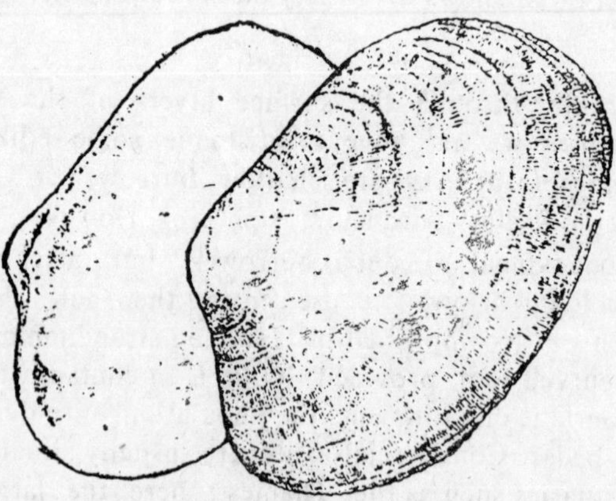

Figure 11·2. Valves of the carpet shell, *Venerupis decussata.*

openings of the siphons just reach the surface, where a slight hollow in the substratum is the only indication of their presence below. The valves are oval, reaching some 10 cm in length and, as the foot of the adult is relatively small, these gapers can be dug up more easily than many other bivalves, such as razorshells, as they are incapable of rapid downward burrowing when disturbed.

We may find a few of the pretty thin tellin shells of sandy shores, provided that sand content is high but in more muddy areas its place is taken by the Baltic tellin *Macoma balthica.* This deposit feeder has heavier, dull shell which is not so compressed as the thin tellin. Occasionally a Baltic tellin may be observed on the surface extending its foot in an effort to drag itself along. It leaves a track about 5 mm wide, which usually loops back to its original position.

Netted dog-whelks may be seen pushing their way through sandy mud in far greater numbers than on clean sand since detritus, which constitutes the bulk of their food, is far more abundant here.

In the lowest regions another whelk *Ocenebra erinacea,* commonly called the sting winkle despite the presence of a siphonal groove, may be recognized by its thick ridged shell. Like the majority of whelks it is carnivorous and its prey consists of bivalves and barnacles. Sting winkles are partial to oysters and are therefore regarded as pests by oystermen.

All these inhabitants are also found in wide estuaries where the substratum is sandy mud and the water fully saline.

Turning now to regions of mud, it is as the sand content decreases that a corresponding decrease in variety of species occurs. However, this does not necessarily indicate a reduction in the number of inhabitants because these animals adapted to a mud environment form large populations.

Tubes of fine mud, about 5 mm in diameter, protruding some 8 cm above the surface on the lower shore, belong to the beautiful peacock worm, *Sabella penovina*. When covered by the tide this annelid extends its crown of feathery tentacles to sift out suspended food and absorb oxygen from the water. When disturbed the crown rapidly retracted. Another tube-worm, *Myxicola infundibulum*, is not so conspicuous since the opening of its larger mud tube is flush with the surface.

The ragworm, *Nereis diversicolor*, recognized by the red line running from head to tail along the centre of its back, glides over the surface of soft mud, preventing itself from sinking by traversing a wide area as it progresses along its wavy path. It is very active during high water in its search for food ; however, when the tide recedes it burrows into the mud for protection, but this is only a temporary home. *N. diversicolor* feeds in the normal way of all ragworms but is also capable of straining of suspended particles from sea water when within its burrow. The larvae of this species, although able to swim, remain in the surface and mud instead of becoming members of the temporary plankton, as is usual with most ragworms.

Disturbance of the surface mud near low water mark may reveal a few shrimps, for these crustaceans, although abundant on sandy shores, can tolerate mud and here *N. diversicolor* probably constitutes their main item of diet.

Corophium volutator, a relative of the common sandhopper, burrows in mud and forms large populations Although a burrowing form, this amphipod crawls over the surface and on

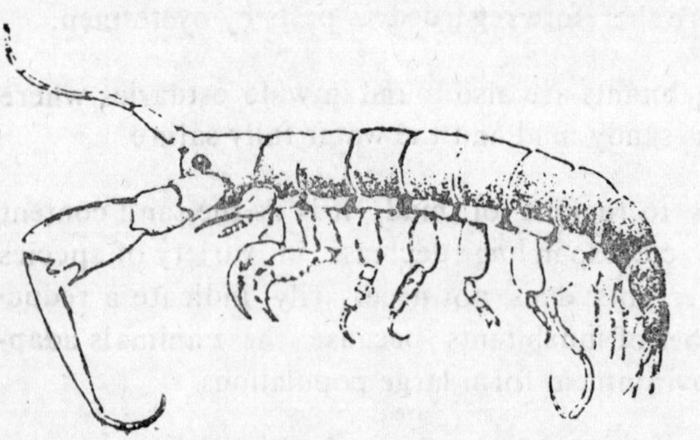

Corophium volutator

Figure 11.3

ebb-tide a few specimens may be found exposed at the water's edge in the wet mud ; as soon as the water drains away they retreat below. *Corophium* is also capable of swimming and records show that whole populations make local movements, probably when there is some adverse change in their environment.

In small shallow pools may be observed long, mobile siphons extending from the mud and encompassing a wide arc in search of organic debris. These belong to peppery furrow shells, *Scrobicularia plana,* bivalve deposit feeders which live in large populations in soft mud. The oval valves are greatly compressed enabling the animals to burrow deeply, perhaps to a depth of 25 cm in large specimens, and once below they rarely move their positions. The valve of *Scrobicularia* may reach a length of 54 mm but such a specimen would be eighteen years old. Growth is rapid for the first few years, but after ten years the rate becomes reduced to about 1 mm per year. *Sacrobicularia* is an edible bivalve, but not much favoured in the country. However, in France it is a popular delicacy and locals may frequently be seen up to their knees in mud, delving up to their elbows in mud in search of the bivalve

Baltic tellins are found alongside *Scrobicularia* since they live in mud as well as sandy mud, but they do not burrow so deeply. In some areas these two deposit feeders are present in equal numbers, but in others the population of one may be so dense that few specimens of the other found. Both suck up any suitable organic detritus, but a proportion of their food consists of micro-organisms living amongst the mud particles.

Variable Salinity. So far the effect of decrease in particle. size on shore inhabitants has been considered, but now this must be discussed in conjunction with variable salinity.

Where rivers meet the sea, intermingling of fresh and salt water occurs, but the extent of this mixing is controlled by many factors such as the shape of the estuary, its geographical situation, strength of the tides, direction of coastal currents, rate of flow of the fresh water, etc. Combination of all these diverse conditions is far too complex for consideration, here, but from the aspect of plant and animal populations there are two basic types of estuary :

1. Estuaries with water of *increasing salinity* from surface to bottom, that is with a vertical salinity gradient. This occurs when the incoming sea water flows beneath the outgoing fresh water and therefore the salt content low on the shores is greater than towards the banks. In these estuaries most of the marine animals inhabit the lower zones, their numbers decreasing towards the upper mud lapped by the freshwater surface layers.

2. Estuaries with water of the *same salinity* from surface to bottom. This occurs when the incoming sea water mixes completely with the outgoing fresh water, so here little variation in salinity occurs over the littoral zone and marine species inhabit the whole region.

The salinity never remains constant at any one point along an estuary, but follows the ebb and flow of the tide so that the salt content is highest at high water and lowest at low water. Even this varies from day to day as sea water penetrates farther upstream during spring tides than during neap tides.

Climatic conditions also play their part in controlling the salinity. Heavy rainfall increases the volume and force of the river outflow thus producing a reduction in salinity along the length of the estuary and in dry seasons the reverse occurs, the outflow of fresh water decreases and the salinity becomes raised.

It is not so much the range of salinity but the *rate of change* of salinity which controls colonization. Provided the lowering of salinity is very gradual, some marine animals can successfully adopt themselves to life in estuaries.

If rocks and stones are scattered in the mud the common shore crab, *Carcinus maenas*, happily migrates into regions of slightly lowered salinity and fishermen sometimes place tins or jars upside down along a stony stretch of estuary in the hope that young shore crabs will use them as protective covering during moulting ; when they are soft-backed these crabs are particularly good bait. When berried the females move seawards and do not return upstream until after the eggs have hatched, which indicates that the larvae are not so tolerant of lowered salinities as the adults.

Rough and edible periwinkles, *Littorina saxatilis* and *L. littorea*, survive in estuaries, but *L. saxatilis* is more tolerant of lowered salinities than *L. littorea*.

Some seaweeds can withstand slight reductions in salt content, and of the brown wracks the brackish water species, *Fucus secranoides*, predominates. The green seaweed *Enteromorpha* may be abundant and extends farther upstream than any other species.

Shrimps do not mind lowered salinities provided the water is warm, so they venture up estuaries in the spring but return seawards in the autumn. However, like the shore crab, females carrying eggs move down into fully saline water.

The small prawn, *Palaemonetes varians*, is a brackish water species found in pools and swimming near the surface at high water alongside the river banks, where they can easily be caught in a fine-mesh hand net. This prawn is almost transparent and only 2-3 cm long.

Several isopods of the genus *Sphaeroma* tolerate reduced salinities and their habit of rolling up into a ball in adverse conditions enables them to survive in cracks in the floor of dried out pools until the tide teturns.

Corophium volutator, the burrowing amphipod already discussed is found well upstream and as the young develop within the brood pouch of the female and emerge as miniature adults there is no hazard of the larvae being carried out to sea by the ebb-tide.

Other amphipods of the genus *Gammarus* live in estuaries, but each species tolerates certain salinities only, so that they are found at different heights up the estuary.

The ragworm, *Nereis diversicolor*, also tolerates lowered salinities and, as mentioned previously, the larvae remain in the surface mud, thus ensuring that they stay in the correct habitat for adult life. If, like the majority of ragworms, the larvae were planktonic, they might drift out to sea never to find their way back into an estuary.

Of the bivalve molluscs, the edible mussel tolerates dilution of sea water and therefore mussel-beds may extend some distance up river. Although mussels can survive in quite low salinities, they do not grow so rapidly nor reach a maximum size under such conditions.

The burrowing bivalves *Scrobicularia* and *Macoma* tolerate considerable reduction in salinity, but *Scrobicularia* penetrates farther upstream than *Macoma*.

The truly brackish-water mollusc is the tiny univalve, *Hydrobia ulvae*, which often forms dense populations. It browses on *Enteromorpha* or any available organic detritus. Besides crawling over the mud it sometimes burrows just below the surface and occasionally it floats in the upper waters, accomplishing this by secreting a mucous raft for itself. This may well be a dispersal mechanism.

Farther upstream freshwater fauna become dominant and once freshwater species only are present, the limit of the estuary has been reached, since an estuary is that region of a river with water of variable salinity.

Salt-Marshes and Their Vegetation. Salt-marshes bound the landward side of mud-flats wherever the tidal flow is not too strong to prevent colonization by vegetation. This depends on the flow at spring tides, for a seedling may germinate during neap tides only to be uprooted at spring tides.

The formation of a salt-marsh commences when seeds, carried by the water and deposited together with salt, germinate and mud particles become trapped around the base of the growing plants. Small areas of stabilized mud are built up, and more and more plants take root, until small islands of vegetation dot the shore. Further sediment collects, increasing the size of these islands until eventually some of them fuse and form a system of creeks and channels along which the incoming tide flows.

Sometimes the islands merge to encircle completely a bare patch of mud, and the incoming water then flows around these hillocks of vegetation, trickling over and filling the central hollow only at spring tides. Thess isolated depressions are called *salt pans.* During neap tides the water within these salt pans gradually evaporates, thus increasing the salt content, and sometimes during extremely hot weather they dry out completely leaving a crust of salt on the surface of the mud During heavy and continuous rainfall the water in these pans may be considerably diluted, making the gap even wider between the lowest and highest salinities. These conditions are too unfavourable for germination of seeds and therefore salt pans usually remain devoid of vegetation. These salt pans are rounded in shape, but elongated pans may be formed when creeks become blocked, either by the vegetation from each side growing across and causing the deposition of mud or by incaving of the sides.

Often the edge of a fully formed salt-marsh gradually becomes so eroded by water movements that a *salting cliff* is formed with bare mud below and salt-marsh vegetation above. In many estuaries indentations in these salting cliffs form excellent mud berths for boats during the winter months, as the water rise only the full height of the cliff and covers the saltings during spring tides.

Now that we have some idea how salt-marshes develop it is obvious that the plant colonizers of such areas must be specialized to withstand regular submergence or partial submergence by see water ; they are *halophytes.*

Glasswort or marsh samphire, *Salicornia stricta,* is a common primary colonizer of bare mud. It is a succulent annual with upright, cylindrical, branched stems, which are notched and bear small scale leaves only ; the whole plant is bright green, though with age it may become tinged with red or yellow. Glasswort may grow to a height of 25 cm and its inconspicuous petal-less flowers appear during August and September. Although an annual, the dead stems remain upright for some while and silt continues to collect around them. From a distance mud with a sparse population of glasswort look rather like a desert with miniature cacti.

Glasswort colonizes only areas of firm mud since its root system is shallow. Therefore in soft, mobile mud it is replaced by cord-grass, *Spartina* spp.. a perennial with deep vertical roots fot anchorage and horizontal rhizomes ramifying throughout the surface layers for stabilization of the substratum. Cord-grass grows in large tufts, from 30 to 120 cm high and its pale yellow flower spikes appear from July to September. *Spartina* is so efficient in trapping mud and debris that man plants it in certain areas to help reclaim land from the sea. Even when glasswort is in primary colonizer, cord-grass becomes established farther inland in regions of softer mud.

In sandy mud sea poa, *Puccinellia maritima*, is the pioneer, forming thick tufts around which silt soon collects. This perennial may grow to a height of 30 cm, but the plants are often prostrate, forming a turf. It is in flower during July and August.

A variety of halophytes become established above the zone of primary colonizers and the following are some of the commonest species forming the general salt-marsh vegetation.

Common seablite, *Sueda maritima*, usually occurs at low levels just above glasswort, though it may be found farther upshore. It is an annual, often very small, but sometimes reaching a height of 50 cm. The branched stem is smooth and bears many short, cylindrical pointed green leaves, which become tinged with red during the autumn. The flowers, which appear from July to October, are green, small and inconspicuous.

Sea aster, *Aster tripolium*, is a perennial growing to a height of approximately 60 cm and its flowers, which bloom during August and September have yellow discs surrounded by pale mauve ray florets, very similar to the common garden Michaelmas daisy. However, in certain localities such as East Anglia a particular variety occurs in which the mauve florets are absent.

Sea purslane, *Halimione portulacoides*, is often very abundant in well-drained saltings, but tends to be confined to east and south coasts. This is a straggly perennial with stems some 20 to 45 cm long trailing over the ground and bearing shorter erect branches with small, eliptical, greyish leaves. The small yellow flowers, arranged in short spikes, are unisexual, but both male and female flowers develop on the same plant. They are in bloom from July to October.

During July and August some saltings, particularly those on the east coast, are a blaze of mauve. This is the beautiful sea lavender, *Limonium vulgare*, in full bloom and even though the individual tubular flowers are tiny they are crowded together towards the tip of the leafless flower stalks and *en masse* give a lovely display. Sea lavender is a perennial growing from 10 to 30 cm high, and its lanceolate leaves are arranged in a rosette.

Sea pink, which has already been mentioned, is also a member of the salt-marsh community, but only in the upper levels as it is not very tolerant of high salinities. It probably survives here because its long roots penetrate below the more saline upper layers.

Scurvy-grass, *Cochlearia officinalis*, a perennial varying in size from 10 to 25 cm, with thick, fleshy, long-stalked, heart-shaped leaves, inhabits the middle zone of saltings. The four-petalled white flowers, which may be tinged with mauve, are approximately 8 mm in diameter and bloom from April to July.

Sea-spurrey, *Spergularia* spp., found on the middle levels

of saltings, is recognized by its five-petalled, deep pink flowers, 8—16 mm in diameter, in bloom from June to September. The much branched slender stems tend to trail and the small leaves are fleshy.

Sea wormwood, *Artemesia maritima*, becomes established in the uppermost levels of saltings and from a distance appears as a delicate silvery plant, some 30 cm high. The stems and slender leaflets are covered with a down of fine hairs and the whole plant has a pleasantly aromatic smell. The small, yellow, daisy-type flowers, crowded into short spikes, appear during August and September.

Sea plantain, *Plantago maritima*, found on spray-washed cliffs also inhabits the middle and upper zones of saltings alongside sea lavender and sea pink.

12

Planktonic Larvae

As we have seen in previous sections, many of the shore animals are sedentary creatures and the majority of mobile forms wander over only a very small area, so for dispersal purposes they depend on their planktonic larvae. These young are free-swimming creatures, entirely different in form from the mature animals, so they undergo considerable changes in structure before reverting to the shore for adult life. When such changes occur during the growing stage in the life-cycle of an animal it is referred to as *metamorphosis*, and we are all familiar with this in butterflies and moths where the young are unwinged crawling caterpillars. Metamorphosis may occur by a series of distinct changes or as a gradul process ; the stages in the life history of a butterfly, that is egg-caterpillar-pupa-adult, exemplify the former, and the development of a frog from a tadpole is an example of the latter. We shall encounter both types in the life histories of shore creatures.

Planktonic life is very hazardous as many marine animals feed on these minute organisms ; to ensure that at least one or two larvae reach maturity, many eggs are laid. Although these tiny larvae are adapted for swimming most of them float in the surface waters, drifting with the currents, therefore some never reach the correct habitat for adult life. Even if sedentary succeed in settling on the wrong substratum or at the incorrect level on the shore, they soon die. These are additional reasons why prolific egg laying is necessary for perpetuation of some shore inhabitants.

When these microscopic larvae were first discovered in plankton they were thought to be new animal species so were given individual names. Although later research determined that they were the young of well-known animals, the names were retained to indicate the various larval forms. Therefore the larvae of gastropods and lamellibranchs are called *veligers*, those of crabs *zoeae*, those of barnacles *nauplii*, etc. A brief examination of these different forms now follows so that the larvae may be referred to by name in the chapters on specific phyla. They are all of very small size and need to be studied through a powerful hand-lens or microscope, though in some species the later stages may be visible to the naked eye.

Planula Larva. This is a very simple type of larva with an ovoid, but somewhat flattened form, completely covered with cilia which are its means of propulsion through the water. This is the typical larva of coelenterates and consists of a solid mass of cells. When ready to metamorphose it settles on the bottom and a central cavity develops which becomes the coelenteron of the adult.

Müller's Larva. On hatching, this is a minute sphere with an upper cap region bearing a band of cilia around its lower edge, that is the equator of the sphere, and a lower gut region, consisting of a simple cavity with *one* opening only, the mouth. It moves around in the water by active lashing of the cilia and feeds on even smaller planktonic organisms which enter its open mouth as it swims. As growth occurs the ciliated band becomes lobed, then a gradual flattening from above takes place and the larva develops bilateral symmetry. Eventually the lobes are lost and it then sinks to the bottom, having metamorphosed gradually into a tiny flatworm.

Pilidium Larva. This is similar to Müller's larva, but more triangular in shape with the ciliated band drawn out into *two* lobes only, which hang down on either side of the central mouth. In this form it swims around, feeds and grows. Eventually a rapid metamorphosis occurs when the inner region containing the gut separates from the ciliated structure, sinks to the bottom and there develops into an adult ribbon worm The discarded part continues to float for a while, but as it cannot feed, soon dies.

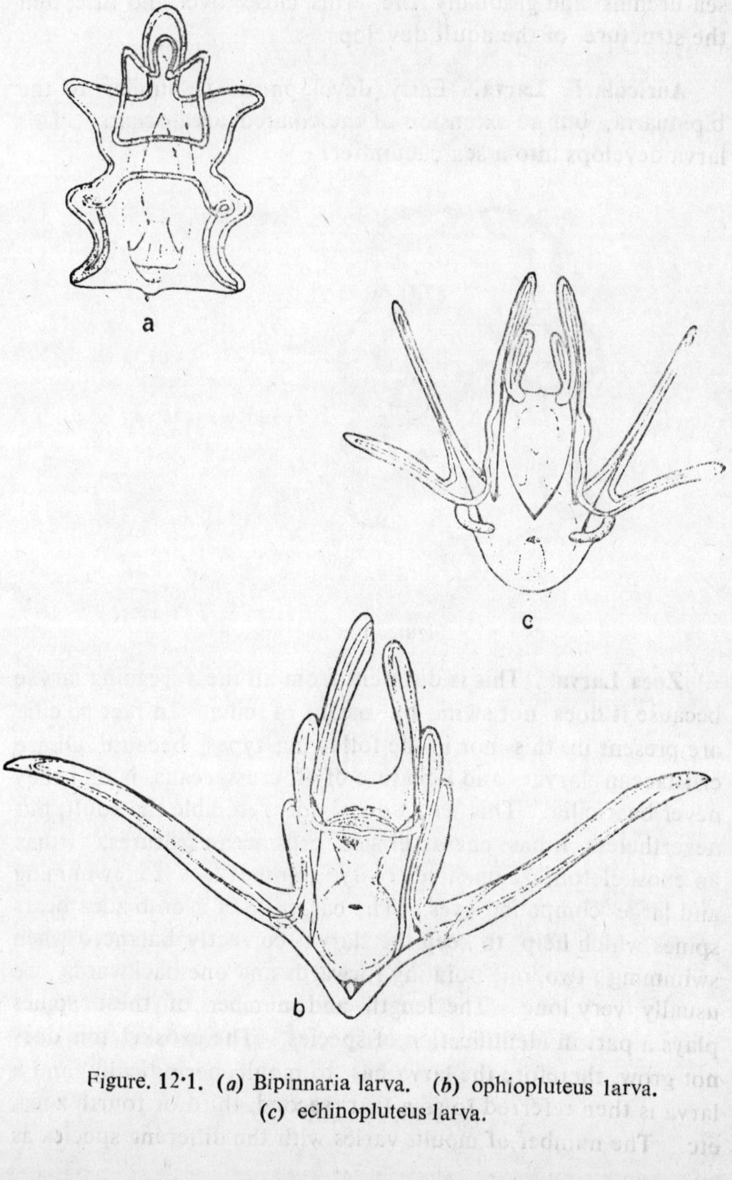

Figure. 12·1. (*a*) Bipinnaria larva. (*b*) ophiopluteus larva. (*c*) echinopluteus larva.

Echinopluteus Larva. This is similar to ophiopluteus, but it has *five* pairs of arms all of equal length and compression is lateral instead of dorso/ventral. This is the typical larva of sea-urchins and gradually the arms close over and fuse, and the structure of the adult develops.

Auricularia Larva. Early development is similar to the bipinnaria, but no extension of the ciliated area occurs. This larva develops into a sea-cucumber.

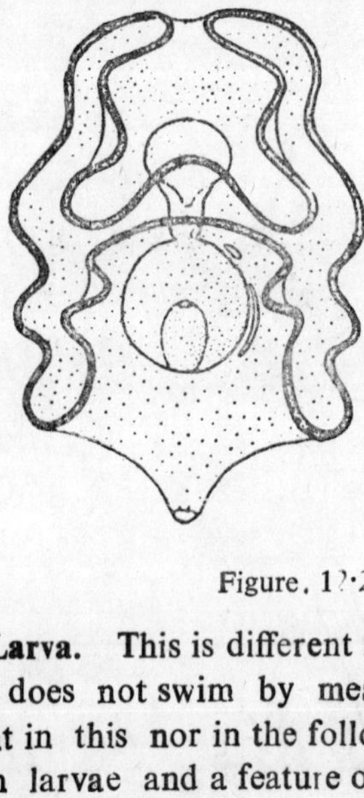

Auricularia larva

Figure. 1?·2.

Zoea Larva. This is different from all the foregoing larvae because it does not swim by means of cilia. In fact *no* cilia are present in this nor in the following types, because all are crustacean larvae and a feature of all crustaceans is that they never bear cilia. This larva does not resemble the adult, but nevertheless it has characteristic crustacean features. It has an exoskeleton, segmented body, jointed legs for swimming and large compound eyes. The carapace of a crab zoea bears spines which help to keep the larva correctly balanced when swimming ; two, one pointing forwards and one backwards, are usually very long. The length and number of these spines plays a part in identification of species. The exoskeleton does not grow, therefore the larva has to moult periodically and a larva is then referred to as a first, second, third or fourth zoea, etc. The number of moults varies with the different species as does the overall shape of the larva. Zoea larvae are typical of decapod crustaceans.

Megalopa Larva. This larva develops after the last zoea moult in crabs. The carapace is broader and flattened dorso/ventrally so it appears more crab-like in shape, the spines are shorter, walking legs with nippers on the first pair are present, but the segmented abdomen is long and held out straight behind. This larva swims by means of abdominal appendages, but eventually sinks to the bottom where after another moult the abdomen shortens and folds under the thorax, thus metamorphosising into a small crab.

Mysis Larva. This larva is very similar to a mysid (a delicate, shrimplike creature described in Section 23), and the thoracic limbs are used for swimming. It develops after the last zoeal moult in swimming decapods (shrimps and prawns) and has to undergo little change to become the adult. Lobsters hatch out directly into mysis larvae, the zoeal stage having occurred within the egg (i.e. zoea of lobsters never free living). After a free-swimming period the mysis sinks, the thoracic limbs become functional walking limbs and the young lobster crawls away over the bottom.

Nuplius Larva. This is a simple unsegmented larva, somewhat oval in shape but with the front end broader and extended

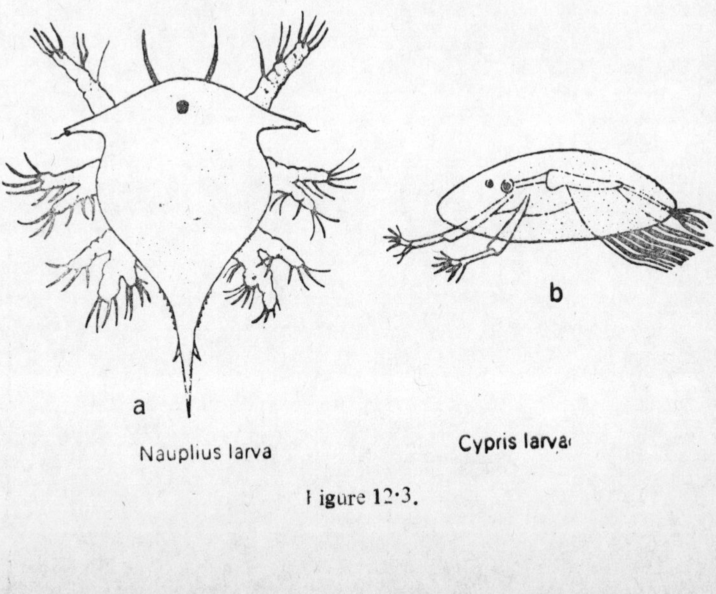

Figure 12·3.

into small spines at the two corners. It has three pairs of appendages only for swimming and a single median eye. For growth, moulting must occur and first, second and third nauplii develop. This is the early larval form of barnacles.

Cypris Larva. This develops after the last nauplius moult. The body becomes laterally flattened and enclosed within a transparent oval bivalve shell It has six pairs of thoracic limbs which in locomotion extend below the edge of the shell, and two of the original nauplius appendages, the attenules, develop cement glands at their tips. When ready for settlement the cypris deposits head downwards, fixes itself in position with cement from the glands and metamorphoses into the adult barnacle.

13

Phylum : Protozoa

Protozoans are the simplest of all animals, each individual consisting of a minute, undifferentiated mass of living material, invisible to the naked eye Although they possess no organs, they are highly successful creatures and constitute a large proportion of the permanent plankton.

There are many different forms of protozoans, including some with delicate limy skeletons, but as all are microscopic in size they do not merit further consideration here.

We will now turn our attention to large creatures whose bodies are composed of a collection of cells, instead of a single mass of protoplasm. METAZOA is the general name for all multicellular animals but, as we shall see in the following sections, great diversity of structure, complexity and habit occurs in the different phyla.

14

Phylum Sponges : Porifera

Sponges are sedentary, aquatic animals, sometimes solitary and sometimes colonial, found in all seas. They are the most primitive metazoans and differ from all other multicellular animals in using their principal aperture as an exhalent opening instead of a mouth for the intake of substances.

Structure. The basic form of a solitary sponge is a vase-shaped hollow structure, attached to the substratum at the narrow end, with its body surface permeated by many minute pores or *ostia*. Water enters the central cavity through these ostia but flows out via the one large terminal opening, the *osculum*. In colonial species one osculum, often situated at the top of a volcano-like hump, serves several individuals.

The many cells are arranged in two layers separated by a stiff, jellylike substance containing minute skeletal rods, the *spicules*, which may be calcareous, siliceous or fibrous. A bath sponge is simply the fibrous skeleton of a colony of *Spongia*, found in warm shallow seas. The shape as well as the substance of these spicules is variable, so classification of the phylum is based principally on spicule structure. The inner layer of cells bear flagella whose beating maintains a continuous flow of water through the body cavity.

The spongy nature of these animals is apparent when they are gently squeezed. On depression of a small area water is expelled through the osculum, but on release water again enters the area from nearby cells and seems to spring back into its original position. Sponges literally soak up water and shore species are always found in sheltered spots where the possibility of desiccation is at a minimum.

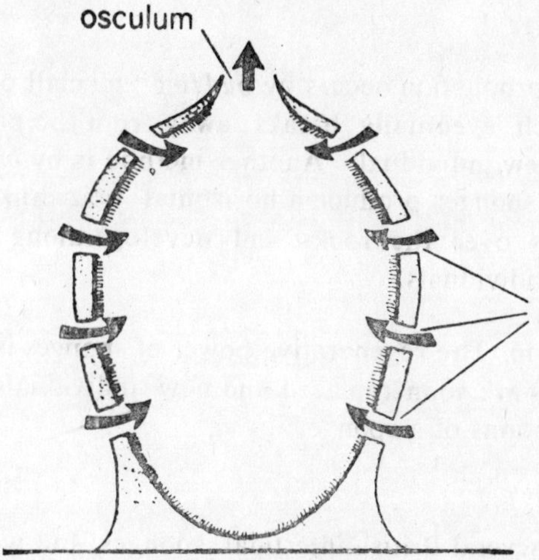

Figure 14 1. Lateral section of a sponge to show its basic structure ; arrows indicate direction of flow of water.

Respiratory Mechanism. As all cells of sponges are in contact with water gaseous exchange is direct, oxygen diffusing from the water into the cells and carbon dioxide from the cells into the water.

Food and Feeding. Sponges feed on plankton and organic detritus suspended in the indrawn water, the particles being trapped around the base of the flagella and then taken into the cells. Sponges, therefore, are omnivorous feeders.

Reproduction. All sponges are hermaphrodites, but usually the male gonads ripen first, thus cross-fertilization in general. Spermatozoa only are shed into the sea via the exhalent current, the ova remaining *in situ* where they are fertilized by spermatozoa from another sponge brought in with the inhalent current.

After fertilization the eggs develop into ovoid larvae covered with flagella, and on discharge into the sea become the free-swimming dispersal stage. Eventually the larvae settle and undergo a most unusual process. The flagellated cells on the outer surface migrate inwards to become the inner layer of the adult sponge !

Asexual reproduction occurs by *budding* ; a small outgrowth develops which eventually breaks away from the parent and grows into a new individual. Another method is by *branching* ; some colonial sponges produce a horizontal branchlike growth which extends over the rocks and develops along its length new, upright individuals.

Regeneration. The regenerative power of sponges is high, so damaged areas are soon replaced and new individuals develop from small sections of a sponge.

Common Species

There are several British intertidal sponges, but we have to search for them low on the shore in rock clefts, on the under-surface of rock overhangs, beneath thick layers of *Fucus* and among holdfasts of seaweeds. This is because sponges survive only in damp, sheltered positions away from the drying effects of sun and wind. *In situ* the oscula are obvious, but the ostia can be seen only with the aid of a hand-lens.

Of the encrusting colonial forms whose spicules are siliceous breadcrumb sponge, *Halichondria panicea*, is the commonest. It covers wide areas of sheltered rocks forming a buff, yellow or pale green crust, perhaps 1 cm thick, with a fairly smooth surface but, here and there, it is raised up into miniature volcanoes with the large oscula forming the craters at their peaks. Small patches may be found on the middle shore under layers on knotted and bladder wrack, but growth is prolific on all sheltered surfaces near low water mark. It also grows in small lumps around the holdfasts of seaweeds. The breedcrumb sponge is found on all British coasts.

Hymeniacidon perlevis (=*H. sanguinea*) is another encrusting colonial sponge found alongside the breadcrumb sponge but, in contrast, it has a rough surface with numerous small oscula.

Its furrowed masses are orange, orange red, scarlet or blood red.

Myxilla incrustans, usually bright orange, forms encrusting patches some 4 cm thick, with large oscula level with the main bulk of the sponge. This species occurs near low water mark and below, in areas where muddy sand is near the rocks.

Suberites domuncula has a smooth surface with only a few inconspicuous oscula, and is yellow or orange, growing in lumps attached to rocks low on the shore. This sponge, sometimes called *Ficulina ficus*, has the habit of growing on gastropod shells occupied by hermit crabs. It gradually grows over the whole surface, except the aperture, forming a spongy lump with no semblance of the original shell. In this way the hermit crab may gain extra protection because the sponge is distasteful to fish and other predators, and the sponge obtains a suitable surface for attachment. This is another example of commensalism. Sponge-covered hermits live in shallow seas, though they may occasionally be found on the shore at extreme low water springs.

All the foregoing sponges have siliceous spicules, but in the following species the spicules are calcareous.

The purse sponge, *Grantia compressa*, has a buff-coloured, flattened, oval, vase-like body with a large compressed terminal osculum and a short stalk for attachment. It is the commonest solitary species of British shores and is found hanging downwards amongst the red seaweeds *Lomentaria* and *Plumaria* from the undersurfaces of rock overhangs near low water mark. Specimens of all sizes may be near together, the average length being 3 cm, though some may be as long as 5 cm.

The urn or crowned sponge, *Sycon coronatum*, is a colonial form with individual grey or cream cylindrical vases, up to 5 cm long, arising rigidly from a common stemlike base. The osculum of each vase is terminal and fringed with spicules. *Sycon* is found near low water mark on all coasts.

Leucosolenia botryoides is another colonial form with bunches of small, stiff vases arising from a common base. Each vase, about 8 mm long; terminates in a large osculum. This species grows on *Fucus* and resembles a bunch of minute bananas.

The last of our shore sponges to be considered here is unique in its habit. *Cliona celata* bores into shells and limestone rocks, riddling them with minute holes from which it protrudes small lumps of its smooth yellow or orange body. *Cliona* inhabits the lower shore on all coasts and most commonly attacks oyster, scallop and venus shells.

15

Phylum : Coelenterata

All the members of this phylum are aquatic and include the the jellyfish, sea-anemones and corals. Many of these are very beautiful in form and colour, often looking more like flowers than animals so it is not surprising that they are sometimes called *zoophytes* (*zoo* – animal, *phyte* – plant).

Coelenterates are one of the simplest groups of metazoa, though more complex than the sponges. Their body wall consists of only two layers of cells separated by a jellylike substance and they are just a bag with one opening like the Porifera, but with the difference that substances pass in and out of this one opening, the mouth. These animals exhibit radial symmetry—appear the same along any radius—and have one or more rings of tentacles around the mouth. These tentacles are hollow because the central gut cavity or *coelenteron* extends into them. All coelenterates are carnivores and the outer layer contains many stinging cells for paralysing the prey —a characteristic feature of this phylum.

The coelenterates are of two forms :

1. the **Polyp**, the sedentary flowerlike form of sea-anemones, and
2. the **Medusa**, the free-swimming bell-like form of jelly-fish.

Sometimes several minute polyps grow on one stiff stalklike structure to form a sessile colony and these are called *hydroids* or *sea-firs*.

The phylum is divided into three classes, the *ANTHOZOA* (sea-anemones and corals), *SCYPHOZOA* (jellyfish) and *HYDROZOA* (hydroids). Nearly all are marine creatures and each class has many shore representatives, except the Scyphozoa. However, the latter will be included, as stranded jellyfish are not uncommon finds on our shores.

ANTHOZOA

Sea-anemones, the best known representatives of this class, exhibit the two principal characteristics : (1) they are polyps with *no* medusa stage in their life-cycle and (2) they are sedentary animals. Sea-anemones are solitary, but corals, also members of the Anthozoa, are usually colonial.

Most anemones need a firm substratum for attachment so they inhabit rocky shores, hiding away in dim recesses between cracks and crevices, though occasionally bright light is preferred. Some attach themselves to stones and shells below the surface of mud or sand and a few burrow and are never attached.

Structure. The simple body consists of the basal disc for attachment to the substratum, the upright cylindrical column forming the wall of the coelenteron and the mouth disc at the free end with the central mouth surrounded by hollow, unbranched, pointed tentacles. The surface is kept slimy by mucus-secreting cells interspersed amongst the numerous stringing cells in the outer layer. Within each stinging cell, *nematoblast*, a fluid-filled capsule contains a fine, hollow, coiled thread which, on stimulation, rapidly uncoils and protrudes from the surface. A sudden increase of pressure within the capsule forces fluid into the hollow thread turning it inside out and making it sufficiently rigid to penetrate and inject poison into an unsuspecting animal which ventures too close. Each capsule and thread is called a *nematocyst*. A similar type of capsule releases a flexible thread used for entangling parts of prey such as the bristles of a ragworm. Each nematocyst can be ejected only once, but new ones develop to replace those discharged. Nematoblasts are prolific on the tentacles, fairly abundant in the mouth region and present on the column, though in decreasing numbers towards the base. Special sensory cells are also present in the outer layer and these are most abundant in the tentacles.

The column and tentacles are contractile as both longitudinal and circular muscles are present. When disturbed the longitudinal muscles contract, pulling the mouth disc and tentacles into the coelenteron, then circular muscles just below the mouth disc contract pulling the wall inwards to close the opening. In this way sea-anemones are able to survive the hazards of exposure during low water. The basal disc adheres to the rocks by means of the mucous secretion and muscular action. In true burrowing sea-anemones, such as *Peachia*, there is no basal disc, the lower end of the column being rounded.

The lining layer of the coelenteron is thrown up into vertical folds to increase the absorptive surface of this simple gut. The partitions formed do not meet and some extend farther into the cavity than others, the numbers and size varying with different species.

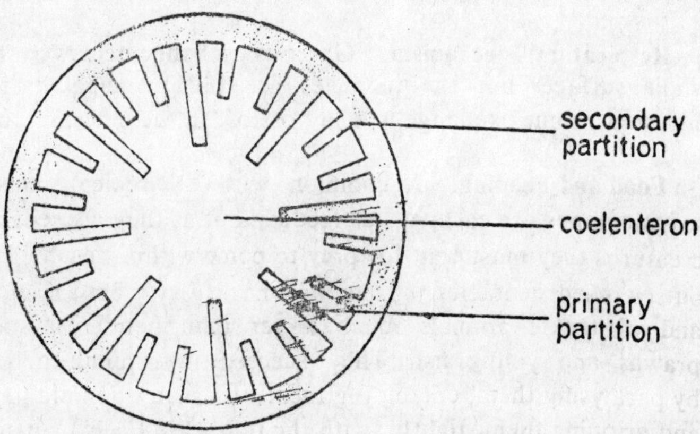

Figure 15.1. Transverse section of column of sea-anemone to show vertical partitions.

The true or stony corals are similar in structure to the anemones but they secrete a protective limy cup into which the polyp can withdraw. Colonies of these animals form the coral reefs, of tropical seas but the only littoral representatives on British coasts are small solitary forms.

The Anthozoa also include colonial forms whose polyps bear eight tentacles only which are branched, thus giving a feathery appearance. These are the soft corals, whose form is supported by small calcareous spicules either laying singly within the tissues, as in dead men's fingers or packed together to form a hard structure as in the sea-fans of deeper water.

Locomotion. Sea-anemones, although basically sedentary animals, are capable of sliding the basal disc over the substratum, but the distance covered is not great.

In burrowing anemones the coelenteron is filled with water and the mouth closed ; then rhythmical contractions of the circular muscles elongate the column, forcing water into the basal end so that it penetrates the sand. This process is then repeated until the mouth disc is level with the surface. Lengthening and shortening of the column and all movements of the tentacles are accomplished by alternate contraction and relaxation of the longitudinal and circular muscles.

Respiratory Mechanism. Gaseous exchange occurs over the whole surface, but the tentacles are the principal areas of diffusion ; some exchange is also possible in the coelenteron.

Food and Feeding. In common with all coelenterates the sea-anemones are carnivorous feeders, but as they are sedentary creatures they must wait for prey to come within reach of their outstretched tentacles. They are not fussy about their food and will tackle animals much larger than themselves, such as prawns and young fish. They succeed in trapping their prey by paralysing them, entangling them with many flexible threads and gripping them tightly with the tentacles. Each nematocyst has a trigger hair on the outer edge and when an unsuspecting animal rubs against it the thread is discharged. Many such triggers are stimulated by one creature, so the prey receives a good injection of poison and its desperate fighting gradually lessens as it becomes paralysed. The flexible threads coil around bristles or any suitable regions, then the tentacles bend inwards and thrust the food into the mouth. Once this has been accomplished the tentacles return to their normal position. Digestion occurs within the coelenteron and the undigested material is later extruded through the mouth, Even the species feeding on planktonic animals trap them by this method.

Reproduction. In sea-anemones the sexes are separate. The eggs and spermatozoa develop within the coelenteron and, when ripe, are discharged into the sea where fertilization

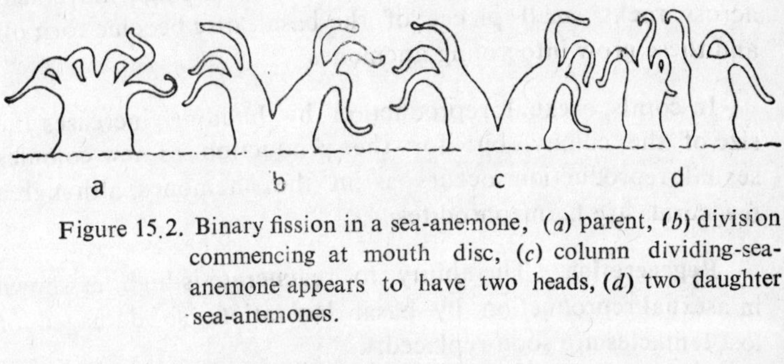

Figure 15.2. Binary fission in a sea-anemone, (*a*) parent, (*b*) division commencing at mouth disc, (*c*) column dividing-sea-anemone appears to have two heads, (*d*) two daughter sea-anemones.

occurs. *Planula* larvae hatch out and swim with the temporary plankton for a period before they settle on the bottom and gradually metamorphose into adult anemones. In a few species, such as the beadlet and daisy anemones, ouly the spermatozoa are ejected into the sea, thus fertilization occurs within the coelenteron of the female and the developing embryos remain there until they are minute replicas of the adult. These species are *ovoviviparous.*

Asexual reproduction occurs in some anemones, but it is usually secondary to the sexual method. *Binary fission*, simple division into two, occurs longitudinally, commencing at the mouth disc and proceeding down the column to the basal disc. *Budding* occurs from the basal disc only; a small swelling appears at the base, elongates and eventually develops tentacles and mouth at the free end. When it is a small replica of the parent, constriction occurs at the point of attachment and finally the young anemone breaks free.

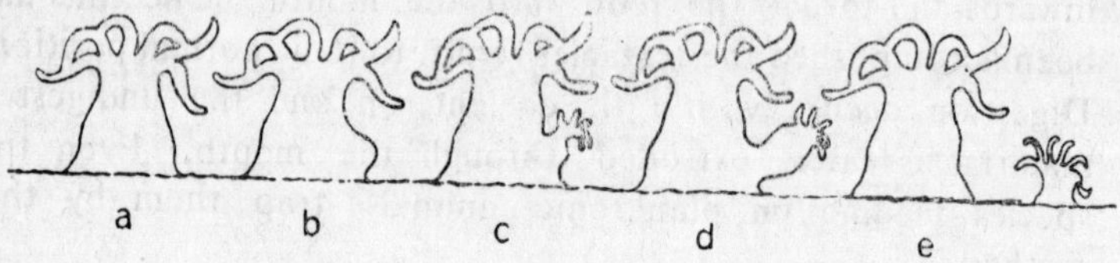

Figure 15.3. Budding in a see-anemone, (*a*) parent, (*b*) swelling at base of column, (*c*) elongation of bud and development of tentacles, (*d*) constriction at base of bud (*e*) daughter sea-anemone separated from parent.

Basal laceration is a third method. During movement across rocks small pieces of the basal disc become torn off and these grow into young anemones.

In corals, asexual reproduction by budding increases the size of the colony, but for the production of new colonies sexual reproduction occurs as in the anemones, although a few corals are hermaphrodites.

Regeneration. The ability to regenerate is high, as shown in asexual reproduction by basal laceration, so damaged or lost tentacles are soon replaced.

Growth. Growth in sea-anemones is very slow and each species has a maximum size beyond which no further increase occurs. Should food resources be low anemones actually decrease in size, but grow again as soon as food is plentiful. Sea-anemones may live for a few or many years and when protected in an aquarium have been known to survive for more than fifty years.

Common Species

Beadlet anemones, *Actinia equina*, are the dark red or greenish brown jellylike blobs, 1—3·5 cm high, found adhering to rocks as the tide ebbs, but on its return tentacles extend transforming them into beautiful 'flowerheads'. Bright blue spots around the edge of the mouth disc are groups of stinging cells. These are seen most clearly as the anemone opens, because they become hidden by the fully expanded tentacles. The basal disc is broader than the short, stout column, giving the anemone a squat appearance. Beadlets are the commonest anemones with the widest range since they inhabit all zones of rocky shores. Their colour varies between dark red, greenish brown, yellowish brown and crimson with green spots. Specimens with the latter colouring are somewhat larger and called *strawberry* anemones. Beadlets are ovoviviparous as the young develop within the coelenteron of the female. When released the young anemones float around before settling, so this probably helps in dispersal of the species.

Snakelocks or opelet anemones, *Anemonia sulcata*, prefer the more open regions of rocky shores, particularly shallow pools. The brown column is soft and flaccid and the long, continuously waving tentacles, also brown though sometimes mauve or apple green tipped with mauve, cannot be withdrawn into the coelenteron. The pinkish mauve tentacles give excellent camouflage when the sankelocks is amongst *Corallina officinalis*. Green tentacles indicate that minute algae are living within—another example of sympiosis. *Anemonia* is particularly suitable to the needs of the sympiotic algae because it does not retract its tentacles and is a sun-lover, living in situations with sufficient light for photosynthesis. The sting of this anemone is more potent than that of other species and its size is variable depending on favourability of the environment, but large specimens may have tentacles of 10 to 12 cm. Sometimes twin-headed specimens are encountered, as snakelocks anemones are capable of binary fission. This species is confined to the west and south-west coasts of Britain.

Dahlia anemones, *Tealia felina*, hide away in deep cracks, usually where fine gravel or sand is present. The column is broad and short, with a sticky, warty surface. Small pieces of shell or stone adhere to this, making the closed anemone blend with its surroundings. The short, thick, pointed tentacles are situated towards the periphery of the mouth disc and when they are fully extended a flat area surrounds the mouth. Colour variation occurs in individual dahlias, but they are subdued greens, crimson, white and grey, with the tentacles banded in grey. The broad base may reach a diameter of 10 cm but the column only a height of 5 cm.

Gem anemones, *Bunodactis verrucosa*, usually inhabit shallow rock pools alongside the coralline seaweeds where their pink, spotted white, column gives a splendid camouflage. These are ovoviviparous anemones, confined to west and south coasts.

Beautiful brown, cream, pink and mauve mottled 'flowers' seen near the edges of shallow tidal pools belong to daisy anemones, *Cereus pedunculatus*, whose basal discs are attached to rocks well below the surface. They also live in mud and sand attached to buried stones. These anemones have a supplementary defence system ; within the coelenteron are long, white stinging threads which can be extruded through the mouth or through special pores in the side of the column. These threads are called *acontia* and the pores *cinclides*. Daisy anemones are ovoviviparous.

The various species of the genus *Sagartia* are, in many ways, very similar to daisy anemones, but although they may be found in rock pools, they are more commonly seen protruding from crevices near low water, as limp columns some 5-6 cm long, terminating in slimy, flaccid tentacles. They are not very attractive, but when the tide returns so does their beauty. Acontia are present and basal laceration is the more usual mode of reproduction.

Peachia hastata may be found among debris after a storm as small oval bodies, 1-2 cm. long, pinkish brown with vertical whitish bands. This true burrowing anemone, with no basal disc, lives in sand on the lower shore and is not often seen because at the slightest disturbance the tentacles are withdrawn below the surface. The column extends to 8 or 9 cm. below the sand and the tentacles, when expanded, lay flush with the surface. The larvae are unusual in being parasitic on medusae and sea-gooseberries, and are not free swimming.

The most beautiful of all British anemones is undoubtedly the plumose, *Metridium senile*. It is a sub-littoral species, though occasionally small specimens are found low on the shore on rocks and in pools. They may be white, cream or delicate hues of salmon pink or orange, and their many tentacles are small, fine and feathery. Their diet is zooplankton and they are capable of reproducing by basal laceration.

Parasitic anemones, *Calliactis parasitica*, attch themselves to edible whelk shells containing hermit crabs, but they are *not* parasitic animals, as the name implies This is an association in which the anemone benfits by having a fairly constant food source from the untidy feeding habits of the crab, and the hermit crab gains a measure of protection from prey by the stinging ability of the anemone tentacles. The large hermits live offshore, but parasitic anemones can live on rocks and may occasionally be located near low water mark. The column is pale brown with cream vertical lines and a few darker spots, and the tentacles cream. Acontia are present and shed freely. This anemone always chooses a shell occupied by *Pagurus* (=*Eupagurus*) *bernhardus*, but the cloak anemone, *Adamsia palliata*, lives on the shell of *P. prideauxi* Cloak anemones are so adapted for clinging closely to hermit shells teat they cannot live a separate existence. The basal disc grows around the shell and fuses where the edges meet so that the anemone is never able to leave the shell. The clock is buff with red spots and acontia are present within the coelenteron.

The soft coral dead men's fingers, *Alcyonium digitatum*, may occasionally be found in sheltered situations low on rocky shores, but normally it inhabits the sub-littoral region. The colonies form lumps of tough, creamy coloured masses, sometimes with long extensions, and appear most uninteresting when exposed by the tide. Under water they display their loveliness as minute polyps gradually show their heads and extend their eight, branched tentacles.

Devonshire cup corals, *Caryophyllia smithii,* are confined to south-west coasts of Britain and, although solitary, are usually in groups. They can withdraw completely within their limy cups, but when open they may easily be mistaken for anemones.

SCYPHOZOA

Scyphozoans or jellyfish are the large free-swimming coelenterates ; the medusa is the dominant stage. Polyps are present in the life-cycle, but these are small and inconspicuous compared with the colourful and graceful medusae.

Structure. Jellyfish are like sea-anemones turned upside down and flattened from the base to squash the column outwards into the umbrella or bell. The quantity of jelly is so much greater than in anemones that it reduces the coelenteron to a small central cavity with narrow radiating canals which link up with a circular canal around the periphery of the bell. Cilia within this system maintain a flow of water to all parts of the animal. Tentacles edge the bell and these, as in sea-anemones, contain numerous stinging cells. Special sensory cells are situated on the edge of the bell at the ends of certain radial canals. The muscular system is will developed with a broad circular muscle band and many radial muscles.

Locomotion. Jellyfish swim gracefully through the water by alternately closing and openiag the bell, a pulsating movement accomplished by contraction and relaxation of the circular muscles. They move with the upper surface of the bell foremost, the tentacles trailing behind.

Respiratory Mechanism. Gaseous exchange occurs over the whole surface as in sea-anemones.

Food and Feeding. Jellyfish are carnivorous, preying on small fish, eggs, larvae, etc., and the method of capture is the same as in anemones.

Reproduction. The sexes are separate and the gonads are situated in the coelenteron in four groups, which can be seen as mauve rings in the common jellyfish, *Aurelia aurita.*

The reproductive products are shed into the coelenteron and pass out through the mouth into the sea where fertilization occurs. In some species the eggs remain in the coelenteron of the female where they are fertilized by sperms brought in with the water current. *Planual* larvae hatch out which, after a free-swimming period, settle and develop into

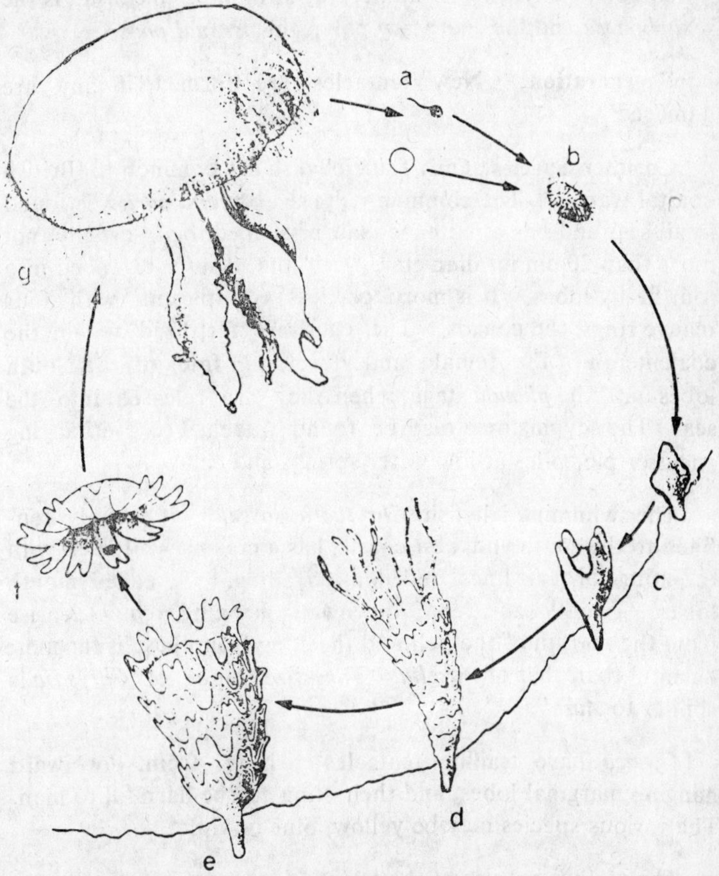

Figure 15·4. Life-cycle of a common jellyfish. (*a*) male and female gametes released from *separate* jellyfish, (*b*) planula larva, (*c*) planula deposites on rock and develops into a polyp, (*d*) scyphistoma, (*e*) ephyra laıva budding off from scyphistoma, (*f*) free-swimming ephyra larva, (*g*) mature jellyfisn.

miuute trumpetshaped polyps called *scyphistoma*. From the free surface of scyphistoma small saucer-like sections, each with eight lobes, break away to become free-swimming *ephyra* medusae. This process is called *strobilization*. Each ephyra is gradually transformed into an adult jellyfish as tissue develops between the lobes to produce a complete bell. In the life-cycle of jellyfish the adult free-swimming medusa is the *sexual phase* and the sedentary polyp the *asexual phase*.

Regeneration. New tentacles are formed if any are damaged.

Common Species. Only four jellyfish are common to British coastal waters. The common jellyfish, *Aurelia aurita*, is found in all seas and has a flattened saucer-shaped bell, usually not more than 30 cm in diameter, with the mouth extended into four fleshy lobes. It is more or less transparent, with four mauve rings, the gonads. The eggs are fertilized within the coelenteron of the female and develop in folds of the mouth lobes until the *planula* stage, when they are released into the sea. The scyphistoma may be found attached to overhanging rocks or pier piles at low water springs and below.

The swimming jellyfish, *Chrysaora isosceles*, is mainly confined to the south and west coasts, has a creamy white bell with radiating brown lines and long, trailing, frilly-edged mouth lobes. Twenty-four long, downward hanging tentacles arise from the margin of the bell and the sting from these is far more harmful than that of *Aurelia*. The size range of *Chrysava* is similar to *Aurelia*.

Cyanea have trailing tentacles arising from downward hanging marginal lobes, and their sting can be harmful to man. The various species may be yellow, blue or violet.

The various species of the genus *Rhizostoma* are the largest British jellyfish, reachiag a diameter of 60 cm. The mouth lobs are fused but perforated by small pores through which water and small prey can be drawn into the coelenteron. The edge of the bell is minutely lobed, but bears no tentacle. The bell is pale green with a darker margin.

One scyphozoan encountered on our shores differs from normal jellyfish in being sedentary with the bell held upside down on a short stalk. *Haliclystus auricula,* the commonest stalked jellyfish, inhabits the lower shore attached to oarweeds, dulse, pod and other seaweeds. The trumpet-shaped bell has tentacles arranged in bunches which appear as knobs at the tips of eight arms formed by deep lobing of the margin. The bell, about 2 cm in diameter, is pale green to pink with lighter rays extending towards the tentacle knobs.

HYDROZOA

These are sedantary colonial coelenterates attached to seaweeds, stones, empty shells and even shells of live molluscs and crustaceans. Both forms occur in the life-cycle of hydroids, but the attached polyp is the dominant stage, the free swimming medusa simply being the dispersal stage. The height of these colonies varies from 5 mm to 15 cm, but the individual polyps are very small and must be studied with a hand-lens.

Structure The colonial polyp is basically the same as the sea-anemone, but the coelenteron is a simple hollow structure with no folding of the lining into partitions and the mouth is surrounded by fewer tentacles which are often solid instead of hollow. The 'stalk' of these colonies is hollow and continuous with the cavities of the polyps, thus the contents of the coelenteron of one polyp can be transported to that of another—a most beneficial feature if some polyps are more successful at capturing prey than others. The arrangement of the polyps along the 'stalk' varies with different species ; they may be opposite, alternate or on one side only.

Many hydroids are supported and protected by a thin sheath of chitin and in some it strengthens all regions of the colony, but in others only the 'stalk'. The sheath around a polyp is referred to as a 'cup' and in some species the polyp can withdraw into it completely. Often it is only this sheath, devoid of living polyps, that we find attached to strandline debris.

In addition to the normal feeding polyps, a large number of hydroids develop wase-like structures which are modified polyps without a mouth and tentacles adopted for asexual reproduction. A few even develop polyps specialized for protection. When modification for various functions occurs in this way the species is said to exhibit *polymorphism*.

Respiratory Mechanism. Gaseous exchange occurs over the whole surface of the tentacles and any other regions in direct contact with the water. As in the other classes, some diffusion also occurs in the coelenteron.

Food and Feeding. The prey is captured as in the sea-anemones, but it consists of zooplankton. Food ingested by one polyp may be carried to any region of the colony where nutriment is repuired

Reproduction. Growth from the tip of the 'stalk' increases the size of the colony, thus the youngest polyps are near the tip and the oldest near the base.

The vase-like polyps reproduce asexually by budding off saucer-shaped structures which are released into the sea. These are tiny medusae bearing sexual organs so it is in this free-swimming stage that sexual reproduction occurs The medusae are of the same general form as jellyfish, but they have four simple radial canals only from which the gonads are suspended. The sexes are separate and, when ripe, the spermatozoa and eggs are shed directly into the water, where fertilization occurs. *Planula* larvae hatch from the fertilized eggs and spend a few days in the plankton before sinking and settling on stones or seaweeds. Once attached, each larva develops tentacles and a mouth, gradually growing into a feeding polyp—the start of a new colony. The life-cycle of a hydroid is shown diagramatically on the facing page. In a few species the free-swimming medusa stage is absent and instead attached reproductive structures develop.

Regeneration. Both polyps and medusae are capable of regenerating small damaged regions.

Common Species

All the hydroid colonies inhabit the lower regions of the shore and continue down into the sub-littoral zone. Hunting through stones, shells and seaweeds thrown up on the beach after storms usually brings to light some of the commonest hydroids though, in most instances, only the empty chitinous sheath, as this survives long after the death of the delicate polyps.

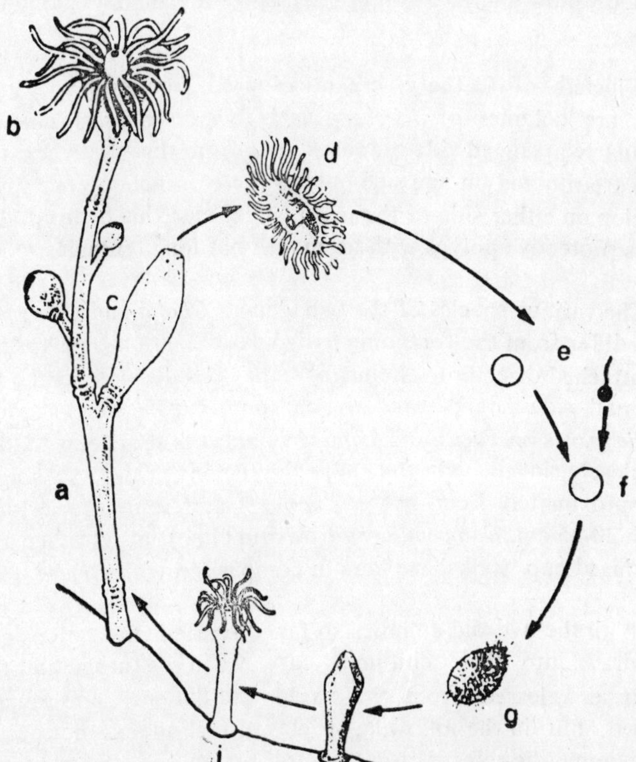

Figure 15.5. Life-cycle of a hydroid. (*a*) hydroid colony. (*b*) feeding polyp. (*c*) asexual reproductive polyp which produces. (*d*) minute medusae. (*e*) male and female gametes released from' *separate* medusae. (*f*) fertilized ovum. (*g*) planula larva. (*h*) larva settles on bottom and (*i*) develops into a new colony.

Dynamena (=*Sertularia*) *pumila* will be found rising stiffly from the surface of *Fucus* in unbranched colonies only about 12 mm tall ; it is easily recognized by the regular arrangement of the minute cups in opposite pairs. It also grows into branched colonies up to 5 cm tall. The vases develop at random along the 'stalks', the whole colony being grey and somewhat translucent.

Sertularella polyzonias grows to about the same height, but is pale yellow and has the cups arranged alternately along the stalk.

Clusters of feathery, cream-coloured fronds up to 12 cm long are colonies of *Kirchenpaueria* (=*Plumularia*) *pinnata*. Regularly arranged side branches arise from the 'stalk' and the cups are situated on one side only of these branches. The vases develop on either side of the main 'stalk' and this hydroid also bears protective polyps with no mouth but long tentacles.

The various species of the two genera *Obelia* and *Campanularia* differ from the foregoing hydroids because the polyps are not attached directly to the main 'stalk' but develop at the tip of small side 'stalks' and the chitinous cups are bell-shaped. *Obelia* grows on *Fucus* and *Laminaria* and the short cup 'stalks' are closely ringed. On the shore the colony grows to a height of approximately 3 cm, but in deeper water some species may reach 20-25 cm. *Campanularia* grows on almost any surface and the ringed cup 'stalks' are long in comparison with *Obelia*.

In all the hydroid colonies so far discussed the polyps can withdraw into their chitinous cups when disturbed and the medusae released from the vases are flattened and saucer-shaped, but in the following species retraction does not occur, so they may be referred to as 'naked' forms, and the medusae are bell-shaped.

Colonies of *Hydractinia echinata* grows on the shells of hermit crabs, forming a whitish pink moss-like covering 5-6 mm high—another example of commensalism. *Hydractinia* colonies include special protective polyps.

Attractive pink clusters of small 'stalks' up to 25 mm tall attached to *Ascophyllum* or *Fucus* are colonies of *Clava*, but these are usually confined to south and west coasts.

Large groups of brown or cream 'stalks' tipped with pink polyps growing from rocks to a length of 7 cm are *Tabularia*. *Tabularia* medusae are *not* free swimming, but remain within the vases from which they release their sexual product into the sea.

Cordylophora caspia, the hydroid found in estuaries, also has no free-swimming medusae.

A rose-pink colony, up to 10 cm tall, found in deep pools on south-west coasts, is *Coryne muscoides*, whose polyps are unique in having knobbed tentacles with the stinging cells confined to the knobs.

16

Phylum : Ctenophora
Sea-gooseberries, Comb-jellies

All ctenophores belong to the open sea but their swimming power is so weak that they drift with the water currents and become stranded in pools are washed ashore during rough seas.

They are small, transparent, spherical animals basically like the coelenterates, but with no stringing cells. Instead they are armed with adhesive cells for catching prey ; all species are carnivores.

Ctenophores are globular bags with one opening, the mouth, but they are easily distinguished from coelenterates by the eight longitudinal bands of swimming plates. These consist of rows of minute cilia joined together along the base like the teeth of a comb. These 'combs' beat in succession giving the appearance of waves spreading along the length of the band. The 'combs' of the eight bands beat in unison, thrusting the animal through the water, mouth foremost. The common name *comb-jelly* originates from these structures.

All ctenophores are hermaphrodites and the sexual products are shed through the mouth into the sea where fertilization occurs. The fertilized eggs later hatch out as free-swimming miniature adults. There is no asexual method of reproduction.

Regenerative powers are considerable in all ctenophores.

Two species are common around all coasts of Britain. Both are transparent and colourless, but their swimming plates are iridescent during the day and luminescent after dark. The sea-gooseberry, *Pleurobrachia pileus*, gets its popular name from its similarity in size and shape to the fruit. Its oval spherical body 12-15 mm long, has one pair of long branching, retractile tentacles bearing many adhesive cells. These tentacles trail through the water during swimming, entangling prey which is then passed on the mouth. Sea-gooseberries feed mainly on small copepods and various planktonic larvae and eggs. They themselves are members of the permanent plankton.

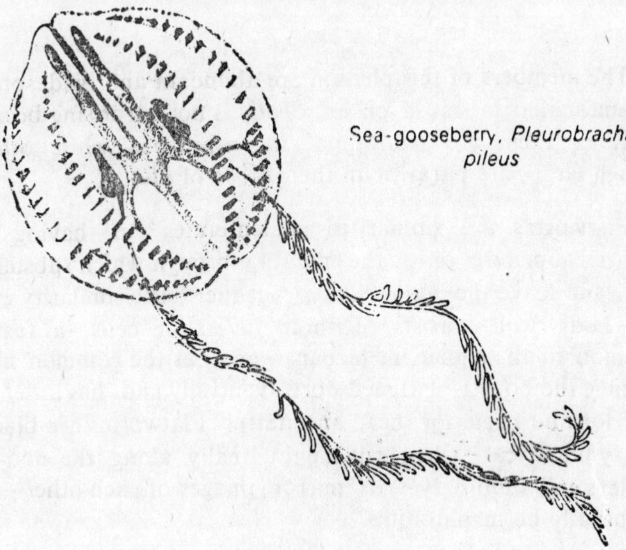

Sea-gooseberry, *Pleurobrachia pileus*

Figure 16,1.

Boroe cucumis is much bigger, perhaps reaching a length of 5 cm, has no tentacles, but a large mouth which is held open in swimming to catch prey.

17

Phylum : Platyhelminthes

Flatworms

The members of this phylum are abundant and widespread, but unfamiliar to most of us. This is not surprising because many of them are small and inconspicuous while others, though large, are parasitic in their mode of life.

Flatworms are similar to coelenterates in having one external opening only, the mouth, through which substances enter and leave the body cavity, but there the similarity ends. The body wall consists of three layers of cells—a feature common to all higher metazoans—and, as the common name implies, the body is flattened dorso-ventrally and has a definite anterior and posterior (head and tail). Flatworms are bilaterally symmetrical—when cut longitudinally along the mid-line the left and right halves are mirror images of each other—and are usually hermaphrodites.

The phylum is divided into three classes, *TURBELLARIA* (free-living flatworms), *TREMATODA* (parasitic flukes) and *CESTODA* (parasitic tapeworms). The few shore forms belong to one order in Turbellaria, the *Polyclodida.*

Locomotion. On the shore flatworms appear to flow over rocks or stones, but in swimming they are very graceful creatures, transporting themselves through the water by undulating movements of the body margins.

Respiratory Mechanism. Gaseous exchange occurs over the whole surface of the body.

Food and Feeding. The mouth is situated on the under-surface, and as flatworms move over the surface they feed on any small live or dead animals they encounter.

Reproduction. Flatworms are hermaphrodites but cross-fertilization occurs and the eggs are laid on the underside of rocks.

Common Species

Oligocladus sanguinolentus is about 1 cm long with a trans-lucent creamy-white body marked with red or brown patches. It has one pair of tentacles.

Prostheceraeus vittatus may reach 3 cm in length and the yellowish-cream body, marked with longitudinal dark lines, has fluted margins. One pair of tentacles is present. This species is confined to the lower shores of south and west coasts where it hides under stones or amongst *Laminaria* holdfasts.

Leptoplana tremellaris is about 2·5 cm long with a buff body devoid of tentacles. It is found on weeds and under stones on the middle and lower shores.

18

Phylum : Nemertini
Ribbon Worms

The bootlace worms found as slimy coiled lumps beneath stones belong to this phylum and exhibit the characteristic feature of immense body extension.

Another common name for the nemertines is *proboscis worms*, relating to the eversible proboscis (extensible structure of the head used in obtaining food) capable of protrusion to great length. When withdrawn, this proboscis lies within a special muscular sheath or pouch situated in a dorsal position above the gut This is unique to nemertines for although an eversible proboscis is present in other invertebrates, when withdrawn it folds back into the gut cavity.

Locomotion. Wriggling over the surface, or burrowing in the mud, is accomplished by alternate contraction and relaxation of the longitudinal and circular muscles, and the ability to extend the body to a great length until it is threadlike enables the worm to squeeze through the smallest cracks. In movement, waves of contraction pass along the body from posterior to anterior.

Respiratory Mechanism. Gaseous exchange occurs over the whole surface of the body.

Food and Feeding. The proboscis is then gradually withdrawn until the prey reaches the mouth and is swallowed. In some species, glands in the proboscis secrete a paralysing fluid which is injected into the victim by means of a special piercing stylet.

Reproduction. The sexes are usually separate and in some species fertilization is internal, the female retaining the developing eggs until they hatch. Generally the fertilized eggs develop into miniature adults, but in a few species free-swimming *pilidium* larvae develop.

Regeneration. Regenerative powers are considerable, and if the proboscis is damaged or lost a new one quickly develops.

Common Species

The bootlace worm, *Lineus longissimus*, is the largest of the shore nemertines. The body is slimy, brown black and capable of enormous extension, normally up to 6 metres, though exceptionally even longer. However, the worms are usually found coiled in muddy gravel beneath stones on the lower shore and any attempt to uncoil them generally leads to disaster as the body breaks easily. Another member of the same genera, *L. ruber*, can tolerate lowered salinities and is therefore found in estuaries, but it is a much smaller species, its maximum length being approximately 20 cm. It is reddish brown.

One of the most beautiful nemertines lives within a tube of mucus below stones or in rock crevices, but only near low water and in the sub-littoral zone. This is *Tubulanus annulatus* with a brick-red or brown body, overlaid with a network of white stripes running longitudinally and circularly ; it may reach a length of 50 cm.

Amphiporous lactifloreus has a whitish-pink body with two darker spots on the head and is found under stones and amongst *Laminaria* holdfasts. The maximum extension of its body is about 7 cm only.

19

Phylum : Aschelminthes Round Worms

Round worms are abundant the world over, living in all possible habitats as well as parasitizing both plants and animals. The eelworms which cause considerable damage to crops belong to this phylum as do the hookworms which live in the intestine of man.

The body is round and tapers to a point at each end, with an anterior mouth and posterior anus. The body wall consists of three layers, as in the ribbon worms, and the outer surface is tough and smooth.

Most of the free-living round worms are small, and as all those of the shore are too minute to see with the naked eye, they do not justify attention here.

20

Phylum : Annelida Segmented Worms

Annelids are readily distinguished from any of the other worms by their ringed or segmented appearance and we are all familiar with one member, the common earthworm of our gardens.

Although the body wall of annelids consists of three layers as in flatworms, ribbon worms and round worms, the internal structure is more complex and exhibits a feature found in all higher animals. This is the presence of a body cavity, the *coelom*, formed by division into two of the middle layer of cells. This fluid-filled coelom separates the gut wall from the body wall, thus allowing independent movement of each.

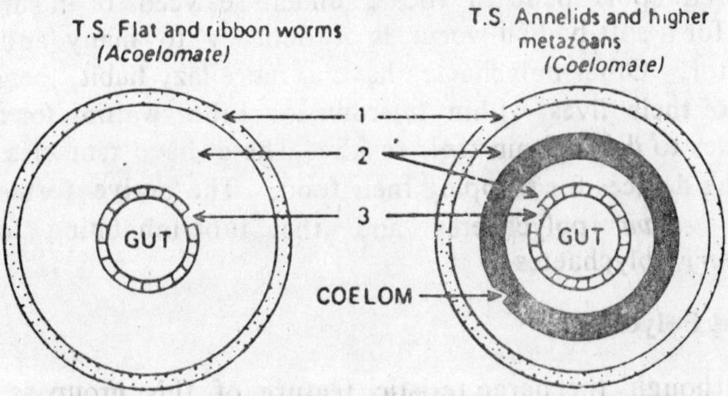

Figure 20.1. The two types of body structure, *Acoelomate* and *Coelomate* (1) outer layer, *ectoderm*, (2) middle layer, *mesoderm*, (3) inner layer, *endoderm*,

The external rings indicate that this coelom is divided by septa into sections or segments, each with the same basic structure, though the organs are in specific regions. Longitudinal and circular muscle layers are present and their alternate contraction and relaxation generates body movement.

The phylum is divided into three classes, *POLYCHAETA* (bristle-worms), *OLIGOCHAETA*) (earthworms) and *HIRUDINEA* (leeches), but all the marine worms belong to the first class.

POLYCHAETA

These are commonly known as the marine bristle-worms, whose chitinous bristles or chaetae arise from parapodia, the paired appendages of each segment. These locomotory 'feet' are developed into paddle-like structures for swimming in some species. All have a distinct head, usually with eyes, and bearing several appendages.

This is a very large and abundant class and some of its five thousand or more members are to be found in every marine habitat. Many of the bristle-worms, such as the ragworms used for bait, crawl, creep or swim in their constant search for food and have well-developed chitinous jaws for capturing their prey. However, they limit their foraging forays to well-sheltered spots beneath rocks, under seaweeds or in surface mud, for a soft-bodied worm is a delicacy to many another predator. Other polychaetes have a more lazy habit, spending most of their lives within burrows or tubes waiting for food particles to drift within their reach. These have tentacles and filtering devices for trapping their food. The active forms are called *errant* polychaetes and the tube-inhabiting forms *sedentary* polychaetes.

Errant Polychaetes

Although thecharac teristic feature of this group is the activity of its members, most of the worms resort to burrowing in the sand or mud for protection, but these burrows are only temporary structures.

Structure. In errant polychaetes he head segment usually bears a pair of small antennae, fleshy tactile structures called palps, one or more pairs of eyes and short feelers called *cirri*. The parapodia are well developed, bear many chaetae as well as dorsal and ventral cirri. In the scale worms, the scales or *elytra* are probably formed fiom enlarged and flattened cirri.

Locomotion. The parapodia of errant polychaetes are muscular, and locomotory movements are accomplished by the combined action of these muscles and those of the longitudinal layer. The two sides of each segment are in opposition to each other ; when the longitudinal muscles on the left contract, those on the right relax and vice versa. When the left parapodium points backwards the right points forwards. The parapodia move in an oarlike fashion, the backward stroke giving the propulsive force. Waves of contraction travel forwards along the length of the worm, but as the two sides are out of phase, instead of progressing in a straight line, the body undulates from side to side.

When crawling, the chaetae are extended to grip the substratum during the backward stroke, but are retracted as the parapodium sweeps forward. The same actions and undulations of the body are effected in swimming, but the lateral movement traverses a wider area and the parapodia function as paddles. However, except in the paddleworms, this appears to be an inefficient method of swimming as the majority soon descend to the bottom and resort to crawling.

When squeezing their way through narrow cracks and crevices the body form becomes thinner and longer by the contraction of the circular layer of muscle.

Respiratory Mechanism. In the majority of errant polychaetes the parapodia are the principal regions of gaseous exchange as these contain networks of capillaries just below the surface, but some diffusion occurs over the whole surface of the body. A few species have small gills.

Food and Feeding. Some bristle-worms are carnivorous, feeding on any small animals such as molluscs, crustaceans or even annelids, but most are omnivorous. Whatever the diet, the food particles are relatively large, and must be grasped and guided into the mouth. To accomplish this the worms have an eversible pharynx or *proboscis,* bearing two strong chitinous jaws for gripping the food, which is drawn inwards as the proboscis retracts. Some species have additional smaller teeth on the proboscis.

This is the normal mode of feeding, but when in its burrow, other methods may be adopted. For instance, *Nereis diversicolor* secretes a mucous cone within the entrance of its burrow and then draws a water current through it. In this way the cone acts as a filter and periodically the worm swallows it and the contained food particles.

Reproduction. The sexes are separate but the eggs and spermatozoa are discharged into the sea, making fertilization a haphazard process. However, many species counteract this by congregating or swarming during the spawning period so that the sexual products are shed in close proximity. The nearness of the females stimulates release of sperms in the males, then the presence of spermatozoa in the water incites the females to liberate their eggs.

Some of the paddleworms stay close together on the mud or sand during spawning and secrete a mucous capsule around the batch of fertilized eggs. *Eulalia viridis* deposits such capsules.

In some of the scaleworms the females retain the eggs and developing larvae in a cavity beneath the scales.

Other bristle-worms which normally crawl around in the mud undergo considerable changes in structure at the time of spawning. The posterior region of the body, which contains the ripening gametes, becomes modified for swimming ; the parapodia develop into efficient paddles. Both sexes then swim to the surface and release their spawn, stimulation occurring as above. When in this form they are called *heteronereids* because at one time they were thought to be a separate species. The time of spawning is often specific, that is during certain weeks only related to the phase of the moon The classical example of this is the *Palalo* worm of the Pacific, where the exact time of arrival at the surface can be predicted, and thus the worms can be caught for food.

In the females there are no special ducts for the passage of the eggs to the exterior, so the body wall ruptures and damage to the tissues is often so great that death occurs soon after spawning.

In the majority of species the eggs hatch out into planktonic larvae, the dispersal stage in their life histories. Some are the simple *trochospheres* which gradually metamorphose into minute segmented wormlike forms and, after loss of the ciliated bands, sink to the bottom to commence adult life. In *Nereis* the larvae are well developed with three pairs of parapodia to help in swimming ; these are *nectochaete* larvae.

Asexual reproduction may occur in some species by simple fragmentation of the body into two parts, each section developing a new head or tail region In some species of syllid polychaetes this split occurs along a predetermined segment, the posterior region then being called the *stolon* and the remaining anterior region the *stock*. Sometimes the new head and tail regions develop before the stolon is liberated and occasionally a second stollon forms before liberation of the first and so on, thus forming a chain of worms.

Regeneration. Some of the errant polychaetes readily regenerate, but others do not.

Common Species

Ragworms. *Nereis diversicolor* has a distinct red line down its back though its body colour may vary from yellow or orange-brown to green and its length from 6 to 9 cm. It is widely distributed and lives in sand or mud on the middle and lower shores ; because of its ability to survive in low salinities it is found in estuaries. It does *not* develop into a heteronereid ;

spawning occurs in the burrows and the larvae are *not* planktonic.

N. fucata is not normally an inhabitant of the shore, but must be mentioned as it is the ragworm found living commensally with the large hermit crab in the coiled tip of the whelk shell. Whed the crab feeds, the worm extends its head over the crab's right shoulder in the hope of gathering a few scraps of food.

N. virens is a much larger worm which may be from 20 to 40 cm. in length and because of outgrowths on the back of the parapodia is sometimes mistaken for a paddleworm. It is basically green, but iridescence gives it purplish tints. It lives in muddy sand under rocks on the northern coasts of Britain.

Paddleworms *Eulalia viridis* is a very common species of these actively swimming worms with paddle-like parapodia. During low water it is found crawling among sponges and other encrustations on rocks of the middle and lower shores. It may be from 4 to 10 cm long and is unmistakable by its grass green colour. Its green spherical egg-capsule, suspended by a thin thread from *Fucus*, is also easily seen during spring and early summer.

Scaleworms. All the members of this family have scales or *elytra* folded across their back, and the body is not typically worm-shaped as it is much shorter and broader. They are most readily identified by the number of pairs of these interlocking scales, but for this a hand-lens and reference book are necessary. Species of the genus *Harmothoe* are particularly common under stones and among seaweeds of the middle and lower shores. They are about 1-3 cm long and some live commensally, sharing the burrows of other animals. Also encountered among the strandline debris is the larger sealeworm, the seamouse, *Aphrodite aculeata*, though is not an inhabitant of the shore.

Catworms. The commonest species of these flattened, pearly-coloured carnivorous worms is *Nephthys hombergi*, which is

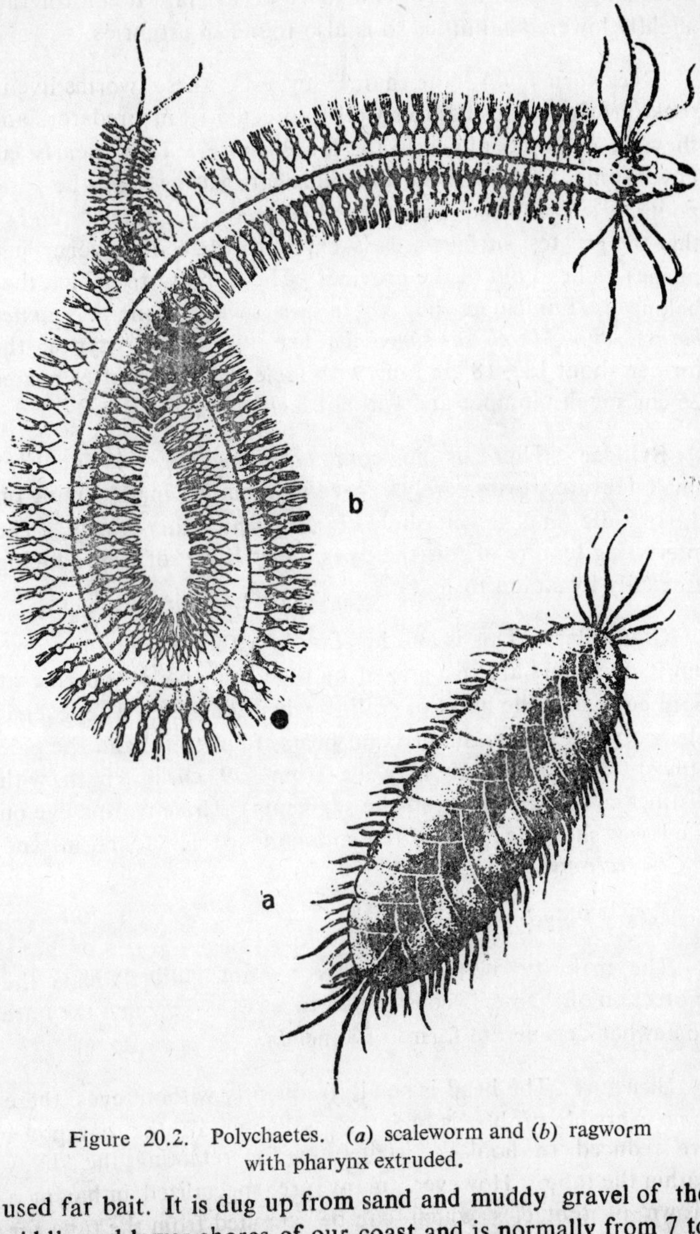

Figure 20.2. Polychaetes. (*a*) scaleworm and (*b*) ragworm with pharynx extruded.

used far bait. It is dug up from sand and muddy gravel of the middle and lower shores of our coast and is normally from 7 to

9 cm long, though it may grow to 18 or 19 cm. It can tolerate slightly lowered salinities so is also found in estuaries.

Rockworms. As the name suggests, these worms live in rock crevices and fissures well protected from predators and they are mainly confined to the lower shore. They nearly all have some form of red gill filaments arising from the parapodia, often with the largest filaments at the anterior end so that the greatest surface area is exposed when the worm just pushes its head out of the crevice. The family to which they belong is Eunicidae, but there are several genera. *Eunice harassi* and *Marphysa sanguinea* are two similar types, the former about 12–18 cm long with feelers, but the latter nearer 25 cm, much plumper and without feelers.

Syllidae. There is no common name for this family of small delicate worms rarely exceeding 5 cm in length, living on the middle and lower shores in sand and under stones. The interesting feature of this family is their habit of reproducing asexually by stolon formation.

Glyceridae. This is another family with no common name, but its members are recognized by their thin body tapering at both ends, and the habit of coiling when touched. The eversible proboscis is pear-shaped and bears four teeth, and the pale almost transparent body may be from 3-9 cm in length, with distinct circular lines on all the segments. These worms live on the lower shore and one of the common species found in sand is *Ciycera convoluta*.

Sedentary Polychaetes

The majority of these worms do not willingly leave the protection of their self-constructed tube or burrow and they are somewhat degenerate forms of annelids.

Structure. The head is small, frequently without eyes, there is no eversible proboscis or jaws, and some of the parapodia are reduced to hooklike structures for retaining the body within the tube. However, many are specialized in having a crown of tentacles which can be extended from the tube for feeding on plankton or detritus, and filamentous gills on the anterior segments for breathing. The body form tends to be broad at the head, gradually tapering off to a point, whereas in errant polychaetes the width is more or less uniform throughout the length of the worm.

Locomotion. Locomotion is confined to wriggling movement within the burrow or tube which may include protrusion and withdrawal of the head region from the entrance. This activity is accomplished by the normal body movements of annelids—alternate contraction and relaxation of the circular and longitudinal muscles.

Respiratory Mechanism. As in errant polychaetes, some gaseous exchange occurs over the whole surface of the body, but sedentary forms also have well-developed gills. In some species these are used solely for breathing, but in others they have two functions—breathing and feeding. In the former group the gills are feathery outgrowths from the more anterior segments. The terebellid *Amphitrite johnstoni* found hidden in gravel beneath small stones has three pairs of these distinctly red gills. The lugworm, *Arenicola marina*, has many pairs distributed along the length of its body which are aerated by the continuous current of water flowing from the rear to the front entrance of the burrow.

In the second group the outgrowths are in the form of a crown of tentacles, bearing fine, hairlike branches, capable of trapping food particles present in the water, while gaseous exchange occurs over their surface. The beautiful peacock worm, *Sabella pavonina*, is a fine example of this type of polychaete.

Food and Feeding. The sedentary polychaetes are either suspension and deposit feeders, and are omnivorous.

Suspension or plankton feeders are the fan worms and other forms bearing a crown of tentacles used for straining plankton from the water. These tentacles also function as respiratory surfaces. Minute cilia on the tentacles beat in such a way that they waft the trapped food parrticles into the mouth. These tentacles are extended very slowly, but can be retracted rapidly at the slightest disturbance. In some worms, such as the small coiled *Spirorbis* found on serrated and bladder wrack, one of the tentacle terminates in a flattened structure, the *operculum*, which closes over the aperture when the worm is safely inside the tube.

Deposit or detritus feeders are of two types : those with long feelers for collecting detritus from the substratum and those which eat large quantities of sand or mud containing fine particles of organic matter. In the former the feelers or tentacles are long and narrow and, while the worm remains protected below, these extend over a wide area in search of detritus deposited on the surface. These very muscular tentacles creep over the substratum as they elongate and contract, but the limit of the exploratory region is determined by the length of a fully spread tentacle. Gland cells secrete a sticky substance for trapping any food encountered and the minute particles are then transported to the mouth by ciliary action down the central groove formed by the inrolled edges of the tentacles. Targer particles are carried to the mouth by inward coiling of the tentacles.

The common sand or mud eater is the lugworm, *Arenicola marina.* It has an extrusible proboscis but no jaws, and continuously ingests sand or mud, digesting any contained organic matter as it passes through the gut, the remaining sand being egested in the form of the familiar wormcast on the surface.

Reproduction. The sexes are usually separate, the eggs and sperms being released into the water without the worms leaving the safety of their homes. Fertilization is therefore external and in most instances planktonic larvae of the *trochosphere* form develop. A few are hermaphrodites and some retain the developing eggs within the cavity of the tube.

Regeneration. Tentacles are often damaged and these are readily regenerated.

Common Species

There are many sedentary polychaetes on all British coasts belonging to numerous families, but for recognition on the shore it is preferable to consider them according to the type of tube or burrow.

Calcareous Tubes. The worms which form a limy tube all have a crown of feathery tentacles with the dual function of breathing and feeding ; an operculum is present for closure of the entrance. This reduces the possibility of dehydration when the tide is out. These worms all belong to the family Serpulidae.

Small white, coiled tubes of approximately 2 mm overall diameter, commonly found on *Fucus serratus* and *F. vesiculosus*, belong to *Spirorbis*. These worms are hermaphrodes, eggs developing in the anterior and spermatozoa in the posterior segments. When fertilized the developing eggs are retained in the cavity of the tube. There are two common species, *Spirorbis borealis* and *S. spirillum*, readily distinguished as the tube of the former coils clockwise and of the latter anticlockwise.

The white tube found adhering to stones and shells on the lower shore with a triangular cross-section, elongated and tapering to a point is that of *Pomatoceros triqueter*. The tubes usually reach a length of 5 or 6 cm, though larger specimens may be found. The sexes are separate and *trochosphere* larvae develop about two days after fertilization.

The tubes of two species which live well below low water mark are often cast ashore after winter storms. These are *Hydroides norvegica* which, like *Pomatoceros*, adheres to stones but has a smooth cylindrical tube only 3 or 4 cm long, and *Serpula vermicularis* with a pinkish cylindrical tube some 8 cm long, several tubes often being entwined together.

Tubes Protruding from the Substratum. Some of these tubes are made of mud only, but others contain small pieces of broken shells or stones ; in either case the worm secretes mucus to hold the particles in position.

The peacock worm, *Sabella pavonina*, has a cylindrical tube of fine mud up to 30 cm and 5 to 6 mm in diameter, attached to stones in mud or gravelly sand of the lower shore, with the upper 8 or 9 cm extending above the surface The worm is only about half the length of the tube so it is well protected when retracted. *Myxicola infundibulum* has a thick mud tube, much greater in diameter than the worm, sunk within the mud so that the head opening is level with the surface. It is found on the lower shore of muddy beaches. *Branchiomma vesiculosum* has many particles of shell and stones embedded in the lower region of the tube which may be 30 cm long, though only about 2.5 cm extends above the surface. It is found in sandy gravel on the lower shore, particularly on the south and south-west coasts. These three worms are members of the sabellid family and have the dual-purpose crown of tentacles.

Sand-masons *Lanice conchilega*, are abundant on the lower regions of sandy shores with their fringed tubes protruding about 3 or 4 cm above the ground. These tubes also contain embedded particles. Sand-masons have fine pale pink extensible tentacles for feeding only, plus three pairs of filamentous gills on the anterior segments. Sand-masons belong to the terebellid family.

Tubes of Sand. *Sabellaria* is the colonial polychaete whose tubes form a honeycomb in sand of the middle and lower shores. Each worm is only 2-3 cm long and has a crown of dual-purpose tentacles.

The tube of *Pectinaria* is conical and open at both ends, and the worm moves through the sand with its tube held at an oblique angle, the narrow opening uppermost. The tube is very fragile, about 4-5 cm long and 5 mm in diameter at the wide end. Usually only empty tubes are found on sandy shores as this species lives in the sub-littoral zone.

Tubes in Rocks and Shells. *Bispira* belongs to the same family as the peacock worm, but it forms its flexible mud tube within rock cracks of the lower shore. The tube is approximately 10 mm in diameter and 20 cm long, though only 2-3 cm protrudes from the rock face.

Polydora is minute in comparison and has the unique habit of boring a small U-shaped tube in rock and extending it with mud to a height of about 10 mm above the surface. When covered with water a pair of threadlike coiling tentacles project from one of the openings, and their waving movements indicate the worm's presence in the sides and floor of shallow limestone rock pools. *Polydora* is also found in shells and, as its body is soft, it would seem that boring is accomplished by a chemical process. Separate gills are present for breathing.

No Tubes—Burrows in Mud, Sand or Gravel Held Open by Mucus. The most familiar polychaete burrower of our shores is the lugworm, *Arenicola marina*, whose U-shaped burrow has already been described. The lugworm has thirteen pairs of filamentous gills along the middle region of its body and it feeds on organic detritus within the sand or mud it ingests. The sexes are separate, the reproductive products being discharged into the burrow and hence to the surface, but during low water only, to ensure that they are washed up the beach by the incoming tide. Here, high on the shore, the larvae hatch out four or five days after the eggs are fertilized. Although capable of swimming, they are not planktonic but bottom dwellers, spending their time in the surface layers of sand. Later the young worms migrate back down to the middle and lower zones, but do not reproduce until they are about two years old. Spawning occurs in the autumn, usually during neap tides, after which many of the worms die.

Redthreads, *Audouinia tentaculata*, burrow in muddy gravel below stones where there is an ample supply of detritus. The body is pointed at both ends and the fine feeding tentacles, usually reddish in colour, explore the substratum for organic matter. When a stone is dislodged these tentacles, which tend to coil, are seen writhing and twisting in all directions, but are rapidly withdrawn below the surface. Threadlike gills are present on most segments of the worm. This species, which is 6—15 cm long, is common on middle and lower shores of the south, but is replaced in the north by the smaller *Cirratulus cirratus* whose tentacles do not exhibit such coiling.

Several species of the genus *Amphitrite* also live on the lower shore in sand or gravel below stones, but the body tapers towards the tail. The anterior region bears a crown of pinkish-orange feeding tentacles, and there are either two or three pairs of filamentous red gills.

21

Phylum : Bryozoa (Polyzoa)

Sea-mats

Seaweed fronds are sometimes covered with a thin, lacework tracery, adhering closely to the surface, in no way resembling animals, although they are bryozoan colonies. Another name for the members of this phylum is polyzoans ; they are commonly called sea-mats.

Each individual of the colony secretes a protective chamber around itself and *en masse* these chambers form the encrusting layer. During low water the animals remain hidden away, but on the return of the tide they protrude their soft bodies, extending their crown of tentacles for food collection. When expanded, bryozoans resemble polyps and are therefore often mistaken for hydroids. However, their structure is entirely different and more complex. Bryozoans have no common connection between individuals of the colony as in hydroids ; their body wall consists of three layers of cells instead of two ; the gut has two openings instead of one ; a coelom is present and the tentacles bear cilia.

Skeleton. The protective boxlike chambers are limy or chitinous. In the common sea-mat, *Membranipora membranacea*, the bottom and sides are limy, but the cover is chitinous, giving some flexibility. The bottom is fixed to the substratum and the four sides are in contact with neighbouring boxes, but there is no link between individuals. Although a colony, each member leads a separate existence.

Respiratory Mechanism. Gaseous exchange occurs over the surface of the tentacles.

Food and Feeding. Bryozoans feed on small particles suspended in the water which may be animals and plants of the plankton or detritus, so these creatures are omnivorous feeders. The ciliated tentacles extend in a funnel shape and water currents, produced by the beating cilia, direct food particles downwards into the mouth.

Reproduction. Bryozoans are usually hermaphrodites, and the eggs and spermatozoa are released into the coelom where fertilization takes place. Some development may occur before discharge into the water via a speciál pore in the body wall. Eventually *cyphonaute* larvae hatch out and spend a period in the plankton before settlement and metamorphosis. This is the dispersal stage in the life history of bryozoans. Asexual reproduction by budding increases the size of a colony.

Regeneration. Bryozoans have an amazing ability to regenerate. Periodically the tentacles, gut and other tissues degenerate into a compact brown mass and new structures are regenerated from the body wall ; the brown mass, now within the new gut, is egested through the anus.

Common Species

Colonies of *Membranipora membranacea* form a crust of whitish, rectangular chambers on *Laminaria* and *Fucus.*

Flustrellidra (=*Flustrella*) *hispida* forms thick greyish-brown crusts around the base of seaweeds, particularly *Gigartina stellata, Chondrus crispus, Ascophyllum nodosum* and *Fucus.* The chambers are more oval than in *Membranipora* and bear horny spines.

Bugula, which is found under overhanging rocks alongside sponges and red seaweeds, particularly resembles hydroids. The colony is plantlike with a main 'stem' bearing spirally arranged branches forming a corkscrew pattern, but the individual compartments are too small to be distinguished with the naked eye. The pale yellow-orange tufts, from 3-5 cm. long, hang downwards and are found on all coasts.

Unlike the other sea-mats, *Alcyonidium* forms a greenish-yellow or grey gelatinous colony, irregularly lobed and finger-like in appearance. It is found among seaweeds low on the shore and at a glance might be mistaken for a sponge *Alcyonidium* may be encrusting or erect. On the shore the colonies are small, but in shallow water they may reach a length of 30 cm.

Hornwrack, *Flustra foliacea,* does not inhabit the littoral zone, but is so frequently washed ashore that it justifies inclusion. The pale yellow or buff colony forms flattened, dichotomously branching fronds, terminating in broad rounded tips, with the rectangular chambers facing outwards on either side. Hornwrack may be 10-15 cm. long and is widely distributed around British coasts.

22

Phylum : Arthropoda

This is the largest phylum of the animal kingdom and includes shrimps, prawns, crabs, butterflies, moths, beetles, grasshoppers, spiders, mites and centipedes, to name just a few.

Arthropods are the animals with jointed limbs (*arthro*—joint *poda*—feet). Their bodies are segmented, but the segments are not all similar as in the annelids and often, at first glance, segmentation is not at all obvious, as is the case when looking at the dorsal surface of a crab. All have an exoskeleton formed of a tough non-living substance, *chitin*, secreted by the outer cells of the animal. This is thickened in parts, but thin at the joints, and movement of the limbs is accomplished by pairs of antagonistic muscles attached to the inner surface of the skeleton. Being outside the soft body an exoskeleton affords the greatest protection, but it has the disadvantage that it does not increase in size and therefore must be shed periodically to allow for growth ; that is, arthropods moult or carry out *ecdysis* Before the old skeleton is shed a new soft one develops below then, as soon as the old is cast off, the animal expands its body to the full, stretching the soft new skeleton before it has time to harden, Once exposed to the surrounding medium—water if aquatic and air if terrestrial—the new exoskeleton begins to harden. The length of time for complete hardening varies with the different species, but during this period the animal is very vulnerable, so it hides away until it is again fully protected. Ecdysis occurs frequently in the larval stages, but rarely once maturity is reached.

In the majority of arthropods the young or *larvae* are of a different form from the adult and sometimes even live in a different environment, as for example the caddis fly, whose early larval days are spent in the bottom of a pond. This means that *metamorphosis* occurs in the life history of these animals.

The Arthropoda have representatives living in all environments and the phylum is divided into five classes : the CRUSTACEA (prawns, crabs and their relatives), INSECTA (butterflies, moths, flies, etc.), ARACHNIDA (spiders and mites), MYRIAPODA (centipeds and millipedes) and ONYCHOPHORA (*Peripatus*) However, with the exception of two or three species, all the marine members come within the class CRUSTACEA.

CRUSTACEA

The crustaceans include barnacles, shrimps, prawns, crabs, lobsters and their relatives, and are readily distinguished from any other arthropods by the presence of *two* pairs of antennae on the head. The body is divided into three regions : *head thorax* and *abdomen*. The head is formed of six fused segments and bears three pairs of jointed appendages which function as jaws Often the head and thorax are indistinguishable ; the combined region is called the *cephalothorax* and its fused exoskeleton the *carapace*. In the large species, such as crabs and lobsters, the carapace is strengthened with lime. Breathing is by means of gills and the many paired appendages are modified for various functions. The larvae are usually pelagic and therefore members of the temporary plankton Most crustaceans are active creatures, but a few are sedentary, such as the barnacles, and some have degenerated into the parasitic mode of life such as *Sacculina*, whose host is the shore crab.

The Crustacea exhibit such great variety in form and habit that they are divided into several sub-classes, but only two have shore representatives of sufficient size for our consideration. These are the *CIRRIPEDIA* (barnacles) and the *MALACOSTRACA* (shrimps, prawns, lobsters, crabs, sandhoppers, etc.).

However, mention must be made of the sub-class *COPEPODA* as these small crustaceans are abundant in the plankton and economically important in forming the basic food of many fish and other marine creatures. These are the 'oar-footed' crustaceans, with the thoracic legs modified for swimming, but with no appendages on the abdomen. The commonest in British coastal waters is *Calanus*, the principal food of herrings. The copepod larval stage is the *nauplius* which forms part of the temporary plankton and thus may be eaten by the adults of its own species.

Sub-Class : CIRRIPEDIA

These are the barnacles which are one of the commonest animals found on our rocky shores. They are sedentary animals—an unusual feature in crustaceans—but the larval stages swim freely in the plankton. The stalked or goose barnacles are not inhabitants of the shore but may be found attached to planks of wood and other floating debris washed up on the beach.

Exoskeleton. The exoskeleton is formed of several small, hard, limy plates, and in most acorn barnacles six overlapping, immovable plates form the boxlike structure containing the animal, with two pairs of movable plates closing over the top to form the operculum. When the tide is out this is all that can be seen as the operculum is tightly closed to prevent dehydration. These barnacles adhere so firmly to rocks that thny are capable of withstanding the fiercest onslaught of rough seas, and it is interesting to note that each stands on its head, being cemented in position by a secretion from glands in the antennae.

In goose barnacles the head is attached to the leathery stalk which suspends the animal from a floatidg object. and there are only five thin, delicate plates forming the flattened shell. In parasitic forms the shell is lost.

Structure. The body within the exoskeleton bears normal crustacean mouth-parts and six pairs of jointed thoracic legs, but the abdomen is greatly reduced and has no appendages.

Respiratory Mechanism. Gaseous exchange occurs over filamentous regions of the thoracic legs.

Food and Feeding. Barnacles are plankton feeders and are said to 'kick the food into their mouths' because the thoracic legs, bearing stiff hairs, sieve the food material from the sea water and then pass it back to the mouth. By watching acorn barnacles below water in an aquarium these in-and-out sweeping leg movements can be observed. Stalked barnacles trap food in the same way.

Reproduction. Barnacles are hermaphrodites, but cross-fertilization usually occurs. Each barnacles has an extensible penis which it protrudes through the open operculum extending it into a neighbouring shell for sperm transference. The fertilized eggs hatch out into *nauplius* larvae and escape into the plankton. These moult several times and develop into *cypris* larvae which eventually alight head downwards on a rock, secrete cement to fix themselves in position and metamorphose into adults.

Although carried about in the plankton, cypris larvae usually settle in areas alredy well covered with barnacles. This gregarious habit ensures cross-fertilization, but it tends towards overcrowding.

Common Species

Acorn barnacles differ in the arrangement and shape of the shell plates so in old, weathered specimens identification is often difficult. The diameter of the base of adult shells ranges from 10 to 20 mm in the different species, but even in individual species there is diversity of size depending on favourability of position on the shore, for although a certain barnacle exists over a wide area, only a small region is the *ideal* environment.

Chthamalus stellatus inhabits the upper and middle zones of exposed shores of the south-west and west coasts so is flatter thaa the other species and the edges of the plates are fluted. When inhabiting more sheltered area, *Chthamalus* does not extend so far down the shore. The larvae settle fairly late in the year around September and October.

In contrast *Balanus balanoides* prefers more sheltered shores of all coasts though it is more abundant in the north and is usually found between MHWN and MLWN. If present on the same shore as *Chthamalus*, it is always below the latter.

B. perforatus is the largest acorn barnacle and it inhabits the lower half of shores of the south-west ; its larvae settle during August and September. *B. crenatus* inhabits the lower shore on all coasts. It is not found on exposed rock surfaces, but attached to stones, shells other crustaceans, etc. Its larvae settle between May and July, though it may be later in northern areas.

Another barnacle which is becoming fairly common high on middle shores is *Elminius modestus*, introduced from Australia in the 1940s. The shell is formed of *four* plates only, so it is easily identified. Its larvae settle throughout the year.

The stalked or goose barnacles which may be found in masses on wood washed ashore belong to the genus *Lepas*.

The commonest parasitic cirriped to be found on the shore is *Sacculina carcini* which parasitizes the shore crab, *Carcinus maenas*, appearing as a pale yellow, fleshy, saclike structure on the abdomen of the host. This contains the reproductive organs, but the main body of the parasite is a system of rootlike sturctures spreading throughout the tissues of the host for absorption of food. The planktonic larvae are typical of barnacles and, when ready to metamorphosise, the *cypris* attaches itself by means of its antennae to a suitable host, then penetrates into the tissues where development occurs. Crabs attacked by *Sacculina* undergo certain morphological changes, so that a male tends towards the female form and a female towards the juvenile form. This is called *parasitic castration* and if the parasite is removed the host returns to its normal form.

Another parasite, *Peltogaster paguri,* appears as a yellow-orange curved sac on the abdomen of the hermit crab, *Pagurus (=Eupagurus) bernhardus.*

Sub-Class : MALACOSTRACA

In this group the head is typical of all crustaceans, but in addition bears compound eyes, usually on stalks. These eyes, composed of many minute lenses, have the advantage of giving a wide field of view but the disadvantage of an indistinct image. The thorax consists of eight segments, each bearing a pair of appendages, with the first two or three pairs, called *maxillipeds,* modified for feeding. The abdomen has six segments, each with a pair of appendages.

As most of the seashore crustaceans come within this large sub-class, for ease of discussion, we will consider them in smaller groups. There are many divisions, but here we are interested only in the following Orders : MYSIDACEA (opossum shrimps), ISOPODA (sea-slaters), AMPHIPODA (sand-hoppers) and DECAPODA (shrimps, prawns, lobsters, crabs).

Order : MYSIDACEA

These are dainty, transparent shrimplike swimming crustaceans, not more than 20 mm long, with large, stalked eyes.

Exoskeleton. The thin carapace extends back over all the eight thoracic segments, but is fused to the first three only.

Locomotion. The mysids use all their abdominal appendages in swimming by a forwards rowing movement. The eight pairs of branched thoracic legs bear *setae*—small bristles—to help in movement through the water, and the abdominal appendages are small swimmerets, with the last pair flattened to form a tail fan.

Respiratory Mechanism. Some species have gills attached to certain appendages for breathing, but when these are absent, gaseous exchange occurs through the thin lining of the carapace. A current of water is directed under the carapace by the first pair of thoracic limbs.

Food and Feeding. The mysids are omnivorous and have two methods of feeding, depending on the size of the food particles. Large particles are grasped by the linner branches of the thoracic limbs and held in position for biting and crushing by the mandibles or jaws. Small particles are filtered from the water by setae on the inner border of the third pair of mouth-parts, then passed to the mandibles and into the mouth. The thoracic limbs are concerned in this filter feeding as their rotary movements direct currents of water towards the mouth. When plankton is in short supply the mysids swim to the bottom, stir up the detritus so that it becomes susbended and then feed on it.

Reproduction. The sexes are separate, and the developing eggs are carried by the female in a special brood pouch formed from flat, incurved, overlapping plates borne on the base of the posteriar thoracic limbs. The eggs hatch directly into miniature adults. Breeding usually occurs in spring and summer ; there may be two or even three generations in one year.

Common Species

Chameleon shrimps, *Praunus*, are 18—20 mm long and hold their body in a slightly curved position. They are abundant all around our coasts in rock pools, among seaweeds and also in esturaries, as they are tolerant of slightly lowered salinities.

Neomysis, about 17 mm long, is abundant in estuaries and frequently many can be seen crowded together at the edge of the sea as it gradually covers the mudbanks.

Ghost shrimps, *Schistomysis*, about 18—19 mm long, are widely distributed, and found at the edge of the sea as well as in estuaries.

Species of the genus *Mysis* and many other mysids do not inhabit the shore, but are planktonic.

Order : ISOPODA

The isopods are small crustaceans not normally exceeding

about 25 mm in length, with the body flattened dorso-ventrally (from above downwards) ; they have sessile eyes (not on stalks). The first thoracic segment is fused with the head, so isopods appear to have seven thoracic segments only and their seven pairs of legs are all similar, hence the name of the order (*iso*–equal, *poda*–feet). The abdomen is formed of six segments only and some of these may be fused together. They are all similar in form to the familiar terrestrial species, the woodlouse of our gardens, and many curl the body just as a woodlouse when disturbed. Some littoral isopods show a marked ability to blend with their background. This ability is due to the presence of chromatophores, but in these animals there is no change in actual colour, only in shade from light to dark.

Exoskeleton. There is no carapace so all segments can be observed from the dorsal surface.

Locomotion. Many of the isopods creep or crawl in between cracks and over the surface of rocks ; their seven pairs of thoracic walking legs are well adapted for this mode of locomotion. Other species swim vigorously by rapid beating of the flattened abdominal appendages. *Sphaeroma* has the unusual habit of swimming on its back.

Respiratory Mechanism. The flattened, broad, plate-like abdominal appendages serve as regions of gaseous exchange.

Food and Feeding. Most isopods and scavengers and therefore omnivorous feeders, using all their mouth-parts in scraping and biting their food. Some species browse on seaweeds which they cut into pieces with their mandibles, while others feed on wood particles, for example the gribble, *Limnoria*.

Reproduction. The sexes are separate and, as with the mysids, the female carries the developing eggs in a brood pouch from which the young hatch as miniature adults.

Common Species

The sea-slater, *Ligia oceanica*, of our rocky coasts is

confined to the upper shore and splash zone where, during daylight hours, it hides up under stones, in cracks and crevices in rocks and sea walls. Further protection from predators is afforded by its ability to blend with the background. After dark is the best time to look for sea-slaters as this is when they venture a little way down the beach to browse on brown seaweeds, their favourite food, though they will feed on any debris, animal or vegetable. Catching one is difficult, as they run fast on their seven pairs of legs and soon disappear out of sight. *Ligia* is one of our largest seashore isopods, reaching some 20–25 mm in length, and is so adapted to terrestrial life that it cannot survive continued submersion.

Sphaeroma is one of the swimming forms often encountered in pools of the middle shore and also in estuarine pools as it can tolerate some dilution of sea water. It swims on its back and curls the body into a ball for protection against predators, or desiccation when the tide is out.

The gribble, *Limnoria lignorum*, about 5 mm long, is a boring form which feeds on the wood particles as it tunnels its way through piers or groynes. The wood is cut away by the action of the mandibles.

Some isopods are parasites and we have already mentioned *Bopyrus squillarum* which lives in the branchial chamber of the common prawn, appearing as a green swelling. This is the female, about 10 mm long, but the male, only 2 mm long, is out of sight as he is attached to the female's abdominal appendages.

Isopods are found on all shores, but for identification of species close examination with a hand-lens is necessary, in conjunction with a suitable identification manual.

Order : AMPHIPODA

The amphipods or sandhoppers are small crustaceans up to about 25 mm in length with the body flattened laterally (from side to side) and the tail region curled under the body. They are similar to isopods in having sessile eyes, seven thoracic and six abdominal segments, though the terminal three may be fused together. The seven pairs of thoracic legs are not identical as they vary in length, and the first two pairs are modified for grasping, having some form of nippers ; thus only five pairs are used for walking.

Exoskeleton. There is no carapace.

Locomotion. The five pairs of thoracic walking legs are used for crawling and the first three pairs of abdominal appendages for swimming, but the amphipods have another method of locomotion which gives them their common name of sandhoppers—apparent jumping or hopping. This is accomplished by the sudden extension of the incurved tail region.

Respiratory Mechanism. Simple gills for gaseous exchange are borne at the base of the thoracic appendages.

Food and Feeding. The amphipods feed on any form of debris, but more particularly on decay vegetable matter. The two pairs of nippers grasp the food and pass it to the mandibles for biting and crushing before it is swallowed. Occasionally an amphipod, such as *Corophium*, filters off fine food particles from mud by sieving it through setae frining the edge of the nippers, and then passing the trapped material to the mouth.

Reproduction. The sexes are separate and, as in isopods developing eggs are carried by the female in a brood pouch. When the young hatch out they have the adult form.

Common Species

The common sandhopper, *Talitrus saltator*, burrows just above high water mark during the day, but comes out at night, foraging for food in the debris of the driftline. A near relative, the shore hopper *Orchestia gammarella*, lives high up on rocky shores among the decaying seaweeds. Both grow to approximately 20 mm.

Corophium volutator is the commonest burrowing amphipod

found on muddy shores, particularly in the lowered salinities of estuaries. Although it lives in burrows, it can crawl over the surface of the mud in search of food and it is capable of swimming. When it is within the U-shaped burrow, its abdominal appendages beat in such a way that a current of water flows over the body from the head backwards, bringing a continuous supply of oxygen and also microscopic food particles. The latter are filtered off and passed to the mouth. *Crophhium* is about 8–9 mm long.

Gammarus locusta, which can be up to 25 mm long, is the amphipod exposed when a stone is overturned on the middle or lower shore. It is not so active as the sand and shore hoppers, but it crawls away on its side when disturbed. There are several other species of *Gammarus* and between them they inhabit areas of all salinities ; each is so specific to its environment that they are salinity indicators.

The rather weird-looking skeleton shrimps, *Caprella*, which we found crawling on seaweeds, hydroids and other sedentary creatures of the lower rocky shore, are amphipods though their bodies are long and thin compared with other members of the group. This helps in camouflage as, when still, they appear to be like fine seaweed threads.

Order : DECAPODA

The decapods include the largest and most familiar crustaceans of our shores, the most characteristic feature of the order being the presence of five pairs of thoracic walking legs, with the first pair bearing *chelae*, that is nippers, claws, pincers.

Before discussing this important order, it will be helpful to look at the basic plan of the decapod body and its appendages.

Head : this bears five pairs of appendages

1. short antennae of antennules.
2. long antennae or feelers.
3. mandibles or jaws.

4. 1st maxillae } secondary mouth-parts.
5. 2nd maxillae }

Thorax : this bears eight pairs of appendages, though the first three pairs fold over the maxillae and appear to be part of the head region.

1, 2 and 3 maxillipeds—additional mouth-parts

4 1st pair of walking legs bearing large chelac

5 to 8 inclusive, walking legs.

Abdomen : this bears six pairs of appendages

1 to 5 inclusive, swimmerets

6 uropods—flattened appendages which form a tail fan with the terminal telson.

Some members of the DECAPODA are swimming forms—the NATANTIA (shrimps and prawns); others are walking forms – the REPTANTIA (lobsters and crabs).

As the head and thorax are completely fused, the only indication of segmentation is given by the paired appendages. In the abdomen the six segments are usually distinct, but in squat lobsters the abdomen is not extended as in common lobsters, but tucked under the thorax. In crabs the body is flattened from above and the greatly reduced abdomen is held tightly under the body, forming the region called the 'apron' by crab-fishermen.

Most decapods move out into deeper water during the winter months.

Exoskeleton The head and thorax are retained within a large carapace and, except at the joints, this is impregnated with lime to form a stout shell in the walking forms. The carapace is fused to the body along the dorsal surface, but not at the sides. This leaves a cavity between the shell and body and within this the gills are suspended—the branchial cavity or gill chamber. In the large decapods ingrowths of cuticle frequently occur to form a delicate internal framework called the *endophragmal* skeleton, which is needed as a base for the attachment of muscles. This can often be seen in partially disintegrated dead crabs washed up on the shore. In the large species moulting is infrequent in the adults ; males probably cast their exoskeleton every year, but the females only every other year.

Although the chelae are of equal size in young decapods, in the adults of some species one grows much larger than the other, as in the hermit crab whose large right claw blocks the entrance when he withdraws into his borrowed shell.

Sexual *dimorphism*, that is different forms in the male and female, is sometimes exhibited and we came across an excellent example of this on the sandy shore in the masked crab, the male having very long chelae, but the female ordinary short ones.

Locomotion. Shrimps and prawns swim by a paddling action of the swimmerets aided by the tail fan.

Lobsters walk along the bottom in a normal forwards direction using their walking legs, but assisted by the vibrating swimmerets.

Crabs progress sideways on their walking legs and are capable of running at a fair pace, if the need arises. They can move to the right or left ; the legs on the side of the direction of movement have a pulling action, while those on the other have a pushing action on the body. Some crabs can swim as well and these, such as the velvet swimming crabs of our rocky shores, have the last pair of legs modified into flattened paddles for moving sideways through the water.

Lobsters, squat lobsters and prawns have another mode of locomotion to which they resort when a rapid retreat is indicated. They suddenly flap and straighten the tail from the bent position, thus forcing themselves backwards through the water at a great rate.

Respiratory Mechanism. Well-developed gills, borne on the base of the thoracic limbs, are enclosed within the branchial cavity. Water enters laterally under the edge of the carapace, is drawn upwards and forwards across the gills so that gaseous exchange may occur, and passes out anteriorly near the mouth. This water current is maintained by regular beating of specially flattened plates on the second pair of maxilae. The normal direction of flow of aerated water is from posterior to anterior. Occasionally this is reversed to meet special conditions, as in the masked crab when it is buried below the sand with only the tips of the antennae exposed.

Food and Feeding. All the decapods are omnivorous feeders, though many feed mainly on live prey or carrion. These large food masses are grasped by the chelae, crushed and ripped into smaller pieces and then passed to the complicated mouth-parts for further tearing and biting until small enough for swallowing. When you watch crabs feeding in an aquarium you will see that this is a very untidy and wasteful method, as much is lost during the tearing processes, although these discarded particles are a ready source of food for neighbouring creatures. As we have already seen, parasitic anemones attach themselves to the shells of hermit crabs to take full advantage of this, as does *Nereis fucata*, the ragworm who shares the shell with the crab.

Filter-feeding is also carried out by a few species whose third pair of maxillipeds bear long setae. In squat lobsters and hermit crabs these are situated at the tip so that fine particles of detritus become trapped in their meshes when the mixillipeds are swept across the bottom. In porcelain crabs these setae are very long and featherlike, forming a fringe around the maxillipeds, which entangle suspended particles as these maxillipeds move through the water.

Reproduction. These sexes are separate and copulation occurs just after the female has moulted. The male either transfers his sperm in small capsules, called *spermatophores*, which he plasters on the body of the female, or injects his sperm into the genital openings of the female, using his two pairs of abdominal appendages modified for this purpose. The sperms pass into a special structure, called the *spermatheca*, where they remain stored in the female's body until she is ready to spawn. Spawning may occur months after mating and often one injection of sperm is sufficient to fertilize two batches of eggs. Females carry their numerous fertilized eggs (counted in thousands) on the abdominal appendages to which they are firmly attached during spawning of a rapidly hardening sticky mucous secretion. A female in this condition is said to be 'in berry'. Periodic movement of the appendages ensures that the developing eggs are well aerated. When the eggs are ripe, minute pelagic *zoea* larvae emerge and spend several weeks as members of the temporary plankton undergoing many ecdyses before attaining the adult form.

Regeneration. Decapod crustaceans sometimes get one of their chelae or other limbs trapped under a rock or grabbed by a predator and in these circumstances can automatically shed it. This is called *autotomy* and is a reflex action causing the contraction of a special muscle which pulls on the leg skeleton, breaking it across a predetermined weak region. There is little loss of blood or body fluid at the cut which rapidly heals. Regeneration commences immediately and at the next moult the minute limb becomes exposed, growing longer at each following moult. Ecdysis occurs only infrequently in adult crabs and lobsters, so it is quite usual to find one with a small regenerating limb

Common Species

NATANTIA—Swimming Forms

Shrimps and Prawns. Sometimes these names are interchanged as if they referred to one and the same animal, but shrimps and prawns belong to two different families and there are three easy ways of recognizing each :

1. Shrimps inhabit sandy shores, whereas prawns are always around rocks or in rock pools amongst seaweeds.

2. Shrimps are flattened dorso-ventrally (from above) but prawns laterally (from side to side).

3. Prawns have a long serrated rostrum extended from the

anterior edge of the carapace, but this is absent in shrimps.

Both adult prawns and shrimps moult every few weeks and their eggs hatch into *zoea* larvae.

Shrimps. During daylight hours, as protection against predators, the common shrimp, *Crangon crangon* (=*C. vulgaris*), buries itself by scooping movements of the limbs, the body sinking down into the sand. By a backward action of the long antennae it attempts to cover its back with sand, but if not successful the greyish-brown body colour changes to blend with the surroundings, giving excellent camouflage. After dark the shrimp walls or swims over the surface in search of food, and almost anything edible is acceptable to it, including ragworms and other smaller crustaceans.

The common shrimp, which may grow to a length of 7 cm, is found on the lower regions of sandy shores, but it can also survive in mud and often invades estuaries. However, it can tolerate only the lowered salinities during the warmer months as it returns to normal seawater areas in the winter. The females do not become mature until the second or third year, and then they may spawn twice in a season. Females live to an age of four or five years, but males only to about three. The young hatch out as *zoea* larvae, moult several times and then become *mysis* larvae before finally metamorphosing into adults.

Prawns. The common prawn, *Palaemon* (=*Leander*), *serratus*, the largest British species reaching a length of 10 cm, is found around the rocks and the smaller prawn *P. squilla*, upto 5 cm long, in rock pools. The body of prawns, which is nearly transparent, is grey with purple dots and lines. Prawns turn pink only after they have been boiled. The inner antennae divide into three and the outer are longer than the body. The second pair of legs are longer than the first and also bear nippers ; thus in walking, the body is supported on three pairs of legs only, with the first two actively searching for food.

The female spawns immediately after mating and remains still until all the eggs are laid. She carries her developing eggs, which may number up to 4000, for about four months and then they hatch into *zoea* larvae. After several ecdyses these become *mysis* larvae, then tiny adults.

The chameleon prawn, *Hippolyte varians*, as its name implies, is adept at colour change and can blend with a background of green, brown, or red seaweed. It lives low on the shore among these weeds, or in pools, and is recognizable by the way it bends the middle of its abdomen so that its back appears humped. It grows to a length of approximately 2 cm.

Athanas nitesceans, between 1 and 2 cm long, has a short, unserrated, sharp-pointed rostrum and is red with a white stripe the length of its back. It lives low on rocky shores among seaweeds or in pools, and is confined to south and west coasts.

Palaemonetes varians grows to approximately 3 cm and inhabits brackish water.

REPTANTIA—Walking or Crawling Forms.

Lobsters. Lobsters and rock-lobsters live offshore, through smallspecimens may occasionally be found stranded in a rock crevice or pool near the water's edge at low water springs. The lobster, *Homarus gammarus* (=*H vulgaris*), is very handsome in its bright blue shell, but be wary of its large claws ! It also has small nippers on the second and third pairs of legs. In addition to darting backwards when startled, swimming in this direction is maintained by alternate flexing and extending of the abdomen, though most of the time lobsters crawl around the rocks. They are not sexually mature until four or five years of age when they are approximately 23 cm long, the minimum size for commercial sales. The female may store sperm in her body for as long as fifteen months before it is used to fertilize her eggs, and then she arries the developing eggs for about nine months. The young hatch out as *mysis* larvae, the zoeal stages having occurred within the egg.

The rock-lobster or crawfish, *Palinurus elephas* (=*P. vulgaris*), is easily distinguished from the lobster as its shell is brown with many spines and the first pair of legs do *not* terminate in massive chelae. The planktonic larva has a unique leaflike form and is called a *phyllosoma* larva. Grawfish are confined to south and west coasts, whereas lobsters are found all around Britain, but both move seawards in winter.

Squat Lobsters. Two species, both belonging to the genus *Galathea*, live low on rocky shores. The abdomen is tucked under the thorax, giving the body an oval shape, and long, flattened, spinous claws are present on the first pair of legs only. The fifth pair of legs is folded within the branchial chamber ; thus spuat lobsters *appear* to have four pairs only. Normally these lobsters, crawl around but can momentarily dart backwards when disturbed by the sudden extension of the abdomen.

The larger species, *G. strigosa* majestic in its red and blue carapace, may grow to a body length of 14 cm, whereas *G. squamifera*, inconspicuous in green and brown, reaches only a maximum of 7 cm.

Hermit Crabs. As mentioned in young hermit crabs are numerous in shallow pools and their antics are fascinating to watch Only the head and thorax are encased in the normal hard crab shell, so hermits live in old gastropod shells to protect the soft, curved abdomen, which snugly fits into the shell whorls and grips the columella with modified prehensile urapods. The other abdominal appendages are lost or reduced ; in the female, four are present on the left side for carrying the eggs, but only three remain in the male. The right chela is larger than the left and blocks the entrance of the shell when the crab is withdrawn. Retreat into the shell can be very rapid. Young hermits inhabit empty topshells, winkle and dog-whelk shells, changing to larger shells as they grow. The adults live in edible whelk-shells, but are no longer shore creatures ; they inhabit deeper water and often have commensals sharing their acquired homes. The common hermit crab,

Pagurus (=*Eupagurus*) *bernhardus*, often shares its home with an anemone, a ragworm and a colony of the coelenterate *Hydractinia*.

Crabs. Crabs need no further introduction ; many different species are found on British beaches, but the commonest and most widely distributed is the shore crab, *Carcinus maenas*. It can be found hiding under stones anywhere in the littoral zone, and even in estuaries, as it is tolerant of lowered salinities. *C. maenas* is typically green, though often mottled or slightly reddish ; in older crabs, when moulting is less frequent, the shell becomes darkened.

As in all crabs, the abdomen of the male is narrow with two pairs of copulatory appendages, whereas that of the female is broad with four pairs of egg-carrying appendages. The eggs hatch into *zoea* larvae, which develop into the *megalopa* form before completing metamorphosis. *C. maenas* may reach a width of 10 cm and live for three or four years,

Our edible crab, *Cancer pagurus*, lives in deep water, but young specimens may be found on the lower shore well hidden under large stones or in rock crevices. The adults travel an amazing distance ; one female, in a period of fifty-two weeks, travelled from Whitby to Fraserburgh, a distance of 230 miles as the crow flies, though probably much farther for the crab (*Yorkshire Crab Stocks*, Ministty of Agriculture, Fisheries and Food Laboratory Leaflet, No. 17). Males grow to a larger size and have larger chelae than females. Edible crabs become mature around five years of age when the shell is approximately 12-13 cm wide. Copulation occurs in inshore waters in summer when the female is sort-shelled, but she does not spawn until the winter migration to deeper off-shore waters. She then carries the developing eggs for several months as they do not hatch into *zoea* larvae until she has moved into inshore waters again in the following spring.

The spiny spider-crab, *Maja* (=*Maia*) *squinado*, is also an offshore inhabitant frequently caught in pots along with *Cancer*, but sometimes young specimens are stranded on the shore. The spiny, reddish-brown carapace is oval though more pointed anteriorly, and the chelae are much narrower and smaller than those of the edible crab, but the walking legs are longer. The meat can be eaten, but is not very popular in Britain, though in parts of America where the crab grows to a greater size, it is much favoured as a delicacy.

We have a few small species of spider-crab inhabiting the littoral zone whose legs are so long and slender that they are truly spiderlike in appearance One, *Inachus dorsettensis*, has the habit of attaching pieces of seaweed to its legs so that it becomes completely camouflaged. The carapace is triangular, rugose and 1—2 cm across the base. The chelae are broad and heavy, a feature which helps to distinguish it from *Macropodia rostrata* which has long, delicate chelae and the carapace extended into a rostrum bearing stalked eyes which cannot be withdrawn. *Macropodia* is a smaller species only about 1 cm across, and the commoner find on the lower shore of all coasts.

Our fiercest littoral species, the velvet swimming crab, *Macropipus* (=*Portunus*) *puber*. is also the most beautiful. It is reddish-brown with blue lines and markings on the legs and has red eyes. Its common name is derived from the short, soft hairs covering the carapace. This species may grow to a width of 10—12 cm and is found on the lower regions of rocky shores of the south and west coasts.

The hairy crab, *Pilumnus hirtellus*, is also confined to south and west coasts where it lives low on the shore under stones and amongst laminarian holdfasts. It is approximately 25 mm broad, brownish-red, with lighter chelae, and covered with hairs.

As we have seen in the masked crab, *Corystes cassivelaunus*, inhabits areas of clean sand and becomes a member of the intertidal fauna only during spring and summer. Dead or dying specimens are washed ashore after storms as is another inhabitant of deeper water, the angular crab, *Goneplax rhomboides* (=*G. angulata*).

Two species of porcelain crabs are found on the middle and lower regions of rocky shores—the broad-clawed and long-clawed forms. These differ from all the foregoing crabs because they appear to have four pairs of legs only. The fifth pair is present, but the legs are reduced and held so close to the body that they are inconspicuous. The broad-clawed porcelain crab, *Porcellana platycheles*, has large flattened chelae and the whole body is hairy, whereas the long-clawed form, *P. longicornis*, has a smooth, hairless shell.

INSECTA

Only two insects may commonly be found on the shore and these are restricted to the upper area and the splash zone. *Anurida* (=*Lipura*) *maritima*, a spring-tail which is unable to leap, has a velvety, dark blue body about 4-5 mm long, and is usually seen floating on the surface of very small rock pools high on the shore, normally in groups. It crawls over the rocks and hides in rock crevices. *Petrobius maritimus*, a three pronged bristle-tail, is larger with a body length of some 10 mm plus a central filament of about the same length. The antennae are long and the body is covered with brownish scales. It can run and jump, and is found under stones and in rock crevices on the upper shore and above.

ARACHNIDA

The sea-spider, *Pycnogonum littorale*, is far from conspicuous, but when found it cannot be mistaken. It is light brown and about 15 mm long with four pairs of thick, segmented legs. It is found on the column of beadlet anemones, on hydroids, under stones and amongst debris.

24

Phylum : Mollusca

This is a large phylum of invertebrates ranging from the edible periwinkle to the eight-armed octopus ; some molluscs are to be found in every seashore habitat. The soft body is usually retained within a shell—the exoskeleton—which protects the animal completely, but in some species the shell is partially or wholly lost.

To the beachcomber the shell is the familiar feature by which the limpet, winkle or mussel is recognized and to the ardent conchologist it is *the* important structure of a mollusc. At first glance this molluscan shell appears to consist of one substance, but a closer look shows it to be three layers : an outer protective horny layer, the *periostracum*, composed of the protein conchiolin, the middle solid chalky or prismatic layer, and the inner layer, which may be nacreous, the two latter composed basically of various forms of calcium carbonate. The shell is secreted by sepecial gland cells in the *mantle*, an extension of the body wall, and cells at its edge form only the middle and outer layers, while those over the whole area of the mantle produce the inner layer. The nacreous layer is the attractive 'mother-of-pearl', and when a sand particle or other foreign body becomes trapped between mantle and body, the gland cells are stimulated to secrete a nacreous layer around it, in an attempt to prevent the irritant effect. Layer upon layer is deposited, and this is how a natural pearl is formed in oysters and some other bivalves. Man cultures pearls by inserting a particle into the oyster so that the animal will deposit nacre around it.

As a mollusc grows, lines appear parallel to the edge of the shell from which it may be possible, in some instances, to judge the age of the animal. Unfortunately this is not always a simple matter of counting one ring for one year's growth as several factors affect the rate of shell formation. Two of these are food availability and temperature, which on their own could be correlated with shell growth, but during the spawning

Figure 23.1. Varieties of Mollusca. (*a*) amphineuran. (*b*) gastropod. (*c*) lamellibranch, (*d*) cephalopod.

period little or no shell may be formed and this is the disturbing factor in the simple calculation.

Two other characteristics of molluscs are the fleshy foot for locomotion and the special gills, called *ctenidia*, for absorption of oxygen from the water.

Many of the molluscs start life as a *veliger* larva, swimming freely in the plankton before metamorphosis into the adult form, but others hatch out as minute replicas of the adult.

This phylum is divided into five classes, three of which contain many littoral species : the *GASTROPODA* (univalves), *LAMELLIBRANCHIA* (bivalves) and *AMPHINEURA* (chitons). The members of the other two classes, the *SCAPHOPODA* (tusk shells) and *CEPHALOPODA* (octopus, etc.) live below the tidal range, but the latter will be discussed briefly as the shell of one, the cuttlefish, is often washed ashore after winter storms.

GASTROPODA

Within this group of single-shelled animals variations of form are so great that they are separated into three sub-classes, two of which have littoral representatives : the *PROSOBRANCHIA* (aquatic snails) and *OPISTHOBRANCHIA* (slugs).

Marine snails are the univalves capable of withdrawing the body completely into the shell for protection. Two well-known examples are the periwinkle and whelk—gastronomic delicacies to some of us. The head of these snails bears *one* pair of tentacles or feelers, which are very efficient sense organs for detecting features of their surroundings. For example, a periwinkle will 'feel' an aperture in a rock to ensure the hole is large enough for the passage of its shell before endeavouring to enter.

Some of the most beautiful gastropods are the sea-slugs which have either a reduced shell or on shell at all. The head bears *two* pairs of tentacles, the second pair functioning as olfactory organs. Unlike our dull unattractive garden slug, many of the sea-slugs are highly coloured and very lovely when seen under water.

In both marine snails and sea-slugs two eyes are present on or near the tentacles.

Shell. Most of these marine snails have the familiar shell form of the garden snail and a body twisted to fit snugly within. From the exterior the shell appears to be a simple cone, but when a section is cut from apex to base the structure is found to be spiral, with a central column, the *columella,* about which the shell is formed in whorls and to which the animal is attached by a strong muscle, the columellar muscle. Contraction of this muscle draws the body back into the shell. In some species the columella is solid, but in others it is hollow and the opening of the latter is called the *umbilicus.* The size and shape of the umbilicus are important features in the identification of marine snails.

When a shell is observed from above, that is looking down on the apex, the whorls are seen to run in a clockwise direction and such a shell is said to be right-handed or *dextral.* A left-handed or *sinistral* shell is abnormal and a real 'find' to the collector.

The shell apex is the first region laid down in the larval stage, thus the lowest and largest whorl is the youngest region of the shell. The latter is called the body whorl and, in most species, on retraction of the foot the aperture is closed by a horny disc, the *operculum,* attached to the foot. This is for protection and to prevent desiccation when left high and dry on the shore by the receding tide. As the shell, and therefore the aperture, increases in size, so must the operculum, and growth lines appear on this at the same rate as on the shell.

The conical-shaped cones of the limpets found on bare rock surfaces do not conform to this structure. Although in the pelagic larval stages the developing shell is spiral, once metamorphosis has occurred and the limpet settles in the littoral region, only the large body whorl remains. Thus there is no columella and the body does not extend outside the base of the shell. Instead of closing the shell with an operculum, the limpet adheres firmly to the rock with its muscular foot, drawing the shell down tightly on to the surface. If the rock is fairly soft the limpet shell eventually wears a groove in it. The gripping mechanism of the foot is so efficient that limpets survive on the most exposed shores ; the greater the battering action of the waves the firmer the hold.

Shell shape and thickness vary with every species, each being adapted to its own particular niche. Variation may even occur within one species ; conditions of life affect shell development and produce different shapes, as in the limpet.

Some of the sea-slugs have a reduced shell, but this may be external or internal. Even when external, the slug is unable to withdraw the body completely. The shell is thin and delicate in comparison with that of the marine snails and, when internal, is reduced to a flattened structure. In some species the shell is absent.

Locomotion. All the marine gastropods have a large, flattened, muscular foot for creeping or gliding over the surface, and movement is accomplished by waves of muscular contraction and relaxation passing continuously along the sole from posterior to anterior. Mucus, secreted by the pedal or foot gland, helps the sole to grip the surface and some minute species, such as *Rissoea*, found hidden in tiny crevices or within barnacles, probably use a thread of this mucus to pull themselves through the water.

In some of the sea-slugs the lateral edges of the foot develop into fleshy out-growths, the parapodia, and by flapping these the slug is able to swim short distances. The sea-hare, *Aplysia punctata*, found on rocky shores, swims in this manner.

Far more expert in swimming is *Akera bullata*, a slug which has much thinner, elongated parapodia, folded around the shell like a skirt, but capable of moving outwards and upwards to propel the animal through the water. When several swim together in this way they appear like minute ballet dancers gracefully drifting through the water.

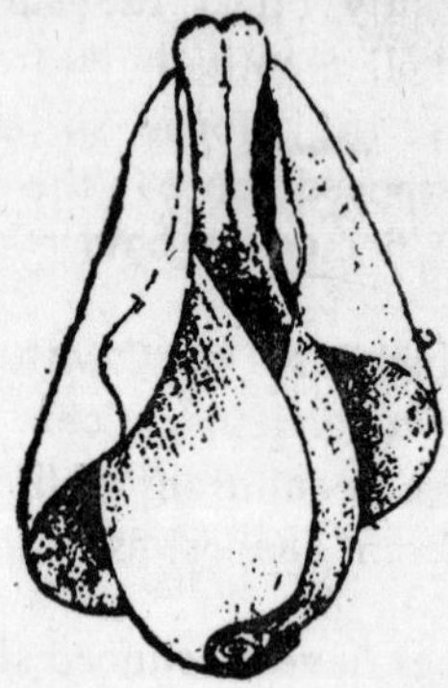

Figure. 23.2. *Akera bullata* with parapodia extended for swimming

Respiratory Mechanism. All of marine snails obtain oxygen from sea water when it is drawn over the gills suspended in the *mantle cavity*, that is the space between the free edge of the mantle and the body. These gills (ctenidia) are very delicate, featherlike structures and must be kept damp at all times.

As the water enters the mantle cavity it is 'tasted' by the *osphradium*, a sensory structure for detecting the presence of chemicals, and, if harmful, the snail takes evasive action.

A few species which inhabit the splash zone have a modified gill chamber for air breathing.

In the true limpets the gills are vestigial, but gareous exchange occurs through folds of tissue, called *pallial* gills, which encircle the foot and extend into the space between the foot and mantle edge.

With degeneration of the shell in sea-slugs there is an accompanying reduction in size of the mantle cavity, so the gills tend to protrude from the surface of the body, as in the sea-hare.

When no shell is present the sea-slug lacks a mantle cavity, so plume-like external gills develop on the dorsal surface, often in a circlet around the anus. In some species, such as the sea-lemon, *Archidoris pseudoargus,* these gills are retractile, but in others, such as *Goniodoris nodosa,* the gills cannot be withdrawn. The grey sea-slug, *Aeolidia papillosa,* and related species, which bear frilled processes called *cerata* on their back, are able to absorb oxygen through the surface of these structures, and if no cerata are present absorption occurs through the skin.

Food and Feeding. Some of the gastropods are herbivorous and others carnivorous, but all have a modified form of tongue, bearing teeth—the *radula.* This toothed, chitinous ribbon is used by herbivores for rasping weed from rock surfaces and by carnivores for cutting flesh and boring holes through shells of their unfortunate prey. The size and number of teeth vary with the different species, but the herbivorous snails such as periwinkles, limpets and topshells, have many small teeth, while the carnivorous whelks have larger, but fewer teeth. Wear on the tip of the radula is great, therefore new tissue, containing developing teeth, is formed continuously and gradually pushed forward as the old teeth are worn away. In a few instances the radula is used as a grasping organ, as in the pelican's foot shell which feeds on plant debris found just above or below the sand or mud.

The anterior region of the head is drawn out into a muscular snout bearing the mouth in a suitable position in the herbivorous species, but in carnivores this is elongated into a long narrow tube, bearing the mouth at its tip. This is the *proboscis* which can be retracted when not in use. The benefit of this extrusible proboscis is demonstrated by the edible whelk when it competes with crabs for the bait in a crab-pot without even entering the pot ! The wily whelk just crawls up the outside and extends its proboscis within and the crabders often bring up their pots with the whelks still attached in this way.

The osphradium helps to detect the presence of any live, dead or decaying flesh in the sorrounding water, and it is particularly well developed in the carnivorous snails.

The slipper limpet, *Crepidula fornicata*, and Chinaman's hat shell, *Calyptraea chinensis*, exhibit filter-feeding, a method more normal to bivalves.

Reproduction. The sexes are separate in all the marine snails and, in many, a penis-like structure is present for internal fertilization. If there is no penis the gametes (sexual products) are shed directly into the sea where external fertilization occurs, but for this to be successful the products from both sexes need to be discharged at the same time. Obviously many gametes never find an opposite number, but in some species of limpets and typshells no gametes are released unless males and females are near each other, thus reducing the wastage to a minimum. Free-swimming *veliger* larvae hatch out from these eggs and float in the plankton for a period of hours, days or weeks, according to the particular species, before finally sinking to the bottom to complete their metamorphosis.

When a penis is present the process of fertilization is less haphazard, but as the sexes are indistinguishable from outward appearances a male often attempts to mate with another male. Eggs spawned as a result of internal fertilization are often protected by an egg-case or capsule, which is deposited on seaweeds or rocks, and within this the young develop and eventually hatch out as minute replicas of the adult. In some species the egg capsules are liberated into the sea, and after floating in the plankton for a while hatch into *veliger* larvae.

One common marine snail, the rough periwinkle, *Littorina saxatilis*, is ovoviviparous. The egg-cases remain within the body of the female and when the young emerge they are in the correct shore zone for adult life.

An unusual habit displayed by slipper limpets is that of changing sex during their life span. They start life as males and finish up as females.

All the sea-slugs are hermaphrodites, but cross-fertilization always occurs. Usually copulation takes place in pairs, but in both *Aplysia punctata* and *Akera bullata* several individuals form a chain ; each animal ejects sperm into the one in front and receives sperm from the one behind. The first of the chain acts as a female only and the last as a male only, but all the others function as both. Occasionally the chain joins to form a circle and then all individuals function as both sexes.

The eggs are small and laid in masses or strings which are easily recognizable. *Veliger* larvae hatch out after a short period and spend a brief time in the plakton before metamorphosis.

Growth. The majority of marine snails continue to grow throughout life, but the rate decreases once sexual maturity is reached. Abundance of food and other factors influence development, but usually the largest shells are the oldest. However, this is not true of the dog-whelk for often a small thick shell is older than a much larger but thinner specimen. This is because the animal ceases to grow once it begins to spawn, but thickening of the shell then occurs around the edge of the aperture. The only other common snails of our shores which cease growth on sexual maturity are the small cowries.

Little information is available concerning the longevity of marine snails, but the edible periwinkle has been recorded as living for periods of four to ten years and even up to twenty in captivity, In comparison the flat topshell survives only for four or five years. Some species may die after the first spawning, as is the case with most sea-slugs which grow to maturity, spawn and die within a year or even less.

Regeneration. Little regeneration occurs in the gastropods, but some marine snails can regenerate eyes and tentacles, though this is a very slow process. However, sea-slugs are capable of regenerating cerata in two or three weeks.

Common Species

Limpets. The common limpets found on rocky shores all belong to the genus *Patella*, but there are three species which are not always easy to distinguish. The shell is conical with no columella and the large aperture is not closed by an operculum. All are herbivorous and move around, feeding on algae when the tide is in, but 'home' each to its own particular niche once the tide recedes. Therefore rock surfaces around limpets are usually devoid of any prolific growth of seaweeds. Some interesting research on the Isle of Man by S.M. Lodge (1948) showed that when limpets were removed from an area of shore normally only sparsely populated by seaweeds, a thick algal growth developed, which indicated that the limpets feed on the seaweed spores before they become established as sporelings. The sexes of limpets are separate, but the sexual products are discharged into the sea, where fertilization occurs.

Patella vulgata has a tall cone, is the largest species, is usually found on the higher regions of the shore and spawns during winter months. *P. intermedia*, smaller and with a flatter shell, is confined to the south-western coasts and *P. aspera*, with an even flatter shell, lives on all coasts, but lower on the shore, though it may inhabit pools higher up.

The pretty blue-rayed limpet, *Patina pellucida*, receives its common name from the bright blue spots which form rays from the apex to the margin of the smooth shell of young animals. Unfortunately these attractive markings are gradually lost with age. The maximum length of the shell is only about 20 mm and this gastropod, which browses on *Laminaria*, is confined to the lower shore and sub-littoral zone.

The other types of limpet are not abundant and they all inhabit the lower shore and sub-littoral region. The keyhole limpet, *Diodora apertura*, is easily identified by the opening at the apex and the slit limpet, *Emarginula reticulata*, by its marginal slit. The tortoiseshell limpet, *Acmaea tessulata*, has conspicuous reddish-brown markings and is confined to northern coasts.

The slipper limpet, *Crepidula fornicata*, is included here because of its common name, but this species is in *no* way related to the common limpets. The larvae are planktonic, but the adults are sedentary animals and therefore rely on food sources near at hand instead of foraging like other gastropods. The highly ciliated gill enables the slipper limpet to filter-feed in the same way as bivalves, but there is one difference, the radula is still operative. Some of the food particles become entrapped in mucus and the mass formed is grasped by the radula and transferred to the mouth (Orton, J.H., *Feeding mechanisms of Crepidula*, Journal Marine Biological Association. Vol. 9). Its method of feeding makes the slipper limpet a pest on oyster-beds because it competes with the oyster for available planktonic food. The slipper limpet is not an indigenous gastropod, but we first brought to the east coast of England from America with oysters imported for re-laying the Whitstable and Colchester beds during the late nineteenth century ; gradually it has spread up the east coast and round the south coast.

The shell has no columella, but half the aperture is covered by a shelf of shell ; probably this shape has led to the use of the name 'slipper limpet'.

Crepidula has the habit of forming chains, one settling on the back of another, until a dozen or so are linked in this way. They are hermaphrodites and in a chain the youngest function as males and the oldest as females ; those in the middle are in the transitional phase. Spawning occurs from March to November, though this appears to be most prevalent in May. The eggs are deposited in capsules, holding up to 250, from which the planktonic larvae escape after approximately a month.

The Chinaman's hat, *Calyptraea chinensis*, belongs to the same family as *Crepidula*, but the shell is circular, growing to a diameter of 2 cm. There is no columella but a shell shelf, and chains are formed with similar variation in sex with age as in *Crepidula*. Small specimens only are found on rocky shore attached to stones in the lowest zone ; this species is confined to the south and west coasts.

Periwinkles. The four species of *Littorina* each inhabits a particular region of the rocky shore as discussed in Section 5.

All have a solid columella and close the aperture with an operculum ; the eyes are borne on short stalks at the base of the tentacles. All are herbivorous, the sexes are separate and fertilization is internal.

The small perivinkle, *L. neritoides* inhabiting rock cracks and crovices of the splash zone, has a smooth black shell only 5-6 mm long, a reduced gill and a gill chamber with blood capillaries in the surface liming for air breathing ; it feeds on encrusting lichens. The female sheds her egg capsules at high spring tides during autumn and winter as only then, during rough seas, is she submerged. The single egg in each capsule develops into a *veliger* larva which lives in the plankton for a considerable period before metamorphosis and pettlement in barnacle area. The young adult then gradually migrates up to the splash zone.

The rough periwinkle, *L. saxatilis* (*rudis*), inhabits the top middle and upper shore regions, though it may venture, at times, to the splash zone, but only the smaller specimens may be found side by side with *L. neritoides* The two are distinguished by the shell form, that of *L. saxatilis* being deeply grooved and varying in colour from white, pale cream, red brown and brown to grey black. Its length from apex to base may be up to 12 mm. *L. saxatilis* is usually found on bare rock and it feeds on encrusting seaweeds. As it is exposed to the air for lengthy periods, there is a slight modification of the gill chamber as in *L. neritoides*. The rough periwinkle is better adapted for life on dry land than the small periwinkle because it is *not* dependent on the sea for development of its young. It is ovoviviparous, the egg capsules being retained in a brood sac within the female's body. Two or three embryos develop within one egg-case and when ready to hatch the young, now minute replicas of the adult, rupture the covering with their radulas. The number of emergent young is relatively small as the dangers of a planktonic life are non-existent, but overcrowding is a hazard as distribution is limited. Breeding appears to occur throughout the year.

The range of the flat periwinkle *L. littoralis*, extends from the upper region of the lower shore to the full extent of the middle shore, wherever *Fucus serratus* and *F. vesiculosus* are present. When the tide recedes it withstands desiccation by crawling among the fronds of these weeds, which are also its staple diet. The apex of the shell is flattened, the maximum length about 15 mm, and its colour varies from white, yellow, brown-red, brown to black. Of all the periwinkles only the spawn of this species is found on the shore, the eggs being deposited in gelatinous oval masses about 7 mm by 3 mm on the fronds of *Fucus*, usually *F. serratus*. With a powerful hand-lens, or under a microscope, it is fascinating to watch the lively movements of the maturing young within this transparent jelly ; when about to hatch the structure of the adult winkle is obvious. Here again, the radula is used to rupture the covering. Each egg mass may contain from fifty to eighty embryos. Development covers a period of three or four weeks.

The edible or common periwinkle, *L. littorea*, is the most familiar and at the same time the most versatile species. Its range is from the lower shore up through the middle shore on exposed rocks hidden under weeds and, owing to the shape of its shell, it can be borne along unharmed by the incoming tide. It is the largest periwinkle and it reaches a maximum length of about 35 mm. Its apex is sharply pointed and the colour dull, varying from red-brown to grey-black, often marked with darker concentric rings. Its diet is seaweeds. *L. littorea* is entirely dependent on the sea for the development of its young because the egg capsules, containing from one to nine eggs, though more usually three, are liberated by the female at high tide and float in the plankton for about five days before hatching occurs. The liberated *veliger* larvae then float in the plankton for about two weeks before metamorphosis and settlement on the shore. Spawning usually occurs from February to June, although the presence of egg capsules in the plankton during all months of the year has been recorded.

Topshells. The topshells, inhabitants of rocky shores, are distinguished from periwinkles by the regular triangular shape of the shell. The columella is hollow in most species, the aperture closed by an operculum and three pairs of *epipodial* tentacles are borne on the foot. Often part of the periostracum is worn away, exposing the mother-of-pearl layer below, which is always present in topshells. The sexes are separate, but fertilization is external and the eggs usually hatch into planktonic *veliger* larvae. All the five common shore species are herbivores and exhibit zonation, though not so distincly as the periwinkles.

The thick or toothed topshell, *Gibbula lineata,* usually inhabits a fairly limited zone from the lower upper to upper middle shore, and is confined to the south and west coasts. The shell, grey with mottled darker markings, is about as tall as it is broad, reaching a maximum diameter of some 25 mm, has an umbilicus and a distinctive tooth on the aperture edge.

The flat or purple topshell, *G. umbilicalis,* has a flattened shell with broad purple stripes and a large umbilicus, the diameter of the base being up to 18 mm. It lives in the zone of its staple diet, *Fucus serratus,* but on south and west coasts only.

The grey topshell or 'silver-tommy', *G. cineraia,* has a more conical shell than the flat topshell and only a small umbilicus. It is silver grey with narrow darker stripes, is up to about 14 mm in diameter and inhabits the lower middle and lower shore, extending into the sub-littoral region.

G. magus is the heaviest of the topshells, having a flattened solid shell about 27 mm broad, with a rough knobbed surface, grey with red or purple wide stripes and a deep, wide umbilicus. It inhabits the lower shore and sub-littoral regions on south and west coasts.

The shell of the pointed or common topshell, *Calliostoma zizyphinum,* is a regular triangle, pale pink with red streaks, as tall as it is broad, reaching a maximum of about 25 mm across the base, the foot bears *four* pairs of epipodial tentacles. The young hatch out from the eggs as minute adults ; there is *no* planktonic larva as in all other species. This species is confined to the lower shore and sub-littoral zone.

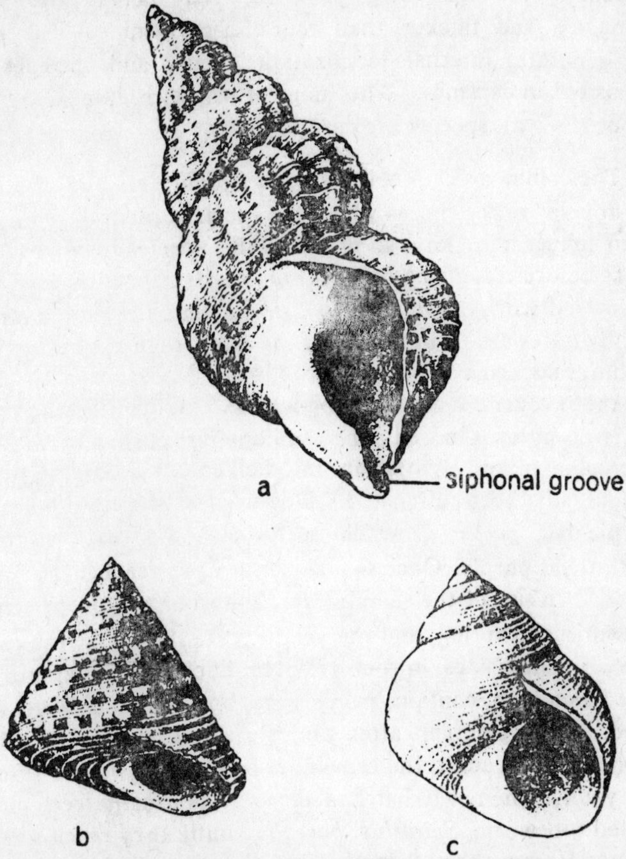

Figure 23.3. Structure of (*a*) welk. (*b*) topshell and (*c*) periwink'e.

Whelks. The shell aperture is the feature by which whelks are easily distinguished from all other gastropods ; it is drawn out into a groove. The purpose of this groove is to allow extension and retraction of the *siphon*, a tubular structure formed by inrolling of the mantle edge. This siphon is extended above the shell so that clear water can be drawn in when the whelk stirs up the muddy or sandy bottom ar it crawls along on its massive foot in search of food. This is necessary because any sand or mud particles suspended in the inhalent water current would soon clog the gills. The shell is also more elongated and thicker than that of a periwinkle. The sexes are separate, internal fertilization occurs and the eggs are deposited in capsules. The snout of whelks is elongated into a proboscis ; all species are carnivorous.

The common dog-whelk, *Nucella lapillus,* inhabits the middle zone of rocky shores where the special function of a siphon is no longer necessary, so probably this species lived in muddy areas before colonizing rocky shores. Its siphon is very short compared with other whelks. In feeding, the radula mechanically bores a hole in the shell of prey, then the fleshy tissue within is sucked up by the proboscis. Mussels and barnacles are the favourite foods of dog-whelks. When feeding on the latter no hole is bored ; the radula is just pushed between the opercular plates. Variation in shell colour according to diet has already been discussed. Dog-whelks secrete a poisonous purple dye, *purpurin,* which in former days was used to dye cloth royal purple. Once sexual maturity is reached no further increase in size of the shell occurs. Spawning occurs principally in winter and spring, and the yellow, vase-shaped capsules are deposited in masses. in rock crevices. Each capsule, approximately 5 mm high, contains many eggs, but only a few are fertilized. They emerge, after about sixteen weeks, as minute replicas of the adult, the remainder being eaten by the developing young. The newly hatched dog-whelks usually feed on the coiled tubeworm, *Spirorbis borealis,* until they reach a length of 9 or 10 mm ; they then revert to the normal adult diet.

Although commonly called the sting winkle, *Ocenebra erinacea,* is a whelk with a solid, ridged shell, living in muddy sand very low on the shore and sub-littorally, but it moves up the shore in early summer to deposit its egg capsules. It feeds on bivalves and is often a pest on oyster-beds. With age the shell becomes thickened, and sometimes the siphonal groove becomes covered over, forming a tube.

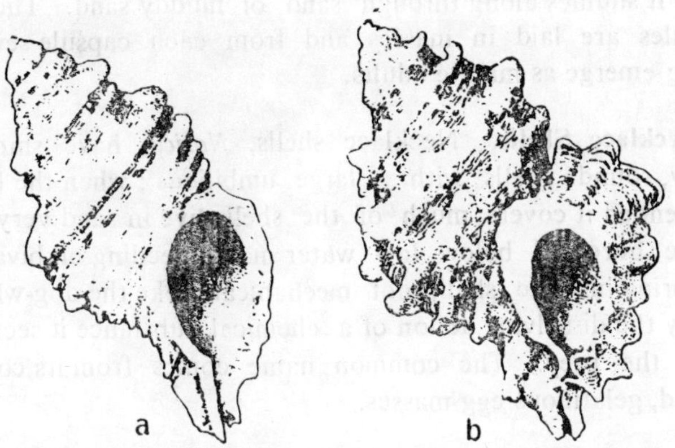

Figure. 23.4. Sting winkles, *Ocenebra erinacea.* (*a*) Young shel showing open siphonal groove and (*b*) old shell showing thickening and growth over siphonal groove forming a tube.

The oyster drill, *Urosalpinx cinerea,* is similar to the sting winkle, but is a far more troublesome pest on oyster-beds. Like the slipper limpet, it was introduced from America, but it is still confined to the coast of Britain.

The netted dog-whelk, *Nassarius reticulatus,* is a scavenger and ploughs its way through sand searching for food on the lower shore, often in regions near rocks. The colour of the shell blends with the sand and its surface is ribbed in a network pattern. The flat, bottle-shaped egg capsules are attached in rows usually to *Zostera* or *Fucus.*

The thick-lapped dog-whelk, *N. incrassatus,* is similar to the netted dog-whelk, but is only about half its size. It deposits solitary egg inhabits the lower regions of rocky shores.

The common or edible whelk, *Buccinum undatum,* is not a true inhabitant of the littoral zone as only very young specimens are found here, but as its shell and egg capsules are frequently washed ashore it is of interest to us. It is the largest of the British whelks, with a long siphon used for the correct purpose of drawing clean water into the gill chamber while it shuffles along through sand or muddy sand. The egg capsules are laid in masses and from each capsule several young emerge as minute adults.

Necklace Shells. Necklace shells, *Natica*, have smooth, glossy, rounds shells with a large umbilicus ; when the body is extended it covers much of the shells live in sand very low on the shore and below low water mark, feeding on bivalves by boring into the shell, not mechanically like the dog-whelk, but by the dissolving action of a chemical substance it secretes on to the prey. The common name comes from its collar-shaped, gelatinous egg masses.

Chink Shells. The banded chink shell, *Lacuna vincta,* is only about 12 mm long and the shell has an umbilicus which distinguishes it from periwinkles lives on weeds low on rocky shores and in spring its yellow or green egg rings are conspicuous on *Fucus*.

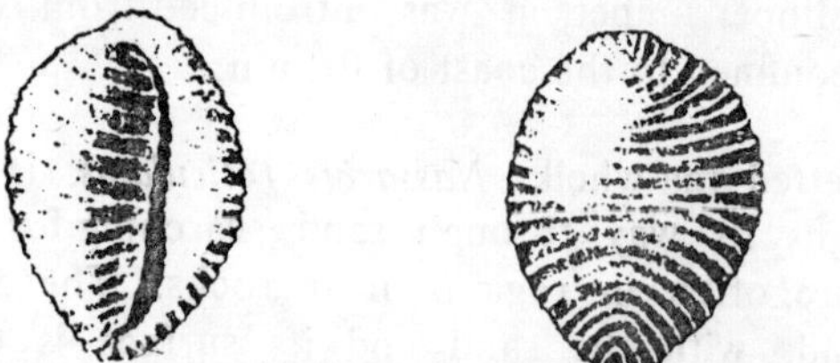

a b

Figure 23.5. Cowries. (*a*) Ventral view showing slit aperture, (*b*) dorsal view.

Cowries. There are only two British species, the spotted cowrie, *Trivia monacha*, with three brown spots on its shell, and the white cowrie, *T. arctica*. Both live on rocks low on the shore, feeding on compound sea-squirts. The shell, about 10 mm in length, consists of the body whorl only and has the aperture drawn ont into a longitudinal slit from which a short siphon projects anteriorly and the mantle tissues extend over the shell. Like the dog-whelk, on further shell growth occurs once the animal is sexually mature.

Pelican's Foot Shell. The shell of *Aporrhais pes-pelicani* is tower shaped with a characteristic extension of the outer edge of the aperture, from which it acquires its name. In young specimens this is lacking and sometimes poses a problem in identification. This species lives offshore in sand or muddy gravel where it feeds on detritus, but occasionally, after rough seas, live specimens are found washed up near the low water mark.

Spire Shells. The laver spire shell, *Hydrobia ulvae*, about 5—10 mm in length inhabits estuaries and salt-marshes feeding on sea-lettuce (*Ulva*), *Enteromarpha*, blue-green algae and diatoms of the plankton and, when on bare mud-flats, on bacteria of organic debris. The eggs are laid in capsules from which veliger larvae emerge after two or three weeks.

Sea-slugs. The sea-hare, *Aplysia punctata*, with a thin flattened internal shell, normally lives in shallow water, but in late spring it comes ashore to spawn, the eggs being laid in long orange-pink strings. The body colour varies from crimson, purple-brown, olive-brown, olive-green, changing with age as the animal varies its diet from red to brown seaweeds during its gradual movement upwards. The animal releases a slimy purple fluid when irritated, so if you touch one, beware ! Normally sea-hares crawl around among the weeds, but they can swim. In some years sea-hares are very abundant and readily found on rocks or in pools low on the shore, but in other years they are scarce.

The sea-lemen *Archidoris pseudoargus*, the commonest British intertidal seaslug, reaching 75 mm in length, is found on rocky shores feeding on the breadcrumb sponge, with which its warty-surfaced, pale yellow body blends. The ring of dorsal gills is retractile. The eggs are laid in coiled wide, white ribbons.

In *Goniodoris nodosa* the ring of dorsal gills cannot be retracted and the body, up to 25 mm when fully extended, is smooth and pale pink or white. It inhibits rocky shores feeding on sea-mats and sea-squirts.

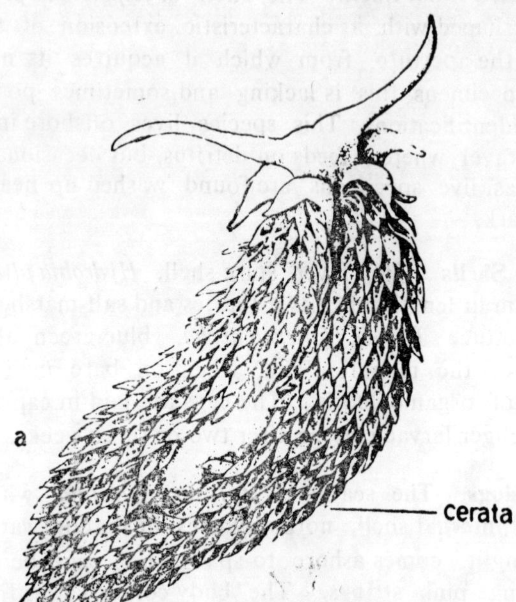

Figure 23.6. Sea-slugs. (*a*) grey sea-slug. *Aeolidia papillosa.* (*b*) sea-lemon, *Aechidoris pseudoargus*

The grey sea-slug, *Aeolidia paoillosa*, which may be 90 mm long when fully extended, is the largest British intertidal sea-slug. The skin of the dorsal surface is extended into many tubular *cerata* which look similar to the tentacles of the sea-anemones on which it feeds exclusively. The gut extends into these cerata, and stinging cells from the anemones become embedded in the cerata walls and so protect the sea-slug from predators, just as the anemones are protected. The eggs are laid in spiral ribbons.

LAMELLIBRANCHIA

This large class of molluscs, commonly called the bivalves, includes familiar edible shellfish such as cockles, mussels and oysters. All exhibit the characteristic feature of a shell composed of two flattened sections hinged together. The laterally compressed body within has no distinct head, thus radula, tentacles and eyes are absent, and the foot is modified for digging or burrowing. The mantle is in two folds, one on either side of the body, out attached to it along the hinge line. Each fold secretes one valve of the shell. These mantle flaps may be joined along the free edges except for inhalent and exhalent apertures, and an opening for the foot. Sometimes the mantle is drawn out into siphons with the ingoing and outgoing opening at the tips. In some species which burrow deeply these may be long, and in others the two may be fused along part or all of their length.

Compared with the active gastropods, the lamellibranchs are relatively sedentary, as most live buried in mud or sand are dependent on indrawn sea water for their food source ; they are filter-feeders. A few species are capable of boring into wood or rock.

Shell. Unlike the gastropods, we do not immediately observe lamellibranchs on the shore as they are nearly all burrowing creatures. The first signs of their presence are empty shells, and usually only half shells, as the two valves become torn apart when carried up and down the beach by the tide In the live animals the two valves are hinged together along the upper or dorsal edge and thus may be closed together tightly or allowed to gape. Closure occurs by contraction of a pair of *adduclor* muscles, one connecting the two valves anteriorly and the other posteriorly. On relaxation of these muscles the elastic thrust of a ligament at the hinge forces the two valves apart. Some bivalves are symmetrical, having adductor muscles of equal size, but others have an irregular form and in these the muscles are unequal. This is displayed by the muscle whose anterior adductor is reduced. In more rounded species, such as scallops and oysters, the anterior muscle is completely lost and the one large posterior adductor has migrated towards the centre. It is this single muscle which forms the bulk of the edible portion.

In some species the hinge is strengthened by small teeth which fit into corresponding sockets in the opposite valve and the size, shape and number of these are important factors in the identification of empty shells.

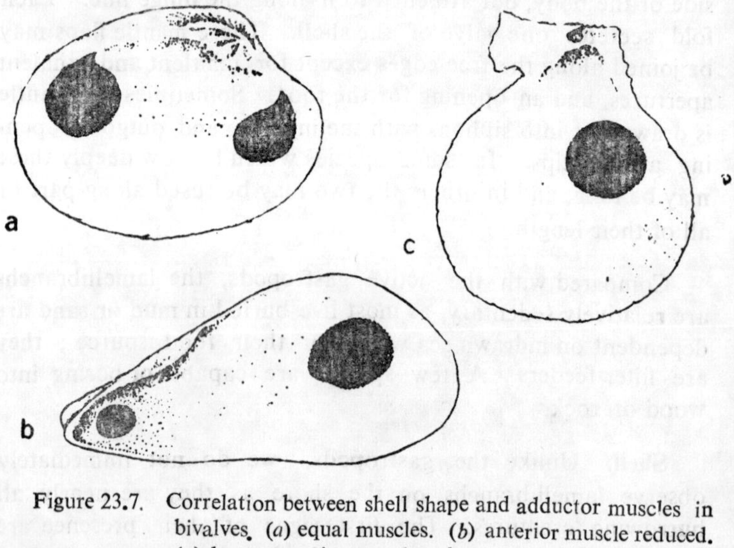

Figure 23.7. Correlation between shell shape and adductor muscles in bivalves. (*a*) equal muscles. (*b*) anterior muscle reduced. (*c*) large posterior muscle only.

Usually the two valves are similar, but in a few species they differ, as in the scallop, *Pecten maximus*, whose lower (right) valve is convex and upper (left) valve is flat.

In the larvae the shells is first formed at the beak, near the hinge, and then laid down around the outer edges so that the newest region is at the free edge, and concentric growth rings may be observed on many shells.

Scars on the inner surface of empty shells indicate the points of attachment of muscles, mantle, etc., and their shape, size and position are also major factors in identification.

When we consider the different species we shall find the deepest burrowers exhibit the greatest flattening of the shell.

Locomotion. The foot of lamellibranchs differs from that of gastropods both in shape and mode of movement. It is flattened laterally for retention between the two valves and for ease of movement through the substratum during burrowing, an action accomplished by alternate lengthening and shortening, as already described in the case of the razorshell. Many species can dig very rapidly in this way. This protrusion and withdrawal between the valves is controlled by pedal muscles which are comparable to the columella muscle of univalves.

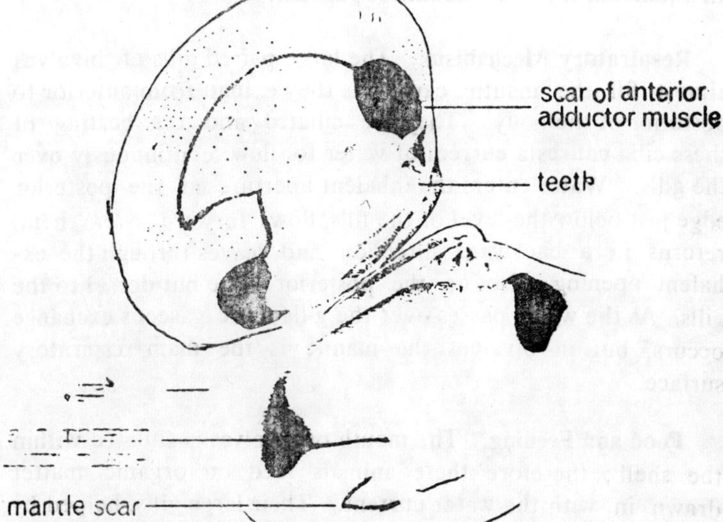

Figure 23.8. Scars on inner surface of a bivalve shell.

A few bivalves live on the surface, the commonest being mussels, and to retain their position they secure themselves to the rocks by tough *byssus* threads. These are formed when a sticky fluid, secreted by a gland within the foot, hardens on exposure. The mussel twists on its foot, attaching several threads in different directions to anchor itself, so that the shell can be swayed by the waves, but not torn from the rock. However, as already noted, in highly populated areas the mussels are too close together to allow any such movement. New byssus threads are produced as the old ones become damaged and, when a solitary mussel is dropped into the front of an aquarium, it is fascinating to watch the extension and retraction of the foot as the animal orientates itself before attaching threads to the glass.

Scallops and file-shells live below water mark and are capable of swimming. This they accomplish by flapping their valves and expelling jets of water through various positions around the mantle edge, according to the required direction of movement. The action is rather jerky, but when observed in an aquarium it gives a beautiful pageant.

Respiratory Mechanism. The large paired gills of bivalves almost fill the mantle cavity as they extend from anterior to posterior of the body. They are ciliated and the beating of these cilia causes a current of water to flow continuously over the gills. Water enters the inhalent aperture at the posterior edge just below the level of the fills, flows forward over them, returns in a backward direction and leaves through the exhalent opening, also on the posterior edge but dorsal to the gills. As the water passes over the gills some gaseous exchange occurs, but in bivalves the mantle is the main respiratory surface.

Food and Feeding. The mouth of bivalves is situated within the shell; therefore these animals feed on organic matter drawn in with the water current. Their large gills, helped by an ample secretion of mucus, sieve or trap the food particles with settle in a groove along the ventral edge and from here they are wafted forward by special cilia towards the mouth. The mouth is bounded by a pair of palps whose function is to direct and control entry of the food. Any undigested food and waste products are carried outside the exhalent current.

Some bivalves feed on plankton. These are suspension feeders which have no siphons or only relatively short ones. Others food on detritus. These are deposit feeders with long narrow siphons, the inhalent being the longer of the two for movement over a wide circle of the sea-floor.

In wood-boring lamellibranchs the gills are very small. Animals have a specialized alimentary system capable of digesting wood cellulose.

Reproduction. The sexes are separate in nearly all bivalves, though a few species, such as oysters, are capable of changing sex during their life span, not just once, but several times ! The productive system is much simpler than in gastropods, the sexual products being discharged into the sea through the exhalent aperture so that fertilization is external. Planktonic veliger larvae, with two tiny valves, develop and float in the sea for a period before settling and burrowing in the substratum.

In oysters, *Osterea,* and a few other bivalves, the females retain their eggs in the mantle cavity where they are fertilized by spermatozoa drawn in with the inhalent current. Early development proceeds in the mantle cavity and is followed by a short period in the plankton before settlement. There is no connection between the embryo and the mother, the mantle cavity purely acting as a temporary blood chamber. In the wood-bores, *Xylophaga* and *Teredo*, the eggs contain more yolk than usual, which enables are developing embryos to remain within the mantle cavity until metamorphosis, so they leave as minute adults.

Common Species

Suspension Feeders. Trough shells are typically triangular in shape, with the anterior and posterior edges approximately of equal length, white or yellowish white in colour, and concentrically grooved. They live in sand, more generally below low water mark in shallow to medium depths, but empty shells are commonly found on the beech. After storm live specimens may be tossed ashore and deposited along the driftline. The siphons are united, of equal length and short ; thus these bivalves are shallow burrowers and they are found on all coasts. Three species, elliptical, cut and thick, belong to the genus *Spisula*, but these are not readily identified from external appearances, though they are easily distinguished from the genus *Mactra*. The rayed trough shell *Mactra corallina*, has smooth shiny shell, much thinner than *Spisula*, cream, sometimes mauvis, with light brown rays from beak to margin. It is the largest through shell, reaching 50 mm from anterior to posterior edge.

Venus shells are more rounded and the beak curves over towards the anterior side. The siphons are short and joined except at the tip. All inhabit clean sand. One of the commonest, the striped venus, *Venus striatula*, is cream with pale reddish-brown rays from beak to margin, and close, fine concentric ridges. It grows to about 30 mm in length and burrows on lower sandy shores and in the sub-littoral region. Empty venus shells are a common find.

Carpet shells belong to the same family as venus shells and therefore have a curved beak, but they are oval with the posterior region wedge-shaped. In all species the shell surface is ridged concentrically, but in the cross-cut carpet shell, *Ven-erupis decussata*, these are crossed by radiating ribs giving a fine network pattern. *V. decussata*, cream in colour, reaching a length of about 45 mm, lives in muddy sand or gravel on the lower shore, and below on south and west coasts. It may sometimes be found in rock pools with a similar substratum. The pullet carpet shell, *V. pullastra* is very similar in size, but the sculpturing is not so distinct and the shell is patterned with purple-brown markings. It lives in the same type of habitat, but is found on all coasts.

Razorshells are long and narrow, have very short siphons only separated at the tip and live in sand on the lower shore.

Cockles need no introduction and the only shore inhabitant the edible cockle, *Cardium edule*, which grows to a length of 5 cm. These cockles are very sensitive to temperature as they burrow so near the surface ; in severe winters the mortality rate is high. The foot becomes less active as the temperature drops and therefore a cockle may not bury deep enough to prevent dislodgement during rough seas. Edible cockles may live to an age of eight years, but in dense populations longevity is reduced. The larger cockles, commonly called the red-nosed cockles, live offshore, but are found stranded ashore after storms.

Ottershells and gapers live below low water mark in sand or muddy sand, but in winter they are found along the strand-line. The common ottershell, *Lutraria lutraria*, is elliptical, reaching a length of 12 cm, yellowish-white, with long joined siphons, marked with purple-brown patches and contained in a transparent sheath. The blunt gaper, *Mya truncata*, has a more solid shell, ridged concentrically and truncated posteriorly, giving a rectangular shape, the two valves gaping widely in this region. The sand gaper, *M. arenaria*, inhabits sandy mud and is the edible clam so much favoured in America. The larvae secrete byssus threads for attachment and the young gapers become very active as young mussels do, but when they reach a length of about 7 mm no further threads are produced and they bury in the normal way of adults. Sand gapers do not reach sexual maturity until five years of age.

Mussels are suspension feeders, but they do not have siphons. However, when submerged the inhalent and exhalent openings can be seen, the former being distinguished by its frilled edge. These bivalves do not burrow, but attach themselves to rocks by byssus threads The common or edible mussel, *Mytilus edulis*, besides living on rocky shores, inhabits muddy areas if stones are present for attachment of the byssus threads ; in estuaries they form vast mussel beds. The shell is dark-blue black and the white inner surface may be tinged with mauve. It is possible for the common mussel to grow to a length of 10 cm, but normally it is much smaller.

Saddle oysters, *Anomia ephippium*, also attach themselves by byssus threads, but these pass through a hole in the flattened right valve and are limy, the shell thus appearing to be cemented in position. As it grows the shell follows the contours of the underlying surface, but retains a circular from and may reach a diameter of 5 cm. The upper of left valve is convex and slightly overgrows the lower shore and below. The shell is white, but glossy inside and when the empty valves are washed ashore they are recognizable by their beautiful pearliness.

Scallops live offshore and although the adults are capable of swimmiing, young scallops are attached by byssus threads.

Another beautiful bivalve, the gaping file-shell, *Lima hians*, also secretes byssus threads, but these it uses to construct a nest amongst *Laminaria* holdfasts.

Hiatella produces byssus threads which are used to secure the bivalve in rock crevices or in the burrow that it bores into soft rock. Boring is mechanical as in the piddocks. The siphons, protected by a horny sheath, are long enough to reach the opening of the burrow and these bivalves may be found on the lower shore and below on all coasts.

Oysters also live on the surface, but they attach themselves to the substratum with cement. The lower left valve is convex and the upper right valve flat. There are no siphons, the foot is present in the young but completely lost in the adult, and only the large posterior adductor muscle is present. The flat or native edible oyster, *Ostrea edulis*, lives in shallow water, but empty shells may be found on the beach.

Piddocks bore their way into rock by a mechanical action controlled by the alternate contraction of the two adductor muscles which socks the loosely attached valves ; the foot is modified into a type of sucker used to grip the end of the burrow. The joined siphons, covered by a sheath along half their length only, are long, thus enabling the piddock to live deep in the rock and still feed on plankton ; although the external opening is small, the burrow widens inwards. Once a young piddock bores into a rock it never willingly leaves its home, so it enlarges the burrow as it grows. The common piddock, *Pholas dactylus,* has a white, brittle, elongated shell, with a ridged surface bearing small spines and may grow to a length of 12 cm. It bores into slate, chalk and red sandstone on lower regions of the shore and below, even in submerged wood, but is confined to south and south-west coasts, this being the northernmost limit of the species, as is the case with the little, white and paper piddocks, *Barnea parva, B. candida* and *Pholadidea loscombiana.*

Flask shells, *Gastrochaena dubia,* bore into limestone, shells and red sandstone, and differ from piddocks by forming a limy tube around their joined and fully sheathed siphons. They also are confined to south and south-west coasts.

Shipworms, which bore into wood, are bivalves and their siphons, separate at the tips only, function as in all other suspensions feeders. However, unlike other boring bivalves, shipworms are not entirely dependent on plankton for food as they also digest cellulose from the wood particles bored out during burrowing. Boring is a mechanical action as in piddocks, but the shell protects only the anterior region of the body and the animal is fixed to the burrow posteriorly. As it bores further into the wood its body elongates, becoming somewhat wormlike, hence its common name. Two small limy plates attached to the hind end of the body close over the entrance when the siphons are withdrawn In this way water can be retained in the burrow when the wood is exposed to air. Shipworms enter the wood as larvae and never leave their burrows during their short lives of about a year. The burrows twist and turn, but never cross, so each shipworm must, in some way, detect the presence of nearby tunnels. Some species line the burrows with a thin layer of lime. The shell of *Terado norvegica* reaches a diameter of 16—18 mm, but that of *T. navalis* only 8—9 mm. Both these species bore into wooden pier piles, groynes and boats, whereas *T. megotara,* with a shell diameter of 12 mm, bores into floating timber only.

The shells of wood piddocks, *Xylophaga dorsalis*, are somewhat similar to those of the shipworms, reaching a maximum diameter of 12 mm, but the body is retained between the valves and is in no way fixed to the burrow. These creatures do not digest wood cellulose and are completely dependent on indrawn plankton for food. Wood piddocks form round, shallow burrows in floating timber only.

Deposit Feeders. In all deposit feeders the shells are flattened laterally and the foot is large but greatly compressed, two features adapted to deep burrowing. The siphons are separate, long and mobile.

In the peppery furrow shell, *Scrobicularia plana*, the inhalent siphon is very long and covers a wide area, drawing in detritus from the sea floor. This bivalve is abundant in estuarine muds and is tolerant of considerably reduced salinities. However, it cannot withstand lowered temperatures, and in conditions as severe as the 1963 winter the populations become greatly reduced.

Another estuarine species the Baltic tellin, *Macoma balthica*, feeds in the same way. Its solid, oval shell may reach a length of 25 mm and is white with yellow, pink or purple concentric bands. *Macoma* is far more tolerant of lowered temperatures than *Scrobicularia*.

All the tellin shells are detritus feeders and the commonest found on sandy shores is the delicate, translucent, thin tellin, *Tellina tenuis*, ranging in colour from salmon pink, rose pink to white. The shell may be up to 19 mm long. This bivalve is found in clean sand only from the middle shore downwards, on all coasts.

Alongside the thin tellin we find the banded wedge shell, *Donax vittatus*, whose shiny, triangular shell reaches a length of 30 mm. Fine grooves radiating outwards from the beak give a toothed edge to the base of the shell which varies in colour between white, pale yellow, brown and purple, with the inner surface white and sometimes splashed with mauve.

Of the sunset shells only one inhabits the littoral region. This is the Faroe sunset shell, *Gari fervensis,* whose oblong shell is angular posteriorly and reaches a length of 45 mm. It is cream or buff with white concentric markings and rays, and a brown band at the periphery. It burrows in sand of the lower shore and below low water mark.

AMPHINEURA

The shell of these small molluscs, the chitons, is formed of eight overlapping plates or valves, which give the flattened, bilateral, oval-shaped body sufficient flexibility to adhere closely to uneven surfaced rocks and also to curl up when detached—a useful practice in rough seas. The tonghened mantle extends beyond the valves to form a *girdle* and, viewed ventrally, the gills are located in a groove between the mantle and sides of the large foot. When disturbed the chiton tenaciously grips the rock by means of its muscular foot, making dislodgement difficult. In this habit it emulates the common limpet.

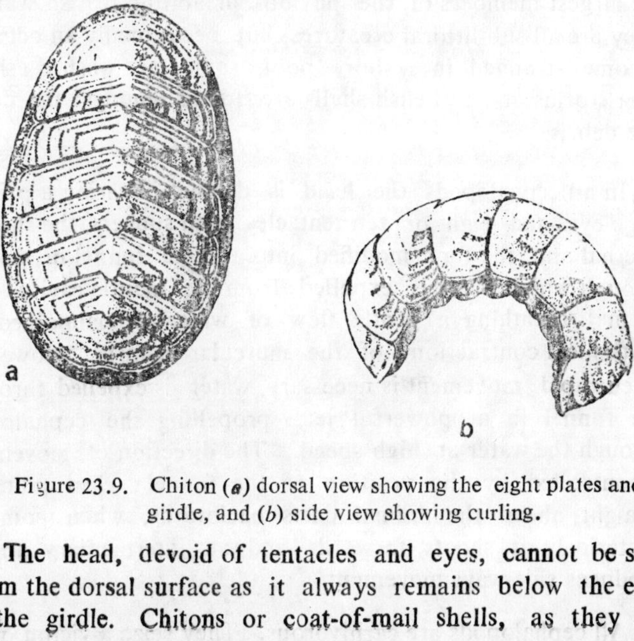

Figure 23.9. Chiton (*a*) dorsal view showing the eight plates and girdle, and (*b*) side view showing curling.

The head, devoid of tentacles and eyes, cannot be seen from the dorsal surface as it always remains below the edge of the girdle. Chitons or coat-of-mail shells, as they are commonly called, move very slowly over rocks, browsing on minute algal growths which they scrape off with the radula. The sexes are separate, fertilization external and the eggs develop into trochosphere larvae.

Lepidochitona clnerea, the commonest chiton found on most rocky shores, is about 12—15 mm long, varying in colour between red, brown and green to blend with the rocks ; the girdle is fairly broad.

Acanthochitona crinitus, also about 12—15 mm long, is common low on the shore, but only on south and west coasts of Britain. It may be brown, yellow or red, and the girdle bears eighteen tufts of bristles which appear starlike on either side of the valves.

CEPHALOPODA

Cephalopoda are the most highly developed molluses and the largest members of the phylum inhabiting British waters. They are all sub-littoral creatures, but occasionally an octopus becomes stranded in a shore pool, squids are washed ashore after storms and cuttlefish shells are found amongst the drift-line debris.

In all cephalopods the head is distinct, bearing a pair of large eyes and eight or ten tentacles with suckers, the shell is internal and the foot modified into a large funnel or siphon through which water is expelled from the mantle cavity. In normal breathing a gentle flow of water is maintained by rhythmical contractions of the muscular mantle. However, when rapid movement is necessary, water is expelled through the funnel in a powerful jet, propelling the cephalopod through the water at high speed. The direction of movement is controlled by the position of the funnel ; when pointing straight ahead the animal darts backwards, when pointing posteriorly it shoots forwards and at intermediary angles produces side-ways movement.

All cephalopods are carnivorous. They seize a victim with

their sucker-clad tentacles, then inject it with a paralysing fluid secreted by some of their salivary glands. As struggling of the prey diminishes, the cephalepod's horny jaws tear the flesh and the radula then cuts it into a small enough size for swallowing.

Chromattophores are abundant in the skin of the upper surface, so cepholopods can rapidly change colour. Besides plending with the background in this way, they have another method of defence, they discharge a dark fluid or ink to form a 'smoke-screen' in the water. Some cephalopods are also luminescent.

The sexes are separate and the male inserts spermatozoa, contained in small packets called *spermatophores,* into the mantle cavity of the female.

Cuttlefish and squids have ten tentacles, two of which are longer and narrower than the others, with suckers confined to the broad tips. These special tentacles are nsed in capturing prey, but when not in use are retracted.

The cuttlefish has a broad, oval body, with lateral fins extending along the whole edge. By undulating movement of these fins, it swims gently or maintains its position in the water. In the common cuttlefish, *Sepia officinalis,* the dorsal surface is black and white, often in stripes, though it can rapidly change the pattern. In contrast, the ventral surface is white. The fluid discharged is the brown *sepia,* at one time used as writing ink. The shell is a white, oval 'bone' formed of a horny substanee impregnated with lime. The eggs are small black elongated spheres some 5-6 mm long, rather like grapes, and are laid in bunches suspended from seaweeds. As cuttlefish like sandy bottoms where they can hunt shrimps, they often swim into shallow water in sheltered bays. The cuttlefish is quite artful in its search for shrimps. It swims slowly along a course parallel with, but a few centimetres above, the bottom and as it does so, it expels a jet of water through its siphon. This is just sufficient to distu b the surface sand and expose any buried shrimp As soon as it spies a shrimp, it whips out its two long tentacles and, if it is lucky, twists the suckered tip of one tentacle around the victim and draws it back into its mouth. The common cuttle may grow to a length of about 30 cm.

The little cuttlefish, *Sepiola atlvantica,* reaches only a length of 5 cm, lives alongside-shrimps at low water mark and below, and exhibits strong luminescence.

In contrast, the body f squids is torpedo shaped with a pair of triangular latteral fins towards the posterior. On account of this form, squids are the faster swimmers of the class.

The common squid, *Loligo forbesi,* has a long, transparent, leaflike, horny shell or 'pen' and it lives well offshore. The eggs are laid in cream-coloured gelatinous, cylindrical masses, attached to stones or shells. Sometimes these fingerlike masses are washed ashore and the developing young can be observed moving within their capsules. The bommon squid is greyish white and is not capable of extensive pattern and colour changes as exhibited by cuttlefish.

Octopuses have eight tentacles only which are webbed for part of their length, and these they spread out like a canopy over unsuspecting prey. The body is spherical and not so streamlined as in the other cephalpods. When swimming the body moves forwards with the tentacles trailing behind, but the more usual method of movement is along the bottom on its tentacles. The shell is reduced to two small vestigial rods. Octopuses live among rocks, hiding in crevices. The female lays her eggs in strings in sheltered rock-holes and then remains on guard beside them. Octopuses have a fantastic ability for squeezing through very narrow cracks.

The curled octopus, *Eledone cirrhosa,* is found in all British waters, but is commonest in the north. Its tentacles bear a single row of suckers.

The common octopus, *Octopus vulgaris,* is not so common as it is found only in the English Channel, this being the northernmost limit of the species. It is easily distinguished from *Eledone* by the double row of suckers on its tentacles.

24

Phylum : Echinodermata

In this phylum *all* the members are marine and none form colonies the parasitic mode of life.

Echinoderms are commonly called *spiny-skinned* animals because small spines project through the skin. These are for protection and are extensions of the simple limy skeleton which supports the body. Most echinoderms appear radially symmetrical and the body is usually five-rayed. A characteristic feature on the phylum is the presence of a water-vascular system for control of the special *tube-feet*, whose functions vary between locomotion, food collection, sensitivity and respiration.

The Echinodermata are divided into five classes, the *ASTEROIDEA* (starfish, cushion stars and sunstars), *OPHIUROIDEA* (brittlestars), *ECHINONIDEA* (sea-urchins), *HOLOTHURODIDEA* (sea-cucumbers) and *CRINOIDEA* (featherstars).

ASTEROIDEA

Starfish are probably the most familiar members of the echinoderms with their typically star-shaped form of a central disc extending into five arms. The body is dorso-ventrally flattened with the mouth situated in the centre of the disc on the ventral surface. The anus, if present, is on its dorsal surface, together with the water pore, and at the base of the arms are the genital openings. Internally the disc contains the

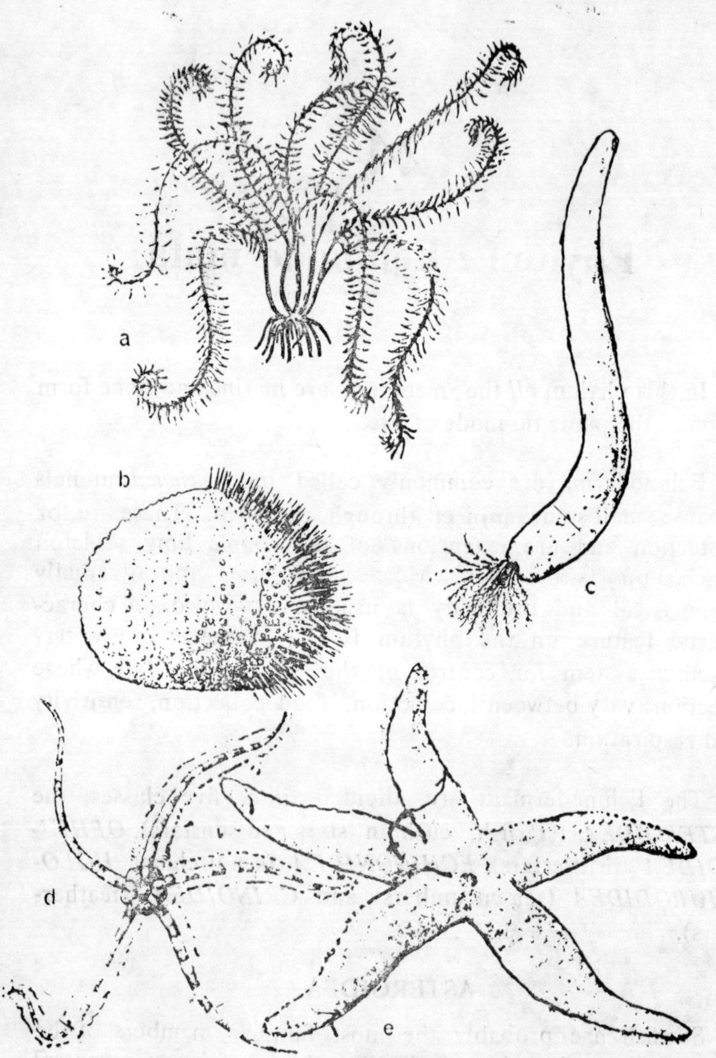

Figu. e 24 1. Varieties of Echinodermata. (*a*) feather-star, (*b*) sea-urchin, (*c*) sea-cucumber, (*d*) brittlestar, (*e*) starfish.

stomach, but the rest of the gut extends into the arms, where the gonads are also located.

Skeleton. The skeleton of starfish consists of many small, separate, calcareous plates held together by connective tissue to allow slight bending movements of the body. From many of these plates project small spines to give further protection. On the ventral surface of the arms the sides bend inwards to form a grave, and on the bounding skeletal plates the spines can be moved up and down across this furrow,

The surface of a starfish is always clean because any pieces of seaweed or particles of sand and shell which become caught among the spines are immediately removed by the *pedicellaria*, special minute gripping organs attached to some of the skeletal plates and spines. In addition to this function, the pedicellaria are also used for holding prey and are a means of defence Not all starfish bear these organs and of the more common British species the burrowing starfish, the cushion star and the scarlet starfish are devoid of pedicellaria.

Tube-feet. When a starfish is turned on its back rows of tube-feet can be seen protruding along the groves of the arms

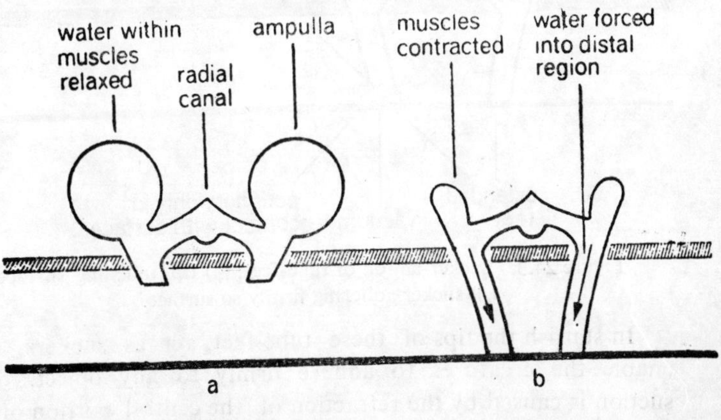

Figure 24.2. Method of retraction and extension of tube-feet, (*a*) retracted and (*b*) extended.

and, as the animal tries to sigh itself, these feet are extended and retracted. The operation of these is most interesting. Within the body of a starfish there is a system of water-carrying tubes called the *water-vascular system.* This consists of a circular canal in the disc from which radiate five canals, one to each arm. From these radial canals a series of paired lateral branches terminate in the tube-feet. Each tube-foot consists of two regions, the upper saclike structure, called the *ampulla,* and the hollow, elastic-walled, closed tube. When the ampulla muscles contract, water is forced into the tube-foot thus extending it, as shown in the diagram facing. Water can flow only in this direction because a valve prevents back-flow into the radial canal. When the ampulla muscles relax, the water returns to the sac and the tube-foot retracts. Some of the fluid within the canals seeps through the walls into the body cavity ; replenishment is, therefore, necessary and water enters through a special pore on the dorsal surface called the *madreporite.*

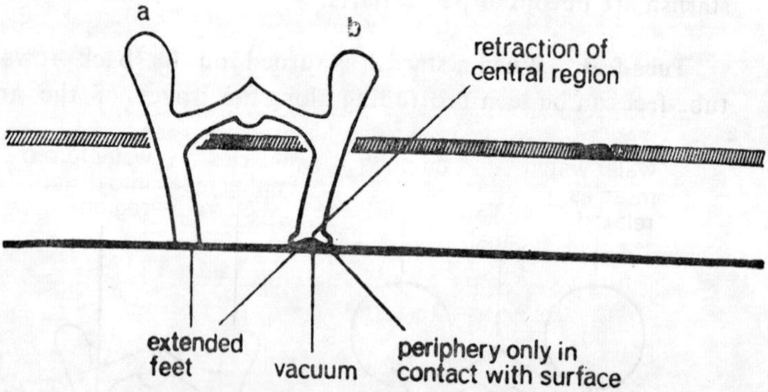

Figure 24.3. Sucker-action of tube-feet, (*a*) tip touching surface and (*b*) sucker adhering firmly so surface.

In starfish the tips of these tube-feet act as suckers, and enable the creatures to adhere firmly to any object. The suction is caused by the retraction of the central portion of the tip of a foot so that a vacuum is produced in the space formed, with the periphery only in contact with the surface. A mucus secreted by glands in the tip also helps in adhesion.

Locomotion. As there is no head nor anterior region in a starfish it can move in any direction, and even though the individual foot movements may appear haphazard, they are co-ordinated so that the animal progress along the required course. The specially modified sensory tube-feet at the tips of the arms are used to seek out the favourable direction. To proceed along a certain path the tube-feet are extanded forward at an angle, until the tips touch the surface and, when the suckers have adhered firmly, the longitudinal muscles of the tube-feet contract, thus pulling the body forward. The suction is then released and the tube-feet are extended forward once more.

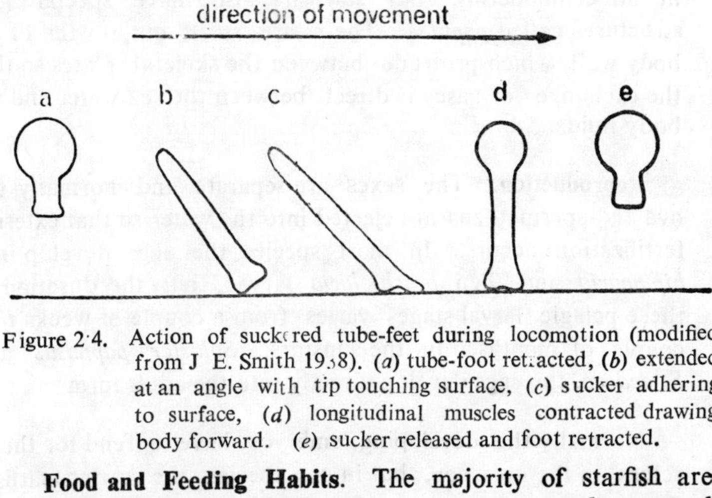

Figure 2·4. Action of suckered tube-feet during locomotion (modified from J E. Smith 1958). (*a*) tube-foot retracted, (*b*) extended at an angle with tip touching surface, (*c*) sucker adhering to surface, (*d*) longitudinal muscles contracted drawing body forward. (*e*) sucker released and foot retracted.

Food and Feeding Habits. The majority of starfish are capable of a most unusual habit ; they can turn the stomach inside out to envelop prey which is too large to enter the mouth. The walls of the stomach secrete digestive juices for conversion of the food material into a soluble form so that it can be absorbed. After the meal the stomach is drawn in again, leaving the waste outside the body.

All starfish are carnivorous and when feeding on bivalves the lube-feet play an important role. First the prey, such as an oyster, is completely enveloped by the arms. Then the starfish grips the two valves with its suckers in such a manner that, when it raises the central disc, a pull is exerted in opposite directions. The oyster tries to keep its two valves closed, but generally has to 'give up'; once a small gap appears, the starfish pushes its stomach through to digest the flesh within. When the gap has widened further the starfish relaxes its grip.

The burrowing starfish is incapable of extruding its stomach so it swallows its prey whol, and the indigestible matter is passed back out of the mouth.

Respiratory Mechanism. Diffusion of oxygen and carbon dioxide occurs through the surface of the tube-feet as in all echinoderms, but starfish also have special 'gill' structures called *papulae.* These are small outgrowths of the body wall which protrude between the skeletal plates so that the exchange of gases is direct between the sea water and the body fluids.

Reproduction. The sexes are separate and normally the ova and spermatozoa are ejected into the water so that external fertilization occurs. In most species the eggs develop into *bipinnaria* and then *brachiolaria* larvae, but the duration of these pelagic larval stages varies from a couple of weeks to a couple of months. In the sunstars, *Solaster papposus* and *S. endeca,* the eggs develop directly into the adult form

Normally the developing embryos have to fend for themselves in the open sea, but in one species, the scarlet starfish, *Henricia sanguinolenta,* the female affords some protection to the young. She forms a 'tentlike' cavity around the fertilized eggs by holding on to a rock with the tips of the arms and raising the central disc. She remains in this position without food for the three-week development period.

Regeneration. All starfish are capable of regeneration and if an arm is lost, a new one readily develops : frequenty a starfish is found with one or two arms shorter than the others. Regeneration is very strong in the common starfish, *Asterias rubens,* and a detached arm, provided it retains a small portion of the disc, will develop four more arms to form the complete animal. A favourite food of starfish is the oyster and in days gone by the oystermen removed starfish from their oyster-beds, cut them up and threw the pieces back, little realizing that instead of reducing the number they were in fact increasing the population !

Growth. The growth rate of starfish varies with the availability of food so size is not necessarily an indication of age. They can survive without food for some months when, of course, there is no growth. *Asterias rubens* is generally sexually mature at one year and lives for five or six years.

Common Species

The starfish most readily found on any shore around Britain is the common starfish, *Asterias rubens*. It also lives in deeper water where it may attain a total diameter of 45 cm, but specimens found on the shore, usually under stones or in crevices, do not normally exceed 12 cm.

The cushion star, *Asterina gibbosa*, is the only other starfish that is a true inhabitant of the shore. It is found low on rocky shores under stones and over-hangs, but it is confined to the south and west coasts. The arms are not so distinct from the central disc, and the body form appears pentagonal. This is the smallest British starfish with a total diameter of about 4 cm though it can grow to 10 cm.

The spiny starfish, *Marthasterias glacialis*, and the scarlet starfish, *Henricia sanguinolenta*, may be found on the shore, but the more usual habitat is the sublittoral region, *M. glacialis* is confined to the south and west coast.

The sunstars are shallow water forms which have more than five arms ; they may have as many as thirteen. The common sunstar, *Solaster papposus*, is found on all coasts, but the purple sunstar, *S. endeca*, on all coasts except the south and south-east.

The burrowing starfish, *Astropecten irregularis*, lives in sand, but belongs to the sub-littoral zone. However it is occasionally found very low on the shore and is recognized by its flattened body which bears distinctive calcarcous plates along the arm edges. The tips of the tube-feet are pointed and modified for burrowing in the sand.

OPHIUROIDEA

The brittlestars are similar in form to the starfish, but the arms are longer and narrower and distinct from the central disc. These thin arms break easily, hence the common name.

The disc is flat with the central mouth on the ventral surface, but there is no anus. The alimentary system and reproductive organs are retained completely within the disc.

Skeleton. Unlike starfish, the calcareous plates on the dorsal surface of brittle-stars are arranged in a definite pattern and the arm grooves are closed over. The consecutive plates have very flexible joints to allow horizontal movement of the arms. Spines may be present but there are no pedicellaria.

Tube-feet. The tube-feet of brittlestars do not terminate in suckers. The tips are pointed and, unlike starfish, mncus-glands are present along the length of the tube-feet.

Locomotion. When brittlestars traverse flat, hard surfaces the movement is dependent on the flexure of the arms. These

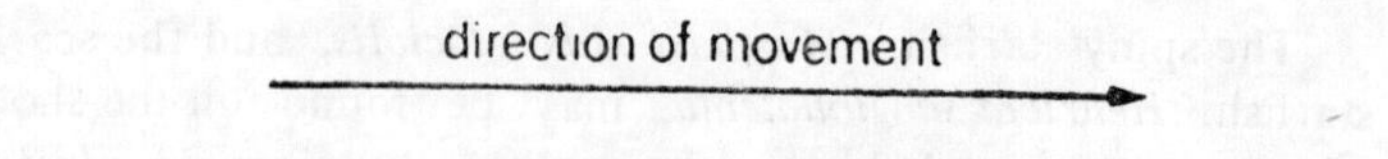

Figure 24.5. Action of pointed tube-feet during locomotion (modified from J.E. Smith 1938). (*a*) tube-foot extended forward at an angle with tip touching the surface. (*b*) side of foot laying along surface, (*c*) foot straightened drawing body forward.

are flung ahead in pairs, forcing the animal forward in a jerky motion. Movement in this way is fairly rapid.

Some species grip objects with a couple of arms and drag themselves forward. *Ophiocomina nigra* moves over *Laminaria* fronds in this way.

Some species are not capable of such rapid movement and, instead of flinging the arms forward, an arm is extended, the gripping the surface with the help of the spines, then contracted by bending in a snakelike manner, thus dragging the body forward over the surface with the other arms trailing behind.

In climbing vertical surfaces the tube-feet come into play and the movement is a gliding progression. As there are no suckers the distal third of an extended foot bends until the side lays along the surface, the mucous secretion helping in this adhesion. The foot is then gradually straightened, thus pulling the animal forward. *Ophiothrix fragilis* climps in this way.

Food and Feeding Habits The stomach cannot be turned inside out and as there is no anus the undigested food is extruded through the mouth. The diet may be detritus or small animals, dead or alive, such as worms, crustaceans and compound tunicates In *Ophiocomina nigra* the tips of the long arms twist around prey and carry it back to the mouth.

Respiratory Mechanism. There are no papulae as in the starfish, but on the ventral of surface of the disc, on either side of each arm, a narrow silt opens into a thin-walled sac. Sea water enters this sac and gaseous exchange occurs through the wall. The tube-feet also act as respiratory surfaces.

Reproduction. In most brittlestars the sexes are separate. The reproductive organs open into the thin-walled sacs mentioned above and these are called *genital bursae*. After external fertilization the eggs develop into *ophiopluteus* larvae.

One littoral species a hermaprodite and also exhibits

ovovivipar ity. This is *Amphicpholis squamata*, which lives on a sandy or stony bottom An ovary and testis open into each genital bursa so it is here that fertilization occurs and the embros develop. The young do not leave this protection until they are miniature adults.

A sand-burrowing brittlestar, *Acrocnida brachiata*, has a peculiar way of discharging the genital products. The arms are extremely long so, with the tips remaining buried below the sand, it raises the disc and upper parts of the arms above the surface and discharges its ova or spermatozoa from this postiion, afterwards sinking back into the sand,

Regeneration. This is strong in all species. Arms are often thrown off, but new ones develop rapidly.

Common Species

Acrocnida brachiata burrows in sand with only the tips of the arms protruding on the middle and lower shores. This species is confined to south and west coasts. The disc is only 12 mm in diameter, but the arms may be 180 mm long.

Ophiothrix fragilis is found under stones and in shells low on rocky shores, on all coasts. The diameter of the disc can reach 20 mm and the arms may grow to 100 mm. The colour of this species is variable, ranging from dark blue or violet to reddish-brown, buff or grey, and its arms may be banded or spotted. *Ophiopholis aculeata* is found in similar surroundings, but is only widely distributed in the north. The disc is five-pointed instead of round, 20 mm in diemeter with arms only 70–80 mm long.

Amphipholis squamatia inhabits the lower shore on all coasts where the bottom is sand or gravel, and is found under stones or in pools, particularly associated with the red seaweeds *Corallina*. In addition to being a hermaphrodite and ovo-viviparons, it is also phosphorescent. The disc may be 5 mm in diameter and the arms 20 mm long.

Ophiocomina nigra and the various species of *Ophiura* are sub-littoral so are found only when washed ashore. The former is common on south and west coasts and, as its name implies, is usually black, although it can be pink, with a disc diameter up to 25 mm and an arm length of 125 mm. The latter are found on all coasts.

ECHINOIDEA

The sea-archins are the only echinoderms in which the skeletal plates are completely fused to form a rigid structure. the *test*. The body is spherical in the *regular* forms such as the edible urchin, but more oval in the *irregular* forms with definite anterior and posterior regions as in the burrowing urchins. The alimentary system consists of a long intestine which encircles the body cavity with the anus on the dorsal surface, as in the starfish.

Skeleton. Although there is complete fusion of the calcareous plates, the radial symmetry is still obvious as the test is divided into ten regular sections. Each alternate section has two series of perforations through which the tube-feet protude and these regions correspond to the arms of the starfish and brittlestars.

The spines are the most distinctive feature of the sea-urchin and are much longer and stronger than in other echinoderms, besides being capable of movement in all directions. To allow for this the articulation is that of a ball and socket joint and on a naked test the raised knobs, or tubercles, are obvious.

In the sand-burrowing urchin, *Echinocardium cordatum*, commonly called the sea-potato, some of the spines are modified into spade-like structures for digging.

Pedicellaria are scattered over the whole surface of the test and function as in starfish, but the gripping structure is more complex.

Five strong teeth surround the mouth and the pointed tips meet and protrude slightly. During feeding the tips are gradually worn away, so the teeth grow continuously from the base.

A pyramidal framework of calcareous plates supports these teeth, known as Aristotle's lantern. The irregular froms lack these teeth.

Tube feet. As in starfish the tube-feet terminate in suckers, but they are far more extensible. Around the mouth there are ten short sensitive buccal tube-feet used in the search for food.

In *Echinocardium* suckers are lacking and some tube-feet are specially modified for the burrowing habit.

Locomotion. In climbing, the method of movement is similar to starfish, but the tube-feet are very long and slender for extension beyond the tips of the spines. On flat surfaces the lower spines are used in stilt fashion, but this method of progression is slow. In *regular* urchins movement may be in any direction, but in *irregular* forms the anterior region is always foremost. By using its tube-feet an urchin is capable of righting itself.

Food and Feeding Habits. The *regular* urchins explore the substratum with the buccal tube-feet and, when food is found, centre themselves over it so that the teeth can come into action. These rasp algae and encrusting animals off stones and cut the prey into small pieces. Favourite foods are hydroids. sponges, barnacles, sea-mats and small mussels, as well as algae and detritus ; the teeth are quite strong enough to deal with the hard shells.

In burrowing urchins living in cavities several centimetres below the surface, food is obtained by modified tube-feet capable of extending up the shaft to explore the sand surface above. These tube-feet are glandular, so any food particles stick to the mucous section and, on retraction of the feet, the food is passed to the spines which direct it to the mouth.

Respiratory Mechanism. There are five pairs of 'gills' only which project through slits in the test around the mouth. The tube-feet are the other respiratory surfaces. No 'gills' are present in the *irregular* urchins.

Reproduction. The sexes are separate and the reproductive organs are situated dorsally, their ducts opening through pores around the centre of this surface. The fertilized eggs develop into *echinopluteus* larvae. The common sea-urchin, *Echinus esculentus,* is often called the *edible* urchin, but it is only the gonads that are eaten by man.

Regeneration. The sea-urchins can regenerate spines, pedicellaria and tube-feet readily and even small breaks in the test.

Common Species

Psammebhinvs miliaris is the regular urchin found under stones on any rocky shore, often with pieces of shell, stone or seaweed stuck to its spines ; it grows to a maximum diameter of about 50 mm. It is green with violet tips to the spines.

The green sea-urchin, *Echinocyamus pusillus,* is much smaller, its greatly flattened, oval test reaching a length of 15 mm only. It is bright green and inhabits the very lowest regions of coarse sand or gravel shores.

The common or edible urchin, *Echinus esculentus,* is sublittoral, but very occassionally a young specimen may be found on the shore. It is nearly spherical in shape and is the largest British sea-urchin, growing to a diameter of 12 cm. The test is red with whitish turbercles, and the spines red and white with violet tips.

Two species are rock-borers and they appear to enlarge existing depressions in rock by a rotary action of the spines, assisted by a digging operation of the teeth. *Paraeentrotus lividus,* common on the south and west coasts of Ireland, is gergarious so that an area of rock becomes honeycombed with their borings. *Strongylocentrotus drobranchiensis,* the other rock-borer, is found only on the east coast of Britain.

The sea-potato, *Echinocardium cordatnm,* buries in clean sand, 15-20 cm deep, with a single shaft to the surface. Secrated much holds the sand particles in position so that the animal is free in the burrow. Usually many creatures of all sizes are found in the same area. The test is heart-shaped and attains a maximum length of 8·9 cm, but specimens found are normally much smaller. Its colour is pale cream to dirty yellow and it inhabits the middle and lower shores on all coasts.

The purple heart unchin, *Spatangus purpureus,* burrows in coarse sand and gravel low on the shore on all coasts. It is violet with whitish spines and many reach a length of 10 cm.

HOLOTHUROIDEA

Compared with the other classes of echinoderms the sea-cucumbers are the least attractive as the body is elongated into a thick tube covered with a leathery skin, often dull in colour. The mouth is at one end and the anus at the other, so the regions corresponding to the arms of starfish are stretched lengthwise between these two external openings.

The mouth is surrounded by a circlet of tentacles formed from modified tube-feet. The body is very muscular and in some sea-cucumbers the mouth region, including the tentacles, can be withdrawn into the body cavity ; in these species the skin is much thinner in the anterior region.

Skeleton. This is reduced to minute calcareous particles embeded in the skin and, when viewed under a microscope, these are found to be of varying shapes. The body is therefore pliable and soft to touch compared with other echinoderms. Spines and pedicellaria are absent.

Tube-feet. In sea-cucumbers the tube-feet are situated on the five longitudinal regions, but normally only those on the ventral surface terminate in suckers. As in sea-urchins, the mouth is surrounded by a circlet of buccal tube-feet but they are modified into extensive tentacles.

Locomotion. Sea-cucumbers are an inactive class of animals living in crevices, under rocks or buried in mud or sand, and their sluggish movements are produced by contraction and relaxation of the muscular body wall. Tube-feet play little part in locomotion, but are important in attachment.

Food and Feeding Habits. The food consists of detritus and small organisms. In the sea-gherkin, *Cucumaria saxicola*, detritus caught in its long, branching tentacles becomes stuck to a mucous secretion and the tips of the tentacles then bend inwards to transfer the food to the mouth.

In some species, such as the cotton-spinner, *Holothuria forskali*, the tentacles are much shorter and just shovel the mud and detritus into the mouth.

Respiratory Mechanism. Diffusion of oxygen and carbon dioxide occurs through the walls of a system of hollow tubes, called *respiratory trees*, located within the body cavity. They extend from the cloaca, a small cavity situated just inside the anus, whose muscular walls enable water to be sucked in and out of the system continuously.

In some species special defensive organs are present at the base of the respiratory trees. These secrete a substance which, on contact with sea water, forms a mass of sticky threads and thus entangles the attacker. *Holothuria forskali* is very adept at this, hence its common name *cotton-spinner*.

In species without respiratory trees the skin is thin enough to allow diffusion over the whole body surface.

Reproduction. The sexes are usually separate, but a few species are hermaphrodites. When this is the case, they are alternately male and female, because the one gonad produces both spermatozoa and ova, but at different times. The fertilized eggs usually develop into *auricularia* larvae.

Regeneration. The ability to regenerate is very great and in some seacucumbers the respiratory trees and part of the gut are ruptured and extruded through the anus when attacked by a predator, but within a short time they are renewed.

Common Species

The nigger or cotton-spinner, *Holothuria forskali*, has a flattened body covered with a thick skin, black or dark brown on the upper surface and pale cream or yellow underneath. It has twenty short tentacles and may grow to a length of 20 cm. Occasionally this species may be found very low on rocky shores of the south-west, but it normally inhabits the shallow waters.

The sea-gherkin, *Cucumaria saxicola*, has a smooth, delicate, whitish skin and the cylindrical body has ten well branched dark tentacles. It may reach 15 cm in length and lives on the lower regions of rocky shores of the south and west coasts. Two other species. *C. normai* and *C. lactea*, live in similar regions, but the former, which is restricted to south coasts, grows to a length of 15 cm and has a wrinkled leathery skin, whereas the latter, found on all coasts, reaches only 4 cm and has a smooth leathery skin.

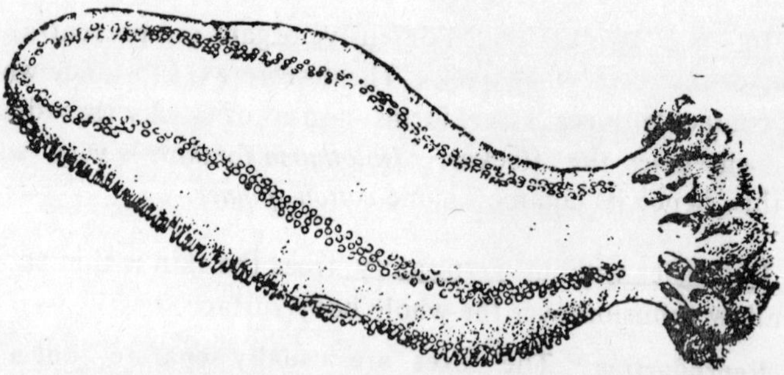

Figure 24.6. Sea-cucumber, *Cucumaria spp.*

In the burrowing forms the body does not bear tube-feet nor are respiratory trees present, but the skin is thin. *Leptosynapta inhaerens* has twelve well-branched, feathery tentacles, and a pinkish coloured body which may reach a length of 30 cm, though normally these creatures are only about half this size. *Leptosynapta* is a hermaphrodite and development is direct, that is there is no pelagic larval stage. It burrows in sand or mud on most coasts. *Lapidoplax digitata* also has twelve tentacles, but these terminate in four digits. It is usually red or brownish in colour, reaching a maximum length of 30 cm and burrows in sand or mud on south-west and west coasts only.

CRINOIDEA

This is the most primitive class of echinoderms and although they are abundant in the seas, only one species is found on British shores. This is the beautiful rosy feather-star, *Antedon bifida.*

Crinoids are the only echinoderms that attach themselves to the substratum. In some species fixture is for life, but in others, such as *Antedon.* only the young are sedentary.

The plates of the skeleton are separate and the body form is cuplike, the arms being raised upwards with the central mouth on the upper surface of the disc. Beneath there are twenty-five short stalks, or *cirri,* on which the animal rests and by which it moves slowly over rocks.

Each of the five arms of *Antedon* divides into two and as these are narrow with many fine side branches they appear featherlike, hence the common name. These arms are grooved and ciliated, so food particles collected from the water are passed along the furrows to the mouth.

In addition to creeping over rocks, the rosy feather-star swims by gentle waving motions of its arms.

The sexes are separate and the reproductive organs are borne on some of the side branches of the arms.

The colour of *Antedon* varies from rosy red to mauve and yellow or orange ; the complete diameter is approximately 10 cm, though it may be as much as 15 cm in specimens from deeper water. This creature is found attached to rocks and stones very low on the shore, but only on south-west coasts.

25

Phylum : Chordata

Man, together with all other vertebrates, belongs to the phylum Chordata whose characteristic feature is the possession of a strengthened rod of tissue, the *notochord,* though this is only present in vertebrates during early development, its function being taken over by the backbone. However, a few animals without backbones do possess a notochord and therefore come within the same phylum.

All these lower chordates are marine creatures and include lancelets, acorn-worms and sea-squirts, but only the latter group, the Tunicata, has representatives living on the shore. Of the vertebrates, only fish are true inhabitants of the shore.

TUNICATA

Tunicata or sea-squirts belong to the same phylum as the vertebrates, but on studying the gelatinous saclike, sessile adults this seems incomprehensible. However, justification for inclusion in the Chordata is found in the larval stage ; the larvae are free-swimming tadpole-like creatures with a notochord.

All tunicates are marine, living either singly or in colonies, and several colourful representatives abound on our rocky shores.

Structure. The body is always protected by a toughened *test* or *tunic* and has two openings, the mouth or inhalent aperture at the top of the sac and the exhalent aperture at the side. During submersion, water flows freely through the animal and when the tide recedes it retains as much as possible to prevent desiccation during exposure. The derivation of the common name sea-squirt becomes obvious on touching an exposed animal ; the body contracts, squirting out jets of water through both openings.

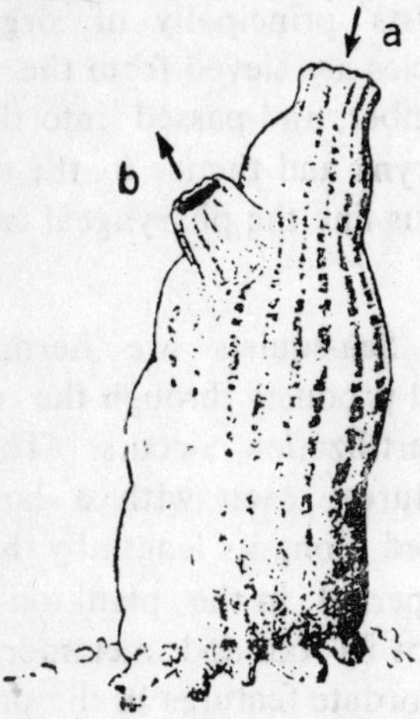

Figure 25.1. Basic form of a solitary tunicate. (*a*) inhalent aperture and (*b*) exhalent aperture.

The mouth opens into an expanded region of the gut, the pharynx, perforated by regular rows of tiny slits bearing cilia at their edges. The beating of these cilia draws a water current into the mouth, through the slits and out via the exhalent aperture. This is the form of solitary sea-spuirts and the internal structures can often be identified through the semi-transparent body wall. Colonial forms are of two types. Some are a collection of solitary forms fused together at their bases, while other encrusting forms consist of a small group of individuals each with its own mouth, but with one common exhalent aperture. These are known as compound tunicates and the star sea-squirt that is so abundant on rocks and weeds exemplifies their structure and beauty.

Respiratory Mechanism. The perforated pharynx is well supplied with blood and, as water is continuously drawn over the surface and through the slits, this is the region of gaseous exchange. The pharyngeal cavity is therefore also referred to as the branchial chamber.

Food and Feeding. Sea-squirts are suspension feeders, so their diet consists of plankton or detritus, depending on their location. On exposed shores the food is plankton, whereas in estuaries it consists principally of organic detritus. These microscopic particles are sieved from the water, drawn through the branchial chamber, and passed into the ocsophagus at the base of the pharynx and thence to the stomach for digestion. Secretions of mucus line the pharyngeal cavity and assist in this filtering process.

Reproduction. Sea-squirts are hermaphrodites and they release their sexual products through the exhalent opening into the sea where fertilization occurs. The larvae are minute tadpole-like creatures, each with a large muscular tail for swimming supported along its length by the internal notochord. After a freeliving period in the plankton a larva settles head downward, absorbs its tail and metamorphoses into the adult form, losing all chordate features in the process.

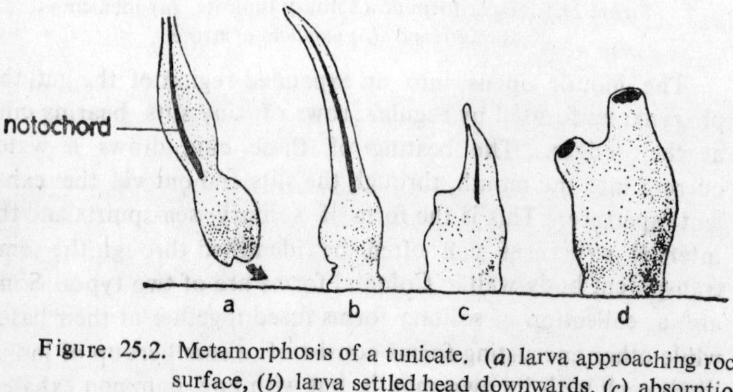

Figure. 25.2. Metamorphosis of a tunicate. (*a*) larva approaching rock surface, (*b*) larva settled head downwards, (*c*) absorption of larval tail, (*d*) adult tunicate.

Common Species

Simple, solitary forms are attached to rocks and stones on the lower shore and in shallow water, and some become exposed on pier piles, harbour walls, etc., at low water springs.

Most species are gelatinous and semi-transparent, and the two external opening are conspicuous. They are easily recognizable as simple sea-squirts, but accurate identification *in situ* is difficult.

Ciona intestinalis, found on all British coasts, is attached at the base and the elongated, cylindrical, yellowish or pale green transparent body may reach a length of 12 cm, with the inhalent opening at the top and the exhalent close beside it.

Ascidia conchilega is attached along one side with the mouth at the tip and the exhalent opening towards the base on the free side. The transparent test is rather rough and the oval, flattened body grows to a length of about 5 cm. This creature is found on all coasts.

Ascidiella aspersa is an estuarine species, but confined to south and west coasts. It is attached at the base and may reach 12 cm in length. The body surface is rough, with the mouth at the top and the exhalent opening about a third of the way down one side.

Dendrodoa grossularia is only 6—12 mm high, bright red or brownish, with a rough wrinkled test. It is a solitary form, but is frequently found in masses under rock overhangs, particularly on south and west coasts.

Some colonial forms, such as *Clavelina lepadiformis*, appear as groups of simple sea-squirts arising from a common base. In *Clavelina* each individual has a soft transparent test, showing the yellow-orange contents below ; the body is attached to the base by a short stalk. This sea-squirt is usually about 1—2 cm high and grows on rocks and stones on the lower shore.

Morchellium and *Aplidium* both have fleshy, mushroom-shaped colonies attached by short stalks and have bright, attractive colours – yellow, orange, red. They may be 1—3 cm long and are usually attached to undersurfaces of rock overhangs.

Of the compound forms the star sea-squirt, *Botryllus schlosseri*, is the commonest. It encrusts rocks and seaweeds in patches up to 15 cm across, or forms pendulous clumps suspended from the undersurface of rock overhangs. Each 'star' consists of from 3 to 12 individuals, each about 2 mm long, around the one exhalent opening. This very beautiful species appears in a variety of colours : deep red or violet with a cream star, green or deep blue with a yellow star. It is abundant on the lower shore on all coasts.

Botrylloides leachi is similar to *Botryllus* but the individuals are not so regularly placed ; they may be in branched lines or ovals.

FISH

The number of species found on the shore is negligible compared with the open sea. Since fish are aquatic creatures, those that populate the littoral zone resort to pools, puddles with stones and weeds for protection, or bury themselves in the sand or mud. They are, like all other shore inhabitants. cold-blooded animals.

Structure. The body of a consists of a head, trunk and tail but these merge into each other giving the steamlined shape necessary for ease of movement through the water. The head is the region anterior to the gills, and the tail that part posterior to the anus. The trunk bears paired pectoral and pelvic fins, comparable to the fore and hind limbs of higher vertebrates, and median dorsal and ventral fins. The tail terminates in a large caudal fin. Some fish, such as plaice or turbot, have become adapted to a less active existence on the ocean floor, therefore their bodies are flattened instead of typically streamlined.

In bony fish the gills have a protective covering, the *operculum,* which is free along the posterior edge for the exit of water after it has passed over the gills. The whole body is protected by regularly arranged overlapping scales which are derived from the skin. These are laid down early in life and increase in size with fish growth. When viewed under a microscope growth rings can be observed and from these the age of fish may be calculated, just as the age of a tree may be determined by the annual rings on a cut section.

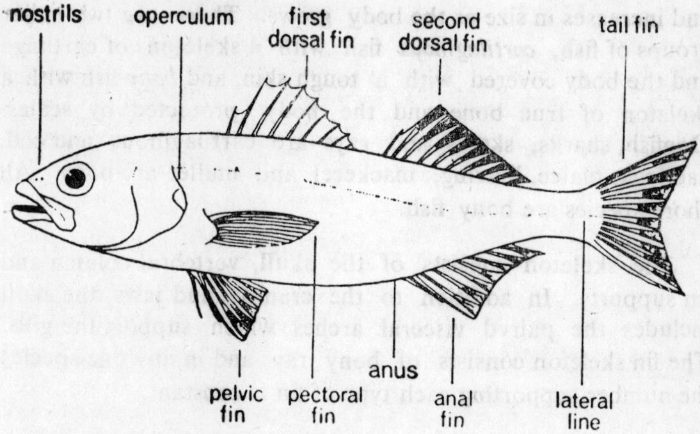

Figure 25.3. External features of a bony fish.

Feeding of fish varies with the season so when food is plentiful in spring and summer, increase in size is rapid and the growth rings on the scales are widely spaced, but when food is scarce in winter, growth is slowed down and the rings are close together. The latter show up clearly so, by counting these close areas, the age in years may be deduced.

The bulk of the body, the flesh of the fish, consists of muscles which are arranged simply compared with the higher vertebrates. The principal muscles, the laterals, run from head to tail, not continuously but divided into segments called myotomes. These strong muscles are used in swimming.

The nostrils of fish are concerned solely with the detection of odours and in some species this is the most important sense for detecting food.

An obvious feature on most fish is the faint line running down each side of the body from head to tail. This is the *lateral line*, the only external sign of the sense organs concerned with the detection of vibrations. This is a special sensory device found only in fish.

Skeleton. Fish and all vertebrates have an endoskeleton as opposed to the exoskeleton encountered in crustaceans. This endoskeleton is embedded within the tissues of the body and increases in size as the body grows. There are two major groups of fish, *cartilaginous* fish with a skeleton of cartilage and the body covered with a tough skin, and *bony* fish with a skeleton of true bone and the body protected by scales. Dogfish, sharks, skates and rays are cartilaginous and cod, haddock, plaice, herring, mackerel and mullet are bony. All shore species are bony fish.

The skeleton consists of the skull, vertebral column and fin supports. In addition to the cranium and jaws, the skull includes the paired visceral arches which support the gills. The fin skeleton consists of bony rays and in any one species the number supporting each type of fin is constant.

Locomotion. In swimming, waves of muscular contraction pass down the sides of a fish from head to tail ; when the lateral muscles at one position on the left side contract, the corresponding muscles on the right relax and vice versa. This causes the body to undulate from side to side as it moves forward through the water. The fins are concerned with maintaining an even keel and controlling direction of movement. The paired pectorals and pelvics control up and down movements and the dorsal and ventral medians control rolling and yawing. During fast swimming some fish collapse their dorsal fin into a groove further to streamline the body.

To enable a bony fish to swim at varying depths it has a special hydrostatic organ, the *swim-bladder*. This is a gas-filled sac in the body cavity just below the vertebral column and the pressure within is altered by the addition or removal of gas, so that internal pressure always equals external pressure. When a fish seems to remain stationary in the water slight movements of the fins only maintain its position because the swim-bladder keeps it buoyant. Cartilaginous fish do not have a swim-bladder and therefore must actively swim, or sink to the bottom.

Respiratory mechanism. Bony fish have four pairs of gills, with blood capillaries very near the surface, and as water passes over them gaseous exchange occurs. To maintain the flow of water over these gills the mouth and opercula work in conjunction. In inspiration the opercula close, the mouth opens and water enters the buccal cavity depressing the floor as it fills. In expiration the mouth closes, the opercula open and the floor of the buccal cavity rises, forcing the water over the gills and out. Some fish do not bother with this mechanism, but swim through the water with mouth and opercula open so that water continuously flows through. However, a disadvantage of this method is that these fish must never stop swimming. The mackerel breathes in this way.

Food and Feeding Habits. These vary with the species because within the class of fish some are carnivorous, some omnivorous, and some filter-feeders. The teeth vary with the diet, but these are used only for grabbing the food which is then swallowed whole. The alimentary canal is basically like that of all vertebrates with a stomach, intestine and associated glands (liver and pancreas) and rectum. There are no salivary glands so no digestion occurs until the food reaches the stomach.

Reproduction. The sexes are separate in fish, and males and females of the same species may differ in external features such as size, colour and markings, or length of fin rays. Fertilization, in most instances, is external, but fewer eggs remain unfertilized than might be anticipated because the males and females of a species collect in shoals at the time of spawning. The number of eggs released is usually extremely high because life for the developing young is very hazardous. In many species, such as plaice and cod, the eggs are pelagic, that is float in the surface waters, and therefore become likely prey for neighbouring marine creatures. In others, such as the herring, the eggs are demersal, that is sink to the bottom, and life is less dangerous. Even so, the eggs of herring are laid in tens of thousands, though this number is small compared with hundreds of thousands or even millions laid by cod and other fish with pelagic eggs.

Shore fish, however, usually lay only small numbers of eggs and these they protect in various ways. Some build nests and then stand guard over the developing young, others lay the eggs in rock crevices and some protect them in a special sac formen by extensions of their own body wall.

Common Species

Blennies. Blennies are true littoral fish inhabiting rocky shores. Although there are several species the common blenny or shanny, *Blennius pholis*, is by far the commonest on all coasts of Britain. It has a thickest body with a dorsal fin

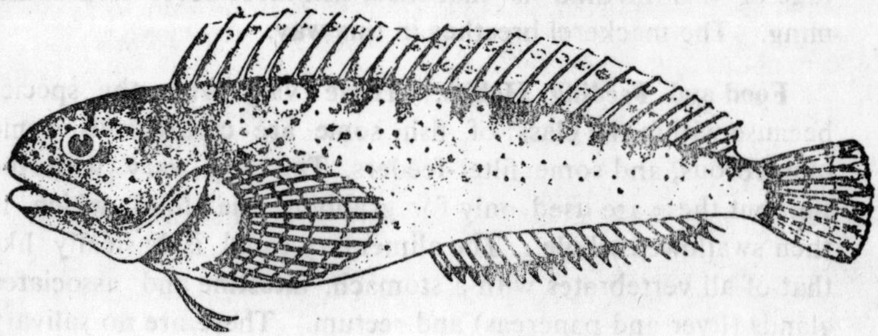

Figure 25 4, Common blenny or shanny. *Blennius pholis.*

running along its length, and an anal fin about half as long. The pectorals are large and rounded, but the pelvics are short and narrow and situated just below the pectorals When at rest on the bottom, these pelvics help to support the anterior region and they are also used in climbing and jumping movements over rocks. The head is blunt and the mouth bounded by thick lips. The eyes are large, and if you watch these fish in an aquarium you can observe the eyes gazing around. Blennies may grow to a length of about 15 cm, but most specimens encountered are shorter than this. The body colour varies and may be dark green, banded or blotched with black, or more yellowish-brown with similar markings. Blennies are carnivores feeding mainly on barnacles and mussels. As mentioned the amber-coloured eggs are guarded by the male.

Butterfish or Gunnels. *Pholis* (=*Centronotus*) *gunnellus* is a close relative of the blenny with a continuous dorsal fin and small pelvics, but it is elongated and flattened laterally. It bears distinctive black spots, circled with white, on either side of the brownish-grey body. Butterfish live on rocky shores under stones and weeds, and the female lays her yellow eggs in small masses which she and the male guard in turn. They are sometimes found curled around their developing eggs.

Pipefish. There are several species of pipefish which inhabit inshore waters, but the worm pipefish, *Nerophis lumbriciformis,* is the only probable find under stones and weeds or in pools on rocky shores. It grows to about 15 cm and is olive brown with ventral markings of white. All species have elongated bodies with tiny dorsal fins and no pelvics ; some are devoid of pectorals as well. Consequently they are not very strong swimmers and tend to be carried along by water currents. The snout is long and narrow, which is a special adaptation for sucking in their food, just as we draw liquid up a straw. Their prey consists principally of small crustaceans and they sometimes hunt them out by prodding around seaweed with their snout. As already discussed it is the male which protects the developing eggs within a special abdominal pouch.

Sand Eels. There are two species, the lesser and the greater sand eel, *Ammodytes tobianus* and *Hyperoplus* (=*Ammodytes*) *lanceolatus*. Both have a long, narrow, silver body with no pelvic fins, but with one very long dorsal fin and one anal fin. They are not true shore fish as they swim in shoals, only coming inshore in sandy areas during spring and summer.

Sticklebacks. The fifteen-spined stickleback, *Spinachia spinachia* (=*S. vulgaris*), is the only truly marine species, though the three-spined, *Gasterosteus aculeatus,* may occasionally be found in the brackish waters of estuaries. In each the name indicates the number of spines which protrude from the dorsal surface. The body, olive green with silvery sides, tapers into a slender tail which terminates in a fan-shaped caudal fin. *S. spinachia* grows to a length of approximately 15 cm and may be found in rocky pools on all coasts. The male builds the nest.

Sea-Scorpions or Bullheads. The sea-scorpion is a vicious-looking fish with a broad, flattened head bearing many spines and with a large mouth. Two species inhabit our rocky shore, *Myoxocephalus* (=*Cottus*) *scorpius* and *Taurulus* (=*Cottus*) *bubalis* ; the former have four spines on each operculum and the latter five. Their bodies are mottled in brown, grey, dark green, black, yellow and reddish-brown, thus blending perfectly with their surroundings of rocks and seaweeds. Here they wait quietly and feed on any unsuspecting small crustaceans which come within reach of their massive mouths. The female lays her yellowish-orange eggs in empty shells, under stones and in rock crevices. Then the male mounts guard and periodically ensures plenty of air is available by disturbing the water his pectoral fins. Sometimes he protects the eggs by reatining them between his pectoral and pelvic fins.

Lesser Weevers or Stingfish. These fish, *Trachinus vipera,* livc alongside shrimps, buried in the sand and are capable of inflicting a harmful sting. The dorsal and opercula spines are grooved, and poison, secreted from glands situated at the base of these spines, flows along the furrows and is injected into the prey or you, if you happen to tread on such a fish. The body colour blends with the sand. Stingfish are about 13 cm long and, unlike most shore fish, their eggs are pelagic.

Rocklings. These belong to the cod family and have an elongated body, narrow pelvic fins anterior to the pectorals, a long anal, a rounded caudal and a dorsal fin running most of the length of the back. The anterior region of this dorsal fin is reduced and withdrawn into a groove lined with sensory cells which detect the presence of food in the surrounding water. Rocklings feed principally on worms, molluscs and small erustaceans. They have barbels on the upper lip and one on the chin, and they swim close to the bottom with the tips of the pelvic fins and chin barbel just sweeping the ground. There are two species, the five-bearded rockling, *Ciliata* (=*Onos*) *mustela*, and the three-bearded rockling, *Gaidropsarus vulgaris* (=*Onos tricirratus*), the former having five barbels in all and the latter three. Five-bearded rocklings are found on all coasts among weed-covered rocks and in rock pools. Their bodies are dark brown or black above, but lighter below, and they may grow to a length of 30 cm, but those encountered are usually only half this length or less. Three-bearded rocklings frequent the shallow seas particularly on south and south-west coasts, have lighter yellowish-brown bodies blotched with darker spots and may be 40 cm in length, although normally they are only 10—15 cm long. The eggs are pelagic in both species.

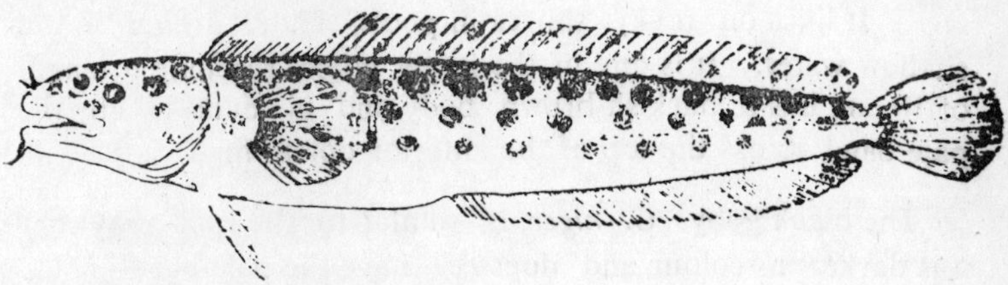

Figure 25·5. Three-bearded rockling, *Gaidropsarus vulgaris*.

Gobies. Several species of gobies live around our shores and non is much longer than 12 cm. They have large eyes situated close together, a feature which makes them look goggle-eyed, and therefore easy to recognize. The body of a goby gradually tapers and terminates in a rounded caudal fin. There are two dorsal fins, the anterior with long spines, and a special characteristic of this group is the fusing of the two pelvic fins to form a suckerlike structure which helps retain the fish in position on the bottom when the water is greatly disturbed. Most species are gregarious and bottom-living creatures feeding mainly on worms and small crustaceans.

The eggs are laid in empty shells or on sheltered rocks and it is the male who guards them. The mating activity is reminiscent of the stickleback because the male finds a suitable spot, attracts and entices a female to deposit her eggs there then, after fertilizing them, remains near by to protect and aerate them. The female takes no further interest once she has laid the eggs.

The sand goby, *Pomatoschistus* (=*Gobius*) *minutus*, is yellowish-brown with a distinctive black spot at the rear of its anterior dorsal fin. It is one of the smaller gobies reaching only a length of approximately 8 cm. It lives in sandy areas along-side shrimps, and also in shallow rock pools where it may be seen shooting through the water at high speed, then disappearing out of sight, its camouflage taking effect once it is motionless. Sand gobies are also tolerant of lowered salinities.

The rock goby, *Gobius paganellus*, is the only solitary species. It lives on rocky shores in pools, under stones and in shallow water. It is one of the larger gobies reaching a length of 10 cm, has a darkish-brown body and is identified by the pale band across the top of the anterior dorsal fin.

The black goby. *G. niger*, is similar to the rock goby, but it is darker in colour and does *not* have the pale band on the dorsal fin.

The spotted goby, *G. ruthensparri*, is not a bottom-living fish, but swims amongst *Laminaria* fronds and in deep pools. It has a dark spot behind the pectoral fin and another on the tail just in front of the caudal fin.

The painted goby, *Pomatoschistus* (=*Gobius*) *pictus*, only about 4 cm long, is similar to the sand goby, but is more brightly coloured and is found only on sandy bottoms on south and west coasts.

Suckerfish or Clingfish. Modification of the pelvic fins is

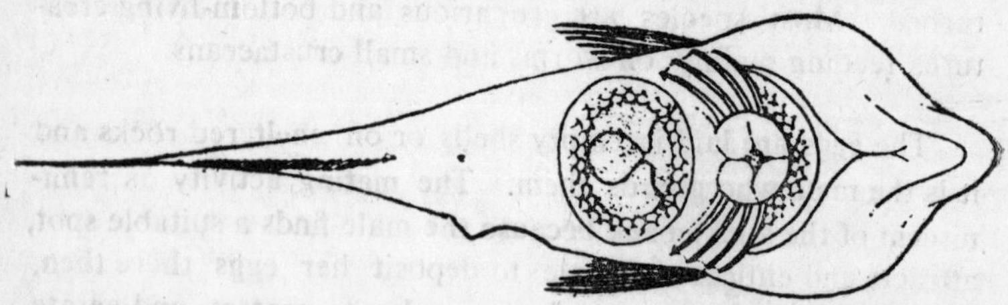

Figure 25·6. Cornish sucker, *Lepadogaster lepadogaster* Ventral view showing sucker formed from modified pelvic fins.

far more elaborate and effective than in the gobies and these fish become firmly attached to the substratum. The commonest found on our shores is the shore clingfish or Cornish sucker, *Lepadogaster lepadogaster* (=*L. gouanii*), which has a dorsoventrally flattened body—a further adaptation to its mode of life. It is typically marked and may be 10 cm long. The eggs are laid in rock crevices and empty shells, and are protected by the parents during development. British coasts are the northernmost limit of these fish, and during winter months they migrate into deeper water.

The two-spotted clingfish, *Diplecogaster* (=*Lepadogaster*) *bimaculata*, is much smaller and only young fish are found on the shore.

Wrasses. Many species of wrasse live in shallow water around our rocky coasts, bui it is only young specimens that are found in rock pools. These fish have a deep body with laternal flattening, a single continuous fin along the dorsal surface and the pelvics situated just behind the pectorals. These are carnivorous fish which have strong teeth for dealing with their prey; the mouth is surrounded by thick lips. Some wrasses are beautifully marked and brightly coloured. Three species build nests of seaweeds, so it is the young of these that are the commonest finds. The ballan wrasse, *Labrus bergylta*, builds its nest of red seaweeds, mainly *Corallina* and *Polysiphonia*, in rock crevices, both sexes taking part in the operation, but once the eggs have been laid and fertilized they are ignored by the parents. Young ballan wrasse are often delicate shades of grass-green, though colour variation is great. This species feeds principally on crustaceans such as shore, edible, spider and swimming crabs, prawns and even acorn barnacles which are scraped off the rocks with the powerful teeth. Mussels, ragworms and small fish are all prey taken by ballan wrasse.

The corkwing wrasse, *Crenilabrus melops*, uses the common wracks for its nest-building and feeds on smaller creatures than the ballan, such as amphipods, *Spirorbis*, gastropods and ragworms.

The cuckoo wrasse, *Labrus mixtus*, is the third nest-builder. but is not nearly so common on our coasts.

Flatfish. These are fish of shallow seas, but small specimens are sometimes found in sandy pools. The interesting feature to remember about flatfish is that when the young hatch out from the eggs they are the normal symmetrical shape of other fish, and that the modifications for life on one side occur during the first few weeks of development. Even the smallest flatfish we find in the sand will have the asymmetrical adult form. Some lay on their left side, for example plaice, dabs, soles and others on their right, such as turbot, brill, topknots.

Other Species. The young of shallow water fish may be found in small shoals at the edge of the sea or in rock pools, but the number of different species is too great for them to be mentioned here.

26

Estuaries

An estuary is where a river widens as it nears the sea and where there is mixing of fresh water and salt water. There are four main types of estuary of which the commonest are drowned river valleys, or rias, located on coastal plains and caused by a rise in sea-level relative to the land. The other three types are less common and include land subsidence, especially along fault lines which allows sea water to invade, estuaries formed behind sand and shingle bars lying parallel to the coastline and lastly fjords. The latter are valleys which have been deepened by glacial action and are typically 'U'-shaped in cross-section with a shallow sill at the entrance restricting the exchange of water between the deep fjord and the open sea.

Typically in an estuary there is a gradation of salinity from the mouth where the water is entirely saline to the head of the estuary where the water is entirely fresh. However, some large rivers such as the Amazon discharge so great a volume of fresh water that all the 'estuarine' mixing occurs at sea and no salt water penetrates up river. Bot in most estuaries on a rising flood tide the fresh water flowing out to sea is insufficient to prevent an inflow of sea water up the estuary. The estuary banks resemble an intertidal coastal area in that the water level rises and falls regularly. This tidal water in the upper reaches of an estuary may be entirely fresh, as water from the river is pounded up by the inflowing tide.

Physical Factors

Salinity. Sea water has a salinity around 35 parts per thousand, fresh water less than 0.5 parts per thousand. The mixing of these two bodies of water may occur in a variety of ways. A wedge may be formed with denser inflowing sea water extending up the estuary below the less dense outflowing river water, e.g. in the estuary of the Mississippi. In this two-layered wedge there is limited mixing at the interface caused by the breaking of internal waves. Alternatively if there is a strong tidal current then an even mixing of both fresh and sea water may occur producing estuaries with vertically homogeneous salinity profiles e.g. in the Thames estuary.

In any estuary more than 400 m wide the effect of Coriolis forces may produce different salinities on opposing banks. The interface between the two water masses is tilted so that looking downstream in the northern hemisphere the fresh water is deflected and flows to a greater extent on the right side of the estuary. This effect has been demonstrated in Chesapeake Bay. Coriolis forces are reversed in the southern hemisphere and in the Hawkesbury River estuary in Australia there is a tilting to the left looking downstream.

The zone of mixing obviously moves up-and downstream with the tide. The degree of mixing will depend on the state of the tide since at low tide the water flowing into an estuary will be fresh river water. There is also run-off from land drainage, the amount of which depends on the season and the topography of the catchment area.

Estuaries may become hyperhaline (salinity >40 parts per thousand, see Table) during periods of intense evaporation over

TABLE

Venice Classification of Saline Waters

	Salinity parts per thousands
Hyperhaline	> 40
Euhaline	40—30
Polyhaline	30—18
Mesohaline	18—5
Oligohaline	5—0.5
Fresh water	< 0.5

large areas of shallow water. Hyperhalinity is often recorded in summer, e.g. in the estuary of the Magorthy River flowing into Chesapeake Bay.

Sediment. Perhaps the most memorable feature of many estuaries to the unwary is the well-known phenomenon of the stuck boot. Much of the coarser material transported downstream by a river will have been deposited in the upper reaches of the estuary ; fine particulate matter or silt with a size range of 4 - 63 μm is carried in suspension further into the estuary and then deposited. Particles clump together, a process known as flocculation, at the halocline where the water mixes. Illite and kaolinite flocculate in salinities of less than 4 parts per thousand, whereas montmorillonite coalesces over the whole range of salinity. The larger floccules sink and form liquid mud on the surface of the submerged mudflats. Estuaries are primarily areas of deposition with an estimated average annual accretion of 2 mm per year. Not all the particulate matter is derived from the river; much is of marine origin and is brought in by the tides, e.g. the Mersey in north west England.

Much research work is funded by oil companies on estuarine deposits such as those of the Mississippi delta in the Gulf of Mexico, since submarine slumping and movement of sediments have potentially disastrous consequences on pipelines connecting offshore drilling rigs with onshore refineries.

Light Penetration. Turbidity is higher in estuaries than in the adjacent open sea as a result of the suspended particulate material derived from the river, from the sea and from the reworking and re-suspension of particles by currents and tides. Nearly all light is absorbed in the first 1—2 m and consequently phytoplankton contributes little to primary productivity. More emphasis is placed on the abundant and constant supply of organic detritus as a source of food to power estuarine food webs. Detritus may be defined as all types of biogenic material (usually fragment of plants) in various stages of microbial decomposition.

Wave Action and Tides. The relatively sheltered nature of many estuaries that narrow gradually further away from the mouth (which itself may be constricted), means that there is limited fetch in most directions. Only small waves lap estuarine shores, thus further encouraging the deposition of mud. The narrowing inland of many estuaries such as the River Severn flowing into the Bristol Channel actually funnels the tidal flow and increases the tidal height. Where the Channel is about 65 km wide at its mouth the average tidal range is about 6 m whereas 130 km further inland the width is only 8 km but tidal range has increased to about 10 m. This funnel also produces a spectacular wall of water or 'bore' 2.5 m high which sweeps up the River Severn at 25 km h^{-1} at every high tide.

Oxygen Both within the sediments and in the overyling water, levels of oxygen are generally low in estuaries. However, during the hours of daylight local pockets of supersaturation may occur in *Zostera* beds as a result of the intense photosynthetic activity. Organisms living among these beds may suffer an oxygen deficiency at night when photosynthesis ceases. Levels of oxygen are further reduced by the micro-organisms breaking down the suspended organic matter in the water. This microbial decomposition of detritus leads to a substantial oxygen demand, depleting oxygen in the interstitial water within the fine sediments deposited already. Anoxic conditions are found 5—10 mm below the surface.

In fjords there may be severe deoxygenation of the water below sill level, a process exacerbated for example in Norway's Oslo Fjord by the presence of sewage effluents which create a high oxygen demand.

Flora, Fauna and Food Webs

Flora. Estuaries are rich environments that may be compared with coral reefs and tropical rain forests, as far as productivity levels are concerned. But here the similarity ends. Reefs and forests have the potential for self sufficiency with algae and flowering plants respectively as primary producers and, by recycling of resources within the system are self-contained, apart from the inputs of plankton to the reef system and sunlight to both. Estuaries, however, derive their richness from a more or less continual input of particulate matter and nutrients both from the river and the sea. Turbidity and clogging deposition reduces overall primary productivity of plankton but a few species of diatom such as *Skeletonema* and the dinoflagellate *Gonyaulax* flourish.

Macroflora includes the eel grass *Zostera* which lives in both temperate and tropical regions. Saltmarsh flora is well developed along the North Norfolk coast in eastern England especially in the estuarine areas behind shingle bars formed parallel to the coast such as Blakeney. Point and the island of Scolt Head. There is a clear succession of plants following *Zostera*. Glasswort or samphire *Salicornia* (the succulent fleshy stems and branches of which are delicious cooked and served with vinegar) follows with sea aster. *Aster tripolium*, sea lavender *Limonium vulgare*, sea purslane *Halimione portulacoides*, annual seablite *Suaeda maritima* and shrubby seablite *Suaeda fruticosa* interspersed with sea campion *Silene maritima* and thrift *Armeria maritima*. However, on these Norfolk marshes and elsewhere this saltmarsh sequence is often distorted by the rapid growth of cord *Spartina townsendii*. This marine grass was first recorded from Hythe in Hampshire in 1878, a natural hybrid between the British *S. maritima* and *S. alterniflora* which was introduced accidentally from North America. The vigorous hybrid was planted deliberately for reclamation purposes in Europe, the east coast of North America in estuaries and on mud flats from Florida to Maine, and in Australia. It was planted in Norfolk originally in 1907 with further introductions of the mainland opposite Scolt Head in 1931–2. By 1939 it was established on the island ; seeds were planted at Blakeney in 1925. *Spartina* increases the rate of mud accretion on colonizing previously bare mud flats but competes fiercely with other saltmarsh species. More recently 'die-back' disease affecting rhizomes and shoots of *Spartina* nas led to problems of saltmarsh instability.

In sheltered muddy estuaries located in areas with less than three consecutive nights of frost, *i.e.* subtropical and tropical regions, mangrove swamps may develop. The black mangrove *Avicennia nitida* [Fig. 26.1 (*a*)] has special aerial roots known

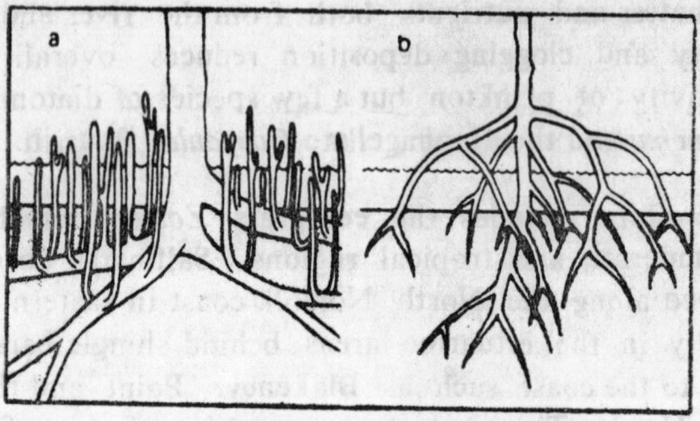

Figure 26.1. (*a*) Pneumatophore roots of black mangrove.
(*b*) Prop roots of red mangrove.

as pneumatophores which enable the mangroves to obtain oxygen while growing in anaerobic mud. The elaborate prop roots of the red mangrove *Rhizophora mangle* [Fig. 26.1 (*b*)] support the tree when the tide is out and provide shelter and surfaces for attachment for the inhabitants of the mangrove community, *e.g.* in the Everglades in Florida. *Rhizophora* is also capable of growing on sand in full salinity. Seeds of the red mangrove sprout while still attached to the tree. Eventually they drop off and float until they lodge in shallow water. Leaf litter forms an important input of detritus into mangrove swamp food webs.

Fauna

Polychaetes. The cat worm *Nephtys bombergi* occurs mainly in the sublittoral but on sheltered muddy beaches and in estuaries extends up to MTL. Penetration up the estuary is limited to levels not greatly affected by the low salinities caused by extra run-off in winter. The Californian species *N. caecoides* is similarly restricted to sheltered muddy bays and estuaries. The rag worm *Nereis diversicolor* and other polychaetes *Scoloplos armiger* and *Cirratulus cirratus* extend to the upper reaches of estuaries. Species of *Nephtys* have planktonic larvae but the larvae of other estuarine polychaetes have abandoned this dispersive phase in order to avoid being swept away from the estuary on the first ebb tide after hatching. The larvae of *Nereis diversicolor* are mainly benthic while the larvae of *Cirratulus* are associated with the gills of the adults. *Scoloplos armiger* produces egg cocoons from which the larvae escape in 10—24 days and burrow immediately. Fertilized eggs and larvae of the lug-worm *Arenicola marina* are deposited high on the shore by the tide. Juvenile worms emerge from these high-level burrows and swim to the zone lower on the shore occupied by the adults.

Nereis diversicolor has powerful jaws, well-developed sensory tentacles and is adapted for life as an active predator. However, it is capable also of entrapping and utilizing the abundant detritus on estuarine shores by creating a filter of mucus. Surprisingly these worms have weak powers of osmoregulation and consequently the cells of the body need to be able to tolerate large and rapid changes in the concentration of cell fluids. However, these euryhaline species are capable of limited osmotic control by regulating the concentration of certain amino acids to correspond osmotically with external levels of salinity.

Molluscs. Alhough small, with a shell less than 10 mm long, the laver spire shell *Hydrobia ulvae* occurs in vast numbers, with over a million m^{-2} in accumulations of shells upto 20 cm thick, on mud flats of estuaries and salt marshes. The specific name *ulvae* is based on its preference for the sea lettuce *Ulva lactuca* as a source of food but it will browse on other weeds such as *Enteromorpha.* It also lives occasionally in shallow pools which are inundated only by EHWs tides. Solinity in the pools may fall to 13 parts per thousand after rain but in hot dry conditions when the water temperature may reach 30°C salinity may rise to 35 parts per thousand. *Hydrobia* will survive if the pools dry out and is a true euryhaline species tolerating these extremes of salinity and temperature. In really adverse conditions the snail always has the option of retreating into its shell and sealing off the entrance with the operculum. When favourable conditions return, *i e.* dampness or a covering by still water, the snail creeps over the apparently bare surfaces of mud, feeding on diatoms, blue-green algae and fine detritus. In turbulence or if the surface dries, the snail burrows. Occasionally the snail has been recorded floating on mucous rafts and air bubbles at high tide and (it has been suggested) thereby exploits the surface film as a further potential source of food. The contribution made from this method of feeding would be slight, however, in comparison with food obtained from the surface of mud.

Some bivalves such as *Scrobicularia plana* have long siphons vacuuming the surface for detritus. This species lies deep in the black anaerobic layer, sometimes oxidized locally by leakage of oxygenated fluids from the shell. Oxygen is supplied via the inhalent siphon. A 4 cm specimen may have an inhalent siphon as long as 28 cm. Filter feeding molluscs tend not to inhabit very fine substrates as the gill filter mechanism would soon become clogged. The cockle *Cerastoderma* (=*Cardium* (*edule* does manage in conditions with a mixture of mud and sand. This species forms the basis of a long-established cockle industry in the Burry Estuary (River Lwchwr) in South Wales. For generations cockle women from Llanridian and neighbouring villages on the north shore of the Gower peninsula have collected these bivalves from the estuary using ponies to pull the laden carts across the marshes. A severe decrease in the population in the late 1950s and early 1960s was thought to be due to large flocks of oystercatchers feeding on up to 350 cockles per bird per day. A controversial cull of oystercatchers by shooting did little to alleviate the declining population of cockles. A shift in the course of estuary channels and some overfishing have both been postulated as more likely causes.

The ability to both filter and deposit feed, already seen in certain polychaetes is present also in the Baltic tellin *Macoma balthica* which normally is a deposit feeder but on occasion may also filter. Deeper in the mud may lie the so-called sand gaper *Mya arenaria* with shells up to 15 cm long.

Crustaceans. The amphipod *Corophium volutator* is the dominant crustacean on the upper reaches of the shore in many European estuaries. On a warm sunny day at low tide whole area of mud appear to be alive with this small crustacean (8 mm) emerging from burrows and looping along using its long antennae to pull the body forward while pushing with the uropods at the rear. On the Swedish coast densities of 50000 m^{-2} have been recorded. It prefers salinities of 10—30 parts per thousand but will tolarate the range 2—50 parts per thousands. In response to temperatures that fall below 4°C it burrows more deeply. It constructs a 'U'-shaped burrow though which it draws water by beating the pleopods, the appendages on the abdomen. Food particles are filtered out from this current. It has two generations a year, the overwintering generation breeding from May to July, producing a summer breeding generation which gives rise to the next overwintering population.

Tropical species of ocypodid crabs show a variety of adaptations to life in fine sediments including elongated eye-stalks that protrude above the surface of the substrate, while the rest of the animal remains securely burried. The tips of the pincers (chelae) are flattened into 'spoons' capable of picking up the surface mud which is then passed to the maxilliped mouthparts. Special hairs (setae) forming a brush on the edge of these maxillipeds help to detach organic matter from the sediment. The organic matter is then carried towards the mouth by water currents. These also form a respiratory stream and the gills in the branchial cavity are protected from clogging by a further screen of feathery hairs.

All the animals considered so far have been permanent members of estuaries. However, some species migrate down river into estuaries to breed such as the prawn *Palaemon longirostris.* Larvae of this species prefer higher salinities than the adults which indicates a relatively recent move into fresh water by purely marine ancestors. Laboratory rearing of this species is enhanced by keeping the larvae in at least half-strength sea water.

Figure 26.2. Cockle women returning from Llanridian marshes, South Wales.

Many of the large penaeid shrimps such as those taken commercially in the Gulf of Mexico, e.g. *Penaeus aztecus* (grounds off Texas), *Penaeus duorarum* (off north western Florida and western Texas) and *Penaeus setiferus* (from North Carolina and into the Gulf), migrate from the sea into estuaries and sheltered brackish lagoons either for breeding or as juveniles. Other non-crustacean species move in and out of estuaries on every tide, examples being fish and birds.

Fish. The grey mullet *Mugil* browses on algae and takes in detritus. Flatfish move into estuaries to feed especially in summer and the plaice *Pleuronectes platessa* and flounder *Platichthys flesus* feed voraciously on polychaetes and malacostracan crustaceans such as *Corophium*, prawn and shrimps.

Two different kinds of breeding migration which involve passage through estuaries are also known in fishes. Anadromous fish migrate from saline to less saline water to breed. This may involve a simple movement from oceanic water to less saline coastal water, but salmon migrate from the sea to the entirely fresh water of rivers, usually in mountainous regions. Catadromous fish migrate to water of greater density than that of the normal habitat in order to spawn, The European fresh water eel migrates from rivers to salt water, undertaking vast oceanic journeys of between 3000 to 5000 km to the Sargasso Sea in the middle of the North Atlantic before spawning. American fresh water eels from the east coast undergo similar migrations with a spawning ground slightly to the west of the European eel spawning grounds. Elvers do not begin their return journey to European estuaries and rivers for three years ; American elvers return after 1—2 years.

Birds. Gulls will feed on fish and also on bivalves picked up and then dropped from a great height to break the shells. However, the dominant birds of estuaries are the ducks, geese and waders, some of which move south in vast flocks to overwinter in relatively equable temperate regions. Many of the Anatidae—ducks and geese—feed entirely on *Zostera* and related marine grasses. Waders are carnivorous and will seek out and remove polychaetes, molluscs and crustaceans from their burrows. Different species specialize in particular groups of prey ; beak shape and size often reflect these adaptations to the preferred food.

All of these animals and plants form part of a complicated estuarine food web. Some of the pathways are still unclear. Others that are known have been indicated.

Estuaries and man

Man has long utilized estuaries both for shipping and commerce, and more recently for leisure. The shelter provided makes estuaries particularly safe as harbours and their use by shipping leads inexorably to the development of docks and industry. Inevitably in this progressive utilization of estuaries there comes a time when man and the natural inhabitants come into conflict. Oil spillage in enclosed waters such as Milford Haven in South Waler or Southampton Water in southern England will have disastrous effects on wildlife, particularly on the populations of sea birds. But estuaries have suffered from much more concerted and long-term pollution than from the relatively recent crude oil spills.

It has been estimated that 30 per cent of the population (more than 15000000) of the British Isles lives near estuaries. Domestic sewage and industrial waste have been dumped conveniently into the waters of estuaries, with spectacularly disastrous results. In 1596, Spenser wrote 'Sweat Thames run softly till I end my song.' Until the early nineteenth century commercial fisheries flourished in the tidal Thames. The smlet, a close relative of the salmon family, was reported in 1797 to be so plentiful in the river that it was sold cheaply 'in the manner of sprats, by coal measure'. Salmon was also caught regularly in modest numbers in the Thames until the middle of the nineteenth century. Eels, trout and whitebait were also taken and byelaws of the Thames Free Fishermen as early as 1697 regulated the dragging for shrimps at Gravesend and Leigh. But in 1854, 500 people died from cholera in Soho, spread by infected water and by 1858 parliamentary committees were abandoned unceremoniously as a result of pestilential odours from the river permeating the Palace of Westminster.

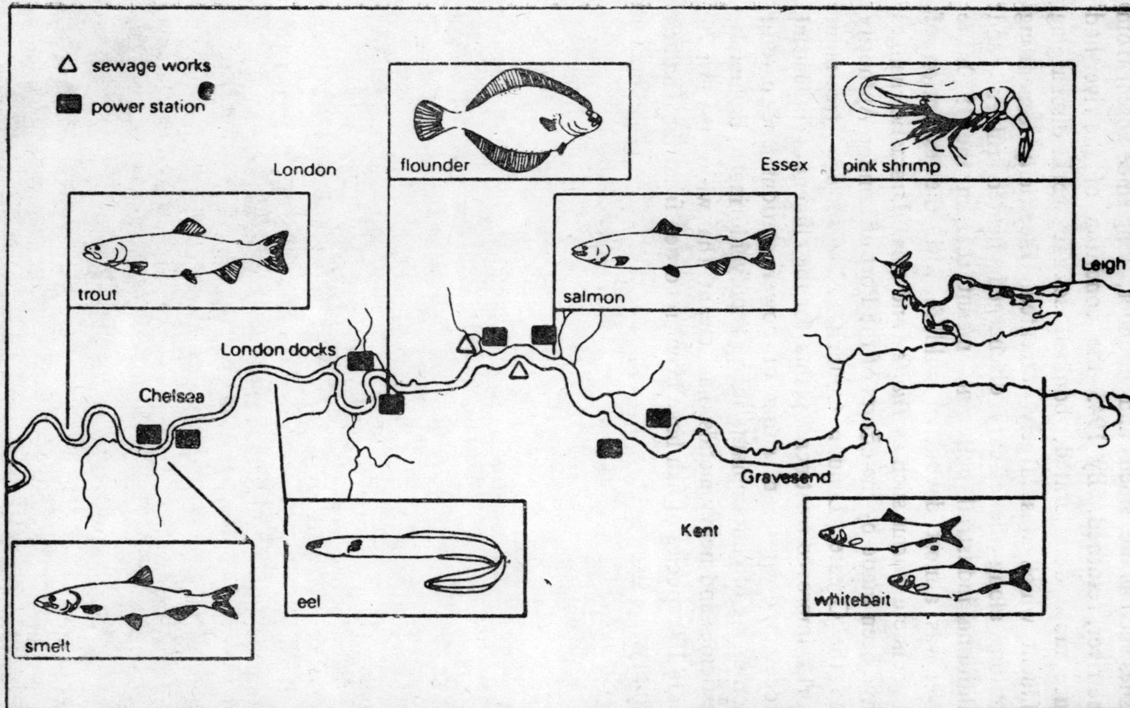

Figure 26·3. The tidal Thames from Teddington Lock to Shoeburyness showing the sites of present-day power stations and sewage works.

By the turn of the century the discharge of untreated sewage into the Thames was being gradually phased out and fishes such as the smelt and flounder, long since absent from the river, returned. By 1945 the condition of the river had once more deteriorated, bombed sewage works discharging effluent which was largely utreated. Electricity generating stations along the estuary discharged heated effluent and additional industrial pollutants meant that in the 1950s the river was almost devoid of wildlife with the exception of oligochaete worms such as *Tubifex* and eels. Dramatic changes have been made by the efforts of the Port of London Authority and the Greater London Council. New sewage treatment works, improved treatment plants for the effluent of industrial processes, downstream siting of power stations and careful monitoring of contaminants such as polychlorinated biphenyls, pesticides and heavy metals has meant that within the last 20 years 100 species of fish have been recorded from the Thames estuary.

Bibliography

Books

Bagenal, T. B., 1972, *The Observer's Book of Sea Fishes.* Warne.

Barrett, J. H. and Yonge, C. M., 1958, *Collins Pocket Guide to the Seashore.* Collins.

Bell, Thomas, 1853, *A History of the British Stalk-eyed Crustacea.* Yan Voorst.

Brightman, F. H. and Nicholson, B. E., 1966, *Oxford Book of Flowerless Plants.* Oxford University Press.

Brightwell, L. R., 1954, *Down to the Sea.* Pitman.

Chapman, V. J., 1964, *Coastal Vegetation.* Pergamon Press.

Clark, A. M., 1962, *Starfishes and their Relations.* British Museum.

Dales, R. P., 1963, *Annelids.* Hutchinson.

Dickinson, C. I. 1963, *British Seaweeds,* (Kew Series). Eyre & Spottiswoode.

Eales, N. B., 1967, *Littoral fauna of the British Isles.* 4th Edition. Cambridge University Press.

Flattely, F. S. and Walton, C. L., 1922—46, *Biology of the Seashore.* Sidgwick & Jackson.

Forbes, E., 1841, *A History of British Echinodermata.*

Gosse, Edmund, 1907, *Father and Son. A Study of Two Temperaments.*

Gosse, Philip H., 1865, *A Year at the Shore.* Strahan.

Green, J., 1968, *The Biology of Estuarine Animals.* Sidgwick & Jackson.

Green, J., 1961, *A Biology of Crustacea.* Witherby.

Haas, W. de and Knorr, F., 1966, *Marine Life*. Burke.

Hardy, A., 1956, *The Open Sea. Part 1—The World of Plankton*, (New Naturalist Series). Collins.

Hepburn, I., 1952, *Flowers of the Coast*, (New Naturalist Series). Collins.

Hyman, L. H., 1940, *The Invertebrates: Protozoa through Ctenophora*. McGraw Hill.

Hyman, L. H , 1955, *The Invertebrates: Echinodermata*. McGraw Hill.

Jackman, L. A. J., 1968, *Marine Aquaria*. 2nd Edition. David & Charles.

Jenkins, J. Travis, 1925, *The Fishes of the British Isles*. Warne.

Kennedy, M., 1954, *The Sea Anger's Fishes*. Hutchinson.

Lane, F. W., 1957, *Kingdom of the Octopus. The Life History of the Cephalopoda*. Jarrolds.

Lewis, J. R., 1964, *Ecology of Rocky Shores*. English University Press.

MacGinitie, G. E. and N., 1949–68, *Natural History of Marine Animals*. McGraw Hill.

McMillan, N. F., 1968, *British Shells*. Warne.

Millar, R. H., 1970, *British Ascidians. Tunicata: Ascidiacea. Keys and Notes for the Identification of Species*. Academic Press.

Miller, R. C., 1966, *The Sea*. Nelson.

Miles, P. M. and H. B., 1966, *Seashore Ecology*. Hulton.

Moore, H. B., 1958, *Marine Ecology*. Wiley.

Mortensen, T., 1927, *Handbook of the Echinoderms of the British Isles*. O.U.P.

Morton, J. E., 1958, *Molluscs*. Hutchinson.

Ministry of Agriculture, Fishries and Food, September 1967, *Yorkshire Crab Stocks*, Leaflet No. 17.